TRUE VINE

TRUE VINE

A Young Black Man's Journey
of Faith, Hope, and Clarity

John W. Fountain

PublicAffairs

New York

Book design and composition by Mark McGarry
Set in Dante

Library of Congress Cataloging-in-Publication data
Fountain, John W., 1960–
True vine : a young Black man's journey of faith, hope, and clarity /
by John W. Fountain.—1st ed.
p. cm.
ISBN 1-58648-084-7
1. Fountain, John W., 1960– —Childhood and youth. 2. Fountain, John W., 1960– —
Religion. 3. African American young men—Illinois—Chicago—Biography. 4. Urban
poor—Illinois—Chicago—Biography. 5. African Americans—Illinois—Chicago—Biography.
6. African Americans—Illinois—Chicago—Religion. 7. African Americans—Illinois—
Chicago—Social life and customs. 8. Fountain family. 9. Chicago (Ill.)—Biography. I. Title.
F548.9.N4 F68 2003
277.3'0825'092—dc21
[B]
2002036952

FIRST EDITION
10 9 8 7 6 5 4 3 2 1

For Grandmother
and
the prayer warriors

I am the vine, ye are the branches: He that abideth in me, and I in him, the same bringeth forth much fruit: for without me ye can do nothing.

John 15:5

CONTENTS

PART 2 LAMENTATIONS

PART 3 EXODUS

PART 4 REVELATION

ABOUT TRUE VINE

As a young man drowning in a sea of poverty on Chicago's West Side, I stood teary-eyed many Sunday mornings during worship service at my grandfather's Pentecostal church to testify, as we called it. Testimony service was filled with the emotional confessions of life's sufferings and ultimately reflected the triumphs that God had given us in our daily lives. In my worst times, my testimony was not so much about what God had done for me but was more a profession of faith about what I believed He would do for me someday. Testimony service was like one big ole group therapy session, complete with tears, hugs, and spiritual dancing that would have knocked the socks off MC Hammer. Fellow Christians encouraged one another with shouts of "Amen" and "Hold on, my brother." During Sunday worship service and at prayer sessions on count-less Tuesday and Friday mornings, the gray-haired church mothers, including Grandmother, who called themselves prayer warriors, shared their life's struggles as well as triumphs. It was their hope that we younger Christians would find through the sharing of their testimonies, the hope, faith, and strength to endure whatever troubles beset us. In time, my own testimonies rang more with victory.

It's funny. Back then I never imagined that I would testify to the world. But that is what this book is, my testimony. Many years have passed since those soul-stirring mornings with Grandmother and the prayer warriors. But in the words of the old church song, sung so many Sundays by Grandmother from the depths of her sanctified soul in the midst of the congregation, I can still "feel the fire burning in my heart." It is that fire that has sustained me even in life's darkest days. My True Vine. To Him be all the glory.

PROLOGUE

1968

I STOOD BAREFOOT at age seven watching the fires from my apartment window. The angry flames licked the pale night sky above the West Side of Chicago. There was an unusual rumbling out on the street, mixed with the voices of unrest, the slapping, sometimes heavy thud of hurried feet beneath our third-floor apartment window on Sixteenth Street and Komensky Avenue in the neighborhood we all called K-Town, though it was more widely known as North Lawndale. I could not see their faces. They could not see mine. We were all in the dark.

From the night came the crashing of glass, the blare of sirens. The screams of human anguish. A symphony of chaos.

The smoke seeped into our living room. It settled over the varnished hardwood floor like fine dust and carried the scent of charred mortar and brick. Mostly ablaze were the Jewish-owned clothing stores and businesses along Pulaski Road near the All Nations Church of God in Christ, a white brick storefront whose sanctuary looked like a movie theater. It was a small neighborhood family church. All of its members were black, even though it bore the name All Nations. All Nations was a Pentecostal church where my grandfather, a stout man with a manicured mustache, was a deacon and Sunday School superintendent, although years later he would receive what he would simply refer to as "the call" from God to pastor his own church.

The fire that April night ran up and down Pulaski Road even as far north as Madison Street. Pulaski Road was the major business strip in K-Town and included the shop where Grandmother had taken my sister, Net, and me one year to buy our mother a dress for Mother's Day with the money we had saved in our fat pink piggy bank. Grandmother, a caramel-complected black woman with strong but tender quilting hands and a deep but soothing tenor voice, was by far the sweetest woman I have ever known. She looked as dignified in her floral sewing smock as she did when wearing her Sunday best with some crowning hat that matched. And she had her own fire, which burned as brilliantly as the one that consumed our neighborhood that night. Except Grandmother's fire was a different kind. It was more infectious than consuming. I call it righteous fire. The fire I witnessed from my window was from hell. That much I could sense even as a child as I watched the embers spit into the sky.

At Pulaski and Roosevelt Roads stood a hamburger joint called Holland's. A neighborhood landmark back then, the restaurant with its blue-and-white windmill marquee that could be seen for miles would be one of the few businesses to survive the flames that spring night. The shop where we had bought Mama's dress would not.

Earlier that day, I saw all the white folks running from Kuppenheimer, the block-long brick building on Eighteenth Street and Karlov Avenue that made men's clothing. Kuppenheimer was where Grandmother worked as a seamstress and where Grandpa and my Uncle Gene, who was shorter but otherwise the spitting image of Grandpa, sometimes moonlighted as security guards—though by day both were friendly neighborhood postmen. An elderly white lady cried as she hurried east on Eighteenth Street toward the bus stop at Pulaski. Some older boys in the neighborhood snatched her purse, moving, it seemed, in slow motion, although in reality it was more like lightning speed. In slow motion was how I processed it. For years, the image played like photographic stills over and over again in my mind. Trauma has always hit me that way.

By afternoon that Friday, enraged packs of black teenage boys were beating up white people who worked in the neighborhood. I have never known the names of either the victims or the perpetrators. But three decades later, I can still see their faces, the angry boys slapping around white men and women as they try futilely to escape. Few words are exchanged. Mostly punches for pain.

I had heard enough at school and from Mama the evening before to know that the older guys and just about everyone in the neighborhood was mad about Dr. Martin Luther King Jr. being killed. The word we kids had learned in school was "assassination." I could pronounce it clearly.

As-sas-si-na-tion.

It had an unsettling ring, like cru-ci-fix-ion.

"Dr. Martin Luther King Jr. was assassinated" was the way the news was synthesized and transmitted throughout the neighborhood.

Assassination. It was a big word, a strange word, in hindsight a word that seemed too loaded, too lethal, and too full of pain to be toted around by a seven-year-old boy. I'm not sure that I fully understood back then what it meant. I only knew that Dr. King, the man who had once lived with his family in our neighborhood just a few blocks away from Komensky, the preacher whose name was on everybody's lips and the object of everybody's tears, was dead. But after the night of fires, the same might have been said of our neighborhood. As I walked to the store the next morning, the National Guard troops I saw riding atop their jeeps up and down Pulaski Road—wearing their green fatigues and assault rifles as the remains of buildings smoldered in smoke and ash—were forever seared into my mind. Years later, I realized that the fires signaled the beginning of the end.

There were many windows in our apartment from which I could have watched the fires that night. I chose the northeast window in our living room, because it had the clearest view of the trouble out on the streets. Mostly, I watched with the lights off, something I had learned early on from my Mama. I witnessed Mama rushing to the window countless times while I was growing up. Whenever there was some new fracas—gunshots, blood-curdling screams, or shattering glass—Mama rushed like a paramedic to the window. But never before she had twisted the switches on the lamps and ordered one of her children to pop the on/off button on the television, submerging our apartment into utter darkness. Only then would she ease back the curtains, crack the blinds, and conduct her surveillance under the cover of the dark from her window perch.

I have long known the value of windows. There are natural windows: a mountain peak or a valley. There are other windows made by man. Windows to other worlds. Windows of darkness. Windows of light. Windows to the soul. Windows high and windows low. Big windows and small windows. Windows can keep out the elements or let them shine in. A house without windows is a prison. Prison is sometimes a matter of choice. Sometimes covering one's windows is a matter of necessity for concealing one's sufferings. My sufferings were poverty and shame.

As a little boy, poverty silenced me. It led me to close the curtains to the windows of my world. It made me hide my worn shoes underneath the desk at school or the wooden pews at church. It made me feel ugly. Poverty sometimes kept me distant from friends when I couldn't afford to do some of the things they were doing: going to the movies or buying an ice-cream cone from the ice-cream truck on a hot summer's day. Or it made me sit hunched over and feeling alone in a school cafeteria because I was seldom able to afford a five-cent cookie to go with my free lunch. I never invited friends home. I figured they would laugh at my despair, symbolized by our tattered dingy sofa, the roaches, and all the mice, everywhere the mice.

Poverty woke me up in the morning like a cock's crow on a sleepy Mississippi farm. Often, there was no soap for baths and no hot water, the lights or gas or one thing or another sometimes was disconnected, my toes poked through my socks and my knees protruded through my pants. I sometimes stood at the silver fence in my front yard where the gate had long since been crippled, dreaming with my arms stretched wide as I watched the moon and stars above. I was a prisoner on a deserted island, watching the ships sail by on the distant horizon. Often, I lay in bed at night amid the creaking of my family's apartment and the scratching of the mice that crept out of their holes and from behind the sink after dark. Sometimes I shut my eyes tight and imagined I would someday become a rich lawyer. With my riches, I would buy Mama a great big house with a big backyard, and I would stock a humongous deep-freeze with meats and frozen greens, then load the pantry shelves full of cereal and cookies and potato chips and stuff. Dreaming eased my pain and I eventually drifted off to sleep, any hunger or unsatisfied longing dissolved until I awoke the next morning to another day of butt-naked poverty and wanting.

Even as an adult, hardship and poverty always seemed like the Jehovah's Witnesses. They were always knocking at my door. Always poverty. I was convinced I would drown in it, be buried in it, maybe even be resurrected in it. In time, I became resigned to dying in it, by natural causes or eventually at the hand of some fool who would blow my head off or knife me in the gut for whatever few dollars I did have. Death seemed the lesser of the evils. For poverty left me feeling hollow, like the winos who lingered at the doorsteps of the liquor stores down on Sixteenth Street, or the dopeheads, or the hookers with hollow eyes down on Roosevelt Road and Cicero Avenue.

I donned an uninviting tough exterior, like a heavyweight boxer. It was my way of scaring away anyone who might otherwise have gotten close enough to find out just how much I was hurting, how difficult a bout of life in the ghetto was for me. My angry facade kept people at bay. It also thwarted any understanding or relief that might have been gained by sharing my pain. I know now that my social abstinence hurt me so much more. I bear the scars.

The private room of suffering in which I had gotten used to licking my wounds made me lock others out, even as an adult. I am still learning to remove the padlocks from the rusted doors of old hurts.

But that little boy still cries sometimes, still cowers in the shame of yesterday's poverty. The man, the writer, knows that somewhere in Chicago or somewhere else out there, there is another little boy or girl drowning in the sea of poverty, gasping for hope. For their sake and mine, I draw back the tightly closed curtains of my windows here and in the pages that follow. I do so in the hope that it will help outsiders understand our world or help someone else to survive it, if not overcome it. I also do so to leave some record of the lives of the African Americans who once called Lawndale their promised land, but whom time, history, and eventually gentrification are likely to render invisible.

Pulling back my curtains has become a lot easier as the frightened little boy in me has found strength and a friend in the man I see in the mirror and has been possible because of the one thing that, even in the days that seemed most dimly lit, has preserved me. Hope. For it is hope that has been the source of sustenance on my life's journey, a journey that ultimately led me away from poverty and my North Lawndale neighborhood but eventually led me back home in a way I might never have imagined.

By then I would be a little worn and weary, but better at least for having made the journey.

PART 1

GENESIS

And the Lord God planted a garden eastward in Eden; and there he put the man whom he had formed. And out of the ground made the Lord God to grow every tree that is pleasant to the sight, and good for food; the tree of life also in the midst of the garden, and the tree of knowledge of good and evil.

Genesis 2:8–9

CHAPTER 1

THE TREE OF LIFE

AN AUTUMN WIND blows through this old apple tree. My eyes have often massaged its variegated ruby red, yellow, and green apples that dangled like Christmas ornaments from its branches for as far back as I can remember. I have studied Mr. Newell's tree next door for many seasons, from my bedroom window, from my backyard, or on idle afternoons from my porch when it was too cold to play outside. I have watched it in the cold dead of winter, when it has been warmed by sun or whipped by wind or rain. And I am still amazed at its life and death, and then its resurrection come each season.

The tree, with its wide brown bottom and sprawling emerald limbs, seems to have always existed. It is rooted in the middle of Mr. Newell's backyard. But it is ours, too. It belongs to the whole neighborhood: to me and to one of my best friends, Elvis. To Mercury, J-Rat, Huckey and Big-Head Ronnie, to my cousins, Arty and Michael. To Blue Moon and his brothers, Horse and Jimmy Lee, to the Stewart boys—Big Mike, Lou, Rob, and David—and to every other man, woman, or child who lived on Komensky Avenue or who hung out here with enough regularity to be considered a resident of the block. A silver fence in the middle of a green grass sea has always shielded this apple tree here in the 1600 block of South Komensky Avenue on Chicago's West Side. The fence wasn't always so stark. Neither was life.

For much of my life, I lived in this place called K-Town, which sits in the heart of a community known as North Lawndale. K-Town is a city within a city, a fifteen-minute drive west from downtown Chicago's skyscrapers and Lake Michigan.

This is the Windy City. In the wintertime, the howling wind licks that icy lake, and on some especially frigid days whips across the city like an invisible twister, frosting everything in its path, turning mustaches and eyebrows into white ice. There is no escaping the cold here, where men in my neighborhood on the most brutal nights of winter disconnected their car batteries and carried them indoors for protection. Somebody a long time ago nicknamed Chicago's glacial winter wind the "Hawk." That's what we called it anyway. When it was really cold outside and the wind was frozen and jagged, we used to say, "The Hawk is bitinnng!" Except you would say this only after having escaped the cold or while warming your nearly frostbitten hands over a space heater, or while walking briskly toward home or school and bundled up so that nothing was exposed, except the whites of your eyes.

Where nearly everything short of gunshots failed to get Negroes in my neighborhood off the street, nothing worked like pure, unadulterated wind-whipped cold. I learned early on that Chicago can be a cold city and that some places here always got a little colder than others did. I suspect that none could be colder than K-Town. I used to joke that the "K" stood for "Kill." I was only half joking. Although it had developed a reputation for being one of the rougher places in the city, K-Town actually got its nickname from all of the streets in the neighborhood named mostly after European heroes, politicians, or cities. The streets all begin with the letter K. There is Karlov, Kedvale, Kostner, Kolin, Keeler, Kenneth, Komensky. You get the picture.

K-Town is where my grandfather, Mr. Newell, Mr. Black, and all the other black folks who flocked to the West Side during the mid- to late 1950s bought proud brick houses on tree-lined streets with crackless cement sidewalks. Most had come to Chicago during the previous decade or so, toward the end of the Great Depression and the start of World War II, from an assortment of oppressive towns in Mississippi, Georgia, Tennessee, Alabama, and even southern Illinois. Chicago was the northern city of promise. It was settled by a black man named Jean Baptiste Point DuSable, the son of a Frenchman and a black woman who built a cabin on the north bank of the Chicago River soon after the American Revolution. K-Town, where Jews, mostly of Eastern European descent, and other immigrants settled in the early years of the twentieth century, was nothing less than the land that flowed with milk and honey—the Promised Land for blacks like my family. But no sooner had black folks moved in than white folks moved out, leaving behind their earthen castles—sturdy brick bungalows and mostly two- and three-flat apartment buildings—which black folks were more than happy to possess. Jews had begun moving into Lawndale in the early 1900s and by 1940 had built a large community that included scores of synagogues, businesses, and community centers. But by the late 1950s, there had been a mass exodus as Jews, with their improved economic status, moved out to the suburbs and newer areas of the city and blacks moved in.

The joy of black folks to land in K-Town was understandable. The majority of blacks who settled there were first-time home buyers just a generation or two removed from the Thirteenth Amendment. Our own family tree was rooted in slavery. Grandpa's grandfather, Burton Roy, who reared him, had been a slave. Burton Roy was father to Grandpa's mother, Easter Roy, who married Eli Hagler, Grandpa's father.

My great-great-grandfather Burton Roy toiled in the fields of Pulaski, Illinois, picking strawberries, corn, and other crops. As a young man, Grandpa worked the same fields, driving mules, plowing the rugged brown earth before marrying my grandmother at age sixteen. She was fifteen and visiting at the time from Tennessee in 1937, when they met in Pulaski and fell in love. George Albert Hagler and Florence Geneva Taylor married on a Thursday evening in the country on April 22, 1937. That same year, Joe Louis defeated James J. Braddock for the heavyweight boxing championship, smack in the middle of the Great Depression.

Back then, life for most blacks in America, where whites were still getting used to the idea of seeing Negroes as red-blooded citizens, wasn't exactly peaches and cream. So when the depression hit, black folks just kept on keeping on. In other words, while white folks shuddered, leaped off tall buildings, and pulled out their hair trying to figure out how they would survive the worst experience of their lives, black folks did what they always did. They made do. In every household, "Mama" stretched the collard or mustard and turnip greens and the greasy fatback that gave the greens their flavor as far as they could. When no greens were left in the pot, black folks sopped up the pot liquor—the nutrient-rich water that the greens had cooked in—with homemade cornbread right down to the last drop. At the fall of a fresh winter's snow, kids filled their cups with the fluffy untouched flakes, then added a spoonful of vanilla flavor and milk for their own version of ice cream, called snow cream. In all my years, I never heard my grandparents speak of the Great Depression as though it yielded some new impossible challenge in the lives of black folks. Black life was hard life, like a sentence to hard labor on a Mississippi chain gang. Except that having someone to share life with—someone with whom you could dream of growing old with, of making good memories along the way, raising a family together and seeing your children's children and even their children rise from your union—could make life worth living, or at least more bearable. There was solace in knowing that you did not have to endure life alone and that when all else failed, no matter how poor you were, no matter what new storm cloud settled over your world, at least you had each other. For Grandpa, nothing compared to Geneva. And for Grandmother, no one compared to George.

During the year my grandparents were married, the Great Flood of the raging Mississippi River swallowed Pulaski and neighboring Cairo, Illinois, and other towns in its path. When the floodwaters receded, it meant good work for Grandpa. He made $2.50 a day, helping hoist houses back onto their foundations. Grandpa would need all the money he could earn.

A year after my grandparents married, Aunt Mary was born. Then two years later came Uncle Gene. Fourteen months later, there was Aunt Scope, whose real name is Gloria. Twenty-two months later, Gwen, who is my mom. Fourteen months later, Aunt Clotee. Twenty-one months later, Aunt Brenda. The four oldest of my grandparent's children were born in Pulaski. Only Aunt Brenda was born at a hospital. The others were birthed at home, ushered into this world by the field-worn but gentle hands of my great-grandmother, Easter Roy, or a local midwife. In 1943, the same year that my mother was born, Grandpa packed up his young family and moved to Chicago.

The family settled at the city's Robert Brooks Housing Project on the West Side. Their home was a two-bedroom apartment at 1332 South Racine Avenue. My grandparents lived there with their oldest four children, including Mama. But by the time the next two children were born, the family had managed to get a place with more space. It was a three-bedroom apartment in the same housing project.

In those days, the projects were not crumbling, urine-smelling buildings with bald lawns and concrete yards festering with gangs and drugs. You could lie out on the plush grass at night, looking up at the stars until you fell asleep without fear of being stripped of all your valuables and waking up butt naked. Fathers and husbands were the norm. Sunday mornings arrived with the chatter of children and their families on their way to church. They arrived with the smell of cornbread or chicken-and-dressing or some other down-home favorite, like pot roast and cabbage, prepared in advance for Sunday supper.

Life was simple. You lived and worked and raised your family. You pinched and saved until finally you had earned enough to buy a house. The projects were not places where anybody ever intended to stay, no matter how green the grass on this side of the Jordan. In the meantime, there would be no such word as *ghetto* in George and Geneva's house.

The Hagler house was always spotless. Grandmother was as fanatical about keeping a clean house as she was about praying or ironing her daughters' ribbons and Grandpa's shirts and baking butter pound cakes and her mouthwatering peach cobbler. After settling in Chicago, Grandpa did maintenance work at a manufacturing company. He eventually went to work at the U.S. Postal Service as a letter carrier, the only job I ever knew him to have when I was growing up. I can still see him: dressed in his postal blues and short-sleeve shirts in the summer, his leather sack slung over his shoulder, whistling on his way home.

For years while their children were small, Grandmother worked during the day, cleaning and cooking at white people's houses. Sometimes she picked up a few extra dollars combing and braiding the hair of little girls who lived in the projects. She eventually got a job as a seamstress. When she began working full-time outside her home, the older Hagler children watched the younger ones and the neighbors kept a lookout on all of them until Grandmother or Grandpa got home. Back then everybody looked out for everybody else. And many of the folks who lived in their little housing project enclave attended All Nations Church of God in Christ, where Elder William Campbell was pastor. With their pastor as well as the church's missionaries and deacons as neighbors, the Hagler kids weren't about to get into too much trouble. Having parents who believed in the attitude-adjusting power of the strap helped, too.

By November 1956, Grandmother and Grandpa had scratched and saved enough money for a down payment on a house. On the day before Thanksgiving, they moved into their own version of a deluxe apartment in the sky: a two-unit, six-bedroom apartment building at 1634 South Komensky Avenue. Mama was just thirteen then. Eight years later, my grandparents purchased a second building several houses down at 1654 South Komensky Avenue. The Compound was what Aunt Mary affectionately named the two apartment buildings that my grandparents bought on Komensky. Everybody in our family lived at the Compound at one point or another.

All of my grandparents' children were grown by the time they bought the second apartment building. But Grandpa wanted his daughters always to have somewhere to live. He must have sensed something about the men in his daughters' lives, or maybe it was just his fatherly sense of wanting to provide for his children. At any rate, he figured that by buying these two buildings, five apartment units in all, each of his little girls would always have a place to call home, man or not.

As a boy, for many years I lived with my family in the third-floor apartment at 1654 South Komensky Avenue. There was Mama, my stepfather, and my three younger siblings.

My sister, Net, is two years younger than I am. Her real name is Gloria, named after Aunt Scope. But we have always called her Net—derived from her middle name, Lynette. Net and I have the same father. We are Fountains. Our two younger siblings are Clincys.

Jeff, my brother, who is seven years younger, was a rambunctious little boy who was never at a loss for getting into trouble. Once, Jeff set the bottom bunk on fire as I lay sleeping in the top bed. I awoke to my stepfather's dragging me to safety and hot flames licking at my mattress. Despite his devilishness and the matching arched eyebrows to prove it, Jeff was always Mama's "Juice," which translates into her innocent baby boy with sugar on top.

The last of my siblings is my youngest sister, Meredith. Eleven years my junior, she seemed to have been born in a different era. On many levels, I would later come to understand this to be entirely true. I also learned that children who grew up in the same house with the same two parents could be reared in totally different environments and how those separate worlds in the same household ultimately could mold in siblings distinctly different lives, perspectives, and even memories. Net and I were children of struggle. Meredith and Jeff were children of gain.

Mama was the kind of woman who loved her children more than anything else in the world and would protect them unto death. A brown-skinned black woman with thick brown lips and pretty eyebrows, she also loved God, a pack of Winstons, a sixteen-ounce bottle of Pepsi-Cola, and snapping her fingers to a slow jam playing over the radio. Mama was gentle and kindhearted, quick to help a friend or family, always willing to give her last. She believed in family and in sticking together. "Family is always first," I can still hear Mama telling her children. "All y'all gonna ever have is each other." Mama was tenderhearted and easily wounded, but also a fighter. If you had to go to war, you would want to take Mama. She wasn't the kind to back down and wasn't one to mince words, either. Mama was a supreme curser. When she was spewing profanities, the words shot out like hollow-point bullets that could penetrate even the most fortified of psyches. She created word combinations of such invention that I have rarely heard the equal, even from some of the most profi-

cient of profanity spewers. Mama didn't curse—she cussed. Her enuncia-
tion was riveting, accent on just the right syllable, and some pronounce-
ments of the most offensive of words was guttural. Mama had a way of
making a person feel they actually were whatever beguiling name she was
calling them at that precise moment. She'd cut 'em up, then walk away,
depending on whether the other person still wanted to tango.

And of course, there was my stepfather, whose name was Eddie Clincy
and who Grandmother affectionately called Eddie Man, especially when
she was asking him to do a fix-it job, which Grandpa was never good at.

Such was the makeup of my family and the beginnings of our life on
Komensky.

Over time, I watched the way life on Komensky and life in the 'hood
in general incapacitated people. It sometimes rendered them as living sar-
cophaguses, sipping gin and white port wine mixed with Kool-Aid or
ingesting some other cheap anesthetic until that time when the pro-
nouncement of death finally was made official. It was clear to me even as
a child that there were only two kinds of people in my world: the living
and the dead. I decided early on that I wanted to live. But sometimes I
wasn't completely sure whether I should be counted among the actual living or the living dead.

Every kid on Komensky Avenue looked forward to the end of summer
when the grownups cordoned off the block at the south end on Eighteenth Street and at the north end on Sixteenth Street with streamers and
two yellow police horses. This was the second-greatest event that took
place on Komensky each year.

At the annual block party, Old Man Newell, who headed the Block
Club, carted out his gargantuan grill and smoked hot dogs and sausages
paid for with donations from each household. We all ate from the same
grill, laughing with friends over a mouthful of Oscar Mayer and a cold
cup of Kool-Aid. Then we ate cold watermelon and homemade ice cream
that melted like cotton candy in our mouth. There was singing, foot
races, and dancing in the middle of the street. Mostly, the kids danced

while the grownups laughed or played cards and snapped their fingers. At first, it was the sounds of Motown: Diana Ross and the Supremes, the Temptations, and the Jackson Five. There was the finger-snapping, booty-shaking music of the Godfather of Soul, James Brown, and the Queen of Soul, Aretha Franklin. As I got older, the music turned to disco, then to P-Funk and to a new blend of booming bass riffs laced with words but no singing, called rap. But there was nothing like the Isley Brothers pouring from speakers on a hot August day at the Block Club party on Komensky. As the Isleys played, time stood still, the melody and the smell of barbecue smoke drifting on a summer breeze.

Then came the band. My best friend was a skinny kid named Elvis, who had a brother named Leon who played drums. Elvis, Leon, and I formed our own group that we named the Funky Souls. I played lead guitar and Elvis played bass, but we weren't good enough to play the Block Club party. Elvis and Leon had a grown-up brother named Willie, who played skins for a Chicago band called the South Side Movement. And no Block Club party was complete until the band had played. I still have visions of Willie, a tall, wiry man with an Afro, beating his glistening drums in the middle of the street, his gangster brim cocked to the side and hanging down over his face, his arms flailing as if on fire. Suddenly, he twirled a drumstick on his fingers, then slung it high into the blue sky to the oohs and ahs of the crowd, smiling as he caught it without ever missing a beat.

As much as we could count on the annual party, we also could count on the annual fight. There was the time when Lori, an average-size girl who punched as hard as a man and was the same age as Net, beat up another girl's mother. There was the time that Gladys and Scooter Mump's mama got into a brawl and Old Man O'Neal came out shooting in the air. There was always an assortment of squabbles that led to fisticuffs and sometimes even to minor bloodshed. No one ever got killed, and usually it was feelings more than anything else that were most seriously hurt.

★

If the second-best day on Komensky was the Block Club party, the best was Apple Day. None of this would have been possible without Old Man Newell and his old apple tree.

My family and I lived only a fence away from Mr. and Mrs. Newell. Their names were Dewey James and Bessie Lee Newell. But for us, every adult's first name was always Mr. or Mrs. or Miss. We kids sometimes referred to Mr. Newell as Old Man Newell, but only when we were beyond earshot of adults. That would have been considered disrespect. Mr. Newell was a dark chocolate, thinly muscular man with a prunelike neck. Mrs. Newell was a high-yellow black woman whom I used to swear was white, though I later learned her father was white and her mother Indian. Mrs. Newell was wrinkled, too. Her hair was white, and she sometimes wore a floral apron. A short woman, she spoke in a syrupy-thick Southern drawl. Her voice was a bit husky. Her husband's was soft, a melodic tenor, smooth as silk. The Newells also had a hound called Spot, black-and-white and sometimes friendly.

In addition to being president of the Komensky Block Club, Mr. Newell was the elder statesman. He also had the best-kept yard and house. The Newell's house was brown brick with a sandy-orange painted front. The Newells were always doing something to that house—painting, fixing the stairs, always something. Even when they were working, Mr. and Mrs. Newell never walked fast, Mr. Newell especially. He sauntered from the front yard to the back, sometimes wearing dress trousers and a handsome straw hat as if he were going out on a date. He was always clipping his hedges, fussing over his roses and beds of flowers, kneeling to pick up every speck of trash and every weed. When he cut the grass, he walked behind his buzzing mower early in the morning or in the cool of a summer evening, carefully trimming in the way a barber does when he is shaving a man close with a razor.

After all of his labor, Mr. Newell sometimes sat on his porch at day's end, spitting brown juice, his jaw swollen with a bite of tobacco. Sometimes he puffed on a mahogany pipe, the scent of cherry smoke blending with the smell of freshly mown grass. He would sit admiring the work of his hands and wearing the same proud look that I would later recognize in young men on Komensky after they had spent the afternoon waxing and rubbing their cars into a hot shine. Mr. Newell's grass sparkled so much brighter than their chrome wheels.

All my friends on the block knew better than to walk on Mr. Newell's grass or to climb his fence to try to get at his apples. Mean when it came to protecting his property, that old man would almost curse you out. I sometimes imagined he might even unleash both barrels of one of his shotguns and then command Spot to drag back your body.

"Young mannn, get off my grass!" he had been known to shout before rising from his rocking chair on his front porch with his hound at his heels. He never needed to say it twice. Sometimes that old man treated his flowers, fat green hedges, grass, and trees like they were human, especially his apple tree.

On some summer days, after it rained, I scooped up apples that had fallen from the apple tree into my own backyard. I couldn't have been older than eight when this ritual began. I would spin the apples around in my fingers, inspecting for worm holes or squirrel and rat bites. If there were no marks, I polished the apples on my shirt or pants leg and ate them as quickly and with as much pleasure as any that had been store-bought. Sweet or not, they were delicious. On rarer occasions, my Aunt Mary's sons, Arty and Michael, got up the nerve to hop Mr. Newell's fence and raid his backyard. Mostly, we had to wait until that day at the end of summer when Mr. Newell invited the whole block into his back-yard on the day we called Apple Day.

On Apple Day, the older boys in the neighborhood, including Arty, who was two years older than I was, climbed high up in the tree and shook its branches until it rained apples. I can still see Arty with his pearly, buck-toothed smile, grinning as he climbed higher and higher and higher, like Tarzan the Ape Man, while my friends and I and all the grown-ups stood around, baking in the sun with anticipation. The air filled with oohs and ahs each time the apples showered down.

"Arrr-daaay! Shake it, mannn, shake it!" I screamed, standing in my yard, where branches hung over.

I was always half-afraid that Arty was going to fall and break a leg while climbing up the tree. In the end, he always climbed down, brushed himself off, and collected his share.

Much of what fell to the earth on those days got turned into applesauce, apple preserves, cinnamon apples, apple pies, and cobbler. Getting food from my backyard was something a poor city boy like me could really appreciate.

In time, Mr. Newell found it necessary to erect a wire-and-pole fence around his front lawn. Later, he took to padlocking his front and back gates to protect the old apple tree as the Promised Land slowly disintegrated into a tarnished land where it was not clear that anyone or even their dreams would survive.

I have watched the wind blow through this old apple tree for many seasons. I have always wondered where it comes from and where it goes after it has ruffled these emerald branches. The apples have glistened for as long as the tree has stood in the sun, a towering symbol of life on Komensky.

As much as I had often wished that life here would stay the same, I realized a long time ago that life here would change. I don't know how I knew this. Whether it was the slowly mounting toll of murder or the decay and poverty that eventually spread like weeds and began to choke out life, or something else, I don't know. I just knew. And I knew early on that if I were to survive, I must surely flee this place.

Except this was home. And there was a part of me that never wanted to say good-bye.

CHAPTER 2

HOLY ROLLERS

GRANDPA was always the provider. He was a kind man with a peaceful, soft-spoken demeanor. Grandpa never drank liquor, although he did at one time smoke cigarettes and developed into quite a marksman with a pool stick long before his preaching days. He had a kind of quiet respectability that said, "I'm a nice guy, but don't mess with me." We kids seldom did and, on rare occasions, only by accident. We understood Grandpa. And he understood us. His mere presence and the occasional turning up of the bass in his voice were enough to evoke the fear of God. Once when most of his children were grown and gone, a drunken man somehow ended up at Grandpa's door late one night, banging and demanding to be let in. Grandmother screamed for the man to go away, saying that he must have the wrong house. Grandpa quietly loaded his shotgun and sat down at the kitchen table, waiting for the man to bust through the door so he could drop 'im.

"Mister, please go away, Mister pleeezzzz," Grandmother begged. "If you come in here, my husband is gonna kill you. Mister please . . ."

Grandpa never uttered a word. And the man, who finally came to himself and went away, had Grandmother and the Good Lord to thank for sparing his life that day.

Grandpa didn't play. But Grandmother was a softy. Sometimes we purposely pushed her to the limits by blabbering on and on even after she had told us repeatedly to be quiet. Sometimes we were having so much fun outside that we ignored Grandmother when she called to us to come inside the house. There were times when we sneaked Grandpa's BB rifle out of its hiding place in a box on the side of the washbasin in the basement, and the time that Arty used the rifle to pick off pigeons in the lady's yard a couple of doors down. Sometimes we pushed Grandmother to the brink with our talk of secularism and our love for blues music and how our greatest desire was to grow up to be sinners and never, ever to go to church.

"Hey Grand-mo-therrrr, I can't wait 'til I grow up, I ain't never going to church," somebody, usually my cousins, Michael or Cheryl, would spout. Their words were soon followed by a "Me too," from the chorus of other grandchildren.

"And when I have kids, I ain't ever gon' make them go to church," another would shout.

"Me neither!" rang the chorus.

"All I'm gonna do on Sundays is lay in bed and watch TV," I would say, followed by shouts of "Yeah!" and snickers from my cousins.

"Yeah!" everybody shouted, slapping fives and laughing as if we were being tickled.

When Grandmother had had enough of our playful vexing and still we would not shut up or when we had disobeyed far too many times, she ordered us into her backyard to pick a switch from a bush. Of course, because she allowed us to select our own whipping tool, we quickly learned to pick the feeblest limbs. Even the idea of Grandmother administering corporal punishment, which was seldom, cracked us up so much that we could hardly keep a straight face even as she raised her hand to do what she deemed to be her regrettable duty, which we knew truly hurt her more than it ever hurt us. Grandmother was good at many things. Whipping was not one of them. But she always had a hole card, one that she rarely ever used. Just flashing it was enough.

"That's all right," she would say in frustration. "Daddy will be here after while." "Daddy" is how she referred to my grandfather. It was a term of reverence and endearment, she had once explained to me as a teenager, adding that in the Bible, Sarah had called her husband, Abraham, "Lord." Grandmother's way with us was always endearing and sweet even when she was threatening. "Daddy will be here after while," she would say.

We always straightened right up.

"Okay, Grandmother, we'll be good, we'll be good," most of us would respond. "All right, all right, don't tell Grandpa."

My cousin Michael was hardheaded. And he often dismissed Grandmother's warnings as quickly as she had uttered them.

"Man, she gonna tell Grandpa," I would say to Michael.

"Grandpa ain't gon' do nothing to me," he'd say, his eyes widening and playful. "I ain't scared of Grandpa."

"Fool, Grandpa gon' kill you, man," I warned, thinking as I did most of the time that Michael must be crazy.

Michael laughed, his fire finally turning into mush.

"I'm just playin' man. I ain't no fool," he'd say. "All right, Grandmother, I'll be good. Don't tell Grandpa . . . For real, Grandmother, for real. Don't tell Grandpa."

Thank God, she seldom did tell Grandpa. It is a strange thing, loving someone and being so full of admiration and yet so afraid of that person all at the same time. That was how we felt about Grandpa. But it wasn't fear in a bad way. We weren't afraid that he would abuse us, or anything like that. We were just too terrified "to act a fool," as my Aunt Mary often characterized misbehaving. It was good fear. And Grandpa was a good man.

He would pile all of his grandchildren into his car or into the church van and drive us to the park, where we played softball. Once, he hit a grounder and was running to first base, then slipped and fell. A look of mild embarrassment spread across his face that was as clear as the green grass and the sun. And we all laughed. He laughed, too.

When Grandpa and Grandmother had their annual "appreciations" as we called them, which were the yearly church-sponsored programs to honor them for their loyal service to the ministry, they always invited the family to their house afterward for pizza. It was always Home Run Inn Pizza, the Hagler family favorite. Home Run Inn is a West Side joint down at Thirty-first Street and Keeler Avenue on the south end of K-Town that I swear still makes the best pizza in Chicago, with its thick sausage and cheese combination and sweet thicker-than-thin crust. Even though Home Run Inn has since expanded, opening a few restaurants in the suburbs, the Thirty-first and Keeler joint is still the best. Grandpa would order about seven pizzas and we would eat them all. Arty and Michael and Uncle Gene ate like pigs at a trough, swallowing down slices like gulps of air.

Everybody came to Grandmother and Grandpa's for pizza. Everybody always came to their house every Christmas and Thanksgiving as well, "everybody" being all my aunts and their husbands and my uncle and his wife, and all the grandchildren, the whole busload of us. All of the adults sat in the living room after dinner laughing and sometimes playing games while the children played downstairs. At the end of the Thanksgiving evening, we wrote all our names on little pieces of paper and put them into a sack for a Christmas grab bag. Grandmother and Grandpa delighted in having their family around. And for a long time, it seemed as if there were few things that we did not do as a family.

On some weekends, we traveled by caravan, each family riding in its car to a smorgasbord in Kankakee, Illinois, a small town forty-five miles south of Chicago—that is, everyone except my family. For a long time, we always piled into someone else's car, or my stepfather drove one of my grandparents' cars because we didn't have one of our own, which meant we didn't get to partake in another family ritual for many years. That ritual was driving by everybody's house and honking the horn whenever you got a new car as the family poured out of their houses and gave it a good look over.

On the road to Kankakee, the men raced south down the Dan Ryan Expressway, the downtown skyscrapers at our backs, past Comiskey Park, past the concrete high-rises that were the Robert Taylor Homes and State-way Gardens, which looked like giant prisons. We eventually turned onto

Interstate 57, the cityscape giving way to green cornfields and flat prairie land that stretched as far as the eye could see. My cousins and I always bet on whose car would arrive in Kankakee first, and we jumped and laughed and waved as our cars passed each other on the highway. Uncle Gene always drove faster than anyone else, his smile glistening like chrome as he sat behind the wheel of his white-and-black Buick Wildcat that screeched and smoked whenever he burned rubber. He was tough to beat. But all of that fast driving made Grandmother nervous. In her own car, she had worn out the passenger-side floor mat and had penetrated even the car's floor by hitting her imaginary brakes mercilessly while Grandpa was behind the wheel and his mind was somewhere else until Grandmother suddenly screamed, "Honeyyy!" to keep him from slamming into another car. We always made it to the smorgasbord safely.

The smorgasbord in Kankakee was a wooden cabinlike restaurant called Redwood Inn. It sat just off Interstate 57, on the east side of the highway. We piled into that place, usually fourteen adults and anywhere from ten to fifteen children. We ate until our insides ached. Once, the men in the family had gone to Redwood Inn by themselves and had eaten so much, piled their plates so high with meats, so many times, that the white folks who ran the place asked them kindly to never come back. They later laughed about it. So did everyone else who has ever heard the story. It is still hard to imagine being kicked out of a smorgasbord.

If we weren't driving to Kankakee, we were driving somewhere else. There were trips to Riverview, the now defunct but legendary Chicago amusement park that existed long before the Great Americas and Six Flags. There was the annual trip to the Burton Roy family reunion in Gary or Indianapolis, Indiana. And there was the annual trip to Memphis, Tennessee, the Mecca of the Church of God in Christ, where the Holy Convocation, the gathering of the church faithful, was held each November.

The Holy Convocation was the equivalent of the Muslim hajj. Every saint of God was encouraged to make the journey at least once in their lives to the church's annual national fall meeting at its headquarters in Memphis. Except many saints kept going back, caught up in the thrill of seeing so many worshipers in one city gathered together for the same purpose and all wearing a week's worth of their Sunday best.

The women wore feathery or lace-draped hats, sequins, and pumps. The older women in the church, who were called church mothers, wore matching scarves that they draped over their skirts to hide their knees during service so as not to reveal too much flesh. Their hair was fixed in fancy buns and French rolls, or it was satin-straight or curly or finger waved. A mink coat or stole accentuated the ensemble, if a sister was so inclined. But the jewelry was modest. Rarely did sanctified sisters adorn their earthly vessels with more than a watch and a wedding ring. Earrings were modest if they were worn at all. Women rarely wore makeup. Sanctified women didn't believe in wearing the paint of Jezebel. That was a true mark of worldliness.

The men were not to be outdone. They wore lizard- and alligator-skin shoes or buffed leather with crisp white shirts, pocket squares and silk ties to match, cufflinks and double-breasted or three-piece suits that made them look like the Hollywood versions of Eliot Ness's men, the Gospel version of the Untouchables. They wore fedoras or other dress hats and cashmere coats. They toted Bibles underneath their arms, looking spiffy and spit-shined, every whisker trimmed and in place. It may have been the annual meeting of the Church of God in Christ, but it was as much the meeting of the Church of God in Fashion. Still is.

But there was also an air of pride and excitement, the likes of which I have seen only when decent, like-minded black folks assemble in large numbers. At the Holy Convocation, there hung in the air a sense of purpose and kinship like a big ole family reunion, with folks greeting each other in hotel lobbies, restaurants, and even out on the street with hugs and kisses. The women were referred to as Sister or Mother. The men were called Brother, or Elder or Minister, although preachers had developed this habit of referring to other preachers as "Doc," which is meant to say Doctor, as in Ph.D. in theology, even if this was not the case. And most often that was not the case. Their terminology was simply vernacular and used much in the same way that as a boy I used the term "Man."

Being in that environment was infectious, and I could see early on how people got hooked on making the annual trek. Down in Memphis, you felt like you were a part of something huge and that this denomination—started by a black Southern preacher named Bishop Charles Harrison Mason, a physically small man who spoke in tongues and believed in the baptism of the Holy Ghost—must have been ordained by God to have grown to this magnitude of people coming from all over the world to worship under the umbrella of the grand old Churches of God in Christ. It truly was amazing.

My grandparents always made the 500-mile drive from Chicago to Memphis, and on occasion carried several grandchildren with them in their car, braving the idea of being confined in close quarters with a bunch of cackling kids for miles on end. But Grandmother and Grandpa loved being around us. And we loved being around them, although I am not sure we kids always realized this.

On the road to the Holy Convocation, we could always spot the saints who were headed to Memphis. There were a few dead giveaways. One sure way was if the car was southbound with Illinois plates. Another was if the car was a Lincoln Continental or a Cadillac. Preachers drove big cars. Another was whether they had spotted us first and honked as we crossed paths on the highway. And last, if there were women in the car with scarves on their heads and big puffy pink hair rollers underneath to keep their dos in place, it was a safe bet that they were Memphis bound.

Whenever we traveled to Memphis, Grandpa always stopped at his hometown in Pulaski to see old friends, and then again in Cairo, Illinois, where we stopped to eat at a restaurant called Whataburger, pronounced by us kids as "Waterburger." This joint had the biggest and best hamburgers in the world. It was Grandpa's favorite—and ours, too. There was nothing like a Whataburger after a few hundred miles of riding across flat Illinois highway for hours, dreaming of the moment when at the southern tip of the state we would pull into the parking lot of the restaurant and partake of this ritual that had become as much a part of the Hagler family tradition as anything else. Grandpa seemed to delight in watching us sink our teeth into the giant burgers as much as he enjoyed devouring one or two himself.

When I was ten or eleven, Grandmother and Grandpa had taken me, Michael, and Arty and my Aunt Scope's daughters, Cheryl and Doris, with them to Memphis. It had been a good trip, but also one in which we had managed to get the best of our grandparents' nerves and one in which Cheryl had even managed to rile up Grandmother enough to get a good smacking from her after we had visited the Church of God in Christ school called Saints Industrial in Lexington, Mississippi.

"I'm glad I don't go to that school. Those kids talk white," Cheryl had said, getting on Grandmother's last nerve and provoking her to smite Cheryl with a hairbrush somewhere across her head as she sat in the back seat of the car. "I'm so mad I could just die!" Cheryl screamed in response to Grandmother's wrath.

Something rose up in Grandmother, and she commenced to whipping Cheryl's butt, working the brush like a pair of martial arts fighting sticks.

"Go 'head and die!" Grandmother huffed and screamed as she laid into Cheryl. "Go 'head and die!"

Provoking Grandmother to that point was nearly impossible, though if anybody could do it, Cheryl, with all of her curt backtalk, surely could. Anyway, on our way back from Memphis, not far out of Cairo and after having just completed our return trip to Whataburger, Michael and Arty started passing gas. Maybe it was the Whataburgers they had eaten, maybe not. They always seemed to have possessed the gift of passing gas at will. I was sitting in the front with my grandparents. My cousins were all in the back. Each time the waft of gas filled the car, Grandpa rolled down the power windows of the Cadillac, the cold November air chilling us to the bone.

"George, let the window up, honey, pleeeeazzz, honeyyy," Grandmother said as my cousins all snickered. "Y'all be quiet and stop all that laughing and talking," Grandmother fussed without any success.

Grandpa sat behind the wheel of the car never saying a word.

Finally, after many more farts and laughing and the rolling down of the windows and Grandmother's pointless pleading, the car suddenly began slowing down and veering off the highway toward the service lane. Fear filled the car. And my cousins all stopped laughing. Grandpa still didn't say a word.

"Uh-ohhh," Michael said.

"I tried to tell y'all to stop," Grandmother said, sounding as if Judgment Day had come.

The car came to a halt and Grandpa swiftly reached across Grandmother and into the glove compartment down by my knees. He pulled out a small rubber flashlight, then whipped around swiftly and played the xylophone on my cousins' heads. Bing-bing-bing-bing, bing-bing-bing-bing, went the flashlight as Grandpa went down the line.

"Didn't your grandmother tell you to stop?" Grandpa said angrily. "Didn't your grandmother tell you to stop?"

Bing, bing, bing, bing . . .

In a flash, it was over. Grandpa shoved the flashlight back into the glove compartment and pulled away, his hands on the wheel, no more farts or laughing, though Doris sniffled from just outside Cairo all the way back to Chicago.

There was nothing Grandpa loved more than his family, except maybe God, or the church, which for a long time was his family. I have wondered many times where that comes from. The more I began to understand him and perhaps even to better understand myself over the years, the less it was a mystery. Grandmother and Grandpa clung to each other because they were all they had. They clung to their family because they understood long ago that family was all they would ever have. They loved their family because of who they were at the core. What's funny is I always looked at them as anomalies, as maybe even being a little weird for their unusual fuss and concern over their grandchildren and the simple joy they seemed to take from all of us being together as a family. I later wondered, looking back, why there weren't more people in my neighborhood who cherished their families the way my grandparents had. But what I could see was how vital men are to their families, and how entirely opposite all the men that Grandpa's daughters married were from him.

We were all known as the Haglers, even though my last name was Fountain and none of my cousins, with the exception of Kim, my Uncle Gene's daughter, bore the Hagler name. For the rest of us, the link to the Hagler clan was through our mothers, who were born Haglers. Then they married and had children, and we inherited our fathers' names and the Hagler traits.

The Hagler physical attributes are as distinguishable as those of the Kennedys or other families whose genetic makeup is easily identifiable. We all inherited the Hagler look, so pronounced that throughout my life folks I had never seen before would walk up and ask, "Hey, are you a Hagler?" Or at times when I have introduced myself to someone involved in some way in the Church of God in Christ and have mentioned that my grandfather was Pastor George Hagler, people have exclaimed, sometimes with a chuckle, "I can tell. You look like a Hagler. You have that Hagler head."

The female Hagler look is slightly different. Hagler women are round, no matter how slim in the early stages. Father Time, fried chicken, and Grandmother's peach cobbler—not to mention Aunt Mary's homemade, triple-decker German chocolate cake—had a way of fluffing them out. Our women have thick thighs, wide bottoms, and coke-bottle-thin lower legs. Eyes brown, like Grandmother's, and almond-shaped. Short to medium length hair of medium to coarse grade. Mocha skin, although varying shades of brown fill the family with a few, like my sister Net, being yellow, our father's genes prevailing against those of the Haglers. That was a rare occurrence.

The men are broad, with wide shoulders, seventeen- to nineteen-inch necks, barrel chests, and size ten to eleven feet. Two hundred pounds is carried with ease on our frames. Our excess is displayed in our cheeks and our guts, though a good suit that accentuates the shoulders and chest camouflages the bulge. Cowlicks have their way among Hagler men. Facial hair is sparse by choice, generally a mustache, maybe some sideburns but seldom a beard.

For Haglers, male and female, round and high cheeks are common. High foreheads and straight, often thick, smooth eyebrows that lie neatly and submissively in place. We all have the same average-sized nose that is slightly pointed and rounded at the base, blending well with a full face. There is the indentation, the pronounced raised lines that look like a paper clip between our nose and lips, which are thick, shapely, and brown.

Even our babies look like Hagler babies: light-skinned with chocolate around the tips of the ears and fingertips, cute round faces with fat cheeks and button noses, curly to straight hair whose curly grade is soon to fade.

Probably nothing is a more telling feature on a Hagler than our heads, round and big. But it is the way we carry them, particularly the men. It is something I perfected as a child after years of studying the way my grandfather walked. It is the Hagler walk: stiff neck, shoulders back, back straight with each foot placed purposefully on the ground, the chin slightly tilted up and a faint hint of swagger that said, "Even if I don't have a dollar, I'm somebody, I'm a Hagler." It is a proud walk. I wanted to be just like Grandpa, not a mailman necessarily, though it was an honorable job. But the man part of him, especially the family man part of him, was what most appealed to me.

For a while growing up, I even wished my name was Hagler. The man who had given me his name—first, middle, and last—gave me little else. And in those times that other men disappointed me or flat out failed and there was no one else to look up to, there was always Grandpa. He was a simple man, one who had not earned a high school diploma but whose language and wisdom and heart shone like gold. Grandpa was not a man of many words. But you could depend on him. He was like a rock: Strong. Solid. Sure. And that was more than I could say of most of the men who had touched my life. However, even having the good image of Grandpa would not be enough for a boy desperately in need of so much more than I could ever have known back then. It would take nearly half a lifetime to understand that I always had much more than I ever realized.

CHAPTER 3

SOUL MAN

"Stop...In the naaame of luuuv, beee-forrre youuu breaaak my hearrrt. Think it o-o-verrrr..." Diana Ross and the Supremes' voices piped through the boxy, wooden hi-fi stereo in our living room. Then James Brown, the Temptations, the Beatles. "I wanna hold your ha-a-and, I wanna hold your hand," I sang as Mama got ready for work, the sounds of the radio sweeping through the apartment like the smell of Dial soap and Mama's instant coffee, which she always mixed with water she boiled in a small uncovered pot on the kitchen stove.

It was still dark outside. Komensky was quiet and still except on the inside of people's houses, where the lights had already begun to flick on as parents readied for work and children stumbled from bed. It was just Mama and Net and me. I was four. Net was two. Mama was twenty-one. Mama helped us get dressed while she danced and snapped her fingers, gliding on the music though moving with a sense of purpose. Our mornings were always tranquil. There were no mice, roaches, or hardship and fussing in those years.

Mama worked as a telephone operator at Illinois Bell, or Ma Bell, as everybody called the telephone company. Mama had to be at work by 7 o'clock. That meant Net and I had to get dressed so we could go to Aunt Mary's house. Aunt Mary, Mama's eldest sister, was our baby-sitter, and she lived a few doors down South Komensky at 1634 on the second floor. On weekdays, Aunt Mary kept most of the kids in the Hagler clan as well as a few other kids, which always made for a packed house. Sometimes there were more than a dozen of us little crumb snatchers at Aunt Mary's. We didn't have to do that much, it seemed, to get on Aunt Mary's nerves. And Aunt Mary didn't mind telling us when we had. Nor did she mind whipping our butts. She used to look extremely relieved when the little hand on the wall clock that hung above the space heater in her living room finally wound around to five at the end of the day and our mothers began returning from work. Then the strained lines in Aunt Mary's face dissolved like two Alka-Seltzer tablets in water and the thunder in her voice was replaced with a syrupy treble. I wonder if she ever knew how relieved we felt, too. We kids used to secretly call Aunt Mary "the warden," but never within her earshot. That would have meant an instant beat-down.

The cycle of going to the baby-sitter's began each morning before 6 A.M. with the smell of coffee and the sounds of mostly Motown. The radio was forever tuned to WVON 1450. Every so often, the half-sung station identification echoed over the airwaves. "Dou-ble U-VONnnn four-teeeeen fif-teee..."

Mama loved music. Our hi-fi was truly one of Mama's treasures. It was one of those rectangular-shaped, mahogany-colored wooden boxes that looked almost like a short bedroom dresser. It seemed that everyone had a hi-fi then. They were as common as the velvet Muhammad Ali "Float like a butterfly, sting like a bee" posters that we all later got at the annual Black Expo at McCormick Place in Chicago or those psychedelic octagon-shaped metallic joints that hung on the wall and that you turned on whenever you turned on the hi-fi, whose lights seemed to flash in time to the rhythm of the music. Our hi-fi sat in the living room against the north wall. Its top was always raised when it was on. Mama had amassed her own collection of 45s and LPs. She had everybody: Martha Reeves and the Vandellas, the Temptin' Temptations, Aretha Franklin, Gladys Knight and the Pips, James Brown. Mama's love for music rubbed off on me. I also picked up her knack for dancing. I especially liked to dance with Mama. She smiled and snapped. I shuffled and shook.

"You gettin' down, boy," Mama used to say in that way that older black folks do when they're watching a little kid boogie down. "Hey now ...How ya' handling it, John, how ya' handling it!"

I never said a word. I just smiled and danced with all my might until I got tired or the music stopped. Mama taught me how to do the Boogaloo, Mashed Potato, Bird, and Funky Chicken and even how to bop. Now the bop was something special. It is the black equivalent of the waltz and is known today as "stepping," which is a big part of black culture in Chicago. But unlike the waltz, the bop is performed with more rhythm and fancier moves like the tango. People who bopped—or "steppers," as they are called—are expected to display the right mixture of cool and technique to be considered bad, which is meant to say, good. When you did the bop, you couldn't be too wild or out of control. You had to be smooth, or "smoove," as we used to say. Every choreographed step and turn was an expression of who you were. When perfected, your moves spoke for you. They said, "I'm the baddest coolest Negro on the dance floor." I loved to bop. But I also loved to do the Bird. Mama seemed to love having me show off my moves to her favorite sister, Clotee, who for a time lived downstairs on the second floor.

But eventually it was hard for even a fancy dancing little brother like me to compete with Tom Jones, who each week made Mama and Aunt Clotee run into the hallway screaming like teenage girls. During the show, so as not to miss a single gyrating move, Aunt Clotee banged on her ceiling with her broom handle and Mama stomped her approval whenever this old white dude in tight slacks did some wiggling dance motion that made his female audience on television as well as Mama and Aunt Clotee go spastic. It was only at the conclusion of the show or during commercial breaks that they dared even take their eyes off the television. Then they ran screaming into the hall to confer and exchange notes.

"Gwennnn, girrrrl, did you see that?" Aunt Clotee screamed.

"Girrrrl, I thought I was gon' lose my mind," Mama fired back.

"Woo-oo-oo! Me too. Uh-oh, girl, he about to come back on," Aunt Clotee said as if she could barely contain herself.

"Okay, I'll see you in a minute," Mama said. Then she slammed the door and ran back to the television, giggling all the way.

Nope. I could not compete with Tom. But when he wasn't on TV sometimes I danced for Mama and Aunt Clotee. I made my legs shake back and forth, with my feet planted on the floor, my knees trembling, as if I was about to start convulsing. Then I'd break out doing the Twist or something else, like the Funky Chicken. Mama and Aunt Clotee laughed and swayed and snapped their fingers and sashayed. But I never had quite the same effect as Tom Jones. It was years before I understood why. But performing for Mama and Aunt Clotee was so much fun. It especially felt good to see Mama belting out one of those hearty, all-consuming belly-aching laughs. I felt the same way whenever I saw my daddy, whenever I heard his voice or saw him walk through our front door, except by age four that had already become a rare occurrence.

There was a rap at our front door one evening. Mama and Net and I sat on the sofa, watching television on a quiet night at home. It was dark outside. The sound of the flickering television filled the living room. Back then, Mama loved watching *The FBI* "in color, with Efrem Zimbalist Jr.," as the announcer's voice blared over the television at the start of every episode, and we sat sometimes with a bowl of buttered popcorn. She also liked watching *Bonanza* and *The Rifleman*. Net and I liked watching whatever Mama watched, especially at night over popcorn, sitting at Mama's feet in our pajamas under the glare of the television.

The knock on the door that evening caught us by surprise. Usually the arrival of visitors at our front door was announced by footsteps on the unpadded wooden stairs that led to our third-floor apartment. There were no footsteps this time. Yet the knock seemed recognizable. I jumped to my feet and dashed to the door.

"It's Daddy, it's Daddy!" I exclaimed.

"Come back here, John," Mama scolded. "Don't open that door."

"But it's Daddy," I answered, puzzled by Mama's tone of voice.

"How do you know who it is? Wait a minute, don't open that door, ask who it is," Mama fired back.

"Whooo izzzz it?" I asked, barely able to keep still.

"It's me," the voice behind the locked door answered. "It's me, John."

"It's Daddy, it's Daddy!" I screamed, jumping up and down. "I told you it was Daddy!"

Mama responded less excitedly.

"Okay, open the door," she said.

I twisted the lock. There he was. Tall, slender, smiling, and wearing a mustache and cap, the patch of pink in the middle of his lips.

"Dad-deee!"

I grabbed his leg and hugged him. He hugged me back, nearly tripping as he walked through the door. He was chewing gum as usual. He smiled.

"Hey boy," he said.

I held onto him all the way to the living room. He spoke to Mama and Net. Then he sat down in a chair in front of the television. He and Mama didn't have much to say to each other. In fact, there was a strange look of unfriendliness or distance or something else in Mama's eyes. Mama seemed nervous. After a few minutes, she rose from the couch and disappeared inside her bedroom. Whatever was their problem didn't matter to me. Daddy was home. I climbed up on his lap. The cinnamon on his breath smelled strong, although there was another strong scent competing against it, each trying to prevail. Years later, I would recognize the smell that had been on my daddy's breath that night as that of a man who had been drinking and had popped a piece of chewing gum into his mouth to camouflage the stale, lingering smell of gin, whiskey, and wine. Sitting there on Daddy's lap, I homed in on the sweet aroma of cinnamon.

"Daddy, gimme some gum," I begged. "Can I have some gum?"

Daddy reached into his shirt pocket and handed me a piece of Dentyne. I peeled back the paper and shoved the gum into my mouth. I felt so secure sitting there, resting on his lap, as if nothing else in the world even mattered. I could not remember the last time I had seen him before then.

Though it was true that by age four he had already become an irregular presence in our lives, there were still fresh memories of being together with my daddy, of his big hand swallowing mine as we walked to my Aunt Margarette's house. Aunt Margarette was his mother's sister and she lived in K-Town, but down off Cermak Road, about a dozen blocks or so from our apartment on Komensky. A tall brown-skinned woman who didn't mince words, she had three sons, all of whom were older than I was. Their names were Clyde, Frank, and Peter. And they were already pre-pubescent boys, with a knack for squeezing my head in their palms and playfully mocking me with a version of the nickname that Aunt Margarette had affectionately given me, "Fur Ball."

"Hey, fuzz ball," my cousins would say, laughing and almost falling over themselves as they spiked my head with their fingers to my own soreness. They thought this was fun and amused themselves at my expense, although I could sense that this was never done maliciously. I loved being around these guys. They were like goofy big brothers.

I had visited their house with Daddy many times and had even spent the night there. Many years later, I can still see my father's image as he lay sleeping in one of Aunt Margarette's bedrooms. Daddy slobbered when he slept, something that Aunt Margarette's boys also teased me about. That hurt some. He was, after all, my daddy. I loved that man as much as any little boy is capable of loving his father. It was innate, I guess. It is hard to describe the sense of ease and comfort I felt in his presence, or the reaffirming power and purpose I felt even as a small child just being around him, as if I was his and he was mine. In all of my years, I have never known that feeling again, never felt completely whole. That is what I felt sitting there on my daddy's lap, chewing cinnamon gum, resting on his chest and pressed close to his face, feeling his mustache, breath, and life. I felt whole, like some man's son. I could have sat there forever.

"Hey, John," Mama interrupted. "Come here." She emerged from her bedroom with a note. "Take this note downstairs to Aunt Scope," she said matter of factly.

"I know what this is," I exclaimed, grabbing the folded piece of paper. "You want to borrow some money."

That was usually the purpose of my mother's notes to my aunt. I knew as much because I had managed to read them all. Mama did not know this, of course. But that was one of the perks of being a smart kid and knowing how to read. I even used to decode the words Mama and other adults spelled around me without hinting that I knew what they were talking about.

"Boy, just take the note to Aunt Scope like I said," Mama said.

"Gwen, if you need money, I got some money," Daddy interrupted.

Mama didn't answer. Her eyes looked almost afraid.

"John, take the note to Aunt Scope," she said.

I hurried to the door, anxious to get back to Daddy. As I walked down the stairs, I thought about reading the note. I even began to unfold it, but decided not to. I don't know why I chose not to read this note. I just didn't read it. I knocked on the door. Aunt Scope answered.

"Aunt Scope, my mama told me to give you this note," I said, handing over the correspondence.

Aunt Scope unfolded the piece of paper and read it.

"Tell her I said, 'Okay,'" she said, half smiling.

I ran back upstairs in my stocking feet.

"Ma," I said, "Aunt Scope said, 'Okay.'"

"Okay," Mama said.

I climbed back onto Daddy's lap. He and Mama were having some discussion. I cannot recall what they were saying. But the tenor of their conversation was strained, Mama's words careful and shaky. We were all sitting there quietly when a few minutes later, suddenly there was another knock at our door. It was a hard rap and unrecognizable. I jumped up and was about to bolt toward the door when Mama stopped me dead in my tracks.

"Johnnnn, sit down!"

I froze. Mama stood up and hurried to the door. I followed behind her.

"Who is it?" she asked.

A man's heavy but gentle voice answered back, "The police."

The police? Why were the police here? I thought. What's going on? What? Why?

"Gwen, you didn't have to call the police," Daddy said, sounding apologetic. "I just wanted to talk, I would have left."

"There is nothing to talk about," Mama fired back, her voice filled with fire. "I just want you out . . . Now!

"But . . ."

"Go!"

End of discussion.

The two black police officers in their blue uniforms led my father away in handcuffs. I watched as they took him out of our apartment and down the stairs, a piece of me going with them. Afterward Mama explained that she was sorry that Net and I had to see our daddy taken away like that, that she had to call the police on him. He had been drinking. And we didn't want for Daddy to hurt Mommy, did we?

We didn't. Neither could we understand, although one of my earliest childhood memories was of my father and mother scuffling at the top of a flight of stairs that seemed like the top of a steep hill and me standing there frozen, afraid that at any moment Mama might go tumbling down. She did not. At least not in the physical sense. But looking back, I can only imagine that was how she must have felt sometimes, left to raise two children, her life spiraling out of control. That night that the police took Daddy away was Mama's attempt to regain control. And how difficult, how brave of her to have summoned the police and kicked this man—who obviously had too many problems to be any good for her and her children—out of our lives. But I did not understand this back then. I could not have understood this back then.

I don't remember if I cried that night. But for years, I would cry whenever I recalled that night. For years, I sat on our porch on some summer evenings, watching the cars go by and dreaming that one day one of those cars would suddenly pull over and stop and that the man getting out of the car would be my daddy. In time, I eventually forgot what Daddy looked like, because any pictures of him disappeared from our apartment and the portrait in my mind became frayed and fuzzy. Faded too were recollections of what he even sounded like, as months turned into years and years turned into what seemed like a lifetime without word from him and with my mother having made the decision that we should not see him and that he should not see us. There was no use in even bringing his name up or even the possibility of seeing him, unless I wanted to encounter Mama's wrath.

In Mama's eyes, Daddy was no good. At least that was the way Mama and the cacophony of other mamas in the 'hood, who routinely pronounced their babies' daddies to be just as good as dead, had simplified it. As a child, I sometimes couldn't help but believe that this was true. That Daddy was no good. But eventually I discovered life to be more complex and have come to see that men in one way or another are the sum of the experiences of their own, sometimes tragic childhoods. I eventually found another way to describe my daddy. Not as being "no good." Just filled up with so much bad that he wound up trying to rinse away his yesterdays with whiskey and cheap wine that left him hung over and staggering through too many todays, until finally there were no more tomorrows.

In all of my forgetting over time, one thing I never forgot: That Daddy always chewed cinnamon gum. Sometimes I would buy it at the candy store just to remember him. Every time I inhaled the scent of cinnamon, I thought of him. Every time I chewed a cinnamon toothpick, or when I sucked on cinnamon candy, or when Aunt Mary sprinkled cinnamon on my toast or on an apple, I thought of my daddy. I still do. Memories of Daddy drift on the scent of cinnamon.

As a child, I vowed that someday when I got good and grown, I would seek out John Wesley Fountain Sr., if only to restore the portrait of him in my mind, if only to find some measure of wholeness for my soul. Someday I would see my daddy again, someday.

CHAPTER 4

GOOD TIMES ROLL

MAMA ALWAYS held some job or other. For a while, she worked as a telephone operator, for a while she worked downtown at Continental Bank in the Accounts Department, and for a while at the Post Office. Mama was a smart lady who read the newspaper every day, always watched the nightly news, and was always ready to engage in some debate about politics or world affairs. She was articulate and slender, with dark brown eyes, and she wore her hair short, sometimes pressed and curled, sometimes not. When she got all dressed up in her high heels to go out on a date, she sprayed Estée Lauder that lingered in the house long after she had kissed us goodnight. She loved chicken and noodles, liver and onions, coffee with cream, chocolate with pecans, and pineapple upside-down cake, which she baked to excess—my own. Her favorite snack was a BLT sandwich with cheese, which she toasted in the bottom oven until the cheese on top had melted and had turned burnt brown at the edges. Her nails were long. And when she painted them, she always removed the polish before she went to church. She fantasized about going on *Let's Make a Deal* until there was *The Price Is Right*, until there was *Jeopardy*. She hated mice, misery, and mopping. There were many things I knew about Mama. But as much as I thought I knew her as a child, I later discovered that I did not. At least, I had no full understanding of who she really was.

As a child, I used to stare at the picture of Mama that hung on the dining room wall in my grandparents' home with the other high school graduation head-and-shoulders shots of her sisters and her brother, each of them dressed in their cap and gown. They all looked so young then, so innocent and carefree. As the years passed, their black-and-white portraits seemed to grow younger. It was hard to imagine that the faces in the frames were actually Mama and my aunts and uncle or that their lives were once as simple and unencumbered as the smiles and youthful eyes in those eight-by-ten portraits seemed to imply.

I studied Mama's portrait more than all the others. I can still see the image of the young woman with the hot-comb-straightened hair and the white collar that showed above the grayish gown, a hint of gloss on her lips and the optimistic eyes that stared back through the glass softly as if she were looking at me through the window of another world. It has always struck me that when Gwendolyn Marie—as Grandmother often called her—posed for that picture she was already my mother or that a couple years after that picture was taken, Mama would be working to support her two children and trying to make a life for the three of us. As I studied her picture, the smooth complexion absent of the tired lines that come from years of worries and heartache, I came to understand that Mama's heart was still young then, still unbroken, tender, hopeful. What I also realized, although not fully until many years later, was that there were so many more dimensions to the young woman in the picture frame whom Net and I knew only as Mama. It was hard to imagine that Mama even had a life before us.

As an adult, I once stumbled across a high school yearbook at Aunt Clotee's house. Sitting on the sofa in the basement of her home, I thumbed through the Farragut High School class of 1962 yearbook and my eyes fell upon pictures of Mama, who graduated the same year as her younger sister, Clotee. Mama had been two years ahead of Aunt Clotee but dropped out of school after getting married in September 1959, a month after her sixteenth birthday. My father was twenty-one. Mama

gave birth to me a year later, at seventeen. Over that next year, Grandmother prodded Mama and pleaded with her to go back to school, insisting that she would need her diploma. A high school diploma was
something that Grandmother had not gotten herself in the years that followed her marriage to Grandpa at fifteen, as life and children preoccupied
her days and dreams. And while Grandmother was probably the most
self-assured woman I knew, one whose joy and lifeblood lay in being a
mother and wife, I later sensed in her a kind of loss or longing regarding
her own lack of formal education. But years after that, I also saw the twinkle in her eyes when in her fifties she went back to school and earned her
GED, though in truth, by then she had already earned a doctorate in life.
But in 1960, she had the foresight to know that things would be different
for Mama, that she might have to earn a living for her children and that
there might be no equivalent of a husband as provider in her life. Finally,
after much coaxing, she persuaded Mama to return to school.

In those times it wasn't acceptable for girls who were mothers, even if
they were married, to be in school. School administrators worried about
the influence that such young ladies might have on other girls at school.
So going back to school meant that Mama had to keep a low profile, especially since she was pregnant again by then, a secret she guarded with
loose-fitting clothes and sealed lips.

When the time came for Mama to graduate, she wanted a new dress
for the ceremony but didn't have the money. Grandmother's money was
tight, too. But because Mama had done what Grandmother had asked by
going back and completing high school, she took Mama to a department
store and let her pick out an expensive beautiful dress for graduation. It
was orange with pretty red and yellow flowers. It was Grandmother's way
of saying, "Thank you. I am so proud of you."

Mama wore the dress to graduation, just two weeks after giving birth
to Net. I sat in the audience at nearly two years old, oblivious to the experience, with Grandpa and Grandmother, who watched proudly as Mama
accepted her diploma. Many years later, whenever Grandmother retold
this story to me, her voice was filled with such emotion and pride that I
have always known that it was not just Mama who graduated from high
school that sunny day in June 1962.

While thumbing through the high school yearbook at Aunt Clotee's, I also came across a biography of Gwendolyn Marie Hagler. It noted that she dreamed of someday becoming a schoolteacher. I remember being stunned by that discovery. Not because I thought Mama was incapable of becoming a teacher. Grandmother had always told me how smart Mama always was, so smart, in fact, that she had skipped a grade. I might have figured as much by the way Mama was always reading books or the newspaper. But Mama never breathed a word of her childhood dreams. Fingering the pages of the yearbook, it was as if I did not know her at all. There was a picture of Mama in the school choir. She was even an honor student. I felt incredibly sad as I wondered whether Gwendolyn Marie Hagler's dream of becoming a schoolteacher was but one of many that got lost somewhere in the gulf that lies between yesterday and today. I once heard it said that life is what happens when you make other plans. Life happened to Mama: marriage, motherhood, and divorce, all within the span of a few years. She dried her eyes, picked us up, and moved on, though not without leaving a piece of herself behind.

Even without my father being around, life was not so bad. Saturdays were the best days for Net and me. On Saturday, Mama gave each of us our $1-a-week allowance. That was a lot of money in the early 1960s. Back then, a dollar could seem like a million bucks to a kid. No sooner had Mama given us our weekly allowance than Net and I hurried out the front door, headed to the Peanut Man.

The Peanut Man was the only name we ever knew for the dark-skinned, wrinkled old man who sat on the corner of Sixteenth Street and Pulaski Road on the steps of the corner dry cleaners, selling dime-bags of shelled roasted peanuts. I later learned that his real name was Claude Hughes, the son of a Mississippi Baptist minister who believed God told him at an early age that he had a calling on his life. The Peanut Man was twenty-seven years old and living in Jackson, Mississippi, when it became clear to him that peanut vending was that calling. I also learned that he was one of my kinfolk in a roundabout way. The Peanut Man was the uncle of my Aunt Brenda's husband, Ollie.

The Peanut Man always wore a pearly smile and a hat. His hat was nothing fancy, just a plain old Sunday gentleman's dress hat to keep the sun out of his face. In addition to peanuts, he sold an assortment of penny bubble gum—hard and soft—and candies, including 5-cent boxes of Lemonheads, Red Hots, and Boston Baked Beans as well as Charms Sweet and Sour Pops. But peanuts were his forte. The Peanut Man sat for hours when he wasn't serving a customer, stuffing roasted shelled peanuts into small red-and-white-striped paper bags. He showed up on that corner every day. As sure as the sun rose, you could count on seeing him. He nodded and smiled as you walked by. Though he seldom spoke a word, he sweetened the neighborhood by his mere presence in a way that I am not sure anyone in the neighborhood really comprehended.

Net and I didn't always buy from the Peanut Man when we got our allowance. Sometimes we walked farther east on Sixteenth Street, about four or five extra blocks, to a dingy storefront that we only ever knew as the "toy store." There we could buy bubbles or some cheap gadget, a spinning top, or a rubber ball and still have plenty left to spend on potato chips or Red Hots and Lemonheads, which were our favorites. Some- times, when Mama asked us, we walked west on Sixteenth Street to Karlov Avenue to Miss Mamie's store. Miss Mamie's was a family run, mom-and-pop operation where we bought candy as well as our mom's grown-up version of treats, an ice-cold bottle of Pepsi and a pack of Win- ston cigarettes. Always Pepsi and always Winstons.

On some Saturdays when Net and I got back from candy shopping, we climbed into bed and built a tent with blankets that we looped on the metal spring between the top and bottom bunks. There we watched tele- vision and ate candy, popcorn, and potato chips for as long as we felt like it—that is, for as long as our supplies lasted. Times were good back then, although my way of measuring good times seems always to have boiled down to whether there was food. As an adult I came to understand the absence of food to be a key difference between the kind of poverty black folks had always known in the rural South and the new brand of urban poverty up North. In the rural South, there were always fields of greens and beans to be picked, maybe a chicken clucking out back, or a pond or lake to fish in. One could find sustenance in the land. But in the big city, the only chicken, fish, and vegetables to be had were at the local grocer and then, only if you had the cash. In those years, Mama always had the cash.

As a little boy, my biggest worry was Mama's bad headaches, which made her really sick. Mama didn't suffer regular headaches. She got migraines. Whenever they came on, the slightest noise hurt her head and the faintest hint of light hurt her eyes. Net and I knew that whenever Mama had a migraine, we needed to keep really quiet. I also knew to bring Mama cold wet towels to place on her forehead while she lay in bed or on the sofa until the pain finally went away. We were Mama's helpers. I got the sense early on that she was all that Net and I had in the world. When Mama wasn't around, Net was all I had and I was all she had, which meant protecting her from my cousins' teasing. Sometimes it seemed that it was the three of us against the world. And early on, Mama began fortifying me for the journey called life, although I did not always understand that was her purpose.

"John, you can be anything you want. You are so smart," she would say, sitting next to me in the living room. "You're the smartest boy in the world."

I absorbed her words.

"You can be president of the United States. You can be anything you want to be," Mama said.

"I want to be a lawyer," I responded, filled with excitement. "I'm going to be a lawyer when I grow up."

"That means you have to go to college, and to law school," Mama said.

"Yup, and I'm gon' buy you a house when I grow up."

"Oh yeah?" Mama laughed.

"Yeah, Ma, a big house, a real big house."

Mama chuckled.

"Well, when you grow up, if you get married, your wife will have to come first," she said.

"Uh-uh!" I protested.

"Sorry, John, but that's the way it is," Mama insisted. "Once you get married, your wife will come first. Mamas come second to their sons' wives."

As a boy of five or six, that didn't sound too much like right to me. I couldn't understand why Mama was already taking a back seat to some girl or woman I had not even met yet. Her counsel on this matter bothered me in much the way that her urging to always walk the straight and narrow, regardless of what anyone else was doing, always bothered me:

Don't worry about who's not going to church, I'm not their mother.
Don't worry about who can go off the block and play. They're not my concern.
Don't worry about him or her or this or that. Worry about yourself.
Do what's right.
Do your best.
I expect more out of you, John.
When you grow up, you have to put your wife first.

Ultimately, it didn't matter what Mama said about some other woman in the future having to be first in my life. I pledged in my heart that someday I would buy Mama that house. After all, she was the most important person in my life. Net and I were the most important people in hers.

Except life for the three of us was bound to change sooner or later.

Mama was getting ready to go out that night, the smell of sweet perfume wafting through our apartment. Net and I were already bathed and dressed for bed in our pajamas. I was six. Net was four. Mama's date was on his way over to pick her up. I remember feeling a little excited over the prospect of meeting this man named Eddie that Mama was dating. I don't know why. I just was.

My little sister and I were sitting on the sofa in the living room when there was a knock on the door. Eddie walked into the living room and sat on the couch. We talked for a few minutes. It was not much of a conversation. Just a meet and greet, small talk between children and an adult who was a complete stranger, smiles and chitchat. I didn't feel one way or another about this man named Eddie. He was just somebody who was going out with my mom. He was dark. He had an Afro and a mustache. He didn't look ugly. He was chewing mint gum. He was a man. It wasn't like he was going to be my dad or anything.

Within a year, they were married. Eddie moved in with us, which I am sure must have been an adjustment for me. But I cannot remember any particulars other than my difficulty in accepting the idea of calling another man "Daddy." Mama helped with the transition. She told Net and me that daddies are men who take care of their children. Mama has always had this saying, "You have to pay the costs to be the boss." Mama essentially told us that there was a new sheriff in town. You didn't argue with Mama about some things.

The first time I called my stepfather "Daddy," I felt sort of queasy. But I soon got used to it as well as the idea of having a man around the house. That he was willing to allow me to call him Daddy and to tell other people that I was his son made calling him Daddy that much easier. Whenever he went to the store, I walked with him. I studied him as he fixed things around the house with his bag of tools. I stared at him through the bathroom doorway as he wiped shaving cream over the stubble on his face and carefully raked a razor over his cheeks, chin, and neck until they were smooth. I sneaked into his aftershave, played catch with his baseball glove. He cut my hair, taught me how to shine my shoes and play checkers, Chinese and the usual way. He lifted me onto his shoulders and carried me to my bed when I fell asleep some nights or when he and Mama had been out and they picked us up from the baby-sitter. He became my dad. In fact, just hearing his voice, a man's voice, resonating through our house had a stabilizing influence, like an anchor on a ship. We didn't share many conversations. He wasn't that kind of man. We played and worked and laughed together. And in time, I grew to love him as a son loves a father. This did not fill the void or heal the pain left by my natural father's absence. But it surely helped sustain me at times.

I only wish that love and memories made on sunny summer afternoons were all there was. That the strains of economics, that unforeseen, untimely, and unpredictable circumstances or errors in judgment, that words or actions committed in anger or haste, were not also as much a part of life's memories. I only wish that the honeymoon could have lasted forever.

My little brother, Jeff, was born in August 1967. Things soon seemed to be rolling downhill. After Jeff's birth, Mama stopped working so she could take care of the three of us. My stepfather had a job at a manufacturing company making spoons and knives and other kitchen utensils, including pots and pans. He seemed to be making decent money. And we seemed to do well as long as he brought his money home. The problem was, he didn't always do that. Then he lost his job, and food grew more and more scarce. If we were on the edges of poverty before, we were certainly about to be thrust into the eye of the storm.

It wasn't long after Jeff was born that we seemed never to have any money anymore, and we sometimes teetered on and off welfare. Sometimes we waited at home hungry, starving, it seemed, for my stepfather to come home with his paycheck on Fridays. It was a great pain seeing the refrigerator and the pantry shelves empty. Sometimes while waiting for supper to materialize, I opened the refrigerator door and stared at the empty shelves, bare except for a spat of margarine and the glow of light. Then, an hour or so later, I would fling open the refrigerator door again, as if somehow I had missed something during my earlier search. Hungry, I stared into the cold emptiness.

On days when there was bread, Net and I made ketchup or syrup sandwiches or boiled grits and stirred in some sugar and butter, which stuck to our guts and kept us from going into hunger shock. In time, we even convinced ourselves that we actually liked eating ketchup sandwiches and drinking sugar water, when our cousins, and we imagined everybody else in our neighborhood, were wolfing down garlic-fried chicken and drinking Kool-Aid. Even a fried bologna sandwich seemed like a delicacy. It's amazing how almost anything can satisfy your hunger when you're hungry enough. Like those potato patties Mama used to make on weekends when there was no money and little to no food.

Mama would mash some potatoes and sprinkle in diced onions, salt, and pepper. Then she'd scoop some of the potatoes out of the bowl and roll them into balls. She covered each ball with white flour, then smashed them into cakes and dropped them into a crackling hot skillet of cooking oil. Mama deep-fried those potato patties until they were a crispy golden brown. The aroma saturated the house. Once they were done, that was some good eating, especially if we had ketchup. But even as I wolfed them down, savoring the crunchy flavor, I still felt in the pit of my stomach the pain of having to eat something that I was too ashamed to admit had been the entire substance of my supper. It bothered Mama, too. But she tried to hide it, humming as she went about making the potato patties, as if she didn't have a care in the world and talking in that reassuring soft voice that for me was only an indicator of how bad things really were. When things got really bad, like when the telephone, the lights, or the gas got disconnected because we had not been able to pay our bills, Mama's façade didn't hold up so well.

There were times when our gas was cut off in the dead of winter. We bundled up in the frigid apartment under mounds of blankets to keep warm for as long as we had to, sometimes aided by an electric space heater. My grandparents seldom knew the extent of our suffering. They would gladly have bailed us out, but Mama was ashamed of having to keep going to them for relief. I could not blame her. So was I. Mama was proud. So was I. Mama figured we could endure. So did I.

When the gas was disconnected, it got so cold inside our apartment that you could see the steam from your mouth when you talked. We washed up instead of taking baths in the morning because there was no hot water. Luckily, we had an electric hot plate that allowed us to at least boil water for washups as well as cook. And lucky for us, the gas and lights were never disconnected at the same time. If you let the water heated on the hot plate get very hot, you could heat four or five pots full and dump them into the tub before the water cooled off. It made for a warm shallow bath. But it felt so good. The only bad thing was eventually having to climb out of the tub and back into the cold, which hit you like a snowball in the face.

There was something I hated even more than being without heat. That was being without lights. The darkness always seemed much more devastating. Perhaps it was more glaring evidence of our desolation. When the electricity was off, we were immobilized. As soon as it got dark outside, we were reduced to stumbling and bumping around, to toting candles in the dark, or simply going to bed. No television. No radio. No glimmer of hope.

The days when there was either no gas or electricity flowing through our apartment always caught me by surprise. I might have left home for school in the morning with the lights shimmering, but I returned home in the afternoon to an apartment that was completely hushed and still. I could tell in an instant that the lights or gas or something had been cut off. And each time, something inside me seemed to die, as we appeared to be sinking lower and lower to a place of no return. Eventually, we always managed to get the utilities reconnected, either by borrowing to pay the bill or because my stepfather surreptitiously reconnected the electric after the utility trucks had safely rounded the corner, which bought us a little more time to find a legal remedy. All of this weighed on Mama. In the absence of being able to help her shoulder any of the responsibility, I vowed silently to at least try to help her hold things together, even if that meant simply helping her to worry.

Early on as a child, I developed a knack for cleaning. It was more like a habit. Call it a nervous habit. Whenever things were bad, I would mop the floors, make the bathroom clean and polished, polish the kitchen cabinets, dust the buffet, scrub the stove, polish the furniture, and finish the job by spraying Glade, if we had it, throughout the house. I cleaned until the sweat and stress poured from my skin and I was purged of my worries. Cleaning took my mind off our problems. It also seemed to make Mama feel better, and it gave my stepfather less to fuss about, although he always seemed to find something. It was years before I finally realized that his fussing was never really about the house not being cleaned or even about something being out of place or dinner not being ready when he got home from work. It was years before I understood that the pain that we as men inflict is only a symptom of something much deeper and that our victims are often scapegoats for misguided anger and misery. It was years before I realized that none of my cleaning could ever have solved any of Mama's and my stepfather's problems any more than my incessant worrying would. But by then, I would be long grown and gone.

But no matter how bad things got, no matter how much we had to do without during the year, Christmas was always special, untainted by our financial circumstance. In the weeks before Christmas, Mama always asked for our list. She asked us to tell her what we *really* wanted. There was not a Christmas that came and went when there wasn't fruit and candy, and just what we had wanted underneath the tree when we awoke on Christmas morning, though there were seldom any gifts for Mama. I still don't know how Mama always managed, and I am still moved to tears as I picture in my mind that wearied but satisfied expression on Mama's face in seeing her children smile at Christmas.

As a boy, I sometimes woke up in the middle of the night for no reason that I was aware of. I climbed out of bed and walked quietly barefoot into the living room, where I discovered Mama, sitting alone in the dark, staring out of the window into the yellowish glare of streetlights, the glow of a cigarette stuck in between her thick fingers, the smoke filtering into the darkness and cloth curtains, the tears falling from her sad eyes. Sometimes I found Mama in her bedroom, sitting on the side of her bed, crying. The pain I saw in her face made my stomach hurt.

"What's wrong, Ma?" I asked, wishing I could make everything all right.

"Oh nothing, John. Go back to bed," Mama said softly, her voice cracking as she dragged from a Winston, turning her wet face to hide her tears.

I never knew the words to say. I went back to my bedroom and hoisted myself back into my top bunk, unable to sleep. I lay awake, dreaming of how I would someday buy Mama a house and take her away from here. In the meantime, I decided to help her cope by doing whatever I could to make her life a little less miserable.

I also started having migraine headaches.

CHAPTER 5

FROM AMAZING GRACE

CRACK! The leather strap slapped hard across my cousin Michael's butt. It sounded like a cowboy popping a whip. Aunt Mary slung the belt over her shoulder, then flung it across his backside. The leather always had a way of burning through pants and through underwear and singeing the skin. My cousins and I waited in line that afternoon in Aunt Mary's kitchen, kneeling over a hard plastic orange kitchen chair for our turn to be whupped. I was about eight. Aunt Mary stood there, seething, with a man-sized belt folded over one hand, dangling deadly at the other end, that familiar wild and determined look in her eyes that showed no sign of mercy.

As the baby-sitter, Aunt Mary was always promising to beat us kids for one thing or another—going out of the yard, talking too much. There was a list of other transgressions: Stealing. Lying. Disobeying. Cursing. Ditching school. Fighting, unless someone had hit you first. Fighting relatives for any reason. Talking back. Disrespecting our elders—which meant any grown-ups. Clowning in school. Acting a fool. The general sin of "getting on her nerve." Whatever that meant.

The way it was supposed to work was when we got "good and grown,"

Aunt Mary assured us, we would come back someday and thank her for beating the hell out of us. Say, something like, "Gee, those whuppings really made me the man or woman I am today." Back then I couldn't see how anything good could ever come of something that hurt so badly. But Aunt Mary was a believer. And she used to beat us like runaway slaves.

"Y'all gon' thank me one day," she used to say.

"Uh-huh, yeah, right," I would think to myself, but not too loud, just in case Aunt Mary could read my mind.

Aunt Mary was "saved, sanctified and filled with the Holy Ghost, and that with a mighty burning fire," she would testify in church on Sunday mornings. But she had mastered the art of cursing us without actually using curse words. She would never do that. She was a Holy Roller who praised God on Sundays with the same fierceness with which she whipped our butts: with all her might. It was like she loved whupping kids, as if she had been ordained by God or something. The only thing she loved more was church. On Sundays, she raised her hands to the heavens, or clapped like thunder, her voice ringing throughout the sanctuary and whipping the congregation up into a frenzy. Then she'd two-step across the floor, Holy dancing in the spirit, her rouge running with her tears as she spoke in tongues, saying something that sounded to us kids like, "Ho-bee-ah-shah-tah." Michael and Arty and Cheryl and Doris and I, the older of the cousins, had mastered the Holy dances—called shouting—and the spiritual language of Aunt Mary and a few other Jesus-loving members of our family.

"Hobeashata! Hobeashata!" we would yell while playing church, galloping, twisting, and jumping. "This how Aunt Mary shout! This how Aunt Mary shout!" another would yell, then give a toe-tapping, booty-swaying demonstration.

"This how Grandpa shout!" another would scream, grabbing his pants at the waist with both hands and leaping for the sky with eyes closed tight like he was on a trampoline.

"Here go Grandmother!" we'd scream. "Woo . . . woo . . . woo!" twisting our arms back and forth, shuffling our feet like we were on fire. We would laugh until our sides ached.

We were smart enough never to mimic our folks to their faces or within earshot. That would have been suicide. Not only would it have been considered disrespecting our elders, but sacrilege. We'd have been killed in the name of Jesus. And we knew it.

Aunt Mary was Michael and Arty's mother. She was a round-faced, pretty woman with chubby cheeks, light caramel skin, and long dark hair. Strange as it may seem, she was one of the nicest and sweetest people in the world, the kind of person who would give you the shirt off her back. She was the best baker in the family, beloved for her sweet dinner rolls that I could eat all day as if they were cookies. And the German chocolate cake she baked for the family on holidays was so good that we all indulged in sinful portions. Aunt Mary was married to Uncle Riddly, a rail-thin older man who was a preacher, though sometimes he sure didn't act like one. We called him "the Doc." We kids all thought the Doc to be a little off, with his tendency to sometimes rant and rave, as well as his eccentric ways and harmonica blowing at church that we all giggled at. I always thought Aunt Mary deserved a medal for putting up with that dude. Such is love and life.

Although she could be as sweet as her syrupy Kool-Aid, Aunt Mary often bragged to other adults about how she could keep all fifteen of us Hagler kids in line and whip any kid—no matter how devilish—into good shape.

"Don't y'all play with me. Y'all know Aunt Mary don't play," she would say in that self-assured voice that could back down a heavyweight boxer, not to mention any of us. I was a believer. Aunt Mary didn't play. That's just the way she was.

Aunt Mary was always vowing to beat the living daylights out of her boys and, for that matter, any other kid over whom she had dominion. At other times, she promised to beat us from "amazing grace to a floating opportunity." On those occasions that we had broken the rules, she would huff and puff and finally spout from the depths of her soul to us kids, "Are you a fool? Somebody bring me that 'stension cord." A pall would fall over the house and all of us kids would immediately drop to the floor in dead silence. "Y'all know I don't play. I 'mo beat y'all from amazing grace to a floatin' opportunity." As a kid, I could always make out the amazing grace part, but not the rest of it, which sounded something like "floatin' oppordunee." We got the message.

Mama was somewhat a softy but had whipped me enough to put the fear of God in me. She didn't play either, but she was more sensitive about burning my skin. Aunt Mary was a whupping machine. She felt it her moral and spiritual duty to keep us walking the straight and narrow. To keep us from growing up to be slaves to the devil. It was part of that old-fashioned beat-a-child, save-a-child mentality that lots of black folks from the South espoused like the Scriptures, especially black church folk.

"The Bible says, beat your child and he won't surely die," Aunt Mary and the church folk used to say, pledging allegiance to the rod of correction. "The Bible says spare the rod, spoil the child . . . the Bible says . . . the Bible says . . . the Bible says . . ."

I learned to take a whupping like a man. Screaming out wasn't cool among the fellas, even back then. However you acted during your whupping, you could count on a mimicking performance by some other kid, who had either heard the ruckus through the walls or had witnessed it firsthand. I sometimes stood with cousins or friends outside the windows of other kids' houses while they got whupped, folding over laughing at their screams of "I-won't-do-it-no-mo'!" Occasionally, a kid might vault from the house like an Olympic sprinter on steroids, chased by his strap-toting Mama, shouting something like, "Come back here, before I kill you!" But for most of us, running was not an option. It only delayed the inevitable and fanned the flames as far as adults were concerned, especially Aunt Mary.

On the day that Aunt Mary had us lined up in the kitchen, she had promised whuppings to my cousins and me. I don't remember what wrong we had done. But none of us felt we deserved a whupping. We seldom ever did.

She lined us up, and I watched fearfully as my cousins took their beatings, one by one kneeling on the floor like they were praying. I probably should have gone first and gotten it over with. As I stood there, I imagined my flesh burning and Aunt Mary getting carried away when my time came around. I sometimes figured she had whupped her own sons so much that it had just plain lost some of its joy. I was fresh meat. And I imagined her licking her chops. Then my rage kicked in. "Who the hell she think she is? She ain't my mama. I'm gonna tell my mama. Old mean witch. You make me sick! I hate you!" I must have screamed this a thousand times—in my mind. But I knew enough to keep my feelings to myself. Aunt Mary forbade us from telling our parents and promised vengeance if we dared. "You bet' not tell it!" she'd fire back at those of us who in some moments of bravery and anger dared speak our minds. "I mean-n-n you bet' not tell it." We seldom did.

"Owww!" I cried, as she blazed my behind.

Whippings were a part of life. If whippings weren't bad enough, Uncle Gene, our mother's only brother, used to threaten us with promises to thump our heads or to smack us with the heavy man-sized palms of his hands. He seemed a big burly guy to us kids. His real name was Harley, but everybody called him Gene after his middle name, Eugene. Uncle Gene was coffee-bean brown, wore a neatly trimmed mustache, and was bald up top but grew his hair long in the back and on the sides. We nicknamed him, but never called him to his face, Tappy Apple, our derivation of Taffy Apple. We called him that because we thought his bald spot looked just like the shiny caramel bottom of a candied apple and his hair was like the partial covering of nuts. We called him Taps for short. His wife was Aunt Emma, a shapely high-yellow-complected woman with long dark hair. She was pretty. Aunt Emma and Uncle Gene had one daughter, Kim. She was a cute girl with thick hair, eyebrows, lips, and bones. A good mix of her mother and father, she was without a doubt a Hagler with the chubby cheeks, wide face, and forehead. Kim was among the youngest of the younger kids and also among the quietest.

My cousin Michael was my best friend. Michael was loud. A practical joker who could find the humor in the simplest of things and was always able to muster a laugh, even when he was fresh from having been slapped across the head or having had a strap laid across his butt by Uncle Gene, usually in church, and in front of everybody.

"Old baldhead," Michael muttered under his breath, as Uncle Gene shuffled away after laying a good one on him. "I hate his baldhead self."

"What you say?" Uncle Gene fired back, hurrying back over and poised to hit him again.

Michael's eyes shifted nervously back and forth. And Uncle Gene walked away.

"Old baldhead, taffy apple," Michael mumbled loud enough for us kids to hear. Then he laughed. Sometimes he couldn't keep back the tears. But even then, he would be laughing. Michael was just that way: crazy. That's at least how everybody seemed to explain it. That would have been understandable. Heck, the boy needed protective headgear as far as I was concerned. I used to wonder how Michael took it. I had visions of killing my uncle if he ever dared lay a finger on me. At the least I would tell my mama, who would have cursed him out thoroughly and kicked his butt herself. I felt sorry for Michael, even when he was laughing through his tears. I could always see beneath his silly facade. What I saw was a lot of pain. But we were kids. And I guess he dealt with it the way kids do.

"I'll be glad when I grow up," we told each other. "I ain't gon' get no more whuppings."

"Yeah," Michael said, "and I'm gon' beat Uncle Gene up if he ever puts his hands on me."

"Yeah! Me too!" I chimed in. "Kick his bald-headed butt!"

But that seemed so far off. In the meantime, I learned to be slick about my talking or playing in church so as not to draw the wrath of Uncle Gene and his palm upside my own head. But I at least had the protection of my mother. For every bit as mean as Uncle Gene was to us, my mother was every bit as mean when it came to protecting her kids. She would have torn into him like a pit bull if she ever got wind of him so much as laying a finger on me. She thought him to be too rough with little boys. He wasn't that way with girls. It was like he was actually two different people when it came to little boys and little girls. I always figured he must have believed that crap about little girls being made of sugar and spice and everything nice and us boys being nothing but snips and snails and puppy dog tails because that's the way he treated us. He never smacked Doris, Cheryl, Net, Donna, Marcy, Kim, or my other girl cousins. He was always gentle and loving with them, laughing, sugary sweet. With us boys—me, Michael, Arty, Pat, Jeff, and Lee—he was gruff, as though he thought he had to be macho-tough with us. Turn us into men. Except we were little boys. Mama once told me that she suspected Uncle Gene was so gruff and brazen with us boys because he never had any sons, that maybe it was the case that because he didn't have any sons he never really understood that boys on the inside are just as tender as girls.

It wasn't just his propensity for barking and smacking that bugged me as a boy. It was his overall brazen exterior. He was like a Brillo pad rubbing against our skin. And although I loved him, I hated him. We boys called him names. That was mean of us. But in our own hurt, lashing out brought us some comfort, at least a good laugh. It would not be until years later as a man that I would understand my Uncle Gene better and also see how much it hurt him that we kids thought he was one mean dude. Truth is, that was not the way we felt entirely.

Despite his gruffness, Uncle Gene was one of the few "good" men in our lives. He had a good job, he worked every day and took care of his wife and daughter. He had a house, money, and a fine car. Sometimes on those hot summer days when we were playing outside on Komensky, Uncle Gene zoomed down the street, tires screeching, showboating in his black-and-white Wildcat, his windows rolled down, the summer breeze blowing, his face wide with a grin and him tooting his horn.

"Uncle Gene! Uncle Gene!" we all screamed.

In a flash, he was gone.

He'd be just showing off. The big man. The cool man. The young man.

We thought Uncle Gene to be rich or something, and as much as we didn't like the way he treated us sometimes, we boys admired him. In a lot of ways, we needed him. Michael and Arty's real father had faded from their lives after their parents divorced. My real father was long gone. And none of us at times found much solace or guidance in the men who had replaced them. There were times while growing up that I had wished

Uncle Gene was my father or at least more like a father to me. That he would maybe take me to a baseball game or something. Hang out. Buy me some candy. But he had his own life, I guess.

Anyway I can't remember much, if any, of that happening, although once in high school he bought me a suit for Easter. Mostly, he was always just kind of passing through in his glistening car, grinning and blowing his horn at us kids and pausing just long enough for us to admire him and all of his trimmings. That's just the way he was. Or at least, it was the way he seemed.

In addition to being good friends, Michael and I were often partners in crime. It was Michael, though, who always seemed to be the one who got caught. One of our greatest misadventures as boys was banging on Aunt Scope's door and running away, to tick off her short grumpy ole husband, Uncle Detie (pronounced Dee-tie). His real name was Willie. I still don't know how his kinfolks came up with the nickname Detie. Aunt Scope married him after her divorce from Ruben, the real father of Cheryl, Doris, and Donna.

Detie loved baseball. When he was in the mood, he used to play catch with other men outside the apartment building on Komensky. Like Uncle Gene, he didn't seem to like little boys. And like Uncle Gene, he didn't have any. Instead, he had three stepdaughters and a daughter of his own, Caryn, whom we cousins, including her sisters, referred to as Miss Prissy. She was a pretty girl, a little on the skinny side, with naturally raised, devilish eyebrows that made her look evil. I affectionately called her Olive Oyl, after Popeye's skinny girlfriend. Caryn was one of the "Little Kids." That group consisted of everybody who wasn't one of the five "Big Kids"—Cheryl, Doris, Michael, Arty, and me. I really didn't have many dealings with Caryn since she was eight years younger. On the other hand, my brother, Jeff, a year older than Caryn, had plenty of encounters. Some were not so pleasant, although he and Caryn later became the best of cousins. In the meantime, Caryn's mean streak and Jeff's knack for fighting were as volatile a mix as a match and gasoline. Once, Mama and her sisters were sitting in our kitchen and Jeff and Caryn were on the back porch playing, when suddenly Jeff let out a howl after Caryn had reached out and smacked him or something. None of the adults moved. Not even Mama. Mama knew that Jeff was more than capable of handling himself and was fast developing a reputation on the block for kicking butt. A few minutes later came Caryn's bloodcurdling scream. Jeff had struck back and everybody knew it. Aunt Scope sprung to her feet. Mama sat calmly and coolly.

"You didn't move when Jeffery screamed, and you bet' not touch him," she growled at her sister.

That was that. Everybody knew Mama didn't play when it came to two things: her card playing and her kids. I guess that's why I was never really worried about Uncle Detie doing too much to me if he ever caught me when Michael and I banged mercilessly on his front door with all our might and then ran like crazy. I don't remember how or when we started banging on Detie's front door, or even why a grown man would even waste the time chasing us. But that's what made it so much fun. We could see the devil in his eyes and hear the thunder in his voice when he tore through the door after us. We could feel the rush.

We knew Detie typically plopped down on the sofa in their first-floor apartment at 1634 after work to watch a color television console that sat in their living room next to the front door. When we got bored, Michael and I would put our plan into action. We'd make sure his car was outside, then creep into the hallway and up to the varnished wooden door. Sometimes Michael did the honors. Sometimes I did. At other times, we both banged.

Bang-bang-bang-bang-bang-bang-bang!

We shot out of the hallway, making a quick right off the front porch and into the grassy yard, giggling as our hearts pumped fear and adrenaline, Detie's footsteps following fast and furious. We ran until he finally gave up and slogged back inside and plopped his tired butt back in front of the TV again. Then we laughed so hard it hurt until we finally collected ourselves.

"Let's do it again!" I said.

"Yeah, man," Michael answered. "Come on!"

We waited until ole Detie got good and settled in front of the television again. But sometimes we would be ready to sneak into the hallway and could see him peeking out.

"He in the hallway, Mike! I see him," I warned. "I see that fool," I said, trembling with excitement. "Run-n-n!"

We took off running, laughing all the way. Ole Detie never caught me. I was lean and mean. But Michael was a little round and bound someday to get caught. That is, if Detie could ever eliminate our element of surprise.

One day, Michael and I were up to our old tricks.

"Hey Mike, is Detie home?" I said looking for his little red car, then spying it parked at the curb. "Let's go bang on Detie's door."

"Okay," Michael said, his eyes lighting up. "Man, let's do it." We tiptoed carefully toward the hallway door, watching closely for shadows. As always, there was a sudden rush of fear and delight, like when you're about to climb aboard a roller coaster.

"All right, man, you go first," I said.

"Naw, you go first," Michael fired back.

"C'mon, Mike. You scared, man?"

I had said the magic words. Michael was a daredevil and if you ever wanted to get him to do something, no matter how crazy, all you had to do was dare him.

"Man, I ain't scared," he fired back, laughing.

Yes he was. So was I. We made our way through the gate, onto the porch and finally up to the hallway door, nervously giggling. We pushed open the big brown door and crept into the dark hallway, me following close on Michael's heels. Cool, there was no sign of Detie.

"Go ahead man. Do it," I whispered. "Go 'head, Mike. Do it, man, do it..."

Just as he knocked on the door, it suddenly flung open. Detie descended on us like an alley cat on mice. We tore out of the hallway, and into the front yard, our hearts pumping much faster than we were running and mean ole ugly Detie on our heels. I was ahead of Michael and running faster. If we could just make it through the yard and out the back gate, I knew we'd have him licked. We could dart down the alley toward Eighteenth Street and he'd never catch us. We kept running. But Detie didn't look to be giving up this time. He was closing in. *Oh my God! Run, man, run*, I told myself. Just ahead was the silver backyard gate, at least the empty space where the gate had once stood. A few more steps and we would be home free. A few more steps. Almost there . . . I made it!

But just as Michael got to the gate, so did Uncle Detie. He reached out and snatched his collar suddenly. *Awww, man, he caught Mike, he caught him*, I thought. *Awww, man*. Detie started yelling and cursing.

"Boy, don't y'all bring y'all butts back here and knock on my door no more, you damn fools," he screamed, smacking Michael upside the head a few times, as I watched from a safe distance. "You ole hardhead kids!" Michael's eyes were filled with terror.

"Let me go. Let me go, man. Let me go," Michael shouted, looking like a frightened animal and struggling to break free of Detie's death grip, though Detie showed no signs of letting go of his fistful of Michael's T-shirt.

Finally, Detie released him and huffed back through the yard toward his house, relishing his moment of vindication. I ran to Michael's side. We stood there for a few minutes, both kind of shaken. Michael wiped away the tears. Then he laughed. So did I.

"Man-n-n, forget Detie," Michael said. "Let's go do it again."

We didn't. At least not that day.

CHAPTER 6

BOYZ IN THE HOOD

"JOHHH-OHNNN," Mama's voice rang out, "Tiiime to get up." I pulled the covers up around my face as I usually did on school mornings and sank deeper into the warmth of my mattress in search of a few more seconds. "Time to geeeet uuu-up," she would sing again. "Johnnn, come on now. Today's a schoo-oo-ool daaay."

I finally relented and flicked off my blanket. I climbed out of bed. My feet hit the cold unforgiving wooden floor. It was February and time to get ready for school. I attended Roswell B. Mason Elementary School, which was four blocks from home and known to everyone as Mason School. I had to be at Mason by 9, which usually meant arising by 7:30. That was time enough to take a washup—a standing bath with a hand towel in the sink—get dressed, eat breakfast, and catch a few cartoons before scooping up my books and heading out the door to school. I was going on ten now and still short in comparison to the boys in my class. Net, who was two years younger, was taller than I was. And I was starting to seriously worry that I was never going to grow any taller. Mama always assured me that I would grow someday, but I had trouble believing her.

Despite my small stature, I fit in with most boys on my block, though being a small dude without the fire for fighting also meant getting picked on some. Sometimes I managed to avoid the bullies, sometimes not. I was grateful that most of the boys on my block liked playing more than fighting.

On many snowy winter days after school, we played two-hand touch football in the street or in the vacant lot on Komensky. There was Michael and Ricky, who were brothers and lived in a basement apartment at the alley near Sixteenth Street. A jovial respectful kid who was a little on the shy side, Michael was short and stout and lifted weights. Both he and Ricky were pro wrestling fanatics back when the Bruiser and the Crusher were big names on the Chicago wrestling scene. Michael was always trying to put somebody in the sleeper or in the figure-four hold. Or he was using the claw—a fingers-spread crushing hold placed on someone's head that was always more crippling on TV than in real life. The brothers were also karate buffs and went berserk when the martial arts flicks came out in the 1970s. A rail-thin dude, Ricky was always thumbing his nose like Bruce Lee, dancing on his tiptoes and kicking. On occasion, he even took off his shirt so he could flex and show us how much his bird chest and skateboard-flat back looked like Bruce Lee's ripped body. Among my other friends was Huckey, a skinny pop-eyed kid who lived across the street from Michael and Ricky. There were also J-Rat, Recee, and all the other fellas.

In the summer, we played baseball every day or we played strikeout, a poor boy's version of baseball. With strikeout, you only needed a wall on which to draw a square for a batter's box with a piece of white chalk. Then you didn't need a catcher. The wall served that purpose, bouncing every pitch that wasn't hit straight back to the pitcher.

When there were no baseball gloves or hardballs to be had, Huckey and Michael and Ricky and I and some of the other boys scrounged up the 32 cents we needed for a Major League rubber ball. We counted our pennies and nickels, everyone chipping in until we had raised the funds. Then we walked to Mr. Penny's store on Sixteenth Street just east of Pulaski Road and bought a red one or a white one, which the old man kept on display near the candy and goods kept behind a glass counter. Usually we bought a white one. We took turns holding it as we walked excitedly back to Komensky. I always squeezed the ball in my right hand, ran my fingers along the seams, and held the ball up to my nose so I could breathe in the fresh scent of new rubber. I can still hear the pound and splat of rubber on brick, filling a summer afternoon on Komensky. We played all day long, or at least until the grown-ups on whose building we were hurling fastballs grew weary of the incessant pounding. Or someone got up to bat and hit a monster homer that sent the white ball sailing into the blue sky and landing way up on top of someone's roof, never to be seen again.

"Mannn, Horsehead," I can still hear Huckey, yelling at Recee.

We sometimes called Recee "Horse" because of the shape of his head and teeth. He was an athletic kid who could hit the ball farther with one hand than most of us could hit it with two, but by junior high he was taking sips from the beer cans of older boys after we played ball games while the rest of us sipped sodas and ate freeze pops.

"Why you have to hit the ball so hard, man?" Huckey said.

"My fault, man," Recee said, trying not to laugh so hard. "I don't know my own scrent," meaning strength.

"Ole horse-head mug," Huckey huffed before walking off.

Recee was cracking up by then and the game was over.

Their exchange was enough to cause an exchange of blows, though it did not. I have seen boys scrap and tussle over less. There was the time that J-Rat—nicknamed after the cartoon character Biggie Rat by the boys in the neighborhood because of the likeness—busted Huckey in the eye over the call of whether a pitch was a strike or not. There were the times that one boy or another called another boy's mama a "ho" (as in "whore") or simply uttered the two words that were the surest to provoke a fight, "Yo Mama!" But after the fight was over, whenever there was a fight, everyone always got up, dusted off, wiped their noses, and walked away. Even gangs back then fought more often with fists and bats than with guns and knives. In those days they fought over who "ran" which street, which amounted to having bragging rights on the block in which they lived and being able to lay claim to a street corner. There were the occasional gunshots in the middle of the night and the knowledge that walking to the store or sometimes to school could be dangerous with robbers, muggers, and "stranger dangers" lurking about, as Aunt Mary and Officer Friendly had warned us in school. By second grade, I had already had the misfortune of being mugged by older boys in the neighborhood. Getting mugged was painless in one sense, though stinging in another. In the half dozen or so times it happened, either on my way to school or walking to or from the store, no one ever punched me. Usually, some big ugly dude grabbed me by the collar and demanded my money. Shaken, I always obliged, reaching into my pocket and handing it over. Usually it was only chump change. But it was mine, and having to part with it left me in tears as I huffed away, happy to have escaped without being punched but angry and saddened over having been robbed.

Gang recruiters also trolled the streets. By the time my cousin Arty was in elementary school, the gangs were chasing him home every day, demanding that he join. Once when Arty was running home from school with the usual trail of boys chasing him, Aunt Mary met them all at the back gate with a baseball bat, then proceeded to allow the boys in, one at a time, so Arty could fight them fairly.

"Come on in here, y'all bastards, one by one, he gon' beat the fool out of all of y'all. I'm tired of y'all chasing my son," Aunt Mary said, poised to handle her business if necessary. "Fight 'em Arty, go 'head, beat the fool out of 'em, go ahead Arthur..."

Arty fought one or two of them that day. But I don't remember that the chasing ever stopped until he moved away and went to high school. I was never recruited, only because I was such a puny dude. And it is a good thing for the gangs, for I suspect that Mama would have killed somebody, or else they would have had to kill Mama.

There were gangs for almost as far back as I can remember. The Black Stone Rangers controlled the South Side, and on the West Side there were the Black Souls, Disciples, Vice Lords, Cobras, and others. By the fifth and sixth grades, some of the kids in my class were professed gang members, lured into the fold by older brothers and in some cases, by their sisters. Teenage gangs still dealt with zip guns and still rumbled then, and no matter how much they screamed black power and claimed to promote unity and brotherhood, there was always the sense that they were a menace. But there was no crack back then, no river of automatic weapons, and no such thing as a drive-by shooting. Komensky was always immune, or at least a sanctuary, from rumbles or shoot-outs and other gang activity. I am not sure why this was the case. It may have been due to the sense of family or community that existed among neighbors and the fact that there were still enough grown men on the block willing to take a stand against thugs. Maybe it was because the sense of respect for adults had not yet been eroded.

I can still remember that summer evening when I was still in grade school and sitting with Mama and Net and some of my cousins on the porch when a car with a load of young men stopped in the middle of the street in front of our apartment building. Suddenly they pointed a shotgun in our direction and scanned our porch. Just as quickly, they pointed the barrel through the opposite window and scanned a porch across the street. All the while, Mama was grabbing at us and trying to shepherd us all to safety inside the hallway. I sat frozen as the car pulled away—no shots fired that time. But it was clear that times were changing.

CHAPTER 7

PUPPY LOVE

AT NIGHT, I read. Sometimes it was schoolbooks. Many nights, it was comic books—*Spider-Man, Captain America, Archie.* Usually, I read by the light that spilled into my bedroom from the kitchen and burned all night because I was afraid of the dark. I always liked reading. It allowed me to go places in my mind. It also lifted the boredom of having to lie in bed wide awake for hours, especially during summer nights when the voices of children still playing outside spilled into my bedroom. We had to be in the house before the streetlights came on, and usually we had to be in bed by 8 o'clock. Those were Mama's rules. You didn't argue with Mama unless you wanted to taste the backside of her right hand, which was so lightning quick that I am not sure even Muhammad Ali could have ducked it. Mama insisted that we get a good night's sleep but had agreed to let us read as much as we wanted as long as we were in bed by 8. The alternatives were listening to the radio or staring at my bedroom walls until I drifted off to sleep, which I did sometimes, but rarely.

The walls of my bedroom were sky blue. They stretched about ten feet from the ceiling—where spiders sometimes spun webs—to the dark-brown-stained baseboard. The wooden baseboard matched the twin beds in the room, which I shared with Jeff. Our bedroom sat just off the kitchen. The kitchen was light yellow and had a high ceiling, too. It was so high that you had to climb up on a ladder in order to change the light bulb in the globe at the center of the ceiling. The kitchen was probably the largest room in the house. It was big enough to hold our washer, dryer, refrigerator, stove, kitchen sink, a kitchen table and chairs, and a slender white space heater with a black grille. Over time, the sooty exhaust from the heater turned the yellow walls charcoal gray, which made painting a frequent necessity. Sometimes Mama turned off the heater and turned on the top stove burners, which I later learned filled the house with carbon monoxide, though it spared the walls of soot.

Our kitchen was the same kitchen where Aunt Mary had whipped my cousins and me years earlier. When I was nine years old, Aunt Mary and her family bought their own two-story house farther north on the West Side, in a neighborhood called Garfield. The same night that Aunt Mary and her family moved out of the second-floor apartment at 1634 South Komensky Avenue, we moved in. I should say it was my stepfather who moved us, for he did all of the work, with a little help from me. For years, Mama would recall how my father had helped Aunt Mary move as well as other folks in our family whenever they needed an extra pair of hands, but how when our turn came to move, nobody offered a finger, let alone a hand. So Daddy moved us: one piece at a time from the third-floor apartment at 1654, where I had watched the fires that night after Dr. King's assassination, to the apartment at 1634, the other half of the Hagler family compound, where Aunt Scope still lived downstairs.

Grandmother and Grandpa were long gone by then, having moved farther northwest to the Austin neighborhood, where black folks with middle-income jobs had begun moving in search of a new Promised Land, fleeing the charred land left by the 1968 fires. Back then, Austin was perceived as the bona fide middle-class neighborhood for blacks on the West Side. It sits on the far western edge of the city and borders the west suburb of Oak Park, the one-time home of Ernest Hemingway and Frank Lloyd Wright. Austin was a quiet urban enclave of brick bungalows with a smattering of Victorian houses as well as well-kept apartment buildings, manicured lawns, and litter-free streets. Austin was not rundown like K-

Town. That is not to say that the folks who could afford to buy homes in Austin were doctors and lawyers. The trickle of black folks moving west were those who had good-paying jobs at the Post Office or were bus drivers and the like. They were blue-collar workers, joined by a slowly emerging class of black white-collar workers who by the late 1960s were starting to get their slice of American Pie after the grand fight for civil rights. They were black folks who drove big fine cars like the "Deuce and a Quarter," which was what everybody called the Buick Electra 225. Or they drove Cadillacs, which everyone called "Hogs." Or they drove Lincoln Continentals, which everyone called "Stankin' Lankins."

I was in fourth grade by then and eager to go to school each weekday morning. But one particular day was special. I was both excited and nervous because this was Valentine's Day. I had bought a box of heart-shaped candy and a card for my sweetheart. She was a little skinny chocolate girl with a pretty white smile. Her name was Henri Chillers, pronounced "On-ree."

Henri was the most gorgeous girl in the world. Her hair was always nicely straightened and fixed in long black satin braids or sometimes with pretty curly bangs. She was soft and girlie, not tomboyish like some of the other girls in my class. I didn't understand this force, whatever it was, that drew me to Henri, that made my legs almost go limp in her presence. The only problem was that I was too shy to say a word to her. I liked her. But she could not have known it. In fact, I didn't say a single word to anyone in our class about my affections for Henri. My friends would have teased me mercilessly for liking a girl. But I could not help myself.

My mother had only recently discovered that there was a sweetie in my life. A few days earlier, with Valentine's Day approaching, Mama suddenly popped the question at home.

"Hey, John," she said.

"Huh, Ma?"

"Valentine's Day is coming up."

"Uh-huh," I replied, without interest.

"Do you think..." she said, her words almost clumsy. "Is there some girl you'd like to give a box of candy to or maybe a card?"

"Uhhh, a box of candy?" I said. "Uh-uh, no way, noooo waaay. I don't want to give no girl no candy."

"Why not?" Mama asked. "There's nothing wrong with that."

I shook my head. "Not me."

"There's nothing wrong with boys giving girls candy or cards," Mama said in her half-lecturing, syrupy voice that had a way of disarming me. "That's what you're supposed to do, John. You are supposed to be nice to girls, open doors, and walk on the side of the street that is closest to the curb so that if a car comes and jumps the curb, you get hit and not the lady."

This all sounded like the same kind of stuff Mama was always telling me I was supposed to do when I grew up. When I asked her why I had to mop our floors and wash the dishes since that was women's work, she had told me it was because I needed to know how to take care of myself. When she taught me how to sort the laundry or how to cut up and fry a chicken and how to braid hair, when she took me grocery shopping and showed me how to comparison shop and calculate groceries within the dollar in my head before the cashier had ever rung up a single item—all things that I had proudly told her my lucky wife someday would happily be handling while I was out making a living—Mama insisted that my wife might have other ideas. By fourth grade, I could thread a needle, clean house, cook a meal, fold the laundry, and even change a baby's diaper in two minutes or less. If Mama was training me to do all this in preparation for when I got grown someday, I wondered what the heck my wife was going to be doing. I used to wonder if Mama wasn't teaching me how to be a wife. Instead she always insisted that she was teaching me to be a man.

"Uh-uh, I'm not gettin' hit by no car. Let her get hit. No way, Ma, no way."

"That's what men do, John."

"I ain't no man."

"Not yet, but you will be, one day."

"Yeah, and I ain't walking on the curb so I can get hit by no car either," I said.

"Okay, John," Mama said, ending our debate. "So, are you sure there isn't a little girl that you would like to give a box of candy to?"

I stood there in the kitchen thinking for a moment. I had never thought about this idea of giving a girl a gift before. It all seemed a little weird, but kind of nice in a way, too. I was torn. Mama could tell.

"Well, think about it. Let me know," Mama said. Then she walked away as if she didn't care either way.

Later on that day, I told Mama that there was a special girl to whom I would like to give a box of candy and that her name was Henri.

Mama and I caught the bus down to Walgreen's at Twenty-sixth Street and Pulaski Road, where I picked out a red, heart-shaped box of choco-lates and a card. I didn't realize it then, but Mama was trying to teach me how to treat women. Some years later, I also reasoned that this had been my mother's way of assuring that I would be a better man than some of those she had encountered in her life. I was an adult when I realized that I had seldom seen Mama showered with a man's affections, peppered with roses and candy or jewelry or the countless things that real men freely give to women they truly love and adore. With her Valentine's Day sug-gestion, Mama was, in effect, working to ensure that there would be one lucky woman someday who would have a man that she had molded with her own hands.

The day seemed to drag on. But the right time to give Henri my Valentine gift never seemed to present itself.

When it came time for dismissal, I walked to my locker and retrieved my coat and the bag with Henri's gift, then lined up with the rest of the kids. Henri was standing nearby in line. It would have been easy for me to pass off the goodies. I tried to convince my arm to move in her direction. But it would not. My arm felt heavy and lifeless. For a second, I thought about taking the candy home and eating it myself. But I really wanted Henri to have it.

From the school's door, you could almost see Henri's house, a brick townhouse that backed onto Mason's playground. As we walked outside the school, the noise of children laughing and playing blew all around me like the wind. I watched Henri and her friends sidle past the green fence away from the school, then turn south toward her home. I walked the other way toward mine.

But as I turned out of the parking lot, tears welled up in my eyes. Then suddenly, I felt a burst of something I cannot explain. I stopped in my tracks, then turned and began running toward the playground, past the school door, past the gate. "I might still be able to catch her," I thought to myself. I kept running, past the throngs of schoolchildren, past the teachers and parents, until finally I spotted Henri. She and three or four other girls in our class were laughing as they walked, drawing closer to the edge of the playground, where Henri would make the right turn and quickly disappear behind her front door. I hurried to catch up to them but was careful to keep enough distance so as not to appear to be obviously chasing them. Then one of the girls spotted me.

"Boyyy, you following us?" she asked.

They all turned around and looked. I stood there without muttering a word with this queer look on my face, holding my books and the paper sack. They resumed walking. I followed.

"Boyyy, why you following us?" the girl turned and asked again, sassily with her hand on her hip.

They all turned around. Henri smiled. They all giggled. My eyes met Henri's. "Man, is she pretty," I thought, although I still could not find the words. Here was my chance. Finally, I reached out and handed her the sack.

"Here, Henri, this is for you," I said.

I stood there just long enough to hear all the girls gasp with excitement as they all looked into the bag and just long enough to see Henri's face light up. Then my fear and shyness returned. I turned and ran away as fast as I could, my head tilted toward the sky, my book bag flailing, my face spread in a wide grin and my insides ready to burst. I kept running, past the school door, rounding the corner of the parking lot at Eighteenth Street, all the way past Kuppenheimer, all the way home. I was so happy that I had given Henri the candy. That day I realized I must be in love.

When I arrived at school the next day, the classroom was abuzz. By then, everyone had heard about the candy I gave Henri on Valentine's

Day. The guys teased me a bunch. So did some of the girls. But it wasn't so bad after all. I could tell Henri was the envy of all the girls. But the best part was when Henri walked over to me during class that morning, her eyes as wide as her smile, her hair pretty and shiny satin as I stood frozen.

"Thaaank youuu, Johnnn," she said, half singing.

"You're welcome," I replied.

But I was the one who felt so grateful.

Back then I wasn't much for words. But as I grew older, I came to see words as powerful tools, especially when it came to the opposite sex. We called it rapping in the 1960s and 1970s. Later it was known as macking and even later as shooting game. Once upon a time, it was called sweet talking. No matter what new slang name each generation of wanna-be-suave brothers coined this ritualized verbosity to woo the ladies, it is all the same.

In those days, a brother without a mack was like a lion without a roar. You got no ladies, or foxes, as we called girls. You had to be able to lay your mack down, to make a girl catch goose bumps from all the sweet nothings you whispered in her ear. Early on, young brothers learned how to play the game, how to be smooth-talking Negroes. We practiced our lines. And eventually, you learned to talk a good game, how to run a game, how to make it up as you went along. You learned to sweet-talk a female teacher into cutting you some slack on the deadline for a paper or how to slide into a female's good graces with soft words and a kind of silky sensuality in that self-assured voice that when perfected was as smooth as butter. Every brother eventually crafted a few golden lines that he memorized like a script. Fake brothers relied on corny uninventive lines that were often brash and distasteful or plain old stale.

I can still see my cousin Michael, raking a sister over with his eyes and trying futilely to impress her with, "Excuse me, miss, do fries come with that shake?"

Still, it amazed me as a young man to see how girls fell for such lines. Years later, it amazed me more that grown women, even so-called sophisticated college-educated types, fell for the same type of shady verses. What I later saw in all of this was not so much the gullibility of women but the almost desperate need that many women had for a man's love, a need that often seemed to grow out of the absence of fathers and ultimately out of some unfulfilled longing for male affection. And what I observed through the years was that amid the desert of real love, sisters fell for the mirage. Except when they realized this, it was often too late.

I still wonder sometimes if some women don't see it coming all along, but simply close their eyes and stumble headlong into a life of heartache, make-believing that some sorry brother is the man of their dreams.

As a boy, love and affection was a box of chocolates, the expectation of nothing in return and the joy of knowing that I put a smile on some little girl's face. It was staring at a pretty face in ponytails and satin bangs on a sun-drenched afternoon at school as the breath of spring was just starting to blow again. Love was holding hands, or a scribbled note from a girl in class saying, "I like you. Do you like me? Will you be my boyfriend?"

In time, life and love would become a lot more complicated.

CHAPTER 8

SUNDAY MORNINGS

IT WAS Sunday morning and ten 'til twelve at True Vine Church of God in Christ. Brother King piped up the Hammond organ, his fingers fluttering over the white and black keys in a soft melody. Uncle Gene collected and stacked the Sunday School books at the wooden offering table that sat in the middle of the sanctuary at the front of the church as the rest of the congregation readied for the shindig at high noon that we called morning worship. Within a few minutes, one of the preachers uttered the call to worship, "Yes Lord," the song known widely as the Church of God in Christ's signature hymn. The preacher stood proudly, looking Godly serious in the pulpit while we waited for the spirit of the Lord to boil like water in a teakettle.

True Vine was housed in a tidy renovated storefront in the 3900 block of West Roosevelt Road, which church folk had nicknamed the "Jericho Road" because of its peril. Its flashing neon sign lit up the strip of liquor stores, drug dealers, and occasional men in drag, some as big and muscular as professional football players. There was even one reverend of a nearby church who was said to carry a gun—Reverend Fizer, a short, dark brown-skinned man with bushy salt-and-pepper sideburns who walked half hunched over in small careful steps. He was pastor of a storefront church across the street from True Vine. Reverend Fizer was one of those countrified preachers, the kind who I imagined had discovered God one humid, spirit-filled night at some small church with dirt for floors in a tiny Mississippi town.

"Country" was how black folks referred to some preachers, particularly those who whooped when they delivered the Lord's word, sounding as if they were gagging on their own tongues. Whooping preachers were the most dramatic. They not only had the gift of gab, they had the gift of making people leap from their seats in frenzied anticipation the way Dr. J did whenever he broke into the open court with the basketball in his hand and nobody on him. Everyone rose to their feet. The right grunt or deep soulful moan, or even the way a preacher stood in the pulpit, the way he wiped the sweat from his brow, or cleared his throat worked like good kindling.

Call it cadence. It didn't work that differently for preachers than it did for a brother putting his mack down on a lady—wooing her with his style as much as his rehearsed, amorous lines. But the most distinct character of whooping preachers was that they half sang their sermons as most black preachers from the Old School did. The best of them could whip up a congregation with their sandpaper voices and make them pop up from the pews like toast simply by singing, "Jeeeeeeeeee-zusss."

Reverend Fizer had the gift. He was a Holy Ghost-filled, tongue-talking, foot-stomping, take-no-prisoners preacher. He once half jokingly explained to my uncle his plan of salvation for the neighborhood ruffians: "If they don't want to go to heaven, I'm gonna help 'em go to hell."

The neighborhood where True Vine was nestled wasn't considered to be part of K-Town, but it was within sneezing distance and just as bad. In fact, it was so dangerous that often when it was time to raise offering, we locked up and posted two deacons at the entrance. The deacons were unarmed, except for the sword of the Lord (the Holy Bible) and the good sense to call the police should the Devil or any of his disciples (in the form of the local assortment of thieves, murderers, and stickup men) ever rear their ugly heads at our church's door. Burglars had ripped us off so often that we took to buttressing the doors with two-by-fours at night. We could never understand how anyone could stoop so low as to steal from a church. But I later came to see that a people's spirit and self-respect can become so eroded by the daily grind of poverty and hopelessness that they care little about themselves, or anyone or anything else. That's how brothers could sell crack to their friends' mamas, break into their neighbors' homes, and, yes, steal from a church.

While the grown-ups readied themselves for worship service in the pause between Sunday School and the call to worship, Michael and I had a ritual of our own for which we needed to make preparation. Usually, the few minutes of transition were all we needed. On countless Sunday mornings, we filled our pockets with paper clips and rubber bands from the pastor's office. While sitting on the back row of the choir stand with the rest of the boy tenors (which helped us go undetected), we carefully and secretly used the rubber bands as slingshots to fire round after round of paper clips through the sanctuary while the grown-ups praised God. We cracked up as our thin metal bullets ricocheted off the walls, occasionally startling people who looked from side to side, and from ceiling to floor, wondering what had been the source of the pops off the walls and pews. It's a wonder we never shot out anybody's eye. Our Sunday slingshot activity was risky business. But it wasn't as serious as faking the Holy Ghost. I wasn't about to move a muscle unless the spirit really moved me. It was partly out of the fear of God, and partly out of reverence for Mama, who would have slapped me silly.

Our pastor was none other than Grandpa himself, who had received God's call to preach a few years earlier. Grandpa got the call one night from God. The way I heard him explain it, usually from the pulpit, was that God had rolled him out of bed late one night and told him that He was "calling him higher." I wondered sometimes if during his visitation from God on that memorable night, a great light had shone around his bedroom and a full-fledged angel dressed in glorious white had stood before him, issuing God's proclamation as Grandpa shivered in awe.

I later discovered that the workings of the Lord, if they were indeed His workings at all, were usually less sensational. I also learned early on that God seemed to have a habit of working late at night, from what I could tell from the testimonies of a lot of church folks. At least that was when He spoke to them, worked out their problems, or revealed to them the long-awaited answer to some question they had been praying about, in some cases, for years. Answers from God came in an assortment of nocturnal ways, in dreams or in visions. And they were crystallized in some impression that fell suddenly on people and shot them out of their beds in that divine moment of revelation. I later reckoned that if this were true, if God truly did speak at night, then this was because most of the time, folks were too busy to hear him in the daytime. If "an idle mind was the Devil's workshop," as Grandpa often instructed from the pulpit, then I imagined that a sleeping soul must have been the toolshed for the Lord. But this much I knew: True Vine was where God manifested himself on Sunday mornings, often in strange and unusual ways.

I was twelve when Grandpa got the call from the Lord. The year was 1973. Richard Nixon was president, Woodward and Bernstein were knocking at the door of the Watergate, Richard J. Daley was still mayor of Chicago, and the *Soul Train* line was doing the Robot and pop-locking to the Jackson Five's "Dancing Machine." It was five years after the fires in K-Town, four years since the bodies of Black Panthers Fred Hampton and Mark Clark were riddled with bullets by Chicago police officers who raided their West Side house as they slept on the morning of December 4, 1969. The year Grandpa got his calling was the year the Vietnam War ended. I still have memories of seeing newspaper headlines of casualties—bold glaring numbers splattered across the front page of the mounting body count of U.S. soldiers dead. At the time, I did not understand the gravity of this war being fought in some faraway place with a strange name. The end of the war carried a wind of change in the country. But as the nation moved toward urban renewal and away from the socially turbulent 1960s, there was the sense that whatever life remained in my neighborhood was being sucked out. There was now the need for car alarms, for burglar alarms, bars, deadbolts, and a loaded .38 Special hidden in the bedroom. Where once it seemed that everyone went to church on Sunday mornings, many people in my neighborhood no longer did, or maybe it was the case that many of those who were left behind never had. It soon became apparent by the still quietness of the streets on Sunday mornings that those who did go to the Lord's house were greatly outnumbered by those who did not, that something got lost in the transition from black folks seeking the Promised Land to possessing the land. Whether it was the loss of hope, faith, and purpose that contributed to a sense of disillusionment, which fueled the disintegration of life as it once had been in K-Town, which led people to believe they somehow had missed the Promised Land, I do not know. Whatever it was, it ignited an exodus.

Although there were still men to look to as role models—working fathers, decent men with some sense of purpose—there seemed to be a shortage of good God-fearing men who didn't live it up on the weekend, have a couple of chicks on the side, or drink to excess and gamble. Not that there weren't any good men, just not enough providers and protectors in my eyes. It also did not help that many of the men who remained were still struggling, working day and night and barely getting by while "the Man" held a foot on their neck and the whole world passed them by. There also seemed to be a shifting of moral ground. The emergence of pimps and players in the movies, which nearly every boy in my neighborhood went to see, chipped away at what moral foundation remained. "I'm a pimp" became the expression of bravado for many of my friends. If that was not sufficient to convey their measure of cool and career aspirations, there was another: "I'm a pimp, I'm a player, I'm a baby layer" is the way the saying went. I imagined that line was probably picked up from one of the pimp movies. Mama wouldn't allow me to go and see "that crap," so I do not know. But one thing Mama could not keep from me was the pimp walk, which every boy and man who wanted to be a man acquired and mastered.

Back then I was never completely dressed until I had climbed into my walk. The transformation usually took place in my bathroom, especially on occasions like Easter, Christmas, and banquets and later at dances and high school homecomings. When I got decked out and it looked good, and I usually deemed it so, I would strut out of the bathroom, feeling like I was going to burst inside with something. Was it joy, cool, pride, ego?

There was something about this metamorphosis from ghetto boy to boy wonder. The cool shot through my veins and my muscles surrendered. The bounce, drag, and tilt took over, like the Holy Ghost. Hallelujah! I'd sidle into the living room. Check me out.

"Ooooh, Johnnnn, lemme see you. Boy, you lookin' sharp," Mama would say, as the family dug my duds. "Don't he look good, y'all?"

Dig it. Watch me walk.

The "pimp." The bounce-and-drag cool swerve, performed in sync. The man. The creased pants. Spit-shined shoes. Splendor, flowing down the runway.

Superfly. That's when it all started. The biggest movie of the century, I had no doubt. And even though Mama wouldn't let me see it, it didn't matter. Ricky and Michael and Huckey and it seemed like every other boy in the neighborhood did go, and they came back with the walk. Brothers started seriously conking and sporting gangster brims and wide lapels with at least two buttons of their shirts open, the collars cuffed over the outside of the jackets of their leisure suits. But it was the walk that talked.

Of everyone I knew, my Uncle Ollie, who was Aunt Brenda's husband, was the coolest. His was a crossover, ear-to-shoulder, graceful swanlike stroll. Throughout his procession while we kids all gawked, he wore a half smile, his white teeth showing beneath his dark lips, brown skin and black mustache and beard. But my friend Morgan, who lived next door to Grandmother, had the baddest walk in high school. Morgan was a tall—about six feet one—slender, dark, smooth-skinned brother, whom even in the dark, even if you couldn't see his face, you could identify by the way he crisscrossed the path in front of him.

Ladies liked a good walk. Or at least that's the way we thought. You didn't just go up to a girl and ask her for her seven digits. You had to pimp a little, let her see a little something before you laid down your mack.

And you couldn't just walk past a group of roughnecks you didn't know without dropping a little bounce and drag for them, just to let them know, "You don't want none of this, homeboys." It's like that scene in *The Godfather* when Don Corleone is laid up in the hospital and young Michael grabs the baker on the hospital steps and they shove their hands in their pockets like they have guns in order to scare away the hit men. Pimp walking is like that when done correctly. Not cool. Cold.

Not every black man or woman liked the pimp walk. Grandpa would inquire of us teenagers, as would some other older men, "What's wrong with your leg, boy?" We knew then that it was time to straighten up and fly right. But only until we were out of sight. Whether the pimp walk was some celebration of male blackness I don't know. I do know that walking so rhythmically, I never felt so good, or so black. But even back then the walk could not compensate for all the negatives of pimposity. And mostly, it was negative.

Superfly ushered in an era of "blaxploitation" that made heroes out of pimps, pushers, and playboys. Wayward preachers on the big screen and in real life, with their skirt-chasing and money-grubbing ways, contributed to the general demise of any notion that black preachers were to be respected. The stereotype became the Right Reverend Chicken Wing, who drove a big shiny Cadillac and kept one eye on the sisters' legs and another on the offering plate. It was said that there were only four kinds of people in the ghetto who drove Cadillacs: pimps, players, pushers, and preachers. In the dearth of professionals, or simply black men whom we could point to as having "made it," the Pimp Daddy became the de facto role model. In fact, real-life pimps and pushers seemed to spring up overnight like weeds and wild grass. And though the boys in my 'hood still played baseball, still licked frozen cups of Kool-Aid, chewed bubble gum, and slap-boxed in the middle of the street, there was change in the wind. It was a wind that might very well have blown me away. I later came to believe that the Lord had called Grandpa to pastor in the nick of time, as True Vine became my anchor in the storm.

At the time Grandpa received his calling from the Lord, the Hagler family was dispersed at several churches. Grandmother and Grandpa were still at All Nations Church of God in Christ, a white storefront on Fifteenth Street and Pulaski Road where they had raised their children. Aunt Scope and her four girls attended North Side Church of God in Christ, where she played the piano and trained the church's choir. Aunt Mary, Uncle Gene, Aunt Clotee, Mama, and for a while, Aunt Brenda were at Greater Faith Temple Church of God in Christ near K-Town, at Fifteenth Street and St. Louis Avenue on the West Side. At some point Aunt Brenda and her family had turned Black Muslim, something that did not sit well with my conservative Christian family and that kept Grandmother on her knees. One day, Grandpa called the family together suddenly for the all-important announcement. He told them that he had been awakened one night and instructed by the Lord to leave All Nations and start his own church.

The name of Grandpa's church, the Lord had told him, should be True Vine, taken from the fifteenth chapter of St. John, in which Jesus says, right there in red writing, "I am the True Vine and my Father is the husbandman" (15:1). And so it was.

Grandpa moved onward by faith. Some church folks at All Nations and elsewhere thought he was nuts or at least had not heard the Lord correctly. The family suspected, however, that the real truth was that some folks were jealous or angry over Grandpa's starting up his own church, particularly those folks whose churches stood to lose something by the Hagler exodus. In asking his family to join him, Grandpa was plucking some of the most valued members out of the North Side and Greater Faith Temple churches. The Haglers had a reputation for being hardworking, money-giving church folk. We believed in tithing, the Old Testament principle of giving one-tenth of all your earnings to the Lord. We were known as the kind of loyal, God-fearing folks who loved the Lord and gave Him our all. So we could understand how certain folks might take offense at the sudden decision by our family to take their tithes and talents elsewhere, even if we were leaving to help the patriarch of our family start another branch of Zion. Truth is, Grandpa did not really have to ask his children to join him in his new ministry. The Lord had called him higher, and by doing so, He essentially issued a summons for us all. Grandpa's five daughters and his son as well as their families were willing to follow. There were no defectors. It was that simple.

Our family was a ready-made church. We had a musician in Aunt Scope, who had played the piano for years even as a teenager, when she earned money for playing at churches or funerals that she gave to my grandparents to help take care of the family. In Uncle Gene, we had a veteran Sunday School superintendent. In Aunt Clotee, we had an executive secretary by training who could help with the church's administrative affairs. In Aunt Mary, we had a spiritual fireball, who, in addition to leading praise and worship service, also had a knack for organizing church plays and Tom Thumb Weddings for children. Aunt Mary was also a registered nurse. In Mama, we had a gifted Sunday School teacher, who was as fervent and passionate about teaching and going to church on Sunday mornings as she was about playing cards. In Aunt Brenda, we had a bellowing alto who didn't need a microphone to be heard. In the chorus of grandchildren, we had plenty enough for a children's choir that would be called the "Sunshine Band." And the older grandchildren, Arty and Michael, Cheryl and Doris and me, would pull double duty, singing in the adult choir as well as in the children's. All the adults with the exception of Aunt Mary would be in the choir. When it finally came time for the choir to sing during service, Aunt Mary was usually fairly well exhausted from having conducted praise and worship.

A number of us tinkered with musical instruments. Arty eventually began bringing his clarinet to church. Donna, Doris and Cheryl's younger sister, who was the same age as Net, brought her violin. Michael beat drums. I twanged on my guitar. Eventually, a guy named Thomas King joined and became our organ player.

Initially, we started having church in the basement of Grandpa and Grandmother's home in Austin before Grandpa found a storefront at 3911 West Roosevelt Road. It was a small building, but sufficient.

Roosevelt Road was a neon-lit corridor for drugs, cutthroats, and all manner of evil. You might see anything out on Roosevelt Road: a stickup, a shooting, a knifing, a fistfight, a stomping, a prostitute sashaying across the middle of the street in the middle of the night, the yellowish streetlights glowing around her. You did not want to be on Roosevelt Road sometimes even in the daytime, and certainly not after dark. Roosevelt Road was the highway of lost souls, Grief Street, the Avenue of Darkness. It was not the kind of place for children and families, and at first glance, maybe not exactly the ideal location for a family church. Except if your desire was to reach people. So it was here that the Lord led Grandpa to hang his light. In a way, he seemed like Noah, leading his family on a calling from God to build an ark in a place where people for years would watch, wonder, scratch their heads, and think that we must all be crazy.

The men in the family worked for months refurbishing and painting the narrow storefront. Then finally one Sunday, we assembled at our new abode. The walls were light gold. The sanctuary was filled with bright white folding chairs and brown-and-white pulpit furniture. The church smelled of fresh paint and a mixture of pine cleaner, carpet deodorizer, and the scent of newness. I had the understanding even back then that the church building and its furnishings were modest in comparison to many other churches. But there was a sense of pride in seeing Grandpa's dream materialize before our eyes. There had been a kind of care and purpose, if not sacredness, that seemed to go into preparing this unassuming storefront for the Lord's service. Grandpa had told my mother and her siblings that he wanted True Vine to always be a place where his grandchildren would not be ashamed to bring their friends, although I did not know this until years later. As we sat there in the tidy, polished storefront on Roosevelt Road that first Sunday in our new church home and the saints began to praise the Lord, I watched Grandpa as his face lit with joy. He beamed more than the shine on his shaved head. All I felt was pride.

The building seated about 100 people, but we soon outgrew it. Two doors down at 3915 West Roosevelt Road was another storefront church whose congregation was moving out. When they moved, Grandpa purchased that building, which had a broken neon sign that we eventually replaced, affixing the name "True Vine." We turned the sign on whenever we were in service. It was white and orange and flashed on and off with the words "Jesus Saves." But long before we could hold service at our new building, there was a lot of work to do.

The men at True Vine went to work gutting it with the help of contractors. The contractors weren't just any contractors, but a guitar-playing father-and-son duo whose names were Lawrence Jones Sr. and

Lawrence Jones Jr. My grandparents had known the Joneses for years. They played the guitar like nobody's business. They only played gospel music. Their style was that rhythm-spitting Southern twang born in the Mississippi Delta out of the secular blues. It had been perfected in dirt-floor country churches where church mothers and little old preachers beat tambourines and played washboards with spoons until the Good Lord had washed away all their troubles. Everyone called them the "Guitar Joneses." Lawrence Jones Jr. even played a double-neck guitar. When the Joneses were playing, they sat down usually with their heads bowed over their axes, their fingers flying and feet patting while little old ladies danced in the aisles and big preachers stomped and jumped up and down in the pulpit until the floors and the walls trembled. The Joneses were born to play guitar. I once heard Lawrence Jones Jr., a delightful man with scruffy sideburns and a short Afro shaped almost in a box cut, remark proudly during a service at True Vine that he had a sure test to determine whether the children his wife claimed were theirs were indeed his. He explained that if he put a guitar in his children's hands, they should be able to play it. If not the guitar, then the horn or the drums, or some other instrument. If gifts are from God, then surely the Joneses had anointed hands. So it always has seemed proper to me that the same hands that God had ordained to play his music should also mold the building that would be the new True Vine, where the saints planned to get their praise on.

It was a slow and tedious process restoring the new building, which was a stale, dreary place that seemed more like a dilapidated dungeon with an upstairs. It was hard to believe that the folks we had purchased the building from had actually held services there. That Grandpa could even envision the building as a church was a miracle itself, at least nothing short of pure unadulterated faith. My stepfather was among the men who helped tear out walls and set the drywall and new floors, who carried out the loads of debris and worked through cold winter nights and on weekends to help build our new church, who strung light fixtures and bolted down pews and made the sacrifice of time or money or both. I later saw the moral in all of this: That even if one man had a vision, it took many hands and hard work to bring his dreams into fruition, and that most often God seemed to work through human hands.

None of witnessing the miracle of True Vine cured my angst about going to church.

I hated Sundays. Having to wear my cousins' oversized hand-me-downs to church often made me want to crawl under a pew. I acquired a scowl that said, "Just leave me the hell alone." But there was one rule in my house: We had to go to church. Mama wasn't saved, but she was still a Sunday School teacher and part of that group of God-fearing black folks who believed that Sunday was God's day. Mama always arose faithfully each Sunday morning for church, even if she had stayed up half the night playing cards with her bid whist–playing buddies, Miss Edna and Mr. Charlie, who lived a few houses down from us on Komensky.

Bid whist is to black folks what bridge is to white folks. If the Joneses were born to play guitar, Mama was born to play bid whist. By an early age, she had taught each of her four children to play. But playing cards with Mama was not for the faint at heart. Sometimes I would be half afraid to put a card into play, knowing that if I wasn't playing up to Mama's standards, I could get a good quick cussing out. Mama was methodical when it came to playing cards. She counted books and knew exactly which cards had been played and which cards had not. She could even detect what cards her partner was holding by the cards he or she put into play.

Mama did not cheat, although she taught my siblings and me how to detect if other people were cheating and to decode their signals. A touch of the ring finger meant one partner was signaling for the other to play diamonds. A hand to the left side of the chest was for hearts. A fist was for clubs and a hand on the table was for spades.

Mama was masterful. She had honed the card-playing lingo and possessed the bravado requisite for being a champion at bid whist. Her weekend card games were full of the sounds of cards slapping a folding table, of the snap, pop, and hiss of another can of Schlitz being opened, and the occasional shout of "Boston!" That meant one team had turned all thirteen books in a single hand. Sometimes my stepfather shouted, "Too late for the camel 'cause the pig's got his eyes closed!" I never knew what that meant, exactly. Except he only said this whenever he was on the verge of winning another hand.

On card-playing weekends, the night was also filled with trash-talking, with the sound of hurried feet moving toward the bathroom whenever the beer had run its course, and with the carefree girlie nature that rang in Mama's voice as her worries got lost in the endless shuffling of the deck. When the night ended and morning crept through the blinds on Sundays, it was time to go to church.

"Joh-honnn," Mama coaxed on Sunday mornings until my reluctance to climb out of my top bunk kindled her wrath. "Get up and get ready for church. *Now!*"

"All right, Ma," I'd mumble, then hit the wooden floor with a thud, dragging and huffing all the way to the bathroom. Sometimes I complained, but not too long and never too loud. Mama, by then a thick woman with quick reflexes, didn't play that. The only time I got to stay home from church was when I was sick or when I faked it. Either way, the penalty was I couldn't go outside to play for the entire day.

But while Mama had control over my body, I had control over my soul. And I wasn't about to yield to all that spiritual foolishness that sent folks spinning from their seats into the aisles and falling flat out in a trancelike state, slobbering and muttering some language that no one, not even the saints, understood. The saints were what we called those who professed to be born again and whose testimonies always included the phrase, "I thank the Lord for being saved, sanctified, baptized, and filled with the Holy Ghost, and that with a mighty burning fire!" The saints clapped and shouted throughout service but were most joyful whenever the spirit fell on someone known to be a bona fide sinner.

When this happened, someone would be sitting in the pew at church, minding his or her own business, the epitome of calm, when suddenly that same person was catapulted from the pew by some unseen force and began twirling like a spinning top, crying, screaming, the facial muscles in a tug of war. Then the saints erupted. The organ revved, Aunt Scope clanged on the baby grand before she leaped from her stool and bunny-hopped in the spirit, and the voices and music blended into a single deafening hum. It was scary sometimes, all of that screaming and tongue-talking. These goings-on had always been explained to me as the manifestations of the Holy Ghost. I eventually got used to it. But I sometimes worried that whenever friends or new people came to True Vine they might be scared to death.

Folks who did not attend our church but who had heard about or witnessed the spiritual display at "sanctified" churches had a way of describing the spiritual manifestations. They called it "catching the Holy Ghost," which has always sounded kind of funny to me, as if it were like catching a cold. Sometimes my cousin Michael faked catching the Holy Ghost.

"Watch this, John, watch this," Michael would say, laughing as he launched into his routine.

He shut his eyes tight and ran into the center aisle, jumping up and down until his mother caught him by the arm or collar and dragged him back to his seat.

"Boyyy, I'm gonna beat you if you keep on acting a fool," Aunt Mary would say, shooting Michael an unholy look and resuming her own holy dance.

I could always tell the beginning of the spiritual fireworks by the way the saints' voices and hand clapping rose to a crescendo, often as the saints sang the same simple words over and over again. "Put your mind on Jesus, we're gon' have a time," they would sing until frenzied. Sometimes I could not help but wonder whether all this trembling of hands and uttering of languages, which sounded to me like a bunch of gibberish, wasn't some crazy stuff that our folks were actually making up. But after a while, I had witnessed this enough to believe there must have been something to it. That still didn't help with the teasing from my friends, who called us "Holy Rollers." Except I wasn't a Holy Roller, just guilty by association.

As a child, the spirit wasn't something I could see or had ever felt. And deep down, I sometimes wondered whether this invisible God really existed at all, although I was afraid to say as much to my relatives. They would have considered me worthy of being cast into the Lake of Fire, and more immediately, worthy of having my butt whipped. As I grew older, I grew bolder about expressing my skepticism about God, at least with Grandmother. She was the Sunday School teacher for my cousins and me and probably the only one in the church with patience enough to deal with a bunch of rebellious adolescents. Still, we sometimes managed to bring Grandmother to the verge of tears.

"What about evolution? What about Charles Darwin?" I asked many Sunday mornings, half smirking, and salty for having to be at church in the first place.

"Hush your mouth, boy," Grandmother would fire back. "Stop all that crazy talkin'."

Then Cheryl would chime in as we double-teamed Grandmother.

"Yeah, Grandmother, how do you know God isn't just a figment of your imagination?"

"Yeah, Grandmother, yeah," we'd all say, then burst into laughter.

Everyone would laugh, everyone except Grandmother. Finally, after having engaged us for longer than she should have, Grandmother would stand there at the head of class, staring blankly, her arms folded, still clutching her Bible and Sunday School book, her eyes welled up with tears.

"We just playin', Grandmother. We know God is real," I'd say, and she'd snap back to life and resume teaching. "We know God is real."

Truth is, I did not.

I had been taught that there was a God as far back as I could remember. My mother had always taken me to church. And the earliest lesson from my mother's bedtime Bible teachings was that "God always was and always will be." I never could wrap my mind around that idea. But I tried to accept it if for no other reason than that Mama had said it was so. She also told us that it was important to pray.

I don't remember the first time I prayed. As a young child, my prayers were more like one-way conversations with God for pocket change, for food, for God to bless Mama and keep her safe, to protect our family, to let me not be afraid of the dark. To bless me with clothes like Arty and Michael and the other boys so that I would not have to try and hide the holes in the knees of my pants with safety pins. I prayed to God to help me to grow up to be somebody.

To my dismay, God never talked back, at least not in such a way that I could hear Him. While waiting to hear from Him, I learned the trick of quelling my hunger by drinking water until my belly was so filled that if I shook my body from side to side, I could hear the water swish inside. I made a deal with God that if He would bless me with better clothes, I would stay in service rather than hanging outside and macking to the girls like most other boys did. I kept my part of the bargain. But in my mind, God wasn't keeping His, if He had at all been listening. All this caused me to grow angry with God. As a young man, I was mad at Him. I imagined Him to be some cruel thunder-spewing dude with a white beard way up in the sky surrounded by white clouds, who dwelled in some faraway place and had no practical answers for my problems down here on earth. If God really existed, why had my father left me? I wondered. Why was there too often no food? Why did I have to wear my cousins' hand-me-downs? Why didn't He talk back when I prayed? Why did we live in the ghetto? If God was so good, why was life so bad?

The older I got, the less I accepted what the saints said about God and the more I began to wonder if there even was a God. Eventually, I began to resent church and a religion that seemed to offer no immediate remedies for present-day sufferings. I found it difficult to reconcile all the talk in church about the hereafter and all of Uncle Gene's singing about the glory days and the streets of gold waiting for us up in heaven when I was suffering so much down here.

If God truly existed, He was going to have to prove Himself to me.

CHAPTER 9

BULLIED BUT BLESSED

ONE DAY while sitting in my eighth-grade classroom, I received a note from the principal, Mr. Riley, asking me to come to his office. My heart beat fast. You only got calls to the principal's office when you had been bad. This had never happened to me before. Had I done something wrong? I wondered as I walked downstairs to Mr. Riley's office. The secretary showed me in. Mr. Riley, a mammoth of a man, sat behind his desk. He was one of those big Barry White–looking brothers, dark brown with a goatee and a short Afro. He drove a Cadillac that slumped to one side whenever he climbed into his car. He was the kind of guy you didn't want to mess with. All the boys at school, even the so-called tough guys, were afraid of him.

"Hey, John, come on in and have a seat," Mr. Riley said.

I sat down, looking at him wide-eyed, as if he might pull out a strap at any minute and order me to bend over while he lashed me for doing God knows what. He sensed as much.

"Relax, young man," he said. He had a husky baritone voice, and when he talked it was as if every breath was laborious. "I just want to talk with you."

"Okay," I said, swallowing hard.

Mr. Riley reached for a stack of papers on his desk.

"I've been going over your reading and math test scores," he said. "Man, your scores are incredible . . . I'm serious. These are incredible, John."

They were. At twelve, I was already reading on an eleventh-grade level. It might have been that all that bedtime reading I had done over the years when Mama made us go to bed while the other kids on the block were still outside playing had paid off. I loved reading and learning. I had always been in the so-called "gifted class" and always excelled in my studies. In seventh grade, I was named "Boy of the Year" for having scored the highest in reading in my school district on annual standardized exams. Mama accompanied me to a big banquet where I was honored with a huge trophy from Congresswoman Cardiss Collins. Days later, my picture with the congresswoman ran in the *Chicago Defender* newspaper.

"John," Mr. Riley asked, "Where are you going to go to high school?"

High school, I thought. Is that all? Man, was I relieved. But his question stumped me. I had never really given it much thought.

"Uh, I don't know," I answered finally. "I guess Farragut."

"Farragut? You can't go to Farragut, John. That's okay for some of your classmates, but you've got so much potential," Mr. Riley said. "You need to go to a good school, one that will prepare you for college," he continued.

"Have you ever thought about Lindblom or St. Ignatius or Providence-St. Mel?"

"No."

"Well, I think you should. Of course, you have to take a test in order to get into these schools," Mr. Riley continued. "But with your test scores, you won't have any problem. Do you think you might be interested?"

"Yes," I said enthusiastically.

I was instantly excited about the prospect of being able to go to a "good school," maybe even the kind of school white kids attended. There were never any white kids at Mason, unless you counted the one or two white families that hadn't fled K-Town with all the other white folks when black folks moved in. Those kids had blended in so well that they even talked like us and walked like us, so much so that I think we all forgot they were white. In fact, a high-yellow black kid or albino was probably as likely to get called "white boy" as a cool white kid.

I had always heard about good schools in white neighborhoods. Mason was okay as a school, despite my having to run for my life from bullies on more than a few occasions. Going to school and learning was still fun. I especially liked history, math, science, and social studies. I felt secure enough to concentrate while in school and felt good about my teachers, who seemed to really love teaching. But soon it would be time to move on. With David Glasgow Farragut High School being the one in my district, it was less likely that my academic good fortune would continue. Farragut was where Mama and her siblings had graduated. But that was a million years ago. And Farragut had since developed a reputation as a not-so-good school with a burgeoning gang problem, the kind that parents would send their kids to only if there were no other options. I didn't think Mama could afford Catholic school. As a matter of fact, I knew she couldn't. And until Mr. Riley called me into his office, I had not known about testing to qualify for entry at a good public school. Wow, I thought to myself. You mean I might not have to go to Farragut?

"Okay, well, I'll call your mother and talk to her, because you can't go to Farragut," Mr. Riley said.

"Okay, thanks," I said.

"You're welcome. You can go back to class now."

That meeting with Mr. Riley would turn out to be one of those pivotal moments in my life that I would look back on many years later and see as much more than chance, as if there was something or someone steering and protecting me. This was not the first time that this kind of thing had happened. In seventh grade, for instance, I was initially in Miss Pettigrew's classroom. Miss Pettigrew was a round, soft-spoken black woman with thin skin and absolutely no bite. This was not a good combination for a teacher of seventh graders at an inner-city public school. I suspect that even a rowdy enough group of kindergartners would have given Miss Pettigrew fits. But the kids in her class were the craziest and wildest group of younguns I ever witnessed at Mason, and Miss Pettigrew had to be the most docile and timid teacher I had ever known.

In class, the kids hurled paper balls at her and at other kids across a classroom that was consumed by chaos. They stood on top of desks and poked fun at her rotund physique. One girl even wrote Miss Pettigrew's name on the board. With chalk in hand and a pointing stick, she proceeded to instruct the class on what Miss Pettigrew's name really meant.

"Petti's-butt-Grew-a-lot," the little chocolate girl explained.

The class burst into laughter. Miss Pettigrew burst into tears. I always thought that girl was lucky it was Miss Pettigrew and not my second grade teacher, Miss Cartwright, whom she was poking fun at, or some other no-jive-taking black woman. Another teacher might have beat the black off that little girl and begged her to go home and get her mama so she could whip her, too. The kids in Miss Pettigrew's class screamed, laughed, and did everything except make her wear a dunce cap while she sat at her desk and cried or stared off into space. This bunch of adolescent ruffians would not allow her to teach. I do not know how I ended up in Miss Pettigrew's class with them. I sat at my desk quietly, fearing that if I so much as farted, the troublemakers might turn their attention from harassing Miss Pettigrew to harassing me. Then one day, just a few days into the school year, Miss Pettigrew handed me a note and told me she was transferring me to another classroom.

"John, you don't belong in here," she said plainly, tears welling up in her eyes.

I gladly took the note and never looked back. I was transferred upstairs to a third-floor classroom with a white woman named Miss Thomas, who didn't take any mess. It was the gifted class, calm and quiet. Here was where I belonged.

I spent the next two years in Miss Thomas's class. My classmates and I advanced from seventh grade to eighth without ever changing teachers or classrooms. That was the way it worked in the junior high gifted class. The class was also very loosely structured, as if learning was some partnership between teacher and student. For instance, we played a weeks-long game to learn about the Constitution and the Revolutionary War.

We could get up in class and walk around, and we role-played. Some of us were the British. Others were the revolutionaries. There was also a gifted class next door taught by a white teacher, Mr. Goodwill. Basically, he and Miss Thomas doubled up on teaching us, splitting certain subjects between them.

Mr. Goodwill taught creative writing, which was my favorite. I had been writing songs or poems for as long as I could remember. In school, I wrote funny stories about talking leaves and just about anything I could dream up. My favorite part of the class was when we all sat in a circle and I could read my latest work. I could hardly wait sometimes, sitting there hoping whoever was reading would hurry up and get done so my turn would come. When I read my stories, the kids always fell over laughing, clinging to every word. I could feel their eyes and attention locked in on me like radar. My stories always ended to thunderous applause. I loved every minute of it—the applause, the power, the ability to entertain with the words that seemed to flow so easily when I picked up my pencil. The only sore spot on those mornings was that sometimes our teachers allowed us to go to the lunchroom to buy cookies to eat while we sat in our writing circle, but I could seldom afford the 5-cent cookie. I sat there sometimes on the verge of tears, too proud to cry, too embarrassed to borrow a nickel or ask a friend for a bite. It would nag me for many years—my inability back then to afford a cookie. It seemed like such a small thing to have desired and a nickel so minuscule that it only made me feel that much lower because I could not afford a stupid cookie that only cost a nickel.

Making matters worse, in seventh and eighth grade, I was picked on some by some of the boys in my class. Usually, it was the dumbest guys in class, the guys who stumbled when they read, who had trouble pronouncing words bigger than "the" and "and." I always felt really bad for those kids because reading aloud reduced them to stuttering, which, looking back, I still find striking since this was, after all, the gifted class.

Sometimes I would be sitting in class and someone would call me a sissy. I was an easy mark: a small kid who didn't like to fight. I looked nerdy with my no-brand-name clothes and sneakers. A kid who spoke in complete sentences in the King's English and often set the curve on tests. Thank God I didn't wear glasses. But I was one of those kids who could read really well and who enjoyed reading aloud. I had been reading aloud for a long time, at home to my younger siblings, at Sunday School, and at other church functions where I might have to stand up before the congregation as a junior deacon and read a Scripture. I later suspected that some of the guys who picked on me were envious of how well I performed in the classroom. It was not unusual for some kid to say, "He thinks he's so smart."

This was true. But I never consciously tried to rub it in anyone's face.

I eventually learned to dumb myself down, a technique that I perfected and carried over even to adulthood. It is something I have used when I have suspected people, usually black people—and sometimes my own family members—of feeling in some way intimidated by who I am, though mostly it is because of who they perceive me to be. Their unease has at times taken on the form of poking fun at my professional speech patterns, which they deem to be "too white." "Ole bourgeois Negro," I have heard them call me. And so they feel the need to put me in my place.

Often, I have tried to cut them off at the pass, to make them feel more comfortable with me, to break up my sentences into ghetto-speak. To withhold knowledge on some subjects during conversations so as not to come off as a know-it-all. I have chosen consciously sometimes to breathe nothing at all of my professional or academic accomplishments for fear that others may think me a braggart. I have rendered myself deaf, dumb, and stupid to the point of paranoia and misery out of fear of offending or being picked on. I have asked myself countless times: Is it me or is it them? Is it me and them?

I later realized that I am not responsible for how people treat me, only for how I treat them. And if being smart or having a nice house or speaking the King's English or reading aloud perfectly or setting the curve on tests bothers anyone, there isn't much or anything I can really do to ease their hang-ups.

As a boy, it didn't help that I was a smart-mouthed, quick-witted kid who could engage in verbal warfare with a tenacity that often left my victims wounded, but no less eager to kick my butt. My troubles sometimes started with some boy in class calling me some derogatory name, then daring me to say anything in my defense. Eventually, I got around to firing my guns. "Big dummy," "stupid," or "yo' mama" were penetrating, but also served as fighting words. Whenever I had so offended, the kid with the bruised ego would promise to bust me in the lip after school, or in the eye. Fighting time was 3:15.

That usually meant running time for me. I never told the teacher if someone was after me. That would have been worse than taking the whipping like a man. Neither could a kid have his mother come up to the school to handle his troubles. You would have gone from being a sissy to being a big sissy. So I ran, and ran and ran. From the school's front door, I bolted like an Olympic sprinter down Keeler Avenue to Eighteenth Street and the three long blocks to Komensky, sometimes all the way to my yard and up the stairs. When I was running, everything and everyone else around me became a blur.

Once, in the fourth grade, my stepfather said he was going to meet me outside the school because a kid named Walter was after me. When the bell rang, I tore out of the school, running for my life. I had already scanned all the faces outside and had not spotted my father. I was doing about ninety miles an hour and rounding the corner of the school's parking lot with Walter hot on my heels when I heard a voice.

"John, come back here."

I recognized the voice. It was my dad. I stopped. And he promptly collared Walter, whose eyes nearly bugged out of his head. Then he lifted him up off the ground, his sneakers dangling. Walter seemed even more afraid than I had been just moments earlier. He looked like he was about ready to wet his pants. He probably did. This much I know: He never bothered me again. In fact, we became good friends after that.

I did not like fighting. I often wondered if this was because of some early exposure to violence, to living in a violent neighborhood, to having heard the sounds of fists hitting and hands slapping, and seeing blood gushing, the dry red stains that it leaves on sidewalks when it isn't quickly washed away. Once, a neighbor stabbed her alcoholic husband while everybody watched in horror on a summer evening when it was still light outside. There was the story of a fat kid busting a dude in the head with a baseball bat. There was the story of another kid who was accidentally shot in the head with a .357 Magnum out on the street one summer day. There was the increasing sound of broken glass and gunshots in the middle of the night or the screams of a woman stumbling down the block late after dark as her drunken old man beat her until the screams dissolved into the stillness that seemed to embrace the neighborhood just before the break of every dawn.

It seemed that almost everybody in the neighborhood liked a good fight. You could always tell when there was going to be a fight after school by the way the large crowds roamed the streets near the school like a bloodthirsty mob. There was a kind of giddiness that rose from the circle of onlookers and that same wild-eyed look I had seen in the faces of Roman spectators in television movies as gladiators fought to the death. I didn't like fighting. I don't know exactly why I didn't. I just didn't. But sometimes a man's gotta do what a man's gotta do.

Huckey and I were not always friends. In fact, he used to pick on me. It is a strange thing how some people prey on those who appear to be weaker. How peers can pressure decent kids to smack around or mistreat a smaller kid everybody knows can't fight, or doesn't like to fight, or doesn't want to fight. Maybe it is human nature. Maybe it is something else.

Huckey wasn't really a bully, like some guys; he was actually a nice, mild-mannered kid. But under the right circumstances, Huckey could be as cruel as anyone.

Once, the boys on Komensky were all playing baseball in a vacant lot at the end of the block near Sixteenth Street. Huckey and I were on opposing teams, and my team was winning. Huckey, who hated losing, especially to a team of so-called scrubs, was pitching. I came up to bat, and for Huckey, it was a foregone conclusion that he would strike me out. Instead I got a hit and ran to first base. The play wasn't even close.

"You're out," Huckey shouted.

"I'm safe," I shouted back.

"He's safe," my teammates cried.

"You're out," Huckey protested again from the pitcher's mound.

"I'm safe."

"You're out," Huckey continued, his eyelids starting to pop with veins. "If you're not off of that base by the time I count to three, I'm going to come over there and knock you off. One . . ."

I was afraid. But I didn't move. "Who does he think he is? He doesn't order me around," I thought. "Anyway, I was safe."

"Twooo . . ."

I didn't say a word.

"Three!"

Huckey ran over and bumped my chest with his. He got so close up in my face that I could feel the heat of his breath. His friends urged him on.

"Kick his butt, Huckey! Kick that nigger's butt!"

Suddenly, Huckey slapped me. And just as suddenly, I lost my mind. I grabbed Huckey's scrawny little neck in a chokehold and began squeezing the life out of him. I squeezed and squeezed and didn't let go. I was swearing and squeezing and crying. But I wouldn't let go. Huckey was crying and slobbering and wiggling. But I could not let go. I would not let go. Every ounce of rage and fear found its way to my death grip.

"I'll kill you," I cried, in between screaming curse words. "I'll kill you! I'll kill you!"

People kept yelling for me to stop choking Huckey. Finally, I looked up and saw Mama running toward me from home and someone pried my arms from Huckey's neck. I walked home with Mama in a fit of rage, still crying and vowing to kill the kid who had slapped me. Word soon spread that John had beat up Huckey. I don't remember when or how we started talking and playing again. But we became good friends.

I never really understood bullies or the desire to bully in those days. But I later came to believe that most bullies were themselves bullied by a parent, by an older brother or cousin or someone. That bullies were kids who in some way had been kicked around so much that one day they found their own sense of satisfaction or vengeance in bullying other people. That discovery didn't make me feel any better. But I could at least understand how this sort of thing could happen, how that cycle might be perpetuated. I also came to understand how another person's success could serve to remind others of their own inadequacies, and how they sometimes tended to lash out, to destroy, belittle, or demean rather than try to improve their own lot. I reckoned that that was the source of a lot of the bullying I experienced as a child. The dumb, cool boys with the cool clothes in some ways wished they could be smart like me.

The irony was that in a lot of ways I envied them.

CHAPTER 10

ST. MEL

IT WAS LATE August 1974, my first day of high school and the dawn of a new day. Fall has always been my favorite time of year. I have always loved the reddening of leaves and the still coolness that lingers like shots of ice water on the last breaths of summer. When fall was knocking at summer's back door and it started to get dark early, the evenings on Komensky seemed to hold a certain peace and calm, especially after a summer filled with noise, gunshots, and fights in K-Town. The beginning of school signaled an end to the hot weather and the muggy days and nights that my family and I had sweated through without air-conditioning in our apartment, finding what relief we could from a rickety Walgreen's window fan. The winds of fall carried with them the slow beckoning of winter, the transfusion of leaves from green to shades of yellow and red until finally they had turned a burnt crispy brown. It seemed even then, at the mere hint of fall that the Hawk would be gearing up for its return, whipping off Lake Michigan and whispering threats of the cold to come. I loved the scents and heartbeat of fall.

In preparation for the first day of school, everybody's mama always took them shopping for new school clothes. You had to have cool threads on the first day. You had to have new shoes, new socks, new pants, and a new shirt. You had to smell new right down to your underwear. I do not know how this tradition started. But getting new clothes at the start of each school year became the expectation of us kids. No one would dare wear last year's clothes to school for the first week of the new academic year, and most certainly not on that first day. You would get laughed at, and people would think you were poor, which was just as bad as being laughed at. Years later, I came to see this ritual of buying a new wardrobe for kids at the start of each new school year as a trap, especially for black families that could least afford it but each season set about decking out their kids in the latest fashions. I would happen upon this discovery years later after my own children began attending school with whites from well-to-do families and saw that they did not do the same. I would look back with one consolation: We hadn't known any better.

I was a month shy of my fourteenth birthday and still a short, scrawny little guy when the first day of high school rolled around. Any hope of being six feet tall might as well have been a wish of someday being seven feet tall. Net was still the taller of the two of us. The fact that she was taller and often mistaken by strangers as my older sister was really starting to make me mad. I also felt embarrassed. Even though I was officially in high school, I looked more like a seventh grader than a freshman.

Going to a new school, I wanted to make a good impression, get off to a fresh start, talk the right talk, walk the right walk, wear the right clothes, and gain the acceptance of my peers. I had gone back-to-school shopping in previous years. And until now, Mama had somehow always managed to buy us something, if only an outfit or two. I would have been grateful for as much this fall. Except this fall, Mama could not afford to buy us even a new pair of drawers.

It bothered me that I did not have anything new to wear on my first day of school, particularly because I was already nervous about going to high school—and I was especially nervous about going to a school that none of my classmates or friends from Mason were going to attend. Most of them were going to Farragut, which was the designated high school for our neighborhood. I was going to attend Providence-St. Mel.

After speaking with Mr. Riley in his office that day a few months earlier, he had indeed called my mother as he had promised. And Mama had agreed that I should go to a high school other than Farragut. Except I am certain she had no idea how she would pay for Catholic school. Lindblom, a public, technical high school on the South Side, had a good reputation. So on a Saturday morning that spring, I took the exam and passed with flying colors. But Mama soon ruled out Lindblom, saying she was too afraid for her baby to take the bus across town. It wasn't just my small size that concerned her but the possibility of my being recruited or beaten up by gangs.

That spring, I had also taken the exam for St. Ignatius High School and for Providence-St. Mel. St. Ignatius was tops among the city's Catholic schools, but it was inconveniently located across the street from the ABLA high-rise housing projects. I would likely have gone to St. Ignatius, but I fell a few points shy on my test, a fact that I wasn't exactly sad about in the end. When I took the test at St. Ignatius, sitting in the cafeteria surrounded by boys, I had wondered where in the heck all the girls were. One fact that Mama and Mr. Riley had neglected to tell me was that St. Ignatius was an all-boys school. But I passed the test at St. Mel, and they had girls. St. Mel was also where my cousins Arty, Cheryl, and Doris attended school. The tuition was roughly $1,200 a year, when you added in the fund-raising that each student was also responsible for. That $1,200 might as well have been a million dollars to Mama. But she said I would be going to St. Mel and not to worry. Somehow, she said, she would find a way to pay for it. That was that. Mama had spoken. But I still worried. It bothered me, too, that my family would be making this kind of sacrifice for me to go to a Catholic school when there were some more practical and immediate needs like food, electricity, and gas.

For my first day of high school, Mama didn't have the 30 cents bus fare I needed for each way, so my stepfather had to drive me to school that morning. That would not have been so bad except his car wasn't the kind of car that a kid wanted to be caught dead in, especially on the first day of school. "The Rambler," as we called it, was a white, semi-rusted Ford four-door that he had bought from someone for $100. It beat having no car at all, but not by much. And it was appropriately named because it rambled and clunked and sputtered along. You could hear it coming from a mile away. I had gone to bed the night before thinking that I was going to catch the bus to school like every other kid. Instead, I climbed that morning into the dreaded Rambler.

As we drew closer and closer to school, I thought about asking my stepfather to drop me off several blocks away. I figured that any kids standing outside my new school would laugh and later tease me for my father having such a raggedy car. I also figured that to make such a request of my stepfather might also hurt his feelings. So I didn't.

Soon we pulled up to the school, the rusted white Rambler clunking all the way. Standing outside on the steps leading to St. Mel were at least a half dozen young men, cool dudes with cool threads and spit-shined shoes. Among them, I spotted my friend Morgan, who lived next door to my grandmother. I thought Morgan was rich. His father owned several racehorses and even two or three grocery stores. His parents drove Cadillacs. Morgan looked like a picture out of *GQ*, his hair neatly trimmed, a hint of mustache, and creased slacks that looked sharp enough to cut steak. I climbed out of the car and shut the raggedy door behind me.

"See you later," I said as I headed toward the school stairs. It seemed like forever. There was Morgan, standing to the left.

"Hey, Morgan," I said.

"Hey, John, what's up man?" he replied.

I walked up the stairs, wearing my double-knit green slacks with one-inch cuffs, worn black canvas sneakers, and a T-shirt. My dad pulled away, the Rambler rambling, sputtering, and spitting as it rolled down the street. The boys on the stairs looked at me and snickered. Morgan smiled. I walked inside, my head hung in shame, but at least glad to be a student at Providence-St. Mel.

St. Mel had a reputation for being a good school and a safe school, especially in such an unsafe neighborhood. In K-Town, gangs had laid claim to certain streets and many kids crossed gang boundaries every day to go to school. For instance, Gangster Disciples pretty much ran things west of Pulaski Road, while the Vice Lords controlled everything east of Pulaski. Once, one of my cousins, who was a Gangster Disciple, was walking with my mother to the Arab store, as we called it, on Sixteenth Street. When they got to Pulaski Road, my cousin told my mother that he would wait for her on our side—the west side—of Pulaski. She asked why. His answer was simple. He was a Disciple, and Disciples could not cross the street into Vice Lord territory short of risking life and limb. Mama understood. When it came to crossing the gang boundaries to go to a school that happened to be in the territory of another gang, schools were not so understanding. Those were just the breaks back then. Not only did you have to elude gang members on your own as you made your way to school but also the guys who were in the schools, sitting next to you in class once you got there.

You did not have to necessarily be in a gang to become a target of rivals. Sometimes simply living in a neighborhood or being seen with friends or cousins who had some gang affiliation was enough. At St. Mel, though, I didn't have to worry about any of that. Gangs were not tolerated. Drugs were not tolerated. Neither was cursing, fighting, or any other nonsense. Even walking on the grass brought a $10 fine. But the greatest comfort in going to St. Mel was its guardian angel—the principal, Paul J. Adams III. He was a goateed, Afro-wearing man with a lot of thug in his heart when it came to protecting his children.

I don't remember the first time I saw Mr. Adams or the first time I heard kids speak about him in the kind of reverent tones usually reserved for God or some bad Negro whom everybody in the neighborhood knew not to mess with. Mr. Adams was a tall man, about six feet, one inch, and kind of scruffy looking at times, especially when he stood in the office on those early school mornings wearing his bathrobe and a five-o'clock shadow, having just emerged from the school's convent, where he lived. He had big eyes that seemed to pop with veins whenever he got mad. He had the stare of an assassin, a cold penetrating look that could make you shiver. His voice was thunderous and he had my mother's command of curse words and the inclination to use them like a .45 automatic. He was my Aunt Mary, John Shaft, and God all rolled up into one—a bad mother-shut-yo'-mouth, which is about what it took to be principal in that neighborhood.

St. Mel wasn't in K-Town, but it was close enough. Pimps, pushers, players, prostitutes, and thugs as well as an assortment of other street-corner hustlers were par for the course in its neighborhood, West Garfield Park, just northeast of K-Town. St. Mel was a yellowish-brick castle towering above Garfield Park like an oasis in a desert.

At St. Mel each morning, we could count on Mr. Adams being there when we arrived, surveying us for book bags, making sure boys wore belts on their pants and that the girls had on clothes that were not too tight or revealing—for which they might be sent home. Sometimes he stood in his office window peering out with binoculars across the street at Garfield Park to identify those students who might be smoking joints before school, which always amazed me. How these kids thought they could get past Mr. Adams, who could sniff out the scent of reefer in an incense factory, was beyond me, especially when they walked in sometimes smelling like burned leaves. High school was an awakening to the drug world for me, even though years earlier Mama had lectured me on the hazards of marijuana and a film in junior high school had discussed the perils of heroin use. But until high school, drugs still seemed foreign, like something that only hippies and strung-out dope fiends used. I didn't know any junkies. But in high school, many kids talked about smoking reefers and getting high as if everyone was doing it. Sometimes it seemed that most everyone was, though at St. Mel, Mr. Adams was in the process of weeding it out.

There was a sense among students that you always needed to be careful even with what you were saying because Mr. Adams always seemed to be lurking somewhere in the shadows like an undercover cop. We could count on Mr. Adams being there at the end of the school day, making sure we were all carrying books and that we got home safely. Sometimes he even walked students to the bus stop, accompanied by his baseball bat when he became aware that gang members were trying to recruit his students. The bat meant we were off-limits. And all the bad and crazy folks in the neighborhood soon learned that Mr. Adams was just as bad, and just as crazy.

That reputation was earned over the years, sometimes with his fists, sometimes with his wicked tongue or with the fearlessness with which he dealt with the bad elements in the neighborhood and occasionally even bullheaded parents. I once heard him tell a parent over the telephone bright and early one morning after the parent's insistence that her child be allowed into class despite not having paid tuition: "If Jesus didn't pay his tuition, he'd have to leave here." End of conversation.

As much as we could count on Mr. Adams being there in the mornings, we could count on him popping up out of nowhere, in the gym, in our classrooms, in the cafeteria, keeping watch for the slightest sign of trouble. The only lunchroom fight that ever occurred in my four years at St. Mel ended with a kid being hit in the head with a pop can when I was a freshman. Mr. Adams nearly went berserk. He halted classes immediately, locked the doors of the school, and ordered all of the students into the assembly hall.

"Somebody knows who hit that boy in the head with a can," he shouted angrily from the auditorium stage as everybody, even the teachers, sat there seeming half afraid to move a muscle. He continued, "Somebody knows something. And doggoned, we gon' find out who did it before we leave here today. Y'all gon' sit here if we have to sit here all day. All day. Y'all think I'm playing? That boy could have died. Y'all must think this is some public school or something. This kind of stuff ain't going on here.

"Anybody care to say who did it?"

Silence filled the auditorium. It was so quiet you could have heard a mouse fart.

"All right, I've got a list of names, and when I start calling these names, anybody's name I call gets one week's work suspension. And every time I come back in here with a new list of names, the work suspension goes up a week."

There was a collective gasp.

Work suspension was the St. Mel equivalent of being sentenced to hard time. Being on work suspension for a week meant that you couldn't go to class, although you were still responsible for your schoolwork. While everyone else was in class, students sentenced to work suspension for having committed some serious school infraction went about mopping, buffing, and cleaning the school. The worst detail for work suspension was the dreaded boiler room. There, students were required to fill the incinerator with trash and emerged at the end of the day soot-stained and smelling like smoke.

Standing in the front of the auditorium and still seething, Mr. Adams called off the names. The students stood up as their names rang out. The rest of us shook our heads, knowing that they were in big trouble. Mr. Adams was really smoking. He stormed out of the auditorium with the students in tow, vowing that he would soon return with more names.

"Awwww mannnn, somebody better tell who did it," somebody said, echoing the sentiment of the student body. The silence inside the auditorium exploded into a smoke cloud of indecipherable chatter. We sat there nervously wondering how this drama would all end. Some of us thought about calling our mamas.

After several more rounds of calling names and ushering students out of the auditorium and into his office for interrogation, the tension inside the auditorium was almost unbearable. Then suddenly, a thinly muscular young man named Dwayne, who was a freshman and had been called out by Mr. Adams earlier, appeared at the auditorium door. Dwayne had a reputation as a troublemaker and a real bad dude. He was the kind of dude I avoided like the plague. He was bad news.

"Cookie, I know you told on me!" Dwayne shouted.

Cookie, whose real name was Diane, was a junior. Diane was a pretty girl but short and petite with a big forehead that she always camouflaged with bangs. She was sitting all the way at the front of the auditorium and didn't acknowledge Dwayne's taunting. The girl didn't even flinch.

"I know it was you, I know it was you," Dwayne continued. "I'm gon' get you girl. You wait 'til we leave school. I'm gon' kick your butt."

Suddenly, Diane jumped up out of her seat.

"I ain't scared a you," she said, whipping her neck around the way sisters do when they are about to get a Negro told.

"I told," Diane yelled. "Yeah, I told on you, 'cause you did it. You threw the can. Why should we all be punished because of you?"

As much as I admired Diane's bravery, I feared for her life. I was looking in Dwayne's face and saw his eyes glaze over. It seemed as if the spirit of a growling Doberman descended on him and took control of his soul. In an instant, Dwayne began loping down the aisle toward Diane.

"Oh my God," I thought. "He's gonna kill her. Where's Mr. Adams? Where is Mr. Adams?"

Students began screaming. Dwayne was moving faster, scowling, growling. Diane looked terrified. But she wasn't running. Dwayne was only a few feet away and moving in for the kill. Then suddenly, something or somebody came out of nowhere moving with lightning speed. It blindsided Dwayne, hitting him with such fierce precision that he looked like a wide receiver being pulverized by a middle linebacker. It was no linebacker, though. It was Sister Carmel. "Oh my God, it's Sister Carmel," I yelled inside my head though my words were reduced to gasps as I watched in disbelief. Everybody was yelling and screaming and scared and cracking up all at the same time. Dwayne, the so-called tough guy, taken out by the flying nun. Wow.

Suddenly, Mr. Adams emerged and grabbed Dwayne by his neck, then led him out of the auditorium, breathing profanities all the way. I never saw Dwayne again.

Mr. Adams was without doubt the baddest Negro on the block. He was known to kick folks out of school dances, which were held on Friday nights in the school cafeteria and which he patrolled with a giant flashlight that he shined in people's faces to make sure they weren't high and nodding out. Anyone who was a student at St. Mel knew better. But not everyone who came to our Friday night dances was a student there. It didn't matter. St. Mel was Mr. Adams's castle. And he was without a doubt king.

At St. Mel you felt safe. And though I would not fully understand it until many years later, Mama's decision to send me to St. Mel was the crossroads for my friends and me. Most of my friends—J-Rat, Huckey, Michael, Ricky, Horsehead, and others—went to Farragut or a similarly deficient public school where there were many adverse elements at war with their getting a good education. It was my sense then that many of my friends' parents did not understand that education separated the wheat from the chaff or that the financial sacrifice of paying for their children's education might yield untold dividends in the future, despite the hardship in the short run. Truth is, some of my friends' parents could have afforded to pay for St. Mel a lot more than Mama could. But few of their parents had Mama's understanding; so that even if it meant that Mama would have to go without so that I wouldn't have to, she made the sacrifice. For years, she wore the same few outfits to church while other women were decked out. For a time, she had no winter coat and often donned Net's coat and shoes when she went to the store. There were no vacations, few trips to the hairdresser, and often not even money for pantyhose. Even back then, I thought I understood how great a sacrifice it was that Mama and my stepfather—who wore a thin summer jacket in the wintertime—were making for my education. But it was more than I could have understood then and much more than I can ever repay.

As I became involved in sports and other activities at St. Mel, my friends and I drifted farther and farther apart. I would leave for school about sunup and return to Komensky long after dark. Sometimes I was so tired that I fell asleep while lying on the floor in front of the space heater in our living room. I waved at my friends on Komensky and they waved back whenever we saw each other coming or going, which was seldom. We were like strangers passing in the night.

St. Mel was my pass to the New World. For the first time in years, I felt like it was okay to be as smart as I could be. Not that I hadn't been encouraged to raise my hand and speak up in class at Mason. But at St. Mel, there was an excitement about learning and doing your best. This was the rule rather than the exception. Students who earned straight A's for any semester were refunded that semester's tuition. And at the beginning of each semester, there was always an honors assembly. The school was small enough, too, that it seemed really intimate, like family. In time, everybody knew everybody. And most kids in the school had a brother or a sister or a cousin also enrolled at St. Mel. There were 150 students in my freshman class, but by the time I graduated four years later, the number had dwindled to sixty-one. That was due in part to students' own inability, although usually it was their unwillingness, to perform academically. It was also due to Mr. Adams's impatience and intolerance with foolishness and his knack of handing out expulsions as readily as he changed his socks.

"Excuse me for a minute," I can still hear Mr. Adams saying, the treble rising in his voice as his eyes widened and he strode toward his office. "I gotta go and put somebody out of my school. I'll be right back. You can't follow the rules, you gotta leave here," he would say as he huffed away.

Mr. Adams had a humorous side, too. I don't know that it was so much that he would try to make us laugh as it was that he did not mince words. Once, in a college guidance class for seniors, which Mr. Adams often taught himself, a kid named Steve stood at the front of the class-room, giving an oral presentation on his career project. Steve had written a paper saying that he planned on becoming a doctor. Standing in front of the class, he had said as much. He had launched into his recitation on the requirements of becoming a physician when suddenly Mr. Adams angrily interrupted him.

"Man, what kind of grade did you get in biology?"

"A 'D,'" Steve answered somewhat sheepishly.

"What'd you get in integrated science?"

"A 'D,'" Steve replied.

"What did you get in chemistry?"

"I didn't take chemistry," Steve answered.

Mr. Adams shot back, "Well, how the hell you think you gon' become a doctor then? Sit down . . . Getting up here with this crazy stuff, man, you must be out your mind," Mr. Adams grumbled. "Sit your butt down, man."

It might have sounded harsh, but it was no less the truth and kind of funny all at the same time. Steve had about as much chance of becoming a doctor as I did of becoming a professional hockey player. You could always count on Mr. Adams for the truth, even if you didn't always like the way it came out.

Mr. Adams was what so many of us lacked and also what so many of us needed: A strong black man who cared about us and loved us, whom we could count on always being there but who did not accept excuses. No matter how poor we were or what our hang-ups were, he expected excellence and also provided the opportunities for success. No matter how gruff he sometimes seemed, there was always an excitement in his eyes whenever we excelled, a genuine joy in his voice over our achievements and a sort of quiet reassurance that said, "I believe in you." For many of us, St. Mel became a safe haven, free from the chaos or despair or drama of our worlds outside of school. It was home away from home and at times my lifeline. St. Mel's real beauty lay not in the number of us who would go on to attend universities like Harvard, Yale, or Princeton, but in its ability to make the dream of college for many ghetto kids who walked through its doors more than just a dream. It was not a school for the elite, but a refuge for the downtrodden, for children whom society had written off, for kids that Mr. Adams saw as diamonds in the rough.

I later learned that St. Ignatius was supposed to be a better school. But what I would come to see so clearly in time was that there was no better place for me than St. Mel and no man who cared more about educating inner-city children than Paul J. Adams.

CHAPTER 11

LOVE AND BASKETBALL

MY GAME was weak. But I was convinced that with a little luck and a lot of effort I could make the freshman team. After the final day of tryouts, my chances still looked good. A couple of days later, the list was posted and I hurried out of class as the final bell sounded at the end of the school day. I ran all the way to the fourth floor, down the hall to St. Mel's gymnasium, up to the wall where the coach had promised to post the names of the boys who had made the team. I knew I had been a long shot all along. Most of the boys who tried out for the team had played for their elementary schools and could perform an assortment of feats with the roundball. I had trouble making layups.

During tryouts, some boys had laughed and poked fun at me as I clumsily fired shots that banged off the backboard. My jumper sometimes veered miles off course. It was embarrassing. But I kept coming back. I showed up every day on time. I jumped at the coach's every command. I ran faster or as hard as anyone and never let thoughts of quitting linger for longer than a few moments. I figured that in the end, when the coach was making his final cuts, hustle and fortitude would count for something. Not every player picked had to be a superstar. And one thing the coach would never have to worry about with me was my ever becoming ineligible because of bad grades. You had to maintain a C average to play at St. Mel, no exceptions. That meant that even some of the best ballplayers, the guys like a lanky kid named Leroy, who could slam dunk and perform wondrous works on the basketball court, might never get to suit up in a million years. So while some superstars laughed at me, I laughed back inside, knowing that some of them would see about as much action in a St. Mel uniform as my mother. Being on the basketball team was my chance to belong, to start over, to be a cool dude, a member of the hoops squad—due all the perks and accolades, including my share of girls. Instead of being the nerdy smart kid, for once in my life I was going to be the man.

I had never played organized basketball before. But I often shot hoops during gym class and in the alley behind our house on Komensky, sometimes nailing a bicycle rim to a wooden light pole and shooting baskets until the sun sank from the sky. I loved basketball and dreamed of playing pro someday, though I never told anybody. The way I figured it, guys who got to be in the NBA played basketball so much that they eventually got good enough to turn pro. Never mind that I was on the short side, just a couple of inches taller than five feet, not extremely quick or athletically gifted.

I don't know how or when the basketball bug bit me. When I was younger, baseball was my first love, and not just any baseball, but Cubs baseball. I used to run home after school each day to catch the final two innings of the Cubs game. I worshiped the Cubs and baseball. So did Mama. But when Dr. J arrived on the pro basketball scene, I about lost my mind and I got myself a peel, started working on my game. The Afro, the glide, the way Dr. J dunked with the ease that other players shot layups was a thing of beauty. Seeing Dr. J in motion made just about every kid I knew want to grow up to be just like him. No matter how deficient our skills or the lack of size or athleticism, we all dreamed of playing pro basketball.

People cheered baseball players, but they worshiped basketball players. In elementary school, the guys who played on the basketball team never got picked on, always got treated as really special by kids and even teachers. Everybody wanted to be their friend. They were like small-town heroes. Everybody else was a zero or a hanger-on. All of this led me to one conclusion: I had to make the team.

That fall day in mid-October 1974, I arrived at the fourth floor to find a crowd of boys surrounding the white sheet of paper taped to a wall. I walked up and scanned the list. Fountain...Fountain...No Fountain. My name wasn't there. My heart sank. I collected myself, fighting back the tears, and caught the bus home. I walked in without saying a word to anyone, shut the bedroom door behind me, then sat on my bed and cried. I had tried so hard and still failed.

I was still sitting in my tears when it dawned on me that I could continue sitting there feeling sorry for myself or I could make the decision to pick myself up and try again next year. I embraced the thought and made a promise to myself that when the team list was posted next year, my name would be on it. Or at least if it wasn't, it would not be because I had not given it my best shot, one last time. "I can get better," I told myself. "I can do it. You can do it, John. You can do it." The words played over and over in my mind and I dried my eyes.

It was years before I understood the significance of that moment and why, even in those times when I have been disheartened or the odds have been stacked against me, a stubborn unwillingness to yield has always sustained me. Whether it was soul or heart, or the will or simply spirit to endure, I do not know. What I do know is that at its root was the belief that I could somehow make it no matter how bleak things seemed. It was faith, not a mountain of faith, or even a mound. Sometimes it was just enough faith to get me through the day. And over time I learned that faith is not a feeling, or necessarily a single moment of inspiration, but a decision. I chose to believe.

Although I didn't make the team, I knew I could learn from the guys who had. I also realized that I needed to play a lot more basketball to have any shot at making next year's team. So I decided to ask the varsity coach if I could be the team's manager. He said yes. Team manager was just a fancy name for waterboy. But I wasn't just any waterboy. I was the varsity waterboy. And being the waterboy meant I got to go to all the games free, attend all practices, shoot around with the varsity, and even ride on the team bus. It also meant the chance to shoot baskets on the court during halftime at games.

But being the waterboy also meant getting teased a bunch. As waterboy, I was typically the butt of jokes. Everyone presumed me to be the team flunky. My first name soon became "Hey!" And my last name, "Waterboy." That never bothered me much. I was happy to be a part of the team. I was always there with the towels during time-outs, standing at the ready with a plastic bottle of chilled water or a warm-up jacket for a player returning to the bench. When I wasn't fulfilling my game duties, I was cheering from the sidelines or studying players' moves, copying them in the pages of my mind. The varsity players took a liking to me and schooled me on the fundamentals of basketball. All the while, I kept thinking, "Wait 'til next year. Next year, I'm going to be wearing a uniform." There was probably not a single other soul who had seen me play who would have believed that.

That fall and through winter, the sting of not having seen my name on the team list as a freshman was my constant motivation. It carried over through summer. Every time I picked up a basketball, it was there, somewhere in the back of my mind. It was there every time I practiced dribbling, or shot layups. During the summer, I spent nearly every waking moment on one basketball court or another, honing my jumper and ball-handling skills. In fact, hitting a layup became a thing of relative ease by summer's end. I could put the ball through my legs without looking. I had even developed a decent jump shot and had picked up a few elusive moves, including being able to put the ball behind my back while inbound for a layup.

I returned to St. Mel that fall as a sophomore with absolutely one goal in mind, to make the team. Tryouts were tough. But I worked hard. I ran as hard or as fast as anyone else, always showed up on time, and was always ready to jump at the coach's command. Finally, the day came for the team list to be posted. I ran upstairs after school. A crowd of boys surrounded the sheet of names. I walked over and scanned for mine: Michael

Brown, Tony Cunningham, Carl Hayes . . . John Fountain . . . John Fountain! "Yes! Yes! I'm on the team! I'm on the team!" I yelled, jumping up and down. I wanted to cry. But I couldn't do that around the fellas. I regained my composure, slapped a five or two.

As I stood there relishing seeing my name on the list, there was a part of me that could not believe I had actually made the team. I was not better than some who hadn't made the final cut, for sure. Many years later, I wondered whether the coach hadn't selected me simply because he admired this kid who had no quit in him. Or maybe he chose me because there are more important things than shooting percentages—like helping a kid with a dream. No one wanted to be on the team more than I did. I'm sure my coach sensed as much. The chance to suit up in one of those nylon purple-and-gold uniforms and run out on the floor as a Providence-St. Mel Knight was one of my greatest goals in life, even if it meant sitting on the bench for an entire season. That first season, I probably did not score a single point. It didn't matter. I was just happy to be on the team.

While I collected my books that spring on the last day of my sophomore year, one year on the basketball team under my belt, I was already looking forward to returning to school in the fall. Not only was I going to be a junior, but also a big man on campus as a member of the varsity.

In the meantime, there would be six weeks of my summer in Project Upward Bound, which meant six weeks of luscious living on the lakefront campus of Northwestern University in Evanston, Illinois, long summer nights, and girls, lots of girls.

When I arrived at Northwestern that summer, I left all my worries back in K-Town. Upward Bound was a federally funded program that introduced promising inner-city kids to college life. It also offered tutoring and college guidance counseling. During the school year, we met on Saturday mornings at the university in Evanston. We attended classes on how to apply to college and how to improve our studying. Tutorial sessions usually took place in the afternoon.

I joined Upward Bound for two reasons. For starters, I planned on going to college and figured that since I would be the first in my family, I would need all the help I could get. Second, Cheryl, Doris, and Arty had already joined and loved it. They bragged about how much fun they were having and how during the summer they got to spend six weeks living on campus, like real college students, away from home, away from parents. I was sold instantly. Once I joined and saw all the fine girls there, I knew I had made the right choice.

During the summer, the idea was to give us a simulated introduction to college life. Those of us who were at least fourteen years old were also offered jobs. We lived in a dormitory and were responsible for getting up and to class on time each day. We were responsible for managing our money, time, studies, and relationships—with some help from staff, of course, if things ever got out of hand. But for the most part, we managed on our own.

Summer at Northwestern was sweet. The school was situated on a lush green campus just off Lake Michigan. Evanston was a hoity-toity suburb with Victorian mansions, picket fences, and white folks who dressed like they didn't have a dime, but who you could tell probably had more money than me and all of my folks put together. It was a quiet place where the sky seemed a little bluer and where the stars under a moonlit night, especially when a breeze was whispering off the lake, seemed like the kind of place where I could live until the day I died. It struck me that this was how white folks lived and that our worlds were far apart indeed. It was amazing how this place, just an hour's train ride from the West Side, could seem an entire world away. The contrast was glaring: Clean streets instead of dirty ones. Peace and quiet instead of murder and mayhem. Grass instead of barren lots. Life instead of death.

During the school year, when my cousins and I and a few other teenagers from St. Mel, who also lived on the West Side, rode the trains to Evanston, we crossed the invisible lines between poverty and prosperity, between city and suburb, between white and black. Those morning rides to Northwestern were the beginning of the opening of my eyes to the universe that existed beyond the horizon of my world, although I did not understand this until many years later. By then, I also understood that to dream beyond the walls of my world would ultimately mean leaving it. Northwestern helped me escape the madness that usually came into full bloom in my neighborhood during the summer months. Like St. Mel, it provided safe haven. Sadly, though, most of the boys I knew weren't so lucky.

At Northwestern, I shared a room with a friend and classmate named Ronald Price. He was a wiry, short kid who wore glasses, and like most of us back in 1976, wore an Afro lifted at the roots with the wire teeth of an Afro pick. Mostly, I called him Price. Teenage boys had this thing of calling each other by their last names. I don't know why or how this started. It seemed like the cool, manly thing to do. Like me, Price also attended St. Mel and had a reputation for being a bookworm. Some thought him to be a nerd and said as much to his face. I always figured myself to be every bit as smart as Price but also realized that if I showed it too often, the same boys and girls who called him "Professor Dingledong" or "Professor Gigglesnorts" would find an equally appropriate nickname for me, too. So I got good grades but knew when to tuck my "A" test that had messed up the curve into my folder without saying so much as a word. Price was a nice kid with a good heart and truly smart. We got along well. And I discovered over the course of the summer that Price wasn't as much the nerd—whatever that meant—as everybody made him out to be. He partied. He minded his own business. And the boy certainly had his share of girls.

Among them that summer was a short, thin girl with smooth brown skin, long lashes, a cute face, and a bright metallic smile. She wore braces and often wore her hair in long cornrows that everybody called French braids in those days. They were thin and shiny, and dangled at her neck. Her voice was as soft as she was petite. She was a real girlie girl, the kind who is afraid of spiders and bugs. Her name was Claudette. Claudette and Price had dated briefly earlier that summer and had since split up.

I fell hard for Claudette. It was more like we fell for each other—although Price would claim for many years, even after we were full-grown men and always with a smile, that I had stolen his girlfriend. We took walks in Shakespeare's Garden, a tiny flower-filled garden on campus with stone love seats. We laughed, played, danced, and ate together and did a few other things when the lights in the dorm dimmed and the usual nocturnal creeping of young men and women began after the counselors had drifted off to sleep. Sex wasn't on my mind, or Claudette's. But the way some of my friends talked about it, it was clear that some of them had been getting busy for quite some time. Oh, I had feelings all right and there was a rush that overcame me when I saw Claudette's pretty face or held her hand. But girls were still to be loved, not made love to.

With summer ending, Claudette and I knew we wouldn't be able to see each other. For one thing, Claudette's parents thought she was too young to date and forbade her receiving telephone calls from boys. For another, she lived on the South Side and I lived on the West Side. For either of us that meant more than a half-hour bus ride each way. Neither of us was old enough to drive yet. I was fifteen. She was fourteen. Even if I had been old enough, I didn't have a car. But the truth was, the distance between our homes was not as great as the perceptions that divided our neighborhoods. South Side blacks thumbed their noses at West Side blacks. In their minds, we were po' unsophisticated Negroes. The mythology about West Siders abounded:

> *There are no pretty women on the West Side . . .*
> *West Side women all have scars on their faces . . .*
> *All West Siders ever do is gang-bang . . .*

The misconceptions cut both ways. We West Siders saw South Side blacks as a bunch of bourgeois, light-skinned, wanna-be-white Negroes. I always suspected that there really wasn't much difference between us. I even understood then that if you went back far enough, our ancestors were probably on the same slave ships from Mother Africa.

That last night at Northwestern, there was one last party in the lounge of our dormitory. The slow sweet melody of the Isley Brothers drifted from the speakers, filling my mind. Claudette and I slow-dragged, holding each other tight in the blue-lighted lounge, wishing the moment would last forever. We soon slipped off to her room for our last good-bye. We sat on the side of her bed, kissing for a while, then cried ourselves to sleep. When we awoke a female staff member was standing over us. I was half in shock and half afraid. Getting caught in a girl's room was a serious infraction, even if it was the end of the summer.

"John," the counselor said, "I think you need to go."

"Okay," I said, stumbling to my feet and rubbing my eyes.

I could tell the counselor was trying hard to keep from laughing.

"Bye, Claudette," I said, hurrying out the door.

"Bye, John," she replied.

The next morning, the parking lot buzzed with parents. I caught my last glimpse of Claudette with her parents as they loaded her suitcases into their car bound for the South Side. I didn't have the nerve to go over and say anything. It was one of the last times I ever saw Claudette.

But even back then I had the consolation of knowing that there are always other fish in the sea.

CHAPTER 12

ROBIN

WE WALKED downstairs, Net and I, both headed to St. Mel for the start of another school year on that cool, end-of-summer morning. Net was a freshman. I was starting my junior year and though I was still on the skinny side, I had finally become the taller with a growth spurt of several inches that seemed to happen overnight. Finances at home were as tight as ever, though my stepfather was working fairly steadily. It's just that the pay for an unskilled laborer was a little hard to stretch for a family of six, not to mention having to pay Catholic school tuition for two kids, particularly when the money my stepfather put into my mother's hands on some paydays was inexplicably short.

Net and I had already signed up for the work-study program at St. Mel to help out with tuition. For Net, that meant cleaning the first-floor girls' bathroom after school. For me, that meant cleaning the school gym, which I figured would work out just fine since I planned on spending a lot of my time in the gym anyway.

Back home on Komensky, my family was now all that was left of the Haglers on the block, the poorest of the lot, last of the Mohicans. Aunt Scope and Detie had bought a gorgeous three-bedroom home on a sprawling lot in Maywood, a quiet suburb west of the city with lush green lawns—following the trail of Negroes fulfilling their dream of getting up and out of the ghetto. They were among the folks who worked long enough and saved their way to greener pastures, fortunate black folks who managed to grab hold of the middle-class crane and transport themselves. Such became the life cycle of the 'hood. Every time anybody got any means, they got out.

Back then, it seemed that all black folks dreamed of moving out someday and into white neighborhoods, of insulating themselves from the troubles that plagued the 'hood. There were still white folks living in Maywood when they moved in, but the majority soon moved onward and upward to escape their new dark neighbors. And it would not be long before the new island began to take on the same unsettling complications of the old one. No matter where blacks moved into places where we had not been before, in a few years it seemed we were ready to pack up and move again, as nomads rather than homesteaders. And so, those who could moved farther and farther west, following the trail of whites. They seemed driven by the belief that white neighborhoods were somehow more desirous and whole. Few of us seemed to understand that the land possessed was only as good as the possessor. That one man's Promised Land is another man's wilderness. It was a lesson I did not understand until years later. When people later wondered how the gang-bangers and drug dealers had followed them in their journey to the suburbs, there was no real mystery: Many had carried them with them in the back seats of their cars.

Net and I had both worked jobs that summer and bought our own school clothes, which meant that for the first time in a long time, we could actually afford clothes we liked. My wardrobe during freshman year had been a disaster, and it was just barely better my sophomore year. But as a junior—a bona fide upperclassman on the varsity, no less—there could be no sneakers, no goofy pants or sweaters, no hand-me-downs. I had to dress the part. And while it wasn't so much the designer craze back then, it was unhip to wear anything that was considered "out of style."

For the first day of school, Net and I had bought matching blue denim jumpsuits. The year was 1976. Platform shoes and bell-bottom pants had just about played out by then but had been replaced by something no less ridiculous: drooping lapels, mod colors, glass-heel shoes for men and denim jumpsuits, although pant legs were still flared.

It was about 7:30 that morning when Net and I walked downstairs on our way to school. We stopped in the vestibule and knocked on our neighbor Adrian's door. Adrian's family had moved into the first-floor apartment at 1634 when Aunt Scope moved out, and Adrian and Net were good friends. I eventually learned that they had no secrets between them. Net had told Adrian about our jumpsuits, and unbeknownst to me, Adrian had bought her own. She soon emerged from her apartment wearing a schoolgirl smile and looking like a carbon copy of Net and me—in her own denim jumpsuit. We walked to the bus, strutting in denim, like Jackson Five wanna-bes. Only there were three of us. I can still picture us—the disco crew—climbing off the bus, walking down Central Park Avenue toward St. Mel. All that was missing was the soundtrack to *Saturday Night Fever*.

Being juniors meant we had dibs on the freshman class of cuties—after the seniors, of course. And there were some darlings. Of course, the girls at that age were not into guys their own age. They were looking for mature men. Most of the guys in my class had little appeal among the girls our own age, who were also looking for older guys. They were nowhere near as impressed with us as some of the younger girls were, even if we were on the varsity basketball team. In my case, it may have been that the girls still saw me as the short kid who wore the green double-knit slacks with cuffs as a freshman and toted water bottles and towels for the varsity—despite my new threads, growth in height, and peach fuzz.

That fall, there was a short pretty girl in the freshman class who soon caught my eye. She was always well dressed and well groomed, a bit on the skinny side but gorgeous. She had a small nose, smooth caramel skin, nice lips, and long hair. As luck would have it, she and Net became good friends. One day Net asked me for a favor. She said her new friend had eyes for someone on the varsity basketball team. It turned out that they weren't for me, but for a guy named Michael Brown. Michael was a shorty, about five foot five, but a decent-looking guy with a big Afro. All the girls thought he was cute as a button. Net asked me to matchmake. Despite my own attraction to her new friend, I said I would talk to Michael. After all, we were friends.

I told Michael that there was this freshie who liked him. Then while standing in the hall one day, I pointed her out. Michael said she was much too skinny for him and that I must be crazy to think he wanted a girl with absolutely no booty. He laughed.

"You crazy, man?" Michael said. "Man, she too bony. Nah, that's all right. You go with her."

It was music to my ears since I liked her anyway and had hopes that Michael wouldn't be interested. I decided to move in for the kill, though I did not breathe a word to Michael.

I soon discovered that another big Afro-wearing dude was interested in my girl, even though she wasn't actually my girl yet. His name was Kent. Kent was a skinny guy whose Afro looked like a football helmet between his shoulders. He was a sophomore and a little on the goofy side. Kent was good friends with my cousin Michael, who was also a sopho-more at St. Mel by then. For some reason, Kent and I never got along. Maybe it had to do with some sort of competitive guy thing. That might explain how we came to bet on which of us would be the first to kiss the little skinny girl we both liked. The bet was for $5. We decided that in order to win, the other guy had to bear witness to the act.

Little did Kent know that I had secretly approached the girl after school one day and let her in on our little bet. She seemed amused. Per-haps she was flattered. I promised to give her half the pot if she went along. She agreed with no hesitation. I figured that had more to do with my charm and good looks than a measly $2.50. Maybe not.

Not long after that, one day after school before basketball practice, I told Kent to meet me on the third floor, but to stay clear out of sight. There was something I wanted him to see. A short while later, I emerged from one of the side staircases—me—and the little cutie. I spied Kent's big ole head, poking around a column of the main staircase. Then I laid a wet one on her. She wasn't such a good kisser. Her lips were a little thin, but it felt good and my mission was accomplished. She walked back downstairs. I ran to collect. Kent's face was twisted with embarrassment and anger. How was this girl that neither of us really knew already giving me kisses? He smelled a rat.

"Pay up, dude," I said.

"Man, how you get her to do that?" Kent fired back. "Something must be up, man. Man, ain't no—"

"I'm the mack daddy, boy. I told you, dude. I'm a playa."

"Whatever."

"I'm tellin' you man. I'm a—"

"Whatever," Kent said.

"Where my money? Pay me. Pay up, boy, pay up," I said, rubbing it in.

"I'm gon' pay you, man," Kent huffed.

I don't remember if he ever did. But it didn't matter. Not many days after the third-floor kissing game I asked the girl after school one day if we could "go together." Translation: Will you be my girl? She told me she had to sleep on it. I told her to write my name on a piece of paper and to place it underneath her pillow and give me an answer in the morning. It was probably a line I had picked up around the older guys at Northwestern. She smiled. The next day, bright and early, she said yes.

She would be the only girlfriend I would have for the rest of my high school days.

Her name was Robin.

Like my grandparents, Robin lived on the West Side just northwest of K-Town in the Austin neighborhood. My first visit to Robin's house was on a Saturday afternoon that fall of 1976. It felt weird going to visit a girl at her home. A million thoughts must have run across my mind as I sat on the northbound Pulaski bus: Will her parents like me? How long should I stay? What are we going to do while I'm there? How do I look? Should I have worn something else?

At Chicago Avenue, I exited the Pulaski bus and walked across the street to catch another westbound. Questions still swirled inside my head until finally the bus's air brakes screeched at my stop. I climbed off at the corner of Lavergne Street and Chicago Avenue. I was about thirty-five blocks from home, in unfamiliar territory. I walked north on Lavergne in search of Superior Avenue for several blocks until realizing that I must be headed in the wrong direction. I turned around and walked the other way. Soon I spotted Superior. I made a right and a few houses down found my destination. It was a nice house, a brick two-story building with a fenced green yard and garage. I rang the bell. Robin answered. I stepped into her world.

There was nice big furniture with no holes or tears, brightly painted walls and carpet, air-conditioning and a shiny mahogany dining room set, complete with a china cabinet. Her mother, Catherine, was a dark-skinned pretty woman with long dark hair. Her father, Bob, had a butterscotch complexion and wore a mustache and a plain short haircut. He had a medium build and a laborer's swollen leathery hands. Bob worked downtown at the People's Gas Company as an engineer, although I later learned that "engineer" was a fancy title for janitor. I could tell early on that Robin's father was a hardworking man who believed in taking good care of his family. I could always tell that about a man by the way his home looked, by the way his wife and children looked and whether he could usually be found at home rather than boozing it up with the fellas or out chasing skirts. Bob smoked cigarettes, like his wife. He also drank a beer on occasion and seemed as easygoing as his own father, whom everybody called Gramps. Gramps lived upstairs in a converted apartment. His wife had died years earlier. He was a quiet, soft-spoken man, to whom I took an immediate liking. Robin seemed especially close to her grandfather.

Of all my first impressions, there was one that struck me about Robin's home early on. That was the number of nieces and nephews who lived there from time to time. On my first visit, a couple of them sat right there with us on the sofa watching television. I remember wondering, "Where did all these little boogies come from?"

They belonged to Robin's two grown sisters. There were only six of them, not including Robin's little brother, though sometimes there seemed to be a dozen or so. Robin's sisters were not Bob's children, but her mother's. Only Robin and her brother, Lamont, were Bob's. In time I came to understand that the presence of her nephews and nieces often annoyed Robin. It wasn't that she did not care for them. Rather it was her sisters' inability or unwillingness to maintain their own homes and care for their own children as well as the frequency with which they readily dumped their troubles and their hungry kids in her mother's lap that bothered her. That sometimes made eating supper a matter of beating "the troopers," as I had nicknamed Robin's nieces and nephews, to the table. Robin's situation at home, though I didn't realize this until later, sometimes seemed to her as bad as mine sometimes seemed to me, although much of my trouble stemmed from our poverty in the cramped three-bedroom roach- and mice-infested apartment. In my mind, Robin had it good—great, in fact. She always had plenty of money and plenty to eat. Her parents bought her clothes. She didn't have to worry about her tuition being paid. What else could you ask for? I wondered.

In time, Robin and I began seeing a lot of each other. Sometimes she stayed after school and we talked and held hands before basketball practice, kissed. Between class we often bumped into each other in the halls and paused long enough to grab each other's hand and say hello.

On the way home from basketball games, girlfriends could ride on the team bus. Robin was my girl. So she always cuddled up next to me. Soon we began arriving at St. Mel early on school days so that we could talk before classes. On non-school nights, we talked on the telephone until we were dead tired, and also on weekends, unless we were together. Robin became my best friend and I, hers.

Little did we know that over the years we would become so much more.

CHAPTER 13

LITTLE RASCALS

WE SAT in a dormitory that lazy warm summer afternoon at basketball camp talking jive, my teammates and I. We had all come to Lou Henson's Fighting Illini basketball camp at the University of Illinois in Champaign. St. Mel had sent the entire basketball team to the weeklong camp to hone our skills, as they had the previous summer, when we were sophomores. Coming up to our senior year and final season, we were being picked as contenders for the Class A state title, which is for small schools. Our coach figured that the camp would give us an edge up. Other schools and coaches had the same idea.

There were some great prospects at the Illini hoops camp that year, but none bigger than Eddie Johnson. Eddie was a tall muscular kid from Westinghouse, a public school also on the West Side. Eddie was a megastar who eventually went on to play for Illinois as well as in the NBA. It was amazing to see all of the town folks, most of them white, come out to the scrimmages each evening and scream out this high school kid's name as if he were Dr. J or Kareem Abdul-Jabbar or the Second Coming. Their eyes followed his every move on the court even during warm-ups. And you got the sense that he knew everybody was watching him, that

Eddie knew he was the man, just by the way he walked—head and nose erect, that smooth gait, that million-dollar swagger. EJ, as we called him, was without a doubt the man. There probably wasn't a kid at camp who wasn't envious of him. EJ had a high school teammate who drew similar attention at camp, though not as much as EJ. His name was Skip Dillard. Skip was a better-than-six-foot-tall guard with calves that were the size of my thighs. Skip went on to star at DePaul University with Mark Aguirre, although Skip's NBA dreams eventually fizzled like almost everybody else's. His fall from basketball stardom would be documented for years in the pages of local newspapers as his life slipped from one tragedy to another.

Back then, we all had basketball dreams. But most of us intoxicated by the prospect of playing in the NBA eventually sobered up. My sobriety came early, during my junior year, when my attention shifted from my studies to hoop dreams and love. In fact, I had all but stopped studying, and my grades plummeted so badly that my grade point average one quarter was less than a C average. For most guys on the team, that would have meant an instant suspension. But my cumulative GPA was high, so my eligibility was not endangered. I still had to face heckling from my teammates. One of them—whose name was Michael Ware—kept calling me "you big dummy," over and over. I also faced the coach's wrath. Coach Art Murnan called me into the office after seeing my grades and explained the facts of life.

"It's not basketball that's going to put food on your family's table one day, John, but what's in here," he said, pointing to his head. "You're not going to the NBA."

His words hit like a sledgehammer.

"The good news is you're going to make it," my coach said, as I sat silently. "It's just not going to be playing basketball. You're probably the smartest kid on the team. I don't want to see you throw it all away."

The words sank in. I ditched the dream and went back to my studies. My good grades returned. In fact, that next semester I made the "A" honor roll. I showed Michael Ware my grades and spoke a few choice words: "Now who's the big dummy, dummy?" I said.

At basketball camp that afternoon, we were lounging in the dorm talking jive when the conversation turned to girls and sex. Sex seemed to be everyone's favorite topic. When guys talked sex, it was mostly locker room talk, the kind of explicit tell-all stuff that if girls knew their boyfriends had shared with anybody, let alone a bunch of salivating dudes, would have made them cry. Their words and voices seemed completely detached from the girls with whom they had lain. Nobody mentioned anything about loving anybody, or protection, or pregnancy. The whole point was to get your groove on. I would later understand that this brand of talk was not much different from the kind that grown men sometimes engage in while drinking whiskey or brews. Mostly, they were hollow words filled with bravado and exaggerations about their prowess among the ladies to make themselves look big, feel good, all at the expense of sisters' reputations.

In the dorm that afternoon, everybody took turns telling tall tales. I was hoping nobody would notice me. But there was no place to hide.

"What about you and your ole girl man?" Leroy asked one of the guys. "Did you hit it? Did you hit it, man?"

"Mannn, you know me," he answered, chuckling and turning up the bass in his voice. He slapped a few fives with the fellas.

"Ahhh nigga, pleeeeazzzzz, you still ain't said nothin'," Leroy said, fishing for details. "You ain't hit that, man," Leroy said.

"All right," the boy said. "All right."

Silence.

"Boyyyyy, I tore it up," he finally confessed.

Cheers filled the room.

"Did you hit it, man?" another boy interjected, the room taking on air of a pep rally.

"Man, I tore it up! Man, she was moanin' and groanin' and scratchin' my back. I still got the scars."

"Let me see!" we all shouted.

That's the way it went on for a while, each boy sharing his sexual experiences in vivid embellished detail. I was laughing, thinking, lost in the moment, when all eyes were suddenly set on me.

"So, John, what's up?" Leroy the Instigator asked. "How was it when you first had sex?"

"Uhhh, uhhh, I uhhh, I was, uhhh . . . " I stuttered.

"You ain't had no sex," Leroy fired back.

"Yes I have," I insisted, though not even I would have been convinced by my lying.

"You lying," several of my friends cried aloud before the room was awash with ridiculing laughter.

"Virgin! John a virgin! Virgin!" they sung over and over as if "virgin" was some dirty word.

They made it seem like a dirty word. I felt deeply ashamed to be the only guy in the group who apparently had not had sex. I knew of guys who had lost their virginity in seventh and eighth grade and were proud of it. Here I was a high school junior having had no trim, as they called it.

Years later, I realized that I should have been proud to be a virgin at sixteen. I also came to understand that while everyone in that room that afternoon had the physical hardware necessary for sex, there was not one of us who was emotionally, psychologically, or socially mature enough. That sex held such potentially life-altering possibilities for the lives of the little girls who were conduits for our exercise of manhood as well as for us. I eventually came to see that so many men measured manhood by how many women they conquered with their penis.

Their chiding continued until almost supper time, then picked up again whenever some guy who hadn't been in the room when the conversation took place asked me if it was really true, if I was really still a virgin. Everybody told me that I needed to have sex and that I would be a better man for having gotten myself a "piece." Michael said it felt so good that once I had done the deed, I would not be able to keep it secret. I returned home with a new determination that summer: to get laid.

Upon returning home after basketball camp, I began work at the Chicago Police Department as a file clerk in the criminal records division at Eleventh and State Streets. It was a white-brick building that was the central headquarters and the brain for the police 911 dispatch. I was hired through the Mayor's Student as Trainee Program, which offered jobs to a select group of students from high schools across the city. Mostly they were smart kids. I worked in the basement of the police department in a dingy cubbyhole of an office with a bunch of old guys, nice guys stuck in dead-end jobs in a section of the building that most folks who passed through police headquarters every day didn't even know existed. There were never any visitors to this unit of the records division, except for the tubes that shot through the air chute that snaked from somewhere up above and contained requests for us to pull records and shoot them back up. I could not believe that these guys spent their lives pulling records, never to see another soul until they emerged from the dungeon to the light on smoke breaks, to go out to lunch, or to go home at the end of each miserable day. Working there that summer was enough to convince me that I was going to college to avoid ever being stuck in a job like that.

During lunch, I liked going upstairs to the fourth floor and watching the police dispatchers who took the 911 calls. I liked seeing all the lighted colorful maps of the city above their desks. On the eleventh floor, at the opposite end of the hallway from the cafeteria, was the women's lockup. On Mondays there was always a trail of prostitutes in the hall or on the elevators after having had their day in court and having just been released from jail following the usual weekend hookers' roundup. Such were the highlights of my job that summer, with the exception of Fridays, when all the trainees who worked at various city government offices got together at City Hall as part of the summer job program. We all got to meet Mayor Michael Bilandic, the man who replaced Mayor Daley when he died in office. From what I knew of Mayor Daley's fiery personality, Mayor Bilandic seemed the complete opposite. He was stoic, almost robotic. By mid-August, it had been a fairly good summer, although not entirely complete, not yet.

Not long after I had returned from basketball camp, I had talked with Robin on the telephone about having sex. I was the one who popped the question. Without much conversation, she said she loved me and would have sex if sex was what I wanted. I remember thinking, "Is it that easy?" I also felt strangely moved. It wasn't just the idea of performing the act itself, of which I had no working knowledge. There was something moving about this girl's willingness to trust me enough to give me her body. We both agreed that we would have sex. But we did not set a date, probably because we were both nervous about the whole idea and that it had never been a part of our relationship. In fact, days and weeks passed before sex came up again.

Later that summer, I was staying with my grandparents, as I sometimes did when life at home seemed more unbearable than usual and the solace and stability of my grandparents' place led me to their doorstep. I later understood that my running away from home to my grandparents' house was caused by my desire to find order, to escape the poverty at home, the incessant worry—and fuss—over the lack of money for food and bills, and my parents' seeming inability to make life more immediately better for us all. At home, I sometimes felt powerless, powerless to change our state of existence—our teetering on and off welfare and the countless disconnections—powerless to do anything, except simply to let life happen to me and to become a victim of circumstance.

So I ran. From a world in which I sometimes felt like I was suffocating, I ran. Away from the mice, the roaches, and the grown-up problems that I, as a teenager, was helpless to solve. And when Mama was angered, frustrated, and overwhelmed by life, and I felt that she was being too hard on me—too critical—or when our family seemed closer to the edge of the poverty abyss, I ran faster. When I was running I never felt like I was running away from Mama or my sisters and my brother. I'd like to think that I was running toward normalcy and peace and for the sake of saving my own life. Not simply fleeing, but escaping. Maybe it wasn't that way at all. Maybe with no other immediate remedies all I could think to do was to run. And the only place that I knew to run to was Grandmother's house, even if it provided only a temporary reprieve.

My periodic stays with my grandparents never lasted more than a few weeks before my grandparents, usually my grandfather, would say that they thought it was time that I go back home, always insisting that things could not be as bad as I had made them out to be. Without saying much, I always packed my things and went quietly back home.

While staying at my grandparents' house that summer, I learned one day that Grandmother and Grandpa were going off to church for a few hours, which meant I would have the house to myself. I called Robin up and invited her over. The day finally had come. We would have sex.

It was a sunny summer day. My grandparents walked out the door, climbed into Grandpa's big blue Cadillac, and drove away. Robin arrived within minutes of their departure. I had timed it perfectly. I met Robin at the door. She was as pretty as ever. She wore a multicolor patchwork leather jacket, pants, and a blouse. Her smooth face was radiant, her long hair shiny and curly. She was chewing gum and smiling as she walked through the door. I could tell she was nervous. We talked for a while. We sat on the plastic-covered sectional sofa in the living room for what seemed forever, watching the color television console.

"Robin, are you sure you want to do this? You know we don't have to if you don't want to," I said, meaning every word.

"Yeah, I know," she said. "You love me, right?" she said, her words soft and searching.

"You know I love you, girl. You're the most important person in the world to me."

We kissed.

"Are you sure?" I asked.

"Yes, John," she replied. "Are you?"

"Yeah, I'm sure."

I wasn't sure. But I wasn't about to back out at that point. I was nervous, too, and with good reason. For one thing, we were at my grandparents' house and I knew there would be a killing if we got caught. The other thing was that I was still a virgin and not quite sure about the mechanics of sex. I feared that things might get downright embarrassing. I had not told Robin this was my first time. She thought I was an experienced man. With my grandparents gone and not due back for hours, I figured we had time to figure everything out.

We kissed some more, then turned off the television and walked upstairs to my bedroom, where the shades were drawn. We undressed, slowly peeling off our clothes, bashfully. I wanted to hide. But there was nowhere to run.

We climbed into bed. Her body was so warm. A soft breeze filtered through the window. It ruffled the leaves in the trees outside. The sun's rays spilled through the sides of the window shade and disappeared into the shadows of the corners of the bedroom. The laughter of children playing outside resounded. There was the engine and wheels of an occasional car rolling past the house. There were no words spoken between us. Only silence and nervous touching. As I looked at this girl chewing the mint gum, I knew that I was completely in love. But I could not resist a fleeting thought: "If the fellas could see me now!"

I nervously fumbled around, trying to do what we were trying to do, but without any immediate success. I was still trying when I heard keys jingling and the heavy wood front door downstairs squeak open, then the voices of my grandparents.

"Oh God," I said. "My grandparents. Get up, get up, girl, get up!"

We leaped out of bed and I began dressing as quickly as I could. Robin didn't have enough time to put on all of her clothes. I told her to hide in the closet, figuring that my grandparents must have forgotten something and that they would likely soon be on their way again. Or if not, I would likely have the opportunity to sneak Robin out of the house at some point. I walked downstairs, trying to act calm. Grandmother went upstairs. For some reason that seemed strange to me at the time, Grandmother walked right into my bedroom.

"Ge-e-eorrrge!" she screamed for my grandfather, who by now, of course, had gone from being a church deacon to a sanctified, Holy Ghost–filled, fornicating-hating preacher.

"Man!" I thought. "I'm dead."

Grandmother found Robin hiding in the closet wearing only her underwear. She had either suspected that something was up, or, given her state of constant communication with God, the Lord had "revealed" it to her. Grandmother walked downstairs angrily shaking her head, moaning under her breath. Robin followed, although she was completely dressed by now. We stood there in the dining room like the rascals we were.

"Nothing happened, Grandmother, nothing happened," I pleaded frantically, watching as my grandfather's face twisted in a manner that I had never seen before.

"Daddy will be able to tell if it did," Grandmother said without blinking. Grandpa headed upstairs to inspect.

"He could tell? How?" I wondered silently, although I would later come to understand that the bed can hold a reservoir of evidence where sex is concerned.

Grandpa found nothing and seemed relieved as he walked back downstairs. I was sure glad he hadn't found any evidence, although the fact that Robin hadn't had on anything except her BVDs when Grandmother discovered her meant that we had been up to no good.

My grandparents lectured and scorned us for a while as we sat there in the kitchen. Then they sent Robin on her way home.

There was the sense that up until that point in my life I could have blamed someone else for my troubles and poverty. I was born into K-Town, a child of circumstance, less in control of my own destiny through adolescence than the adult forces all around me, though still responsible for my choices. As time went on, the choices became weightier and my decisions held more implications for my life and future. Some things Mama could not shield me from. Some battles she could not fight. Some decisions eventually would be mine and mine alone to make. Except all of the ramifications are not always known. And while there are many paths to destruction, finding the way back to the road of redemption can take years, if not a lifetime. At seventeen, my life was already starting to spiral, to veer from the path of hope. But looking back, the saddest thing is that I didn't even have a clue.

After the smoke had finally cleared that day, I felt really bad. It wasn't just that I had been busted. I had lost something more important than my own pride: my grandparents' trust.

That evening, Grandmother telephoned Mama and told her what had happened. Grandmother also warned that it would not be long before Robin and I would have something tangible to show for all of our unfruitful works of darkness. I had enough sense to know that she hadn't needed the Good Lord to tell her that.

PART 2

LAMENTATIONS

For these things I weep; mine eye, mine eye runneth down with water, because the comforter that should relieve my soul is far from me: my children are desolate; because the enemy prevailed.

Lamentations 1:16

CHAPTER 14

RATED PG

THE YOUNG MAN in the mirror was taller, thinner, with noticeably more mustache and sideburns than the guy I had seen there only four years earlier. I stood in the bathroom at home that May evening, studying myself in the mirror above the sink, fixing my cream-color bow tie that matched my cream-color tuxedo with the floppy lapels and wide-leg pant bottoms. I wore a cream-color cummerbund, socks, and new shoes, a pair of those slip-on joints with slits on the sides that looked like formal sandals. It was a 1970s thing. But I was dressed to kill for back then. My face was a smooth chocolate brown. My eyes looked young and fresh, still filled with naïveté. A boy's eyes in a man's body, they bore no hint of the weight of responsibility that was already settling in on my broad shoulders like a millstone.

It was prom night. My senior prom fell on a warm evening that spring of 1978. My senior year at St. Mel was finally winding down. The years seemed to have flown by, and I felt as if I had been a freshman only yesterday. It all happened so quickly, much faster than I had wanted it to, in some ways.

In a few months, I was going off to college, headed to the University of

Illinois at Champaign, where I had been accepted at the end of my junior year through an early admissions program. My admission to the university was contingent upon my not totally bombing out in my classes during my senior year. Of course, I wasn't about to do that with so much at stake. Attending the University of Illinois was at the center of my college dream. I fell in love with the university during my summer basketball camp visits there. Already, my cousins Doris and Cheryl were students there. Arty was living in Champaign as well, although he was attending Parkland, a nearby junior college. I was so sure of my desire to attend the University of Illinois that it was the only school to which I applied for admission. In those days I was always full of certainty and confidence when it came to planning my future, especially where academics were concerned. But I would soon learn that the earthquakes of life, which strike when you least expect them, can shake you to the core, challenging even the very essence of who you thought you were. That not even the best-laid plans are foolproof and that sometimes the momentum of life and bad decisions can send you in a downward spiral that can take years, if not a lifetime, to overcome.

At St. Mel, I was the first senior in a class of sixty-one students admitted to college, which impressed my classmates. Most important, my acceptance to my college of choice alleviated any college-admission worries that many of my classmates carried until the end of the school year and allowed me to concentrate on my studies, at least to enjoy a senior year less encumbered by the college crunch. But I also took great pleasure in being the first in my class admitted to college. One of my proudest moments came at the end of classes on the day the loudspeakers blared: "And we would like to congratulate John Fountain on being the first member of the class of 1978 admitted to college. John will be attending the University of Illinois in Champaign." Miss Johnson, the school secretary, announced this, and the applause of teachers and students spilled into the halls.

During senior year, at the end of school each day, Miss Johnson ritually announced the names of the seniors who had been accepted to college. I soon began to notice the look of fear mixed with a tinge of embarrassment and trepidation that spread across the faces of those who had not yet been admitted. I also saw in many of my classmates who had not yet received a college acceptance letter a growing sense of humility. Reality was setting in, and I sensed that we all understood that our lives were going to take divergent paths upon graduation. The kids who had studied and gotten good grades got into the better schools. Those who did not, in most cases, were still awaiting word on their fate.

Going to college was something I had planned for and dreamed about for as long as I could remember. But at one point during my senior year, I seriously thought about quitting school, although Mama never knew this, only Robin. One night, while talking to Robin on the telephone, I told her that I was tired of school, tired of my mother being on my case about one thing or another, tired of it seeming that no matter what I did, no matter how good my grades were, no matter how much I had accomplished in school, my mother was always going to find something to criticize me about, though I later understood that Mama never meant me any harm. I told Robin that given the poverty and trouble at home, I would be better off quitting school and getting a job.

"Don't quit school, John, you can't," Robin encouraged.

"I'm tired," I said. "What's the point?"

"But you have worked so hard, John. You can't quit now," she said. "You've been accepted to college and everything. It'll be all right. Just hold on."

"I can't—"

"John in a few months, you'll be gone. You have come too far. Don't quit."

I found comfort in Robin's words. But ultimately, the greatest deterrent to quitting school was that I wanted to go to college more than I wanted just about anything else in this world. More than getting to college, I wanted to earn a degree. I always believed college to be the key to a better life, something that Mama had drilled into me for as far back as I could remember.

But another thing was weighing on my mind that winter. Robin was pregnant—or "PG" as we called it. That December, Robin had missed her "monthly friend," as she referred to her period. We got confirmation through a pregnancy test. The doctor determined Robin's due date to be sometime in August, the same month that I was to pack up my bags and head off to college. Neither of us was at all ready to bring a child into the world. But Robin and her folks apparently didn't believe in abortion.

Robin and I didn't always use contraception. Before she got pregnant, we had even talked fondly about what it might be like to become parents someday. We were young and dumb, at least naive about the costs of engaging in some adult behaviors— being only kids ourselves and totally oblivious to the realities of parenthood, let alone teen parenthood. But at the ripe old ages of fifteen and seventeen, we would become Mama and Daddy, even if we were clueless to what this would mean for our lives and our child's.

To say that Mama was shocked when she learned of Robin's pregnancy is to put it mildly, even though Grandmother had duly warned her months earlier. Mama hadn't said much by way of deterrent before Robin got pregnant, except to say that if I ever knocked up Robin, or any other girl, I would have to handle my responsibilities. That was it. Not that discussing sex with a teenage son is easy for any mother. It certainly wasn't for Mama. And even if she had been brave enough to broach the topic, I am not so certain that I wouldn't have run out of the room. One time, Mama found a pack of condoms in my dresser drawer. She told me never to bring that kind of stuff, although she didn't say stuff, into her house anymore. Had I been considering talking to Mama about sexual matters, I would have dropped the idea like a hot potato after witnessing her explosive reaction to a simple pack of condoms. I didn't feel comfortable just bringing the topic up out of the blue with my stepfather or any of the other men I knew, either. And sex simply wasn't talked about in the open in an era where even on television, seeing a married couple in the same bed was something that people were still getting used to. In fact, I had not had the proverbial birds-and-bees talk with any male other than my teammates that day at summer basketball camp. I had listened to my homeboys and was on the road to becoming a father, though the same could not be said of them. But if there was anyone to blame, it was myself. That much I understood even then. And for some reason, the idea that I would soon be a father didn't seem so bad.

It wasn't long before our families and everyone at school and on our respective blocks knew that John and Robin were having a baby. Pregnant girls were not allowed to stay at St. Mel during their pregnancy. I never thought about it at the time, but it seems unfair to have expelled pregnant girls from school when some boy had been equally responsible for her pregnancy but faced no such consequence. Fortunately, Robin showed very little in her first five months and was allowed to finish out the academic year at St. Mel.

Upon learning that Robin and I had a baby on the way, Mama didn't start to shout. Nor did she say that I would have to quit school and go out and get a job, which was the way I had seen such scenarios played out in television movies. I was still planning on going to college. I planned to do the best I could to take care of my child until I finished college and got a good job. I never minded working. In fact, I had held a summer job every summer since my freshman year. I figured my summers would continue to be filled with jobs and that I would take care of my responsibilities to the best of my ability. For starters, Mama insisted that with the earnings from the job I was planning to work that upcoming summer, I buy the things my baby would need, beginning with diapers, clothes, and a crib. In the meantime, there was the prom.

Robin was my prom date. That was another of the things that Mama had insisted on. She forbade me from even getting calls from other girls while Robin was pregnant, though once or twice I talked to a girl other than Robin without Mama knowing about it. While Robin was pregnant, Mama urged me to buy Robin flowers or candy and to be extra kind. The way she explained it was that pregnancy did strange things to women, in addition to stretching their bodies severely out of shape. Pregnant women were prone to mood swings and were extra sensitive, Mama said. So being extra kind and considerate, especially since Robin was carrying my child, was the least I could do, Mama explained. I complied with Mama's wishes, though it was really my good pleasure to shower Robin with candy, flowers, and kindness.

On prom night I stood in the living room, anxiously waiting for my friend Morgan to pick me up in his mother's cream-color Cadillac. I still hadn't gotten my driver's license. I took driver's education at school but was so busy between my studies, sports, and dating Robin that I hadn't made the time to get my license. Then my learner's permit expired. Out of the blue, a month or so before prom, Morgan asked me how Robin and I were getting to the Chateau Royale on prom night. I told him that I hadn't yet figured out a plan. Without hesitation, Morgan volunteered to let us ride with him and his girlfriend, Alicia, who was also a senior at St. Mel. I said yes.

The plan was to pick up our dates and swing back around to our parents' homes to let our mamas admire their grown-up, dressed-up sons. Morgan pulled up and I strolled downstairs to his ride. Mama seemed almost as excited as I was, as she waved good-bye while everybody on the block watched me strut to the Caddy. Mama had that look in her eyes that other mothers did as they watched their sons and daughters in their tuxedos and flowing gowns wave good-bye on prom night, their adolescence faded, adulthood looming so clearly on the horizon.

Robin looked beautiful, her hair pinned up, her lips shaded with rose-colored lipstick. Her gown was a shade of cream, flowing and full enough to conceal the bulge in her waist. There was no sense in flaunting the fact that she was pregnant. She and I had already encountered the stares of people when they detected that she was with child. Just seeing someone so young and so pregnant turned heads. The stares and whisperings of people whenever they noticed Robin's stomach often made me feel bad. I imagined that Robin must have felt that way sometimes too, especially since she caught most of the public scrutiny. Whenever we were together in public, riding the bus or the elevated train, called the El, or walking down the street, I held her hand or sat really close to her and stared people down when they looked her way. I figured that was the least I could do since she was carrying my baby and bearing much of the shame.

The ballroom was filled with candlelit tables and a live band. At the place settings on the table sat memorial white mugs with purple writing that read, "Goodbye to yesterday." We danced that night to our favorite song, "Always and Forever." Later, Robin and I took pictures in the lobby, crystallizing the moment. Years later, I studied our prom pictures to see whether you could tell from the photographs that Robin was pregnant. It was hard to tell from the pictures. She was a petite girl even when she was pregnant. And the dress had done its job.

Later that night, some of the guys talked gregariously about renting hotel rooms after the prom. For Robin and me, the idea didn't have the same appeal. I took Robin home and we watched television for a while. Then I went home, climbed into my bed and fell asleep.

On graduation day, St. Mel's auditorium was filled with television cameras. My classmates and I sat in the middle row way up front, waiting for our names to be called so we could strut across the stage. The mood was bittersweet. I never imagined that graduation would carry with it such a mixture of emotions. I was glad to be finishing high school and excited about going on to college but sad to be saying good-bye to the classmates and teammates with whom I spent the last four years, many of whom I might never see again as life carried us on our different journeys. And on that Sunday in June, even the future of the school was uncertain.

The Catholic Archdiocese of Chicago had decided to close St. Mel, saying that it had become too much of a financial burden and that it was no longer viable. Mr. Adams and St. Mel's staff and faculty, as well as students and parents, had decided to fight the archdiocese's decision, largely because it was the last Catholic school on the West Side and, for many of the West Side's poor, the best alternative to the Chicago public schools. Our fight to keep St. Mel open drew national attention. We held rallies and marches and made the headlines of local and national newspapers and even the nightly news. The news cameras and reporters showed up on graduation day to cover what many assumed would be St. Mel's last class.

All the media attention and the protests to keep St. Mel open made my senior year pass quickly. But even during senior year, money was tight. Mama scrounged up enough for deposits on my senior pictures and class ring, though in the end we could not afford either. I kept the proofs of my pictures, wallet-sized photos etched with the name of the studio and the word "proofs." I never laid eyes on the ring. But at least I was getting my diploma. Mama couldn't afford that, either. But true to her word, sometimes through borrowing, penny-pinching, and always sacrifice, she had found a way to pay my tuition at St. Mel.

On graduation day, Mama sat inside the auditorium, beaming. Net was there, too. So were Robin, her mother, and her sister Diane. Finally, my name was called.

"John Wesley Fountain," the voice rang across the auditorium.

The crowd applauded. I got to my feet, wearing my purple gown and cap, my gold tassel dangling. Then I made my way to the stage as the announcer read from my list of activities and honors:

"'A' honors, 'B' honors, Who's Who Among American High School Students, Project Upward Bound, Chess Club . . ." the announcer read.

I climbed the stairs of the stage, shook hands, and received my diploma, then walked back down, the announcer still reading.

"Basketball, track, cross-country, Mayor's Student as Trainee Program . . ."

The announcer was still reading when I took my seat. The crowd applauded.

"John will be attending the University of Illinois in Urbana–Champaign."

More applause.

After graduation, I took pictures with Mama and Net and then with Robin, who wore a white maternity dress that day. The best picture that I took that day is one that I have kept all these years safely tucked away behind the plastic preserving pages of an old photo album. In that photo, Mama stares at the camera. I hold my diploma, kissing her on the cheek, looking sideways at the photographer. Mama's face is spread in a girlish smile. But it is her eyes that move me. They are so happy.

It was August 7, 1978. Robin was meeting me after work for dinner and shopping on a summer evening. I had gotten a job that summer working at my mother's place of employment. Mama had been back to work for a couple of years now at a nonprofit organization downtown on Wabash Avenue called SPUN. SPUN was an acronym for Society for the Protection of the Unborn through Nutrition. It was ironic that the gig at SPUN turned out to be my job for the summer. In hindsight, it was probably an appropriate place for a father-to-be to be working, especially one whose girlfriend was a black teenage expectant mother, which coincidentally was at the top of the list of high-risk pregnant women. In my job, I eventually began visiting schools for pregnant teens and showing films on the importance of prenatal nutrition, then handing out brochures and fielding questions from young expectant mothers. I shared with Robin every ounce of information that I learned while working at SPUN.

When Robin arrived at my office, we headed to the downtown department stores to shop for the baby. I had already bought a crib. It was a collapsible wooden deal with blue trim. I had also bought clothes and boxes of disposable diapers, although we did not know whether we were having a boy or a girl. That evening, we were in search of more T-shirts and sleepers; the baby was due any day.

Earlier that summer, I accompanied Robin a few times on clinic appointments, which always seemed to make her happy. As we sat in the clinic's waiting room making small talk while waiting for her name to be called, there were plenty of other teenage expectant mothers in the clinic, but few if any, accompanied by their boyfriends. There were no husbands that I can recall, nor any women who looked like they were even old enough to be married, though all of them had round bellies, swollen feet, and that scared and lonely look in their eyes. Being at the clinic with Robin, I felt like an oddball sometimes. It always seemed strange and even shameful to me that more young men were not there with their baby's mamas during clinic visits. But such was the norm.

After shopping that evening, Robin and I went out to dinner. Robin was always hungry. We went to one of our favorite downtown restaurants, a little place off State Street whose lights blinked on and off called Ronny's Steak House. Ronny's wasn't ritzy by any stretch of the imagination. The word was that Ronny's had mice and even big, fat cat-sized rats, but I always thought Ronny's to be a decent sit-down restaurant where a lot of black folks ate whenever they went downtown to the "show," as we called movie theaters back then. Robin and I ordered pizza and steak. We were almost finished eating when Robin complained.

"My stomach hurts," she said.

"Yeah?" I asked. "You think it was the food?"

"I don't know," she said.

"Awww girl, you probably just have to drop a bomb," I laughed. "Go on to the bathroom. You'll be all right," I said.

Robin shot me a half-embarrassed, disgusted look. We both burst out laughing.

"It doesn't feel like that," she said.

The pain seemed to go away. But a few minutes later, it returned.

"My stomach's hurting again. It feels like cramps," Robin said. "I-I-I think I might be in labor."

The pain stopped again. I looked at my watch. Several minutes later, it started again. It didn't seem unbearable. Could it be labor pains? Neither of us had ever had a baby before. We weren't sure. But we figured that it had to be labor pain. We quickly left Ronny's and caught the Lake Street El to Robin's house, where a short time later her water burst. It was time.

At the University of Illinois hospital, Robin's mother sat in the waiting room while I walked the halls with Robin and held her hand. The contractions were more frequent than earlier and much stronger—so intense that they made Robin cry. She sank to the floor whenever they hit. And each time, I sank with her, holding her hand, crying my own tears to see her in so much pain.

"I love you, Robin. It's going to be okay," I said until another contraction passed. Then I helped her back to her feet.

Finally, it was time and the nurses whisked Robin through a set of doors at the end of the hallway.

A short while later, I was standing just outside the waiting room when a nurse rolled our baby out of the delivery room for me to see. It was a little baby boy with a head full of straight black hair, reddish skin, and squinty eyes. Born at 9:45 P.M., August 7, he weighed six pounds, seven ounces. We named him John Wesley Fountain III, although we later began calling him John-John, my childhood nickname.

Standing there in the hospital, seeing my son for the first time, I was filled with joy. I could find no words, only tears.

A few weeks after John-John's birth, I kissed my little son and his mother good-bye and trotted off to college. Actually, my stepfather and Mama drove me to Champaign. As the wheels rolled past the city landscape and miles of cornfields to the University of Illinois campus, I wondered whether I was doing the right thing, whether college was really where I belonged, now that I was a father.

After carting my suitcases and boxes to Room 364 in Forbes Hall, I walked back downstairs to say good-bye to my parents. Mama seemed so quiet, distant even, sitting in the front seat on the passenger side. I didn't understand then that as hard as it was for me to say good-bye to my infant son, it was just as difficult for Mama to say good-bye to me, the son to whom she had given birth just eighteen years earlier and upon whom, in many ways, she had come to rely—as a late-night companion to the store for cigarettes and Schlitz, for moral support, to kill the mice. As my parents pulled away that morning, I was thinking that Mama must be mad at me for some reason, not realizing that her quiet façade was probably all that kept her from bursting into tears and sobbing uncontrollably.

I waved good-bye and walked back upstairs to my room. Only half of me was there. My heart was really with Robin and my son, 150 miles away. And it felt like I was on the other side of the world.

Sitting on my bed inside Forbes Hall only minutes after having arrived at college, I felt very alone. And even though I had landed squarely in the middle of my dream, it was bittersweet.

CHAPTER 15

SCHOOL DAZED

I WAS STANDING above the silver water fountain on the third floor of my dormitory, casually sipping water, when it happened. It had a familiar ring. But it carried an unusual sting from the lips of a white boy. "Hey nigger!" yelled the tall blondish young man. He stood there in the hallway boldly, he and a friend, smirking, laughing. "What are you going to do, nig-gerrrr?"

I saw red. I vaulted toward my room.

"I got something for you," I huffed.

"He's going to get a gun, man. Run!" yelled the other white guy.

That was just another one of their stereotypes. That all black guys had guns and that we even brought them to college with us. I'm not sure which of the weapons in my room I was running to retrieve. But I felt that I needed more than my bare hands to teach these white boys a lesson for having called me a nigger. It was an unspoken rule. If a white person had the audacity to use the "N" word, you had to help him feel the consequences of having said it. No sticks and stones may break my bones crap. You had to handle your business. That a white boy had the nerve to call me that to my face meant that I had no choice but to respond. That much was easy.

I was filled with rage from head to toe as I ran toward my room. I kept hearing that word over and over in my head. It rang with the white boy's stinging inflection. It wasn't that I'd never heard the word before or that no one had ever hurled it at me as an insult. Just never anyone white, although I always imagined that the word floated freely in the air of some white social circles behind closed doors and well beyond the earshot of black folks. I knew that the possibility of some white person calling me a nigger face-to-face always existed and that being on a campus of 30,000 mostly white students, it was bound to happen sooner or later. I wasn't naive, only stunned and caught off-guard when it did happen.

It was not like the zillion-and-one times when my friends and I used the term, slapping fives and teasing, using it as a term of endearment that slipped from our lips with ease and with no second thoughts. For hours, we carried on with our expression of "nigger this" and "nigger that" with no offense meant. Even Aunt Mary or my cousins sometimes called me a "mean ole black nigger." That hurt some, although it was the adjectives in that phrase rather than the noun that hurt most. Yet, shot from the lips of white boys, "nigger" was lethal. I wanted to kill them, to shoot back. "Stupid white boys . . . Honkies!" I said to myself, running toward my door.

"Wait right there," I said, "I'll be right back!"

I rushed inside my room and flung open my closet door. Then I grabbed it, took it out of its case, the slender .22 caliber rifle that a friend had asked me to hold for him for a few days. For a few moments, I held it in my hands, feeling the cold metal and wood, seeing the fire spit out at the end, the two white boys falling dead, a nigger's vengeance paid in full. Then I put it down, my better judgment leading me back to my good senses. These were two stupid fools not worth going to jail over. I picked up a bat instead and hurried out of the room back to the spot where they had disrespected me. They were nowhere to be found. In a way I was glad, because otherwise there would have been consequences for us all.

The one good thing about being a poor college student was that I qualified for every cent of financial aid available. Government grants covered my tuition and fees as well as the lion's share of costs for room and board.

But that still left me with a shortfall of several hundred dollars. Also, I had to buy my own books, pay fees, and take care of incidentals, as well as Sunday supper. The dormitory cafeterias only served one meal on Sunday. That was brunch. And no matter how much you consumed at brunch, by the time evening rolled around, you wanted to eat again, especially as the pizza-delivery dudes scurried through the hallway to the rooms of other students, the smell of cheese and sausage wafting through the dorm.

I saved part of my earnings from my summer job and had gotten two cash scholarships totaling about $1,000. But I quickly made a dent in my modest nest egg after a single trip to the bookstore. And that was just for the first semester. I figured that before too long, money would get tight. Any finances from home would be scarce or nothing at all. That meant that at some point I would have to get a job, which worried me some, because I had never worked while in school at the same time. I had no idea how I would finance the second semester. But I reasoned that this would work itself out in due time.

The campus was lush and green, especially the Quad at the center of campus, where on warm sunny days students tossed Frisbees as some of the white kids sunbathed and read books, or the black fraternities and sororities performed step shows—stomping, dancing, and barking—on some Fridays at high noon. The campus was a world away from K-Town. And in many ways, it soothed me. It gave me the same sense of comfort I had felt during those summers at Northwestern, when life seemed less filled with worry and there was some song drifting on a breeze. Of course, the stakes were higher now that I was a full-fledged college student. And I understood that I needed to get down to business if I had any intention of staying around.

Among the first things I did when I got to campus was to open a checking account. I had been instructed in my guidance class and my consumer economics class at St. Mel that I should do that once I got to college. I had never had a checking account before. When I worked summer jobs in high school, I had cashed my checks at the currency exchange on Sixteenth and Pulaski, where everybody else in my neighborhood conducted their financial affairs. Having a checking or a savings account was a foreign concept to me. Terms like stocks and bonds or mutual funds and diversified portfolio were Greek. I never saw Mama or my stepfather write checks. Whenever Mama purchased money orders at the currency exchange, she handed over cold hard cash. When she paid the telephone or electric bill in person, she slid a wad of money to a cashier on the other side of some usually bulletproof partition. In fact, I knew of no banks in our neighborhood, only the neon-lighted storefronts with the flashing signs that read "Check Cashing" and shone like beacons in the night. I never wondered why there were no banks in K-Town, although I did wonder why currency exchanges charged so exorbitantly to cash a paycheck. Their charge was an escalating percentage based on the amount of the check to be liquidated. I always had the feeling that these joints overcharged and that this was not the way things worked in white neighborhoods. At one point, even getting change for a dollar at the currency exchange on Sixteenth and Pulaski cost a dime.

I resented currency exchanges and the often snotty people who sat behind the impersonal bulletproof glass. I hated sliding my money into the silver tray at the slit beneath the glass and the way the fingers of the cashiers dipped into the tray at the precise moment that yours withdrew without so much as grazing your hand. I do not know why I had not thought of opening an account at a bank before my freshman year in college. Maybe it was more a question of access, or exposure, or knowledge or the lack thereof. What I do know is that it quickly became clear to me that most kids in college had bank accounts of some kind. And it was a thing of admiration and beauty the way they whipped out their checkbooks at the bookstore or at the supermarket or with the pizza man, exuding an air of privilege as they signed their John Hancock. The only paper I had ever seen at grocery stores other than cash was food stamps.

At college, it made sense to open an account at a bank, particularly if you did not want to seem like an odd duck. But it was scary walking into the bank at Fourth and Green Streets in Campustown and actually filling out the requisite paperwork. Opening an account was a simple thing but an entirely new one for me. In addition to fear, I was filled with a sense of excitement and also embarrassment. I felt the same years later when I took my first airplane flight, although by then I was a full-grown man. I walked through the airport that day feeling out of place not knowing so much as how to check in for my seat assignment. As I stood there in the airport, it seemed as if everybody was at ease and I was an alien. It was as if there was this whole world that existed that I knew nothing about. I had descended from Mars. And I imagined that everyone could tell I was green and out of place.

Even a simple thing like opening a checking account was opening the door to a brave new world. And in some ways, I was amazed. With a checking account, I could cash a paycheck at no cost. I didn't need to worry about having safe places to hide my money, such as in a ball of socks or underneath a mattress, both of which I had known people in my family to use. A couple of weeks after I opened my checking account, I was issued bright blue checks stamped with "John Fountain." There was something righteous and endearing about having my own checks. Banks seemed noble. Currency exchanges were ghetto. And although I once imagined that they were a service to poor communities, I began to see them as part of the system that either by purpose and design or by default profited from the poor much more than they should have.

I was soon whipping out my blue checkbook and writing checks like the white kids. However, I quickly learned that writing checks was only part of the equation. The other was making sure you had the cash in your account to cover them. I also learned the meaning of the big bold letters, "NSF," stamped on the back of a check.

My meager finances were hurt by the fact that Robin and I talked frequently on the telephone. By second semester, the phone was disconnected.

My first year at college was a lot harder than I could ever have imagined. I found I had to actually study to pass tests, whereas my brilliance in quick memorization had saved my hide in high school many a day. In college, there was always a paper due in this class or that class. Then there was class itself. On many mornings, I felt an irresistible urge to cut class since there were no parents to ride me and no fines for skipping class. In fact, I learned that most teachers basically did not care if you attended class or not. Either way, they were getting paid. And if you were too lazy to come to class, that was considered to be your problem, not theirs.

That first semester, it was hard balancing my time. Unlike at home, where my days during the school year had been structured either by my coaches, my teachers at school, or Mama, time at college was my own. And it seemed to be my enemy. There were so many things to fill my day with. Mostly, they were distractions: girls, basketball, parties. I wasn't the only one having trouble. A lot of students I knew who were goody-two-shoes, Christian, churchgoing kids came to college and got their first taste of freedom, only to go buck wild. Some guys smoked a lot of pot. Some girls became fraternity groupies, or little sisters to fraternities, which basically meant that they cleaned frat houses and were sexual playthings for the brothers. I didn't go exactly buck wild. But I definitely got my groove on.

My studies soon took second place. Or was it third or fourth? Nothing much stopped me from shooting hoops or from going to every party I could when the weekend rolled around. Many of the campus parties were held at the Illini Union at the center of campus, on the edge of the Quad. Black fraternities or sororities sponsored nearly all the black parties held at the Union. The best parties were always those thrown by the brothers from Omega Psi Phi, known more commonly as Qs or Q-dogs. There were always plenty of sisters at a Q-party, and you could always count on things getting wild and the Q-brothers flailing their arms above their heads and barking whenever the song "Atomic Dog" blared over the speakers. Although the Qs were the envy of many young black men on campus and the lust of many a coed, not everyone cared for their antics. There were stories that some mothers, who came to campus and happened to witness their Q-sons barking and crawling around like dogs during their ritualistic dances, openly wept. Yet becoming a Q was my fantasy. Qs were usually dark-skinned muscular brothers who possessed all the cool in the world and got all the ladies. And they knew how to party better than any other group of brothers on earth. I quickly decided that at some point in my college career, I would pledge. From what I had been told and had observed, that would mean weeks of being a gofer and to some extent a whipping boy as the brothers already in the fraternity indoctrinated the new pledges into the brotherhood. I figured that such were the meager costs of joining the brotherhood.

My cousins cautioned me against pledging any fraternity, saying that arms and legs as well as grades were known to have been casualties for many a brother who had gone before me. But I was drawn to the Qs by the toughness they symbolized. Just as appealing was the unity they displayed. I liked the way they stuck together and admired their quickness to bust a white boy in the face over messing with one of theirs. I wanted to be a Q so badly I could taste it. But pledging would have to wait because first-semester freshmen were forbidden by school regulations from joining a fraternity or sorority.

In hindsight, much of what was beneath my passion to pledge was the desire to fit in, particularly in a place where I think many black students felt like oddballs. At St. Mel, I always had my homeboys on the basketball team. Although two of my St. Mel classmates had accompanied me to the University of Illinois, they were both females. Even though Cheryl, Doris, and Arty were in Champaign, they lived off campus, which was a different world. We seldom saw each other and usually only when I visited them. Living on campus meant having to make new friends, though I would have been happy to find just a few good ones.

Before long, I met a dude in my dorm. He lived on the fourth floor. He was black like me and, like me, had grown up poor. And like me, his name was John. He was from East Chicago Heights, a suburb about thirty-five miles south of Chicago. John was just shy of being six feet tall and was brown skinned, with a cotton candy Afro. Johnny or JB, as I called him, and I became such good friends that we became known as the Brothers J. We shot hoops together and partied together, and on weekends when there were no parties and money was too tight to mention, we jimmied the pinball machines at a joint near our dorm called The Snack Bar, which we had nicknamed the "snatch bar" for the frequency with which shoplifters confiscated food.

On many weekend nights, pinball machines were our recreational salvation. With an older pinball machine, if you picked it up, raising its two front legs a few inches from the floor, then dropped it, a game suddenly registered on the screen. Usually, all we needed was one game to get us going. Then we racked up high scores and won additional games legitimately. We bumped and shook pinball games sometimes until the wee hours of the morning.

I don't remember how John and I met. Probably it was in the dorm cafeteria where nearly all of the blacks, including athletes, sat together in one section. It was voluntary segregation. A few blacks sat with whites, but we looked at them as "sellouts." Sellouts were black students who were trying to be white. We also usually referred to them as Oreos. Although nobody had appointed any of us to be judges of black students' blackness, most of us who were from Chicago—the Mecca of black folk in Illinois—took it upon ourselves to be both judge and jury. The reality was that many of us likely felt intimidated by the ease with which we saw some blacks engage in social intercourse with whites. Maybe our shunning of students whom we considered to be Oreos stemmed from jealousy on our part. Maybe it was out of ignorance. Maybe it was a combination.

Most black students in Champaign were from Chicago, and most of us had spent the vast majority of our lives interacting with and surrounded by other blacks. I was shell-shocked by the sheer number of whites compared to blacks and found living around so many white folks to be a strange new experience. In Chicago, you could grow up without ever seeing anybody white living next door, sitting in the pew at church, or standing in line at the grocery store. Imagine going from that to having to use communal showers with white dudes and being conscious—or paranoid—that every time I walked in, there would be some white boy peeking at my private parts to see if the myth was true. I imagined that our presence took some getting used to for white students as well, some more than others, especially those from small lily-white towns who had never seen a real live Negro. Some white students seemed no more comfortable with us than we were with them. But we were vastly outnumbered.

It didn't help that Mama had told me years ago that I was never to trust white people. That some of them were okay but that ultimately, if it was my hide on the line or some white guy's, they would always choose to save their own rather than mine. The Gospel according to Mama was that no matter how nice whites seemed, there was always that great racial divide to contend with. I shared Mama's wisdom with John, warning him about the white dudes on his dorm floor who befriended him. But John, who had gone to school with whites before and seemed much more comfortable than I was, was not so convinced.

Sometimes it felt as if I was in some foreign land where everyone talked and looked so different from me. The white students at school seemed so smart. They used words I had never heard before. In class, I was sometimes so intimidated that I was often afraid to raise my hand to answer or ask a question. It seemed as if every white college student had an expensive stereo system, lived in the suburbs, and got dropped off at school by their parents in expensive cars or drove their own. In some cases, one or both of their parents had graduated from the University of Illinois. And there was a kind of cockiness, or maybe it was confidence, in the way they carried themselves and articulated their dreams and aspirations.

What shocked me even more was that some black students seemed to have more in common with the white students than with the black students. These black students were not like any of the black kids I knew back in Chicago. They sounded more like white folks than black folks. They even acted more like whites and in many cases frequently hung out with them. In some cases, their mothers or fathers or both were college graduates, and they lived in the middle-class Hyde Park neighborhood of Chicago or in some white suburb. They seemed every bit as confident or cocky, or entitled, as the white kids. In fact, one black guy who lived in Forbes Hall hung out with Jesse Jackson's sons and bragged about riding around in a limousine. He was somebody.

The effect of all this was that I felt isolated and alone, and for the first time in my life, even kind of dumb. In the first few weeks of college, I found myself with many more questions than answers, uncomfortable questions about my own life and existence in this new world filled with all of these proper-talking folks and their big life's dreams. Oh sure, I had dreams, too. But I had the sense that their dreams and the way they wore them like a gun on their hip carried more weight.

I imagined that back home, while I was worrying about food, eating ketchup sandwiches, and sipping sugar-flavored water in place of supper, many of the students who surrounded me at college—both black and white—were dining out. That while I was scrounging up bus fare to high school, they were probably being dropped off in expensive cars or driving their own sports cars. While I was working summers so I could buy school clothes for the fall and give a few dollars to my mother to help out at home, they were probably studying abroad or hanging out at the beach. From conception, college had been their destiny. And their daddies, in some cases, already had jobs lined up for them. Sure, my cousins were there at college, but we seldom saw each other, and it was clear that I was on my own. Sometimes, it felt like college was the last place that I should be. I felt out of place. All the other students were still just kids. I was already a father. Before too long I was consumed by feelings of inadequacy.

If anybody could understand, my friend John could, though I never let on to him just how poor I actually was. I had a few more possessions than John, a Crock-Pot, a hot plate, and a small stereo that my parents had bought me the previous Christmas. John had a small portable television, but we were pretty much in the same boat.

"Man, I ain't got nobody to help me," John said as we sat in his room, talking one day.

"My uncle and my grandparents help me out sometimes. They got big money, man," I said, speaking only half the truth.

In fact, during my freshman year I sometimes visited Arty or Cheryl and Doris's apartment to discover bags of groceries on their tables. When I inquired about where they had gotten the goodies, they said that my grandparents and their mothers had visited them. I seldom said a word to my cousins, but I always wondered why my relatives, visiting from Chicago, never bothered to stop by my room, even to say hello. Mama wondered, too. She also wondered why they never called to say they were going to Champaign in the first place or to ask her whether she wanted to send anything to her son or at least to ask whether she would like to ride along, especially since she didn't drive. It was hard to understand why they never stopped by my room or mailed me a care package, especially since I was the poorest of the lot. On the Sundays that I was without money to buy supper, I sometimes wrote rubber checks to the pizza man. At other times, I sat in my room crying, too ashamed to ask a friend, even John, for help and feeling more sorry for myself than hungry.

"Yeah, man, my folks look out for me," I bragged.

"Man, you're lucky," John said. He paused. "It's just me and my mother and my little brother and sisters. They all depending on me."

I could sense his strain and sense of responsibility.

"I gotta make it," John continued.

Although I did not say the same, I sensed we were both captains of sinking ships. Except mine was sinking faster. I already had a son.

It was lobster day, the day when the cafeteria served fresh lobster and all the trimmings for supper. This was the one time during each semester that everybody showed up to eat, causing long lines that stretched outside the dorm's front door and beyond. John and I cut in line with the permission of friends. It was no big deal. Everybody did it. I was walking with the help of crutches at the time, having hurt my hip while playing intramural basketball. John and I had been standing in line for only a few minutes when suddenly a voice rang out from somewhere in the line behind us. It was a white boy's voice.

"Hey, you guys can't cut in line," the voice said.

We looked at each other and laughed.

"Who the hell does he think he's talking to?" John asked.

"I don't know, man, dude must be crazy," I said, still laughing. "You think he talking to us?"

"Man, I know he ain't talking to me," John barked.

The voice called out again.

"Hey you guys, I'm talkin' to you!"

"Man, that white boy must be crazy," John said, snickering with a bit of a snarl. "Silly mother..."

The voice interrupted.

"You guys better get to the back of the line," it rang again, as we turned and spotted some muscular-looking white dude spouting off at the back of the line. "If you guys aren't back here by the time I count to three, I'm going to come up there and move you back here myself."

The entire line grew dead silent.

"One!"

John and I looked at each other in disbelief. Here was a white boy with balls, a white boy bold enough to confront some black dudes when he wasn't inside a pickup truck with his friends and doing sixty miles per hour while shouting "nigger" as they sped by on campus on weekends.

"Two-o-o-o!"

"Okay," I thought. "I would have to be on crutches when a white boy decides to act a fool." But I knew John was more than capable of handling the situation. A former All State wrestler who also practiced kung fu, he was basically Steven Seagal and The Rock rolled up into one. "No problem," I thought.

"Three-e-e!"

We waited. But we didn't have to wait long. In a few moments, the muscular white boy with near shoulder-length brown hair, who looked like a middle linebacker, emerged from the three-deep line. He walked right up to John and grabbed him, which was his first mistake. The two young men tussled for a few moments like Greco-Roman wrestlers before John was on top of him and attempting to make his assailant's body one with the floor. Finally, a group of young men in line broke up the fight, at which point the white boy began to make his journey back to the back of the line whence he came. By then, John was feeling his oats and standing there in the cafeteria line, basking in the thrill of victory, when suddenly a few other white voices rang out.

"John, you're wrong," said one.

"You're wrong, man," said the other. "I don't care if you hate me for the rest of your life, John, man, you're wrong."

We turned and looked. The voices belonged to the white dudes who lived on John's floor and who had befriended him. John huffed, turned away, and cursed.

"Come on, man," he said to me.

Together we walked all the way to the front of the line, cutting in front of everyone, strutting into the cafeteria as if we owned the joint. No one would dare say a word now, and there was no sense in being even remotely discreet about cutting in line.

"Man, I ain't believe you. I thought them dudes was my friends," John said as we headed to get our lobster.

"I told you, man, you can't trust 'em," I said.

"Shhhoo-o-ot, now I know," John replied.

I later learned the real truth about trusting white folks. And that was that true friendship does not boil down to race and that for as much as you could not trust all whites, the same could be said about blacks. In fact, the black dudes who let us cut in line that day to begin with had literally turned their backs and stared straight ahead, their necks becoming as stiff as boards at the first sign of trouble. They didn't turn to look our way again even while the ruckus was going on. I understood why Mama had said what she had and even why she felt the way she did. She wanted to fortify me against the inescapable realities that confront a black man in a white society. But the problem with Mama's advice was that every time I had been robbed or beaten up in my life, it was by someone who looked a lot like me. Yet I still trusted black people and had learned to decipher whom I could trust and whom I could not. I discovered that if I was going to survive in a white world, ultimately I had to learn to do the same with white people.

I met Robin at the Greyhound Bus terminal on a cold winter's Friday night. She climbed off the bus, carrying my son, wrapped in blankets, and a small suitcase. I smiled. Her face lit up. My heart danced. We kissed. I held my son in my arms. Robin smelled like sweet perfume and mint. Her hair was curly, her face smooth and clear. John-John looked very different from when he was first born. He seemed to be changing so rapidly. We walked the ten or so blocks to my dorm room, where we spent much of the weekend.

The few times that Robin came down to campus to visit me, I didn't tell Mama about it. She would have blown a gasket. What I did not know immediately was that when Robin visited, she had told her folks that she was staying with Doris and Cheryl. But even if I had known that Robin had lied to her folks, it would not have mattered much. I missed her so badly that when I did decide to study it only made it hard to concentrate.

When Robin and John-John visited, we sometimes strolled around campus, ate pizza, laughed, talked, and cried. The time always passed more quickly than either of us ever wanted, Sunday mornings arriving with no sympathy.

On Sunday afternoon, we walked the ten or so blocks back to the Greyhound Bus terminal in downtown Champaign, past Green Street and Pizza World, past University Avenue, wiping away tears, holding hands.

"I love you, Robin," I said, giving her and my son one last hug and kiss.

"I love you, too," Robin answered.

I ushered them aboard the big bus northbound to Chi-Town. The engine revved. The door closed tightly with a dull thud. I watched as the bus pulled away. Then I turned and took my lonely, teary walk back to the dorm.

CHAPTER 16

RATS

ANOTHER trap popped. I lifted the copper wire from the neck of the little gray mouse and slid it into the plastic garbage bag with all the other bloodied and disfigured corpses. Then I reset the wooden trap and climbed back into the bottom bunk with my anxious little brother. Jeff didn't know it, but I was just as afraid as he was. I have always been afraid of rats and mice, ever since the first time I spotted one scurrying through our apartment when I was a little boy. But I have never had the freedom to show such fear. Somebody had to be brave. Most of the time it had to be me.

It was after midnight. I was eighteen, Jeff, eleven. I was home from college on winter break, and we were trying to trap the little critters that ran amuck in our apartment when everything and everyone else stilled and the lights dimmed. Just when things got really quiet and dark, you could hear their little feet. Their teeth and nails ripped through food packages. They tiptoed across tin pots and dishes, rummaged through the garbage, gnawed at chicken bones, squeaked. By day, the apartment was ours. By night, it belonged to every creeping thing. It seemed as if there had been some unspoken agreement between the mice and us.

"Don't y'all mice come out in the daytime" was the way I had imagined our agreement had been cut with the Head Cheese, who had squeaked back in agreement, "And don't y'all even think about coming into the kitchen at night!"

If you had the choice, you would choose to live with mice rather than rats. Rats were bigger and acted differently from mice. Mice scurried. Rats strutted, pimp-walked, came out in the middle of the day, stared you in the eye, and dared you to say something. Thank God we mostly had mice. Mice were more agreeable.

We watched the mice under the glare of the old black-and-white portable television that sat on our bedroom dresser. The television's knobs were long gone, worn out from turning and since replaced by a pair of pliers that worked just as well. We used a wire clothes hanger for an antenna. The picture usually showed well enough for us to watch television, which on Friday nights was *Creature Feature,* a weekly show that came on after the news at 10:30 and showed horror movies like *Frankenstein, Dracula,* and *The Curse of the Werewolf.* We sometimes jimmied the hanger on the television, contorting it beyond recognition. When even that failed to produce decipherable sound and picture, we slapped the television hard, either with a good whack on the side or a closed fist on top. When I was Jeff's age, the glare and buzz of the television had rocked me to sleep at night. I'm not sure if that was because the light from the television gave me some sense of comfort since I was mostly afraid of the dark as a child. Or maybe it was because the voices that emanated from the television helped drown out the sounds of the mice that crept in our house for hours after midnight.

The Meeces—our pet name for them—sometimes seemed to be everywhere. Little gray shadows danced on the stove and in the oven. They darted across the washer and dryer with near bionic strength. They climbed on top of the refrigerator and dangled from the kitchen curtains, their rubbery-looking tails always a dead giveaway. Between the mice and roaches, it was a wonder that we even had room for us humans.

By the time we climbed out of bed on most mornings, the sun had poked through the dirty blinds, lighting up the kitchen. The visitors were gone, having crawled back inside their holes after a night of siege. We were always relieved. But I always felt a little queasy about putting my bare foot on the wooden bedroom floor, where I imagined one last mouse on his way back to his hole might brush across my flesh. After arising from bed some mornings, we would soon discover that the beady-eyed invaders had rumbled through our cereal boxes or had left their droppings on the pantry shelves. Half asleep, we opened the cereal boxes and a few roaches crawled out. Or sometimes there were holes in the bottom of the boxes or bags where the mice had barreled through and had their fill. After a while, we got used to it. At least we stopped crying.

But life at home had worsened in the four months I was away at college. Either that, or escaping it for the first extended period of time in my life—other than a few short summer stints away—had only made things seem much worse. However bad it seemed before, there were never this many mice before, or this many roaches, nor was it this dark and depressing.

I wondered if my college friends had gone home to similar circumstances. I imagined they did not. And I felt sorry for myself, so sorry and depressed. As usual, there was enough of that to go around at our house even when there wasn't much food.

A kind of dark coldness had hung in the air as I walked through the door a few days earlier, carrying my bags fresh from my first semester at college. My stepfather picked me up at the downtown bus terminal. It was busy as usual. The bus station always seemed to buzz with travelers and students going to and from college. Then there were the smelly homeless men and women and dressed-down pimps with roaming eyes who prowled the station for wide-eyed young girls who had run away from home and landed in Chi-Town. The ride to the West Side was uneventful, although I sat silently on the passenger side with mixed feelings, trying to reconcile life in my two worlds. And strangely, as my stepfather rounded the corner near home, I also wondered whether Komensky was a place where I belonged anymore.

Inside the hallway leading to our apartment, the air had the same stale and flat odor, the paint was still peeling. I walked up the wooden stairs, my footsteps and the squeaks announcing my arrival.

"Johnnnnn," my sisters and brother screamed.

"Hey-y-y," I answered, dragging my bags. "Hey, Ma."

"Welcome home," Mama said, smiling, although she seemed tired and drained.

Their eyes fixed on me as though I had been away at war and had finally come back home, and now everything was going to be all right. It was as if my mere presence breathed a fresh wind of life into the apartment, with its gloomy faded walls soiled by the soot from the kitchen space heater. It felt weird that my family seemed so happy to see me, not that they should not have been happy. But it was as if I had made it back to the island where we had all been stranded. And though my one-man life raft had just barely sufficed for me, there was the sense that somehow I could help make life on our island more bearable until a ship big enough for all of us came in. I was happy to see my family, too, but not to be donning my cloak of responsibility to try and make everything better—a burden that had been at the root of my adolescent migraines. But as much as my family needed me, I too needed something or someone to help me out of poverty's quicksand.

Mama seemed more depressed than ever. The rise in our mouse population did not make it any better. Mama was terrified of them, dead or alive. Once, when I was no older than four or five, sitting at the kitchen table eating cereal one morning with my feet dangling over a chair, I was watching Mama iron clothes when she let out a scream that nearly scared me to death. As suddenly as she yelled, she leaped onto a kitchen chair.

"What's the matter, Ma?" I asked.

"Nothing, John," she said, still quivering atop the chair.

I knew better. I knew she had seen a rat or mouse or something. But she wouldn't say. She didn't want me to worry about her or anything else that she considered "grown-up" stuff. It was her way of shielding me, keeping it inside and bearing her burdens, hardships, and fears alone. I surmised years later that it was this way because there seldom was any man in our lives whom Mama could truly count on. And it seemed to me even as a child that many days, the only reliable male in the house was a little boy. What Mama could not see was that whether she told me or not, I always saw things the way they were. And they were bad for a long time.

My having become a father did not help matters any. At the ripe old age of thirty-four, Mama became a grandmother, at my hands, no less. I did not give this much thought back then. But years later, and with teenagers of my own, I would understand how scary a concept this could be for a parent such as my mother, who was still years from reaching middle age when her babies suddenly started having babies of their own. To Mama, it must have seemed like only yesterday that she was burping me on her shoulder, changing my diapers, and wiping up spills. Then, there I was at seventeen, the smell of milk still on my breath and so incompletely ready to handle the responsibility of fatherhood, in some ways still just a child myself and yet also a father.

Mama could do little to help me with my new financial responsibilities. We were struggling as it was. In fact, I had long taken it upon myself that I would be the one who someday would make good and help Mama. I would buy her that house I had promised and set in my heart long ago. I sensed even as a child that Mama believed me in those times when I promised as much, or that at the very least, she was touched by a son's dreamy promises. But I now sensed that with my new status as a teen father, Mama saw my hopes and dreams as being on life support. She said as much in her own way, telling me that I needed to stay in school and that I should not compound my mistake by marrying Robin, whom she thought to be totally selfish and "not the one" for me. She also warned against getting Robin pregnant a second time, and to be especially careful over the next two years. That's the way it always happens, Mama told me. "Be careful," she said.

Mama could not have been more right in cautioning me, although most of the time I thought she didn't know what she was talking about. Within weeks of my son's birth, I began to feel the strain of an adult world that I could not comprehend. It felt as if I had jumped off the diving board at the deep end of the swimming pool without knowing how to swim, and I was fighting the water only to feel myself being hopelessly pulled under, swallowing more water than air, and starting to wonder if I would survive.

Back in August, just days before I went off to college, I warned Net against getting pregnant. I knew a baby was the last thing she needed and also the last thing that Mama needed to worry about. It was not as if I was exactly the poster boy for any anti–teen pregnancy campaign. Still, I figured that messing around with that old boyfriend of hers, she too would soon have a beach-ball belly, and I didn't want that for my little sister.

"Net, don't get pregnant," I told her in scolding tones. "Mama don't need another grandchild."

Net looked at me and batted her big brown eyes, the way she always did when Mama was trying to talk some sense into her head and Mama's words seemed to bounce off her like a rubber ball on a brick wall. Net had a way of removing herself from the room without actually leaving, of escaping conversations as if her mind and soul temporarily left her body. The girl could just bat her eyes and float away. I recognized the signs and I knew Net was about to go transcendental on me.

"Net, don't get pregnant," I barked again.

"I ain't!" she fired back.

"Okay, now," I said, unconvinced and still trying to exert my big-brother control that had always worked when we were kids. Like those times when I was mad at my cousins for some reason or other and did not want Net to play with them either, or when I wanted to watch my favorite show on television. "I'm serious, Net," I continued. "Don't . . ."

"I ain't," she muttered, then smiled.

For some reason, I didn't believe her.

A few days after I arrived home for winter break, I was sitting on the sofa in our living room when suddenly Net rushed out of her bedroom and into a closet to retrieve a dress for church. I couldn't believe what I saw. My eyes widened as I caught a glimpse of her belly, which, though fully cloaked with a robe and partially camouflaged by her arms and the swiftness with which she moved, said it all. It looked as if she was hiding a beach ball underneath her clothes.

"Net," I asked matter-of-factly, "Are you pregnant?"

She stopped in her tracks, and her eyes filled with what first appeared to be amazement, although I soon determined it to be my sister's look of terror.

"Shhh," she said, putting her index finger on her lips.

"Mama don't know?" I asked.

"Uh-uh," she said.

"How could she not know? Girl, you big as a house."

"Shhh," Net said, trying to shush me again, her eyes growing wider.

"You kiddin', right? How could Mama not know?"

"She don't know. John, I'm too scared to tell her," she said, her words rinsed with anxiety.

I shook my head. I could not see how Mama could not know, how she could live in the same house and see Net every day and never notice that her stomach had become as big and round as a watermelon. But I later came to understand how the severity of pressures in everyday life can make people blind to change even in familiar surroundings. That when you dam the river, leaks can spring from the unlikeliest of places and that sometimes you just can't see it, or maybe you try hard not to see it even when it is staring you in the face, until it undeniably, unavoidably explodes.

"Net, are you crazy?" There was no response. "Net, Mama gon' kill you. She gon' kill-ll-ll you. Net?"

I searched for more words. Then I looked into her eyes. They looked frightened and teary, though Net was still smiling. There was nothing much else to be said. But telling Mama was what I knew she had to do, and soon. To say there was going to be a killing was to put it mildly. And I only wished that Net and Mama had gotten this out of the way before I came home. I didn't want to be a witness to my sister being murdered.

I ultimately reasoned that Net must have planned it this way, to break the news to Mama while I was home on break. This way, when Mama commenced to beating her, I could rescue her from the jaws of death. I did not appreciate the idea of being drawn into the middle of this, especially since I had warned her not to get pregnant. But I could not half blame my sister for waiting for me to come home before she told Mama. If I were in her shoes, I probably would have done the same thing.

Still, years later I wondered why there was going to be a killing over Net getting pregnant. There was no killing when I announced that Robin was with child. Not that I did not get a good verbal lashing and that stare of disappointment that every parent knows how to shoot their kids. The difference, of course, was that Robin was someone else's daughter. Robin's family, not Mama, would be stuck with caring for a new baby, should Robin and I shirk our responsibilities. Net being pregnant was a different matter. At worst, Mama was having another baby. At best, there would be a new addition to our household until Net and her boyfriend got married and moved into a place of their own.

Eventually, Net got around to telling Mama. Or I should say that Mama got around to figuring it out, when in her presence Net opened a gift for Christmas from her boyfriend's mama that to her surprise and Mama's turned out to be maternity clothes. Mama went ballistic. And in the end, I was glad that I was there to stop the killing.

On Mother's Day the following spring, Net would give birth to my first niece, a healthy baby girl named Kamika. But in the meantime, the fuss over her being pregnant would simply add to our platter of hardship and drama.

I already had a lot on my mind that December. If my computations were correct, and I knew they were, all of my partying and lack of study the first semester had landed me on academic probation. At best, I was on the high end of a D average and I felt pretty troubled about it all. Not to mention ashamed. I decided not to tell Mama. It wasn't that she would smack me or give me a whipping. I had gotten too old and big for that. If she got really mad, I figured that she would probably curse me out, which was even worse than a whipping.

Later that winter break, I was in the living room and Mama somewhere in the rear of the house near the kitchen when suddenly she screamed, then summoned me.

"Yeah?" I said, hurrying to her.

"What's this?" she said, holding a small white sheet of paper that looked familiar. The paper came into focus.

"My grades," I responded, shocked to see them dangling from Mama's hand as she stood, leaning on the broom.

I had actually received my college grade report in the mail weeks earlier and had hidden it after it confirmed my fears that I was on academic probation and in danger of being expelled from school. Somehow the grade report must have fallen out of my drawer and onto the floor. Either that, or Mama had sifted through my dresser drawers and discovered it. Before, whenever she had asked me why I had not received my grades in the mail, I told her I didn't know. Now there was no more hiding.

I stood there, my heart pounding, waiting for Mama to pull out a belt and whup me the way she did when I had done something bad as a child, or just curse me out. Seconds passed. It seemed like minutes. And still there was no lecture, no slapping or beating. Then suddenly the tears began pouring down Mama's brown face. It was an incessant river that made me wonder if and when she would ever stop crying. She just hung her head, slumped, and sobbed. I never saw Mama cry like that before, never saw her so wounded and hurt. She didn't say another word. She didn't have to. I shuffled away feeling punished enough.

The mood inside our apartment on Komensky that December was like the long melancholy wail of Miles Davis's horn. As Jeff and I turned the lights off in the apartment and went to bed, the fuss of the television was all that could be heard until the tin-tipping of the mice began. It grew louder, more repetitive, like Morse code.

"Man, what's all that noise?" I asked, knowing it had to be mice, but not wanting to believe it could have gotten so bad in a few months.

"It's the Meeces, man," Jeff replied, peering out of bed at the mice crawling on top of the kitchen sink under the cover of a mostly dark kitchen. "Them four-legged soul brothers," he said, laughing.

The light from the flickering television gave way to their furry bodies.

I stared into the kitchen, pulling my feet securely into bed. There were too many mice to count.

"Gol-leee mannn, look at all them suckers," I said, my skin starting to crawl.

We laughed and laughed some more. Then we decided to have some fun. We climbed out of bed and flicked on our bedroom light first, then the kitchen light. The mice scattered. We went to my stepfather's toolbox and grabbed a couple handfuls of metal staples and some rubber bands, then turned out the lights and jumped back into bed. The mice quickly reemerged. We looped the rubber bands around our index finger and thumb the way Michael and I had done on those Sunday mornings at True Vine and fired away. Our shots ricocheted off the kitchen appliances, dinging the washer, the dryer, and the refrigerator.

"Did you get 'em, man?" Jeff shouted.

"Nah, man, he got away," I said. "Man, I'm gonna kill them suckers."

"Me too," Jeff said. "Gimme some more of them staples."

"Man, it seem like a million of 'em," I said, firing off more rounds. Pop! Pop! Pop!

"Yeah," Jeff said, laughing. "It's a lot of em..." Pop! "Look at that sucker on the stove." Pop, pop! Pop!

We quickly discovered that the mice were both too fast and too small, and our aim too imprecise. And after a while, I stopped laughing. In fact, we both stopped laughing.

"I can't believe this, man," I said, scratching my legs and arms. "I can't believe the mice done got this bad."

They were so bad that Net had picked up her shoe one morning only to discover a mouse had taken up residence there. They also occasionally climbed atop her bed and scurried across the blanket. She was half afraid to sleep at night.

"So, what Daddy do about it?" I asked Jeff.

"Nuh-thin," he muttered and shrugged.

"Nuh-thin?" I said angrily. "Man, how come he ain't do nuh-thin?"

Jeff answered. "He put some traps out, but he ain't catch none."

I could not believe it—yes, I could. Still, it seemed next to impossible to understand why my stepfather had not ridded the apartment of the mice. It wasn't enough simply to have set the traps and allow the mice still to exercise dominion. *Why hadn't he caught them? Why hadn't he done this simple thing to make things better for his family? Why, even while the mice were doing the Boogaloo in our kitchen, was he not even home but out somewhere, who knows where, doing who knows what?* It was the same way many nights on payday, when there was nothing to eat and hours turned into days without a word from him until Monday when he showed up a few hours before dawn with excuses but nothing to eat. *Why tonight wasn't he here with us? Where was he? Where in the hell was he? And why should I have to catch these mice? Why always be the man?*

I got mad.

"I'll kill 'em," I said. "I'll kill 'em."

I rushed out of bed again and flicked on the lights. Behind the dryer and the refrigerator sure enough, I found the traps that my stepfather had set to no avail. They were still baited. But the cheese was as hard as a rock. If I were a mouse, I thought, I would not nibble from these traps either. I cleaned the hardened, cracked cheese out of the traps, then soaked the traps in the bathtub in water. I did so, thinking that maybe the traps carried a human scent from being handled and needed to be cleansed, so to speak. I don't know how I came up with this idea. Probably it was from watching too much television. Anyway, I got a couple of strips of bacon from the refrigerator and rubbed it over every inch of the traps, then fitted a few small pieces into the bait hook. I placed one trap behind the dryer and another behind the refrigerator. We climbed back into bed and waited for action.

A few minutes passed. Then pop!

"We got one of them suckers!" I said, dashing out of bed with Jeff close on my heels.

Sure enough, there was a mouse in the trap, his head partially severed by the metal wire. I emptied the trap and reset it, blood-stained and all, without rebaiting. It popped again and again and again into the morning light.

In the end, there were twenty-three corpses in all. Mama was ecstatic the next day when I told her I had caught all the mice and was even happier that next night when the kitchen was still and quiet after the lights dimmed and we'd all gone to bed. I also went out and bought a can of Raid and killed a few hundred roaches that fell from the ceiling like raindrops and were swept up into a pile, then properly disposed of. Mama was so happy. So was I, except I knew that old problems, no matter how joyous the reprieve, would eventually come creeping back into our lives. Just like the mice.

CHAPTER 17

DEAD RINGER

AT 12:15 A.M., John Wesley Fountain was pronounced dead. It was a snow-blown winter's day on campus, the blizzard of 1979 having painted the landscape a frosty white. I had just arrived back at Champaign that winter when the snow began to spill like an endless waterfall from the skies. It was as if I went to bed one night and awoke the next morning to a vast sea of snow that blanketed the Midwest. But life on campus went on, though in considerably slower motion. Students waded through thigh-high snow, making their way to the center of campus for classes.

I was glad to be back at school but felt considerable pressure, given that I was on academic probation and possibly facing expulsion from the university unless I brought my grades up. I made a pact with myself that there would be no party-hopping this semester, only serious study, and, of course, working to keep a few dollars in my pocket, maybe even enough to eventually get my telephone turned back on. The pressure weighed heavily on me: being in college and a father, being on probation, my lack of finances, and my worries about my son and Robin, Mama, my sisters, and brother. In hindsight, I know that the effect of all of this was that I was sinking into a depression. Sometimes you can be sinking and not know it, aboard a boat that is slowly filling with water before you realize that there is a problem. And by the time you do, it's virtually too late. Weary and laden with the weight of the world was how I felt as I lay across my bed in my dorm room on Sunday, January 28.

I had lain down fully dressed and with no intention of going to sleep, but I awoke sometime after midnight and was shocked to see that I had slept so long. It was a deep, almost eerie sleep that I will never forget. It felt as if I had been drugged. I got undressed and climbed back into bed. The next morning I awoke, showered, dressed, and went to class. When returning from class later that day, I checked my mailbox and found a handwritten message that read, "John, please call home." I knew that something was wrong. I thought that maybe something had happened to John-John or Robin. I rushed a few feet away to a public telephone.

"Hello-o-o," Mama's voice rang finally on the other end.

"You have a collect call from John," the operator said. "Will you accept the charges?"

"Yes," Mama said, her voice bearing a hint of urgency.

"Go ahead, caller."

"Hey, Ma, I got the message to call. What's wrong?"

"John Fountain is dead," Mama said just like that. *John Fountain is dead.*

There was nothing except silence for a few moments. Mama's words were hard to process. John Fountain is dead? John Fountain is dead. John who? What? What is she talking about? I wondered.

"Huh?" I responded aloud finally.

Mama continued.

"I got word from Alabama that John Fountain was killed in a car accident last night," she explained.

Finally, it hit me. And I understood what she must have been saying: that my father was dead. Perhaps it was the deadpan way in which Mama had first spoken when relaying the news that made it hard for me to grasp. Perhaps it was the fact that she used his full name, which is also mine. Her words were without detectable sympathy or emotion.

"What?" I asked, more rhetorically than actually seeking an answer as Mama explained in more detail.

I stood next to the telephone, students passing by, all of life seeming to pause. I was stunned as Mama talked. Her words buzzed like static. My thoughts floated a million miles away, back in time and space to memories of holding my father's hand, to the smell of cinnamon gum on his breath and the reddish spot at the center of his lips, to memories of me sitting on my porch on Komensky Avenue on summer days, watching the cars pass by and hoping that someday some car would stop suddenly in front of my house and that the smiling man climbing out of the driver's side door would be my father. Mostly, there were blank pages in my mind, empty spaces and questions, a million questions that I dreamed of erasing someday when I got the chance to sit and talk with the man whose name and seed I carried. I had no illusions about him or any dreamy misconceptions about the kind of relationship the two of us might ever have established. I simply wanted to hear his voice again, to see his face, to touch him, to look into his face to see if I could see any of me. I needed to know that he was not a mirage, to at least restore to my memory the portrait of the man who had long since faded. As I stood there on the telephone, talking to Mama, tears streaming down my face, I began to sob some.

My reaction shocked Mama and also stirred her wrath.

"Why are you crying?" she fussed.

"He was my father," I answered.

"He ain't never done nothin' for you," Mama said, her anger rising.

"It doesn't matter," I answered. "He was my father."

It was hard for Mama to understand, and perhaps even harder for her to express much sympathy, given that my father had essentially deserted her with two children to raise on her own. I could understand Mama's perspective even back then. But I am still convinced that parents often lack the same understanding about their children's feelings for an estranged parent, particularly in cases where one parent has hostile feelings, even justifiably so, for the other parent—feelings that they tend to try and impose upon the child often unknowingly. That can place children in an emotional vise, hold them hostage, not free to love, feel, or think as their heart dictates.

"You are so stupid," Mama shouted.

Click! I hung up the telephone.

Later that day, calmer heads prevailed and I called back. Mama said that services for my father were going to be held later that week and that my stepfather had offered to drive Net and me to Alabama. Still swirling from a mix of emotions, I said I did not want to go.

"I think that would be a mistake, John," Mama said, although I really didn't want her advice at that point. "Okay, so he didn't do anything for you, you can do for him the only thing you could do for him as a son. You can go to his funeral. If you don't go, you'll regret it later."

After some thought, I decided to make the trip to Evergreen, Alabama, to see the man that Grandmother had told me I looked so much like, even walked, talked, and laughed like, even if he was now dead.

We walked up the stairs of the tiny church filled with soft white light. The faces of the people inside were all a blur, and my mind filled with fog. At the front of the church in Evergreen was an open coffin filled with the remains of the man I had waited all these years to see. With my mother and stepfather following closely behind us, Net and I walked down the church aisle past the faces on both sides, inching closer toward the coffin.

I was filled with an eerie sense of anticipation. In one sense, I dreaded the moment when my eyes would meet my dead maker. In another, I was anxious to affirm the ghost in my memory.

A few more steps, a few more blurry faces and I stood above the coffin.

My eyes rushed toward the face, to the sealed eyes that were unfamiliar. They ran from his hair to his forehead and the cold skin caked with makeup that stirred no memories within. I followed the lines to his lips, the mustachioed cold lips with the reddish spot in the middle that I recognized instantly. In that moment, it was as if I could smell the scent of cinnamon, and a veil was lifted, my amnesia suddenly enveloped in living color and memories of my father brought back from the dead to life. But he was dead. And our reintroduction, delayed by years and a lifetime, was reduced to a few seconds' meeting between a living son and his dead father, relegated to a tearless silent good-bye.

As we drove that next morning toward the interstate, bound for our twelve-hour ride back to Illinois, I was filled with more turmoil than peace. The accident report Mama got from the local police station— where I had been mistaken for one of my father's relatives because as much as I may have looked like a Hagler, I apparently also looked so much like them—at least bore more answers about what happened that night my father was killed. Mama said she got the police report because she intended to hire a lawyer to find out if there was anything that Net and I might eventually gain financially from our father's being killed in the accident. For many years after my father was killed, whenever I heard the Temptations' song "Papa Was a Rolling Stone," I always thought of my father, particularly the latter half of the hook: "And when he died, all he left us was alone." If there was anything to be inherited, Mama, in her doggedness and tenacity, would surely find out. Upon leaving Evergreen that day, all we had was a police report. Interspersed in the details of a violent collision, contained in the four-page report written in ink in an officer's squiggly penmanship, I at least found a sketch of the mystery man:

I learned that John Wesley Fountain was driving a 1973 two-door Chevy station wagon. He was unemployed. Drinking—yes is circled. On the night of the accident, the weather was clear, dark, and dry. It occurred on a four-lane asphalt highway, Highway 31. My father was going about five miles per hour in a fifty-five mile per hour zone as he pulled onto the road from his mother's driveway. A truck, which was transporting produce, was doing about forty and coming over a hill.

The truck struck the station wagon. My father was not wearing a seat belt, and he was ejected from the car. His head struck the asphalt pavement. He was taken by ambulance to Evergreen Hospital, where he was pronounced dead at 12:15 A.M. on Monday, January 29, 1979—almost precisely the moment I woke up from my eerie druglike sleep.

The other thing I learned about my father during our visit to Evergreen was that his nickname was "Crack." At least, that was what everybody called him. "Crack" had an uncomfortable ring in my ear. I wondered silently how my father acquired such a nickname. I imagined that he might have gotten it from falling down drunk and hitting his head time and time and time again. Or maybe it was something else. I could have asked someone for the answer. But I did not want to know.

As we rolled farther and farther away from Evergreen, down a stretch of lonely highway, I was admiring the hills of red clay dirt, which I had never seen before. Mama asked if I wanted to take some back with me as a keepsake, something to remember my father by—red clay dirt. In my haze, I said yes. So my stepfather pulled off the highway to the side of the road. Net and I climbed out of the car and scooped up several handfuls in the Alabama sun. Then we resumed our journey home.

I sank into the white leather seat, having a greater sense of where I came from but no real sense of where I was going, and still many tears and years away from finding any resolution about John Wesley Fountain.

CHAPTER 18

INSUFFICIENT FUNDS

I RUSHED from building to building at the end of the spring semester, collecting my grades from professors and calculating my grade point average in my head. I needed to earn at least a 3.4 GPA (on a 5.0 scale) this time around to raise my disastrous first-semester grades to a C average in order to be completely off academic probation. I could have waited several weeks to receive my grade report in the mail and learn of my fate, but I could not have endured the suspense.

I could not have picked a worse time to be on academic probation. The previous few months were the worst in my life—being away from Robin and my son, being on academic probation combined with my lack of finances, despite a part-time job, and the death of my father. But I managed to keep my pact against party going. Some days, especially early on in that spring semester, I sat in my room crying and feeling sorry for myself, often too depressed to study. I wanted to quit school. But I could not. Something inside me would not let me quit. Whether it was my belief that without a college education I was doomed, or whether it was that graduating from college had always been my childhood dream, or something else, I did not know. What I did know was that giving up held severe, if not catastrophic, implications for my future. And that frightened me. So maybe it was fear.

But one day I simply decided to stop crying. At least, I decided that I could not substitute crying for studying. I told myself that no matter how difficult things seemed, no matter how bad I felt, I would feel a lot worse if I had not made the grades to be able to return to school in the fall. I let the painful thought of not being able to return to school drive me to study in much the same way I had psyched myself up to make the basketball team in high school by reminding myself what it felt like when I had not made the cut the previous year.

Despite my newfound commitment to studies, my social life did not suffer entirely. I still played plenty of basketball with the fellas. John and I still bounced pinball machines into the wee hours of the night some weekends. And I talked to a few girls on campus, though none of my conversations ever resulted in any serious relationships. The giant poster of my son, a picture that I had blown up and hung on the wall of my dorm room, as well as the pictures of Robin, didn't exactly help me with the ladies. Anyway, going to classes and working nights at Burger King occupied most of my time and kept me away from trouble, which had a way of sneaking up on you sometimes.

Working at Burger King put some funds in my pocket. I also no longer had to worry about a meal on Sundays, with my access to as many Whoppers and fries as I could eat. A number of university students worked at Burger King, including the older brother of one of my classmates, Zack. Zack's brother was a couple of years older. He was a short, brown-skinned dude whose nose was always running, so everyone thought he was heavily into drugs. One night as I was getting off work, he invited me to smoke a joint with him.

I occasionally got high, though it was always at other people's expense and at their invitation. During the fall semester, on some weekends, another black kid named Cornell, who lived on my dorm floor and whom I called Corn, got high with some white boys at the end of the hall while we played Risk, a board game in which the object is to conquer the world. The white boys had shoe boxes full of weed and hash. They were happy to share for the sake of a good time. And Corn and I were usually more than happy to oblige. We gurgled on a bong and passed joints like Indians smoking a peace pipe while we strategized and made pacts until finally someone had won the game and I stumbled, stoned, back to my room.

It used to amaze me how much reefer was around even back in high school. Mama warned me about marijuana use many times before I took my first puff, always insisting that it would only lead to a craving for more potent drugs. I believed Mama but succumbed to peer pressure and curiosity. I smoked my first joint with Arty and Michael while spending the night at their house one evening while we walked their dog, a black cocker spaniel named Blackie. After that first time, I couldn't figure out why people got high. I still felt rather ordinary, and sober, with no desire to giggle or act real smooth like the way I had seen other teenagers act after they had smoked a joint. That night I swore that smoking weed had no effect on me, but I later learned that I had not inhaled.

When it came to getting high, I had a rule against smoking weed in the daytime because I did not like the feeling of inebriation with so many hours of daylight to burn and so much to do. As much as getting high relaxed me and made me feel cool, or at least made me think I was cool, it also made me sluggish, both in mind and tongue, not to mention what it might have done to my brain cells.

As I got ready to leave work at Burger King that night, I said yes to the offer from Zack's brother. We lit up in the bathroom, fanning the smoke with our hands. Because I was trying to walk the straight and narrow and to be a more conscientious student, I took only one puff and headed home, carrying a bag with a few Double Whoppers with cheese for my homeboys.

I had walked only a block or two south on Fourth Street when I looked into the sky and caught glimpse of what appeared to be a shooting star. It startled me. I kept walking. Then suddenly I saw another, then another and another. Then just as suddenly, I started hearing the stars sailing through the sky. It was like something out of *Star Wars*. The sound of whizzing rockets filled my head. My heart beat fast. I knew something was wrong. So I picked up the pace.

As I walked, I looked to my right at a house that I was just about to pass. For some reason, I began to imagine myself walking up and down the stairs of the house. A few moments later, I awoke from a trancelike state only to find myself going up and down the stairs in a kind of bouncy motion like a bobble-head doll. It scared me to death. And suddenly, in a moment of clarity, I deduced that the joint from which I had inhaled only one puff was no ordinary joint but one that had likely been laced with PCP (called angel dust), which was said to be increasingly popular on campus at the time.

"Oh my God," I said to myself.

I started running. And I didn't stop running until I got to my dorm. Along the way, I had visions of the Devil trying to pluck my heart right out of my chest with charred fingers and razor-sharp fingernails, something I had seen in a horror flick once. I ran to my room, holding my chest. I shut the door behind me, hurled my bag of Whoppers across the room, dropped to my knees, and immediately began to pray.

"God please help me . . . Oh God, please take this away . . . I'll never get high again . . . I promise, Lord," I cried with my eyes shut tight. "Oh God, I'm sorry for all the things I've done . . . Save me, Lord. Help me, Lord. Please . . ."

After a while, I began to feel better and the effects of the high wore off, likely because I had taken only one puff. Eventually, I got up from my knees and lay across my bed, vowing to never get high again.

A few minutes later, there was a knock at the door. I climbed out of bed, staggered over, and twisted the doorknob. Standing there were two guys. To be precise, they were two tall and slender white guys whom I had never seen before in my life, dressed in shirts and ties. They said they were missionaries and asked if they could come in.

"Uh-h-h, no," I answered, half stunned. "I go to church."

They shared a Scripture. Then they walked away.

I shut the door, feeling as though I had seen two ghosts, though I knew that I was not still hallucinating.

★

Months later, as I loaded up the last of my things in my stepfather's car, a refreshing breath of spring hung in the air. I looked forward to going home, to seeing my son, now nine months old. I looked forward to working a summer job and to earning some cash. I looked forward to seeing Robin. I also felt proud. I had gotten every grade I needed and I was off academic probation! One year down, three to go.

As we drove away from Forbes Hall that May morning, I was beginning to feel as though college was where I belonged after all. And after a long and bittersweet first year, I was already dreaming of campus life and classes and my return to Champaign in the fall.

I had a pocketful of cash, money I had saved for books and incidentals. I worked at the notorious Cabrini-Green housing project that summer through the Mayor's Summer Youth Program, supervising youths who lived there. Working there gave me a deeper appreciation for K-Town and its relatively milder brand of poverty and despair compared to life at Cabrini.

Once during the summer, I had taken the teenagers I supervised to see a movie at a downtown theater, only to discover that many of them had never been downtown before, even though it was just a few blocks away, which seemed unbelievable. From the courtyard in the middle of Cabrini-Green, you could look up and see downtown skyscrapers surrounding the complex in the distance. There were no fences barring the residents of Cabrini from entering downtown, only the fences inside their heads. I suspect they were the same invisible barriers that kept many poor people around the city from straying too far outside their worlds into places where they felt they did not belong. The inhabitants were in effect prisoners. But their bondage first took up residence in their own minds. That was the lesson I would take with me from my summer job.

I was about to learn another, more painful, lesson. A few days before I was due back on campus, Mama called me into the living room as I was packing my things.

"I don't know how to tell you this," she began. "We don't have the money to pay your school bill." I still owed the university about $700 in tuition from the previous semester that I had to pay before registering for fall classes. Earlier in the summer, Mama had told me that she was going to take care of the bill and not to worry.

"I'm sorry, we just don't have it," she continued. Her words were slow. Her head was bowed, and her eyes drifted from mine to the floor. "It doesn't look like you're going to be able to go back to school."

"What?" I asked, feeling as if I had been slapped. "What do you mean? How about Grandmother and Grandpa? Did you ask them?"

"Yeah, I did."

"And?"

"They said they don't have it," Mama said.

"What about Aunt Clotee?"

"I asked her, too," Mama answered. "She said she doesn't have it either."

I began doing the calculations inside my head. Maybe I could use the money I saved from my summer job for books and incidentals, I thought. I still had one more check coming in two weeks that would be enough to tide me over until my job on campus kicked in. But how would I buy books? I had to buy books. After a few minutes, by my calculations, if I used what I could to pay my back tuition bill, I was still $300 short.

"Ma, all I need is $300," I said. "Do you think someone will let you borrow $300?"

"I don't know, John. I'll ask," Mama said.

I went to my bedroom, feeling stunned. I wondered why Mama had waited so long to tell me that she might not be able to pay the bill. If I had known, I would have saved more money or made payments on the bill myself. I suspected that Mama was probably too ashamed to tell me, and that time and money had simply run short. Seven hundred dollars was a lot of money, especially for a family with one foot in the welfare office and the other in the poorhouse, although I reasoned that it was not a lot of dough for my well-to-do relatives. I figured somebody would lend Mama a measly $300. I had seen preachers raise more than that with a quick pass of the collection plate. I figured that somebody in the family would come through. The thought eased my worries.

A short while later, Mama summoned me back to the living room.

"John, everybody I called said they don't have it," Mama said, her words ringing hollow. We went through the same litany.

"You asked Grandmother and Grandpa?"

"They said they don't have it."

"What about Aunt Clotee?" I asked.

"She said she doesn't have it," Mama answered sounding exhausted. "You can call her and ask if you'd like."

I called her. But she said she didn't have it. I suspected she did. I suspected that other family members had the money as well.

I have never understood why no one would loan Mama, or, for that matter, me, the money to return to school unless it was the case that Mama was plum borrowed out and considered a bad risk. Whatever the case, I could not comprehend the sudden lack of available financial resources in a family in which the majority were homeowners with decent-paying jobs. I always figured that they might have taken up a collection at True Vine for a needy young college student.

Slowly, the idea of not being able to go back to school began to settle in and filled me with great pain. In all the times I had dreamed of someday going to college, I had never considered that I would be unable to pay for it.

Years later, Robin told me that her father would have given me the money to go back to school, if I had asked, if he had known at the time that I needed such a paltry sum. I also learned later that I could have used part of the fall semester's financial aid to pay the remainder of my bill from the previous semester.

For weeks, I walked around dazed. Eventually, I found some sobriety and solace in understanding that the only person I could truly depend on was myself.

CHAPTER 19

BORN AGAIN

In the weeks after not returning to school in Champaign, I began reading the Bible. Actually, I started reading the Book of Revelation, which as a child had always frightened me with all that talk of beasts and signs and fire and brimstone. But I found a new appreciation for the end-times book of prophecy while visiting Robin one evening. I picked up the giant white Bible that sat on a coffee table in her family's living room and started reading. I began to see the Book of Revelation for what it was—a biblical foretelling of events to come. And strangely, I wasn't afraid to read it anymore. The more I read, the more I wanted to read. I could not put the Bible down. Within a day or two, as I continued to read the Bible, something strange and unusual seemed to be happening to me. But it wasn't in any hocus-pocus or extraterrestrial kind of a way. I began to feel more strongly about God and what I had been taught in Sunday School about his love for me and the plan of salvation through his son, Jesus Christ.

This was not exactly in character for a recalcitrant sinner like myself, who was still a bit skeptical about all the spiritual goings-on that I had witnessed at church for as far back as I could remember. Even when we had our annual monthlong revivals at True Vine, they came and went without me feeling so much as a buzz. As a kid, many times I had walked up front to the church's altar where the saints prayed over me and slobbered while waiting for the Lord to rain down His holy fire from heaven, only to return to my seat without feeling a spark.

In those times, I was always the last man standing, watching in amazement as my cousins Arty, Cheryl, and others caught fire and seemed to be consumed by the spirit. They went from clapping and yelling "Thank you, Jesus" to dancing and speaking in tongues to rolling around on the floor and being slain (knocked out cold) in the spirit. When they came to, they testified about how brand new they felt, but not me. The spirit and its manifestations always seemed to pass me by. I used to wonder why I had not been so touched. I figured that it probably had a lot to do with the fact that I often came to the altar to confess my sins and "invite Jesus into my heart" only because of peer pressure or some arm-twisting by the visiting, hell-spewing evangelist. Once the night's revival ended, I always arose the next morning with God being the least of the things on my carnal mind, no matter how strongly I had professed my commitment to turn from my sinful ways and walk in the way of holiness while standing before the saints the night before.

One night during my Bible-reading binge, I got down on my knees in the bathroom at home with the door closed. Kneeling over the bathtub, I said the Sinner's Prayer, which meant confessing aloud that I was a sinner and that I was sorry for all the wrong I had ever done. I asked God to forgive me for my sins.

"Jesus, come into my heart. I know you are the Son of God and that you died for my sins on the cross and that you rose from the dead. I am sorry for my sins, please forgive me. I want to live for you the rest of my life, Amen," I prayed.

I arose from the floor feeling no different than I had before I prayed. But I believed that God had heard me and saved me as His word promised: "If we confess our sins, he is faithful and just to forgive us our sins."

Robin wasn't unnerved at all by all my new Jesus talk. She was a believer, too, though not yet a convert. She attended a Baptist church but had accompanied me to True Vine numerous times. So she had been exposed to the tongue-talking, charismatic goings-on of sanctified folks. Besides, there was nothing that I did in my newfound love of the Gospel that remotely compared to the way my folks carried on at church, although my new religion did come with a major stipulation for our relationship. I told Robin that we could no longer have sex because that was considered fornication and that all I wanted to do now was to live for and love the Lord. She was shocked, to say the least, but entirely convinced of my sincerity and commitment to a new way of life.

During that time, I was attending Wilbur Wright College on the city's Northwest Side, where I had enrolled not long after my Champaign dreams had been shattered. Of all the Chicago City Colleges, Wright had the best reputation. That still did not lessen the shame of attending a City College, especially after having been deemed by my high school classmates as one of those most likely to succeed. City College was viewed pretty much as a court of last resort. If you couldn't get into anywhere else, the saying went, "you can always go to a City College." They took all comers. No questions asked.

I walked around in a fog for much of the semester at Wright, hoping as I caught the bus to school that none of my former high school classmates would see me and discover that I had sunk so far. Robin no longer attended high school. She had dropped out months earlier, while I was in Champaign. She had kept it a secret from me. I made the discovery that spring only while talking to her oldest brother, whom everyone knew as Junebay (as in June Baby). Junebay, who was at least ten years older, often sat up rocking our son at night while Robin slept so that she could go to school. Finally, the strain of single parenthood and working, or Robin's lack of interest in school, led her to stop going. After dropping out, she started working full-time at Burger King for a while, then at Montgomery Ward as a clerk. When I asked Robin why she had dropped out, she said that there was no one to watch our son and that she was tired of the struggle. When I asked her why she had kept it a secret from me, she said she was ashamed. I suspected that she also wanted to shield me from more strain.

Life at home for me was not good, either. Tensions between Mama and me reached epic proportions. At the heart of our strife was that Mama disapproved of my spending time with Robin. She also wanted me to stick around the house whenever I wasn't at school or work. She even insisted that if I was outside the house and wanted to walk to the store with my friends, that I tell her where I was going. At the time, it seemed like the equivalent of asking me to wear women's underpants. I resisted. Mama fought back. What Mama did not understand back then was that I needed more space to grow. What I did not understand was that Mama needed more time to let go. Unfortunately, we found neither, and neither of us was willing to yield.

Mama was convinced that Robin and her mother were trying to snag me before I became college educated and successful and met some other young lady somewhere down the road whom I wanted to marry. We had numerous fallings-out over the subject, the most memorable in the living room at home late that autumn.

"John, I just don't think you need to be spending so much time with Robin," Mama said. "You need to finish school and get out and live before you settle down.

"That woman sees you as a husband for her daughter, I'm telling you now. You better listen," Mama said, sounding like a broken record. "I've seen it happen so many times. I just don't want you to get trapped."

I couldn't see it.

"Ma, ain't nobody trapping me," I said. "You just don't like Robin."

"It's not that I don't like her, John. She's just so spoiled and selfish. She's no good for you," Mama said, almost seething. "You don't even know what to look for in a mate 'cause you don't even know who you are yet. And let me tell you, John, believe me, she's not the one."

As much as Mama knew how to wound with her cursing, she also knew how to get under my skin without ever uttering a single harsh word. And she was trying to get under my skin. At least that was how I perceived it, rather than seeing Mama as trying to save my life.

"Ma, Robin is my girlfriend. I love her. Can't you understand that?" I shot back. "I ain't no fool. We ain't going to get married anytime soon. I plan on finishing school," I said angrily. "Mannn!" I huffed.

Mama was relentless.

"Look, John, Robin is going to cause you a lot of pain," she said, sadly and sounding resigned. "Remember what I'm telling you. You'll see."

"Okay, Ma, what-e-verrr," I barked.

Mama looked so defeated. And I must have looked so smug.

Mama's protests always had the opposite effect. The more she pushed, the more I pulled. The more she insisted that I separate myself from Robin, the more I clung to her. I also soon left home again for the umpteenth time, living with Aunt Clotee for a while and then with my grandparents, though I continued spending a lot of time with Robin in between work and school. We also started talking about marriage.

Sitting on the sofa in Robin's living room talking about the Lord one evening in November, I had never been so excited, at least not about God. I fasted all that day, asking the Lord to save me and fill me with the Holy Ghost. It was just the two of us sitting there alone, which was a rare moment in her family's house. But on this night, her goo-gobs of nieces and nephews happened to be sitting in the kitchen, talking with the door that led to the living room closed. Her dad was at work and her mother had already gone to bed and had closed the door of her bedroom.

"I am just so happy to be saved. I know the Lord has a calling on my life. And all I want to do is to live for him," I said excitedly to Robin, who responded mostly with nods and smiles.

"I really love the Lord," I continued. "I know the Lord is going to fill me with the Holy Ghost. I am so happy. I have never felt like this before."

In that moment, suddenly, I felt a sensation. It felt like a gentle hand resting on top of my head. For a second I was afraid, unaware of what was happening to me. Then, suddenly a sense of warmth and love surrounded me. It seemed to be reassuring me, speaking to me, telling me not to be afraid. It is hard to explain. All I know is that I closed my eyes and yielded to it, to whatever it was. I believed it to be the Holy Spirit. And instantly I was fully enveloped with the greatest sense of joy and love I have ever known. It was as if time froze. With my eyes closed tight, I suddenly seemed to lose control of my tongue. Actually, I yielded. And before I knew anything, I blurted out some language that I had never heard, nor can recall to this day. Then in a moment, as quickly as it had happened, it was over.

I opened my eyes. And the joy that I had felt before that moment when I felt this power come over me seemed magnified to the tenth power. I was certain that God had filled me with his Holy Spirit. I didn't dance. Nor did I scream or run through the house, knock over chairs, and stand on top of the tables, all of which I had seen the saints do at church. But sitting there on the sofa next to my girlfriend, I felt invincible, so incredibly changed on the inside and filled up with such joy that I wanted to go out and tell everybody about Jesus. Robin cried. And we quietly rejoiced and praised God.

Later, my folks were startled to learn that I had supposedly gotten saved. What shocked them even more was hearing my claim that I had been filled with the Holy Ghost in Robin's house, especially since the saints hadn't been slobbering over me and calling on Jesus at True Vine when this all supposedly happened. It also did not work in my favor that I had a reputation as a bona fide fornicator.

For a long time, the saints at True Vine wondered whether I had fallen off the deep end, but in time they would come to see that I was every bit as saved and Jesus-loving as they were. But in the meantime, I too had doubts about my so-called conversion experience. I wondered if what had happened to me really was God's doing. Why hadn't He simply allowed His spirit to fall upon me while I was in a worship service at True Vine and spun me around while I spoke in tongues so that all the saints might bear witness? Why did he save me right then? Why there?

In time, I would understand why and would see that my conversion was one of the many things in my life that happened in the nick of time.

CHAPTER 20

WEDDING BELLS

ROBIN WALKED slowly down the aisle at True Vine that sunny Saturday in a powder-blue wedding gown and veil, her father by her side, wearing a brown polyester suit. I stood anxiously at the front of the sanctuary near the black baby grand piano. I wore a dark blue suit, white shirt, and blue silk tie. My cousin Michael, who was my best man, stood beside me. Across from Michael stood Robin's sister Diane, the maid of honor, holding an arrangement of white flowers. Grandpa stood nearby, everyone waiting for the bride to complete her walk down the aisle. I was nineteen, and my bride, seventeen.

Aunt Scope played "Here Comes the Bride" on the piano. I studied Robin as she approached, strolling past the faces of family, friends, and members of True Vine in attendance at our modest wedding ceremony. There were about 100 people in all, almost filling the church. Even through her blue veil, I could see Robin smiling, though she looked nervous. I had butterflies, too. But I was happy that this day had come.

Robin looked very pretty in her dress. It was unusually draping around her midsection, much like her prom dress had been. And just as it had been the case at prom, this dress was designed to conceal something,

although this time it was more a matter of good taste than fear of exposing any secret. Nearly everyone who gathered that day—March 22,
1980—to witness us join hands in holy matrimony knew that Robin was
five months pregnant. Apparently my conversion experience and decision
to become abstinent months earlier had not come soon enough to keep
Robin and me from creating our second child in less than two years, as
Mama had feared.

In truth, I never planned on this day coming so soon. Whether Robin
had planned it is a matter open for debate. But once she told me that she
was pregnant again, there was only one thing left for me to do. I wasn't
about to let Robin bring another child of mine into this world without
our being married. It wasn't just the child I was thinking about. I also
knew that if people looked at a woman shamefully for already having had
one child out of wedlock, they would have no mercy on such a
woman—or in Robin's case, a teenage girl—for having two. We should
never have been having sex in the first place. That much we both knew.
But the deed was done. And there was only one thing for me to do: the
right thing. That I loved Robin deeply only made my decision that much
easier.

I don't remember how I proposed, or if I ever proposed. As best I can
recall, it seemed to have been a mutual agreement that became more an
extension of our circumstance and love.

Ours was not a shotgun wedding. Robin's parents did not demand that
we get married. In fact, I don't remember them saying much of anything.
I'm sure they were disappointed, to say the least. But given the amount of
time Robin and I spent together, it is only a miracle that we did not have
more children.

One afternoon, months before our wedding day, I spoke to Robin's
parents about marrying their daughter. I can't imagine some knucklehead
Negro approaching me about marrying my seventeen-year-old daughter
or even having the gumption to come within a few hundred feet of my
house after having impregnated her once, not to mention twice. But with
the damage already done, I might react in much the way that Robin's parents did.

I told Robin's parents that I loved her and that I could not let her bring a second child into this world out of wedlock. I promised to work and to take care of their daughter. In the end, with little debate, her parents agreed to sign for her to marry since she was still underage by Illinois law.

Mama eased up on the idea of marriage once she learned that Robin was pregnant again, though she was still not as sold on the idea as my grandparents. That was understandable. My grandparents got hitched when they were barely pubescent and many years and a quiver full of grandkids later, they were still happily married. Mama got married at age sixteen and was long since divorced, remarried, and converted from romantic to realist. I was both a romantic and a pragmatist. I believed that love could conquer all. But I also realized that love would not pay the bills.

I found a decent-paying job at Bekins Van Lines as something called a rate-audit clerk. My job was to compute the salaries of drivers. I found out about the job through my cousins Doris and Cheryl, who had dropped out of school and were also working as lightweight auditors. I had dropped out of Wright months earlier. In fact, I skipped my final exams after I learned that Robin was pregnant, and my life seemed to be spiraling out of control. I had no illusions of the job at Bekins turning into some sort of career. It was just something to pay the bills.

In preparation for my new role as husband and provider, I also leased a one-bedroom apartment in a two-story building that Uncle Gene owned. The building was in the Austin neighborhood and only a few blocks from Robin's parents' home. We still didn't have furniture, but we figured on using whatever money we received as gifts at our wedding to buy something to sit on. Robin's parents promised us a bed, and we had a small rollaway bed for John-John, who was going on two by then. We were set.

As Robin walked down the aisle, tears welled up in my eyes. There were no bridesmaids. No flower girls. No ring bearer. Just the two of us, a best man, a maid of honor, a preacher, and a set of rings I picked up for under $20. Yet it all seemed perfect.

Soon Robin and I were holding hands before the altar at True Vine, every eye in the church fixed on us. We exchanged vows and prayers, then we kissed. We were married.

We took pictures that day. Years later, I was shocked by how much we looked like children. I know now that we had no business getting married, no business making babies or even having sex in the first place. We were high school sweethearts who rode the love roller-coaster to teenage parenthood like so many other teens we knew. The only difference was that we ended up getting married. But neither of us had any inkling of the responsibilities and the complexities of adult life, nor what we were really in for on the road that lay ahead.

Outside, on that sun-drenched Saturday, Uncle Gene drove us around for a spell in his big brown Cadillac, which he decorated with blue and white ribbon, honking all the way. We returned to True Vine, where we had a reception upstairs in the church's dining hall. Later that day, Robin's folks and mine held separate receptions at their homes, where they served liquor. Our parents probably needed a stiff drink or two.

Tired and worn, Robin and I hopped a ride to 704 North Waller Avenue, our new address. We could not afford a honeymoon.

We quickly undressed, too exhausted to talk, let alone do anything else. It wasn't long before we fell asleep, just the two of us, on our wedding night, on a pile of blankets on the floor.

CHAPTER 21

THE CLEAVERS

THE ALARM CLOCK rang early Monday morning, awakening me to life, love, and the real world. I showered, shaved, and dressed. Then I kissed Robin good-bye as I headed off to catch the bus to my nine-to-five, for the first time as a married man. As I walked out the door into the morning air, I was still trying to digest the idea that I officially had a wife and family. It was hard to believe that just a few days earlier, Robin and I lived in separate households, that not long ago we were only kids, or were still kids in some people's eyes. It seemed that adulthood had arrived with lightning speed, maybe even too soon. I still liked playing video games, eating Now & Laters, and chewing bubble gum. I even enjoyed watching a good cartoon now and then, playing alley ball until it was too dark outside to see the basketball anymore. Years later, it would seem as if my teenage years had whizzed by. It was as if one day I was in high school. The next day I met Robin. Then I graduated from high school, I got a job, we got married, and a couple days after our wedding, there I was on my way to work.

I still had a lot of kid in me when I got married. All that meant was that I had a lot of growing up to do in a hurry. My indoctrination to married life began with working eight-hour days and living for the weekend and for holidays, the way of life for most adults I knew.

Still, I relished marriage, especially the idea of being the breadwinning, dragon-slaying, way-making man. As I stepped aboard the Chicago Avenue bus that honeymoonless Monday morning, I was proud to be headed to my job as a rate-audit clerk at Bekins Van Lines in the west suburb of Hillside to earn a living for my family. But little did I know how little I knew.

At work, I sat at my desk most days, tapping a ten-key calculator as time crept by. I glanced up at the clock more times than I could count, only to discover that barely fifteen minutes had elapsed since I last looked. It wasn't long before I started thinking that this full-time work thing was a lot harder than it looked. I got two fifteen-minute breaks, one in the morning and one in the afternoon, plus an hour for lunch. I didn't smoke like almost everyone else, so I spent my breaks drinking pop before I returned to more hours of boredom, clock-watching, and despair over how much truck drivers made compared to my paltry, entry-level salary as one of the mostly black staff of audit clerks.

I quickly came to see how much office politics and gossip occupied people's minds and conversations. Women were the worst. Maybe it seemed that way because the vast majority of people in our department were women. Anyway, they were always talking about who was sleeping with whom and trying to find out who was getting promoted to what job. The few men who worked in the department didn't seem as preoccupied with shoptalk. But they were no less interested in trying to move up from coach to first class in the company. I quickly saw that there was no future for me there. What I had was a job, plain and simple. There were no illusions.

In fact, it wasn't long, maybe a few months, before I started to hate my job at Bekins. That did not keep me from being proficient on the calculator, fluttering over the keys with one hand while I flipped through pages of receipts. I was always good at math in school. So this number-crunching thing was a piece of cake. I ran the numbers and then ran them again, then sometimes once again, for good measure. Then I plucked another batch of papers from my endless pile, sometimes racing against the other audit clerks working in my department, although the race was mostly in my own mind.

One day, my supervisor called me into his office. He was a stout black man in his thirties who was actually my immediate supervisor's boss. I was worried by his sudden summons and wondered if maybe I wasn't about to be canned for being late a few times, though I had not received any previous warning.

"John," he said. "Come on in and sit down. I want to talk to you."

"Okay," I said, taking a seat in his cushy office.

"I've been going over your work, and I've also been watching you work, and I just wanted to ask you a few questions."

I swallowed hard.

"Tell me something, John, and I want you to be honest. You calculate the salaries of the drivers, you use the formulas that you're supposed to, and everything looks fine," he said, sitting behind his big desk. "But I bet you don't even know why you use those formulas, do you?"

"Uh-h-h . . ."

"It's okay, you can be honest. I've stood back and watched you. I bet you do this stuff without even thinking, don't you? Don't you?"

"U-h-h-h, yeah, I do. I mean, yes, I do."

"And you don't even care, do you? As long as you get it right? Is that true?"

"Yes, that's true," I said, half smiling.

"I knew it," he said laughing out loud, his shoulders shaking. "I knew it."

I didn't get what was so funny or even the point of the discussion. I am sure the expression on my face said as much. His laughing dissipated.

"John, I called you in here to talk because you are smart as heck," he said, starting up again. "You're smarter than anybody in that room. You do this stuff better than most of your coworkers and you don't even know why the heck you do what you do."

I sat quietly, not knowing whether to smile or to keep a straight face.

"John, the reason I wanted you to come into my office is to tell you that if you really applied yourself, there is a place for you in this company. There's nothing you won't be able to do, nothing. You hear what I'm saying?"

"Yes, I do," I said, perking up some as he waxed on about my potential future at Bekins.

"Thanks," I said finally, adding something like, "I'm really going to work harder" before I returned to my desk and more thoughtless auditing.

I didn't mean what I said. I only said what I thought he wanted to hear or perhaps what I thought to be the most courteous and respectful thing to say under the circumstances. Had I said what I really felt, I'm sure he would have fired me on the spot.

It didn't take me long to realize that I was in a crummy, dead-end job that I found about as interesting as a sermon in which any preacher went on longer than an hour. I wondered, too, what I had gotten myself into with this whole marriage business. As I rode the bus back and forth to work, and the workdays seemed to grow longer while weekends flew by, I couldn't help but think back on all the awards I had received throughout school and all the hopes I had had for my life and career. It was hard to accept where I was, which at work amounted to being surrounded by people for whom being a rate-audit clerk was their best option. In hindsight, I know that I looked down on my coworkers, though I should not have. I simply had difficulty coping with the growing realization that I was far from where I was supposed to be and had not even the faintest clue of how to get back on track.

I found comfort in my supervisor's pep talk, though not fully in the way he had intended. He gave me the hope that where I was at that point in my life was not necessarily my destiny. His words were like shock treatment to my dreams, which were already on life support and failing, while life at home seemed almost as shaky.

From the first day that I came home from work, any illusions about having a Ward Cleaver kind of household had been properly dispelled. When I arrived home that evening, I had expected a king's welcome after I had been out slaving all day. In the dream that existed in my mind, my wife stood at the door with my slippers in hand, the newspaper, and a pre-dinner cocktail. Well, not exactly. But the smell of garlic-fried chicken, spilling into the hallway, would have been nice, maybe the smell of meat loaf and cornbread. Instead I arrived to the smell of nothingness. There was not even the sound of water boiling on the kitchen stove. At first I thought that maybe my sense of smell was off as I wandered into the kitchen. Nope. There was nothing there, all right, not even a fried bologna sandwich.

Robin was there. That is, Robin and our son and her younger brother, Lamont. In the days that followed, her sisters or her little brother or someone else in her family were always there when I got home from work, which I soon found annoying. What bothered me even more was that Robin seemed to lack any domestic skills whatsoever. Figuring that it was the lack of skills that was more likely behind Robin's culinary inactivity rather than any unwillingness, I could more easily deal with my meal-less evenings. But on the other matter, I told Robin that her folks were already starting to wear out their welcome. I am sure that the less-than-cordial expression on my face when I came home from work did not hide my feelings. Eventually, they all got the hint.

On July 10, on a summer evening, I rushed Robin to Cook County Hospital. At 1:33 A.M., our second child was born—a boy who weighed six pounds, nine ounces. We named him Demetrius Rashad. Robin liked the name Demetrius. I liked Rashad, which is what we ended up calling him. Rashad was born at Cook County in Ward 51 because we had no medical insurance and Cook County was a free hospital. Robin had been covered under her father's health insurance for John-John's birth. Now we were on our own.

I was sitting in the waiting room when a nurse wheeled out my newborn son so that I could see him. He looked so tiny and precious lying there just minutes after having come into the world. He was light skinned with dark curly hair. And although I was already father to one son, seeing my second son lying in the translucent rolling crib made me feel as if I had become a father all over again. I loved that little dude as much as I loved my first son. Both held a special place in my heart, John-John for being my first and Rashad for being my second, as well as the first child I would carry from the hospital to my own home. This time, I would be there when he said his first words, when he crawled and took his first step, all things with which I had played hit and miss with John-John.

Being free was the only good thing about Cook County at the time. The County, as many people called it, had a reputation for long lines in the emergency room and for being grossly overcrowded and sometimes not very clean. When I finally got to see Robin, she was in a barracks-style room alongside several other women. The room felt like a barn, as if my wife was just one of the poor heifers there recuperating after having dropped her load. I hated Robin having to be at the County. But it was the best we could do. And at least it was free.

A few days after giving birth, Robin was discharged. But our baby had some sort of abdominal obstruction when he was born. The doctors wanted to keep him for what they said would be a few days of tests and observation. We felt empty leaving Rashad behind as we left the hospital that summer day. We both wondered whether we would ever get to bring him home, though neither of us dared speak a word of this to the other. Robin took leaving our baby behind especially hard. And though I was disturbed too, I tried not to let on.

"Awww girl, he'll be okay. He'll be home in no time," I said, trying hard to sound convincing.

I worried each day. Each day I found it hard to think. Each night I found it hard to sleep. Each morning, we called the hospital. And each morning, the answer was the same, "Maybe tomorrow." So each night we prayed.

The doctors never said exactly what was wrong with Rashad. In hindsight, there were a great many questions we should have been asking, so many answers that we should have been demanding. But we were simply too young to know any better.

Finally, more than a week after Robin had been released and after seeing her worried to the point of tears, I said I was going to the hospital, and that no matter what, they were going to give us our son. I marched in and angrily demanded to see the doctor. He said they had just completed their tests and that finally, we could take our baby home. We dressed our baby boy, then wrapped him in blankets and carried him home that day. He was a bundle of joy for the Fountain household, where joy sometimes seemed in short supply.

With two children, there was always plenty of housekeeping and chores to be done. Robin seemed allergic to housekeeping. And I found it easier to do it myself than to fuss and fight about it. Fact was, there was a part of me that really didn't mind doing it. And I figured that this simply went along with being a "good man." I wasn't sure what that term meant exactly, but I knew that it best encapsulated what I wanted to be.

The closest likeness of the man I wanted to be was Grandpa. Mama had often told me how Grandpa combed his daughters' hair when they were young and helped his wife with the chores, doing whatever was necessary in the kitchen, or otherwise, to raise their family. He did all of this apparently with no threat to the status of his manhood. For in most folks' eyes, Grandpa was always a man's man, without a doubt the embodiment of masculinity, a pragmatic black man who could bring home the bacon, fry it up in a pan, and protect his family to the fullest extent of his butt-kicking and shotgun-shooting ability. That was the kind of man I wanted to be. I decided to pattern myself after Grandpa. I drew what I could from my knowledge of my grandparents' relationship and their loving care for their family.

I liked my new role as husband and family man. I especially liked the idea of trying to be the kind of man to my family that I had wished as a child some man had been to my mother and her children.

As the man of the house, I arose bright and early on Saturday mornings to do laundry, usually while Robin was still asleep. I carried the pillowcases and laundry bags stuffed with dirty and soiled clothes on my back several blocks to the storefront laundromat near Chicago and Central Avenues. While the clothes churned, I read the *Sun-Times* amid the whir and rumble and tumble of washers and dryers. Eventually, I loaded the clothes into dryers. As they dried, I folded all our T-shirts, diapers and socks, panties and shorts, jeans and towels until everything was done. Then I carried the clothes clean and fresh back home and put them away.

John's unofficial School of Culinary Arts and Good Housekeeping opened soon after marriage, with me acting as head chef and instructor and Robin as the only student, though she was seldom an eager participant. I set about trying to teach Robin to cut up and fry a chicken, to make hot-water cornbread, to sort clothes, mop and clean, grease a baby's bottom, all of the things that Mama had taught me and that I had once insisted that my wife would do someday.

"You have to put your hand inside the commode with the rag to really get at the grime and grit," I instructed on cleaning the toilet the way Aunt Mary had shown me.

"Put a little bleach in your dishwater."

"Put a little pine cleaner in your mop water."

Such were my instructions as I gave demonstrations.

I didn't mind teaching Robin. But my hands-on instruction made me seem more like a father than a husband, and Robin resented and resisted me. I tried talking less and doing more. Except the more I did, the less there was for Robin to do. So the less she did.

Sometimes, in the heat of argument, Robin made it clear, in all the sassy, neck-twisting pomposity of a fed-up black woman, that she was not about to accept the role of cook, housecleaner, laundress, nanny, or domestic servant.

"You ain't my daddy! You don't tell me what to do," she said for the purpose of reminding me, in case I had forgotten.

Years later, I understood clearly what I could not see then. That Robin and I were on totally different pages about marriage and that we were both so young and unprepared that even if we had a how-to manual, we would still have been sinking in troubled water. Aside from our youth and immaturity, I was operating from some Cleaver family concept of marriage. In actuality, we were more like the Little Rascals playing house. And unfortunately, no matter how mature and responsible I thought myself to be, I was ill prepared for the rigors of work and being father, husband, provider, lover, counselor, finance director, teacher, cook, cleaner, and disciplinarian. It wasn't long before I started having chest spasms and Mama's warnings about Robin seemed to be coming back to haunt me. In my anguish, I thought about divorce. I even talked about divorce. So did Robin, who let me know almost from day one that she could always go back home.

"You ain't doing nothing for me that my daddy can't do for me," she yelled.

"Well, go on back to your daddy, then!" I shouted back, trying to hide the sting.

I surely know that we would not have made it through that first year of marriage had it not been for the prayers of my grandparents, and at times, their insistence that I remain with the woman I was so intent on marrying.

"Nobody could keep y'all apart," Grandpa scolded one day when they came to our apartment to counsel us. "Now y'all act like you don't want to be together."

"Y'all might as well go ahead and stay together," Grandpa continued, his words harsh. "Don't nobody want either one of you, don't nobody want either one of you!"

Grandmother played good cop.

"Might as well go ahead and settle on in," she said, her voice soothing. "Ain't neither one of you going nowhere. Just hang on in there, baby dolls. Might as well settle on in."

Grandmother and Grandpa did a lot of praying for us that first year. Robin and I decided to stick it out.

We figured it could only get better. Little did we know it would only get worse.

I walked into the crowded storefront office on North Laramie Avenue, carrying a yellow envelope stuffed with papers and the weight of the world on my shoulders. I was crying on the inside and cringing on the outside. I didn't want to be there. But my wife and kids had to eat. I no longer had a job and not even any good prospects were lined up. I had to do something to ensure there was at least food on the table.

"May I help you?" the woman at the desk asked.

"Yes, uh-h-h, I'd like to apply for welfare," I answered.

"Take a number and wait for your name to be called," she said.

I walked away with my eyes angled toward the floor, finding a seat among the swarm of other welfare recipients and applicants.

After less than a year of work at Bekins, I had grown frustrated with its mundane routine, and one day I simply stopped going, not having the good sense to keep working until I found another job. I immediately began looking for another job. I looked and looked and looked. But days turned into weeks, and weeks into a month or so of borrowing to meet ends. With relatively no savings, we quickly borrowed ourselves into debt.

Initially, Robin came up with the idea of going down to the Public Aid office and applying for welfare. But I figured that being the man of the house meant taking all the responsibility on my shoulders. If somebody had to go down there, I figured that it should be me. So with babies to feed, I took a deep breath, gathered up all the necessary documentation, then trudged down to the "aid office" as we all called it. It's funny that in all of my years, I have never heard anyone refer to the trip to the welfare office as going "up." The word was down, always down.

The idea of signing up for welfare troubled me. It wasn't the idea of welfare itself that I hated so much, only the idea of me being on welfare. I remembered the ridicule I had gotten from kids in my neighborhood when they caught me spending food stamps at the store. In fact, any kid seen in the store with food stamps quickly became a target of merciless teasing. Food stamps were seen as evidence that you were poor and not just ordinarily poor, but part of the lowest class of folks, so po' that they needed the government to feed them. In fact, everyone joked that the acronym AFDC—Aid to Families with Dependent Children, the fancy name for welfare—stood for "AFter Dad Cut out." That actually wasn't far from the truth.

As a child, I vowed that my children would never know the shame of welfare. Yet there I was at the aid office with the likes of drug addicts and transvestites, and the whole platter of poor folks waiting for hours on end to apply for government assistance. As much as I may have been in denial, I was one of them. And I figured that we were all likely to end up staring across a desk at some crabby old caseworker who believed that all of us were trifling Negroes who were trying to milk the system. I was only trying to keep my family fed until I could find something better. Mama had encouraged me to look at applying for welfare that way, which turned out to be a lot more difficult than it sounded.

At the aid office that day, I applied for emergency food stamps, for a medical card, and for monetary benefits for the four of us. Even though it felt like I was doing the right thing, the only thing at that point, it also felt as if I was being stripped of every ounce of manhood.

The food stamps were issued almost immediately. But we would have to wait six to eight weeks to get any money, providing there were no glitches, the caseworker said. We had to survive until then.

Money was so tight that I could not even afford to buy a key chain for my house key, which I kept on a strip of hard wire that I twisted at the end. Robin stopped going to the beauty shop and instead started giving herself a permanent from the store-bought hair kits. The baby always seemed to need milk and Pampers, and the rent man was knocking at our door. Thank God, the rent man was my uncle.

Christmas that first year fell on a depressingly broke Thursday morning. We were receiving help from Public Aid by then, about $350 a month, plus about $200 in food stamps. It was enough to cover the bills and fill our cupboards. We managed to buy a few toys for our two sons with help from our parents, but little else. I wished that I could buy something for my wife, maybe a coat or some shoes, something. But on Christmas Eve, we were down to $10 between us.

Robin and I decided to take $5 apiece to buy each other a gift. I scoured the aisles of the nearby Walgreen's on Chicago and Central

Avenues before finally coming up with a gift for Robin that I was almost too ashamed to give to her as a Christmas present.

Early Christmas morning, after we had set out the toys for the boys in our living room underneath the tree, I handed Robin my gift-wrapped box. Then Robin, with much the same sheepish, half-ashamed face that I was wearing, handed me a tiny box.

"You go first," Robin said.

"No, you go first," I insisted.

"No, you go first."

I peeled off the paper and opened my box. Then I cracked up laughing.

"Now open yours," I insisted, trying to stop laughing.

Robin stripped off the gift wrapping, then bowled over laughing.

Robin had given me a golden key chain and I had bought her a box of do-it-yourself permanent. We both laughed, at ourselves, at our poverty, at the meager gifts we had given each other. We laughed, hugged, and cried. And we found solace in our belief that next Christmas would be different.

While receiving our monthly welfare check, I kept looking for a job. On Sunday nights, I scoured the Sunday *Tribune* and the *Sun-Times* for ads. I initially started off searching for anything that was auditing or accounting related because I had some work experience in that area. I also figured that my year of college at the University of Illinois, plus a high school diploma from a Catholic school as well as all of my awards, both academic and otherwise that were displayed prominently on my résumé would count for something. But I quickly discovered that most employers seeking people in their accounting departments were looking for people with degrees.

I soon modified my job hunt. I began looking under the "clerk" heading in the classifieds. I circled any prospects and laid my clothes out—a crisp white shirt, pants, and a tie—before going to bed on Sunday night. I also buffed my shoes into a hot shine.

When I awoke on Monday mornings, I climbed out of bed, got dressed, and scooped up my satchel, which contained my search list and pile of résumés. Then I hit the streets, catching the bus to as many prospective employers as I could visit in a single day.

While I hunted, Robin stayed at home with the boys. She might have looked for a job, too. But we figured that if I was having such a hard time finding a job, she wasn't likely to find any job worth anything without a high school diploma. So she waited at home for my return, hoping and praying for good news.

So many days, I arrived at the doorsteps of prospective employers bright and early, only to be told they had already filled that vacancy. "Man," I thought. "They sure filled that position overnight."

Every time a door was slammed, every time I was turned away, every time I came home without a job, I internalized the way I thought people perceived me. And that amounted to being just another poor dumb nigger for whom there was no place in a white man's company. What also became clear was that if rudeness and having doors slammed in my face was what I encountered as a brother who spoke the King's English and who had some experience in maneuvering in the white man's world, a brother fresh out of prison didn't stand half a chance and even less than that without a high school diploma.

It didn't take long before this all began to take an emotional and mental toll. My head soon swirled from self-doubt. I lost confidence and began to wonder if it was me or them. Or was it the system, controlled by that infamous white man who was said to be always trying to keep a brother down?

I didn't know. I only knew that I could not find a job. It didn't help that the economy was slumping. But I figured that if my face had been white or if I had been looking for something more suitable for a black man without a college degree, like a janitorial position, or something mindless, I would probably have had fewer problems landing a job.

I kept looking and eventually expanded my job search to include any entry-level position with benefits. I took Civil Service exams. I was on the waiting list at the U.S. Postal Service and had been turned away by prospective employers at personnel offices more times than I could count. Once, I stood outside all night warming my hands over a flame in a garbage barrel to put in an application at a new company. The call for an interview never came. But for weeks, the stench of the fire and smoke by which I had warmed my hands over the garbage barrel that night lingered in my clothes and on my skin, no matter how many times I tried to wash it off.

Before long, each day that began with anticipation and hope ended tearfully and wet with despair as I made the journey home a little more broken. Sometimes I could not make it home before the tears would start to fall. Sometimes I wiped them away as I sat at the back of the bus, staring out of the window. Sometimes Robin and I cried together.

I found solace in prayer and a Gospel song that seemed to ring inside my head whenever I was most despondent, "Never Alone." Such was my comfort as I walked into the storefront bank on Chicago Avenue near Laramie Avenue after hearing through a friend of Robin's who worked there that they were seeking to hire new tellers. I was spiffily dressed as usual, tie straight and dimpled in the middle, shoes shined.

I filled out the application and turned it in with my résumé, which was usually about the point at which the prospective employer basically said, "Don't call us, we'll call you." But to my surprise this time, a bank manager, a middle-aged white man, invited me to sit down at a desk. I sat there, chin up and back straight, watching as he perused my résumé. He nodded and smiled as he gave my credentials a good looking over. I could tell he was impressed. Finally, someone was impressed.

"So I see you're seeking a job as a teller," the bank manager said.

"Yes," I replied.

"We do have a position open, and from what I see, you're certainly qualified," he said taking in my clean-cut, white-shirt-and-tie appeal.

A job, at last, I thought. Yes! Yes!

Then it happened.

"What are you doing here?" he asked, looking at me strangely.

A job, you big dummy, I thought to myself. What do you think?

"You should be in college," the bank manager said.

I should have been. I searched for words to explain but found none.

"I could give you a job," the man said, bearing not even the slightest hint of animosity in his voice. "But I think if I did, I'd be doing you a disservice. You're better than this. This job is a dead end. You have something special."

I walked out of the bank and trudged back to my apartment and unemployment, feeling like kicking the bank manager. Some years later, I would feel like kissing him. But by then, the bank had closed and been replaced by a liquor store.

CHAPTER 22

BACK ON THE BLOCK

BY THE SPRING OF 1981, we were feeling cramped in the small, one-bedroom apartment in Austin. Rashad, a bubbly little baby, was crawling and beginning to take his first steps. John-John, a smiley kid with long skinny legs and a quiet disposition, was growing more active and wanting to play outside more. We soon discovered that the apartment building we lived in was not exactly conducive to family living. There were a total of eight units in the building. The apartments were more like small condominiums. They were great little places for singles or a married couple with no children, but not for a growing family.

The building had no backyard, or even any space where our boys could play out front. Outside the door of the building's entrance, the narrow sidewalk was barely wide enough for pedestrian traffic. There was not room enough for us to stand outside with our children or to sit and simply to take in a cool breeze and the sunshine rather than be holed up inside our apartment when the warm weather finally returned. The nearest park was too far away to walk to and we had no car. We weren't exactly park-going types, anyway. Some of the city's parks had developed a reputation as places where gangs hung out, along with young men with too much liquor to drink and too much weed to smoke as well as too much time on their hands. It all made the idea of taking your family to the park too dangerous. We definitely needed a bigger place—some place with a backyard where the boys could play and we could feel less constricted. But I had little money, no real credit history, and still no job.

I don't remember how the idea was first hatched or from whom it sprang. I do know that Grandmother and Mama conspired to convince me to move my family back to Komensky. I do not mean that they conspired in a bad way. Only in that way in which mothers and grandmothers, who, in their worry and private discussions about you and your well-being, always figure out what is best for your life, then make suggestions to you, whether you care to hear them or not.

I had all but forgotten about the Compound on Komensky. Although my mother was the only member of the family who still lived there, the other apartments had since all been rented to nonrelatives. The new tenants were not necessarily even close friends of the family, just tenants.

Grandmother said that one of the apartments would be coming open soon, that they were evicting some tenants largely because it had become well known on the block that these folks, who lived on the second floor at 1654, had been dealing drugs out of the apartment. If I wanted the place, Grandmother said, I could have it.

That apartment was the same spacious place where Aunt Scope had lived when I was a little boy, where Aunt Clotee later lived when Mama, Net, and I lived on the third floor. It had a huge eat-in kitchen, a sizable living room, and even a back porch. There was a backyard and a front yard, too, although, as I last remembered, the lawn was almost completely bald. Moving to Komensky would also put us only seven blocks from True Vine, where I was beginning to spend more and more of my time. It didn't hurt that Net was still living at home with Mama at the time. Since Net and Robin were friends, I figured that if we moved to Komensky, having Net nearby would help make Robin's transition easier in that she would already have one friend on the block. The rent was $150 without utilities. Although it had been years since I last saw the apartment that Grandmother and Mama thought to be the perfect little place for my family, I sensed that it would need a lot of work. I also knew that if I wanted it to be exactly the way I wanted, I would have to do much of that work myself. For $150, and to have my grandparents as landlords, the apartment on Komensky seemed like an option worth considering. But I had a ton of reservations.

For starters, the Promised Land was by then a tarnished land. Vacant lots and crumbling buildings that dotted the landscape of K-Town symbolized the decay and ash from the night of fires in 1968. That an openly public dope house had even existed on the 1600 block of South Komensky Avenue reflected in itself a kind of infection of the moral fiber of a place that may always have been poor but whose inhabitants never seemed so destitute that they would accept whatever evils life and man dredged up.

Growing up there had been tough enough. Thoughts of my own sons having to grow up in K-Town unnerved me. I imagined them having to fight their way through school or having to dumb themselves down to avoid getting bloody noses. Mostly, I feared for their lives amid the growing menaces of gangs and drugs and a mounting body count of young black men and boys. As much as the idea of returning to K-Town worried me, it was incomparable to Robin's reaction when I first mentioned it.

"No way, uh-uh, I'm not moving over there. Are you crazy? Why would we move to Komensky? You barely made it outta there," Robin said, looking at me as if I had lost my mind or as if I had asked her to jump off a twelve-story building. Actually, that might have sounded more reasonable.

"No way . . . I'm not moving over there. It's too bad, uh-uh, I ain't going," Robin barked. "Go by yourself!"

She went on and on and on.

"It ain't like Austin is that much better," I said finally, feeling defensive. "Y'all got more drugs over here than we ever had. I really don't think it would be that bad," I argued. "The boys would have a yard, they could go outside and play, we could sit on the porch . . ."

"You go! Shhhh, nigger, you must be crazy if you think me and my sons gon' move over there," Robin protested. "You must be outta yo' cotton-picking mind. I didn't live there before you married me. Why would I move there now? It's too dangerous. No way, uh-uh."

We argued some more. Mostly, I warred against myself. Robin's concerns were legitimate. But we desperately needed to find a bigger place to live and we weren't exactly brimming with possibilities. Even with all of its drawbacks, the idea of living on Komensky held the promise of a lot more mobility and freedom for us than did living in a multiunit apartment building where we hardly knew anyone and there was no yard where our kids could play.

In the days that followed, I began to pray about it, meaning that I got on my knees numerous times and asked God what I should do. At the same time, I also continued to ask God for a larger place for my family to live. I even made my inquiries of God when I wasn't on my knees, my prayers silently resonating in my mind throughout the day.

Then finally, one day I thought I heard from God, though I could not be certain. There was no audible voice. Only a kind of peace that seemed to surround me and fill me up, even though cognitively there were more reasons to stay as far away from K-Town as possible than to return. In time, I told Robin that I thought that moving to Komensky was what I believed would be best for our family, that if we stayed on Waller Avenue we would not be in a position to move forward. What I also understood, even then, was that to move forward you sometimes had to go back.

I asked Robin to trust me. She cried in protest. But I had made up my mind and finally put my foot down. That was that. We were moving, although my insistence probably did little to help squelch Robin's perception of me as a tyrannical, insensitive brute of a husband. Eventually, Robin gave in to my insistence to move to Komensky. At least we stopped arguing about it. I suspected that probably had more to do with her knowing that once I had made up my mind, she had no option other than to go back home to her parents as a single mother with two babies.

But knowing that we would soon be moving to Komensky was no cause for celebration. In fact, I was even more afraid, convinced that if something bad happened once we got there, I would always be the one to blame. And yet, as I prepared to lead the covered wagon back to Dodge City, I could not afford to show how concerned I was, for the sake of the women and children.

★

The hallway was dark and dingy even in the middle of the day. As I entered, I was socked by a foul odor that saturated the hall. It was the mix of stale vomit, cheap perfume, and the faintest hint of pine cleaner that seemed to be trying unsuccessfully to mask the smell of something dead. I accepted Grandmother's offer of renting the second-floor apartment at 1654 South Komensky Avenue. It was a binding contract between relatives sealed with a "yes." There was no lease to sign and no need really for me to have seen the place beforehand. In a sense, I knew what I was getting and was completely aware that I would have to do some work on the apartment before I could even think about moving my family in. Just how much work it would need was the question.

Normally, the landlord handles repairs and such. But since the rent was so cheap and my landlords were my grandparents, and because I wanted to make sure everything was perfect before I moved my family in, the burden of whipping the apartment into shape was mine. I figured I would have to paint and clean, throw out garbage the old tenants had left behind, and patch up a few holes in the walls. Grandmother forewarned me that the previous tenants had damaged the apartment some upon their departure. But how bad could it be?

As we walked up the stairs to the apartment, I began to wonder whether I had not made a mistake. The hall walls were cracked and strewn with cobwebs. They looked as if they had not been painted for many years. Dust was everywhere, on the stairs, windows, and walls. The hall seemed strangely unfamiliar, though I must have run up and down its stairs a thousand times as a child. Finally, Grandmother stuck the key in the lock, but not before bracing me for the shock.

"It's going to need some work," Grandmother said in that cheery tone that always precedes bad news. "Just a little work, and it'll be all right."

My jaw dropped as I scanned the apartment. The decrepit linoleum floor in the kitchen was torn out in patches. The kitchen walls, which appeared at one time to have been yellow, had turned filthy black, or were they brown? The bathroom was a dark hole. The living room was just as dark, the walls covered with 1960s pastel wallpaper that had long since faded and the floor with a stained nasty carpet that looked as if it should have been yanked up and thrown out long ago. It was hard to see how anyone had lived here under these conditions or to believe that the previous tenants had been the bona fide, high-rolling drug dealers the whole neighborhood had thought them to be. If they had so much money, why would they have lived like this? Why would anybody have lived like this? Even my grandparents had been stunned by the apartment's condition after it was vacated. Although the rental offer Grandmother made had seemed reasonable at the time, after seeing the condition the apartment was in, to pay even $150 a month rent seemed $149 too much.

"Oh God. Mannn, I can't believe this," I said. "Grandmother, this place is terrible. Those folks should be ashamed. They tore this apartment up. Look at this," I said moving from room to room and pointing out one thing after another. "Look at that," I sighed.

There were mouse and rat droppings on the pantry shelves, roaches crawling out of the woodwork. The toilet was caked with grime and dirt so that the inside of the bowl looked like molten lava. The bathtub was just as bad. The master bedroom bore the same long-outdated wallpaper as the living room walls. The kitchen's built-in china cabinet was embedded with dirt and badly stained. The glass in its doors as well as the handles of its drawers was missing. The kitchen sink cabinet was yellowed and rusted. The whole apartment smelled as stale as a musty sneaker mixed with a septic tank and a rotting dead mouse or two.

"Grandmother, I can't bring my family up in here," I said, tears welling up in my eyes.

"It'll be all right, baby darling, you'll see," Grandmother said, sounding like the eternal optimist. "Awww yeah. It'll be all-ll-ll right."

"Grandmother, look at this. There ain't nothing we can do with this place," I said, looking around and shaking my head in disbelief and starting to get upset with Grandmother, who seemed to not be standing in the same apartment as I was.

"You'll see," Grandmother insisted. "A little paint and bleach and some disinfectant will work wonders. Awww yeah, this is going to be a real nice place for your family, John Wesley, believe what I tell you, now."

"I can't see it, Grandmother," I said. "I can't see it."

"Believe what I say, child," Grandmother encouraged. "Grandmother wouldn't tell you nothing wrong."

"I hear you, Grandmother, but I sure can't see it," I said. "This place is terrible."

Grandmother promised that day that she would work with me until we had transformed this rat's den into a habitable home. I was not a believer. But there seemed little else to do except to get started.

For weeks, I rode the bus from our apartment on Waller to Komensky. Grandmother and I had already transported pails, a mop, rags, and other cleaning materials to the apartment. We began by mopping and cleaning—deep-down sanctifying cleaning—throwing trash out, sterilizing and disinfecting the china cabinet, the sink drawers, and all the floors. I must have mopped the floors a dozen times, trying to extract the funk. I donned rubber gloves and scrubbed the toilet, the sinks, and bathtub with steel wool and kitchen cleanser. The stench and grime almost made me puke. I poured a concoction of ammonia, bleach, and other cleaners—a gaseous combination that made my nose and eyes run—into the toilet one night so that it would loosen up the deposits. But cleaning the toilet, especially, that toilet, filled with someone else's years of grime and only God knows what else, was still a nasty proposition. I cursed silently, wondering over and over again how anybody could be as nasty as the folks who had lived in this joint. I gagged several times as the grime slowly washed away, giving way to sparkling white porcelain.

I washed the windows, removing layer after layer of dirt until the sun splashed on walls I was certain hadn't seen the light of day for many years. There were holes in the walls, some of them ulcerous cavities where pictures once hung. Grandmother told me not to worry about trying to fix the walls. Elder Campbell, a short, frail elderly man who had been their pastor at All Nations Church of God in Christ, did drywall work and other house repairs on the side, and he was going to patch up the walls and in some cases hang new drywall. Grandmother also said that Aunt Mary's husband, Elder Riddly, would do some of the painting. I had not done much painting and had never sealed holes in walls or hung drywall. So the notion of someone else handling these duties suited me just fine. There was still plenty of work for me to do. Not the least of my tasks was to get rid of any rodents so that my sons and wife would not have to worry about a mouse scurrying across their feet.

I set about carefully going room by room, examining the apartment's floors and baseboards, looking for holes where mice or rats had made tunnels. I removed the drawers from the kitchen buffet and scanned for holes with a flashlight. As a child, I had discovered that mice could squeeze through the smallest of holes. I disconnected the kitchen sink from the water supply and drainage pipes and pulled it out of its place in my search for vermin holes. I shone my flashlight behind the toilet, scouring the walls behind doors and every inch of the apartment. Wherever I found holes, I filled each with a batch of poisoned bread. I don't know exactly what this clear liquid poison was that my uncle gave me to use to kill mice and rats. But I knew it was said to work wonders and also to embalm rodents so that I did not have to worry about smelling them if they lay in the walls and died once my venom had run its course.

I must have laced an entire loaf of white bread with the poison. After filling each hole with a good portion, I stuffed coarse-grade steel wool into the holes. My stepfather told me that the steel wool or crushed glass would have the same effect. Any rats or mice that tried to enter the apartment again by trying to eat their way through my fortifications would be butchered and bloody. Finally, I sealed up every hole with wood putty, or, in some cases, laid new baseboard or quarter round. Still, my task was not done. I had learned that the likelihood of an apartment being besieged by rodents was greatest during late fall at the first sign of cold. That's when mice and rats sought a warm refuge from the Chicago cold. I wanted to cut them off at the pass. In other words, I wanted to make sure that they encountered plenty of poison once they managed to get into the building and long before they had made it to my last line of defense.

On the back porch of the first floor, which at the time was occupied by a woman named Hattie and her young son and daughter, I littered the cubbyhole underneath the building with poison. For it was in the cubbyhole that I imagined all the rodents assembled at some point after gaining entry through the various cracks at the base of the building for their marching orders. With the perimeter secured, I baited the outdoor garbage cans, both inside and around them. Alongside the building, in every visible hole, I dropped a batch of my poison. My aim was to kill every rodent, to create essentially a rat-free zone around my apartment building, even if I could not save everyone else's house in the neighborhood. Rodent abatement was really the city's job. But the green poison pellets the city workers had occasionally left near garbage cans to kill neighborhood mice and rats seemed more like little candy treats for rodents than anything else. At least they did not work to any noticeable effect.

My deathtrap worked. A couple of days after dropping my poison, I returned to Komensky to search for results. In the backyard and around the house and alley lay mice and rats that would soon be joined by some unintended victims. A few days later, there were dead squirrels, birds, a stray dog, all manner of fowl and beasts that lay dead or dying. Witnessing the carnage, I was half afraid that my poison had killed just about everything in the neighborhood. Truth is, it would not have bothered me if every dog, bird, or any other four-legged creature had eaten my poison bread if that was what it took to keep my family from having to live with mice and rats.

The next step was to get rid of the roaches. There were plenty of them, although my grandparents had had the apartment exterminated several times in recent years. That there were still goo-gobs of roaches was no surprise. In fact, I was convinced that so-called neighborhood exterminators were in cahoots with roaches. The exterminators often watered down their poison juice so that the roaches would disperse, retreating to a safe distance inside the walls until the smoke had cleared, and the job would seem well done. A few days later, they returned, free to roam, the extermination man long gone, but well paid, and the roaches wreaking havoc once again.

When I was a child, the exterminator, usually a smiley, little dark-skinned man named Mr. Petty, would show up with his little backpack and shower the place with roach juice. The roaches dropped like flies for a day or two and the pungent odor of the poison lingered so that everyone smelled it in your clothes when you walked into a public place. Slowly but surely them bad fellas would start creeping around again, then multiplying before you knew it, until finally it seemed as if they held a full-blown dance party whenever the lights in our apartment were turned out. As a roach-conscious teenager, I learned to shake out my coat and book bag before walking out the door on my way to school to avoid transporting any of them to my own embarrassment as they suddenly crawled out in public. As much as I hated rats and mice, I also despised roaches. I was like my Aunt Mary when it came to roaches, or "roy-ches," as she called them.

"Kill that roych, kill that roych!" Aunt Mary yelled whenever she had spotted one in her house, and she always swore one of the kids she baby-sat had brought it in.

I knew that I could not live with royches.

Robin's father had a professional exterminator's can, which I borrowed, then went to a neighborhood pest control store and bought my own juice. There would be no dilution on my part, despite the warning on the label. Since we had not moved in yet and I did not have to worry about the chemicals affecting anyone except me, I filled the gold-colored can with poison without adding the water that the instructions called for. I drenched the walls, floors, and halls. Poison ran like a waterfall. I even went to the other two apartments in the building and sprayed them. The infestation of roaches in an apartment building is communal. If one apartment had them, it would not be long before they all had them. My poison worked like magic. The roaches disappeared. *Presto!*

I went to work on the aesthetics, removing what seemed like centuries-old wallpaper. Elder Campbell fixed the walls, although one day while working alone at the apartment building, he was jumped by a mugger and knocked to the ground. As the old preacher later told it, the mugger was atop him with a screwdriver when the preacher, fearing the worst, began chiding his attacker in the way that the saints rebuked the Devil on Sunday mornings.

"Loose here, Sa-tan," he ordered the mugger in groveling tones.

The would-be mugger dropped the screwdriver and ran like the devil, giving Elder Campbell one more praise report in his testimony about the goodness of the Lord.

Elder Riddly then came in to do some of the painting. He painted the walls of the living room and front bedroom a light shade of gold and the ceilings white. But his job was done after that. The rest was up to me. Several friends and relatives had volunteered to help me out whenever I needed them. But when the time finally came, they were nowhere to be found. I sat around, stewing some and feeling sorry for myself, wondering how I was going to do all of that work. After a while, it occurred to me that I might as well get started, or the work might never get done.

I spray painted the kitchen-sink cabinet bright white. When it came time to paint the rest of the house, I drenched the kitchen walls in a white semigloss, painting the bottom third of the walls a soft peach. The walls drank the first couple of coats of paint but eventually shone so brightly that they seemed to smile. Slowly, the apartment began to metamorphose and the pall that had captivated it when I first laid eyes on it began to lift. Robin helped some. But mostly, Grandmother and I did the work.

Early into the renovations, when I was left alone working in the apartment by myself, I sometimes cried, feeling as if the apartment might never come together. I felt like I was in way over my head and that God was probably standing back with his arms folded, watching me struggle in all my despair. It was in times like these that peculiar things sometimes happened, things that I always attributed to being more than just simple luck and coincidence and more like the hand of God.

One day, as we neared completion after more than a month of repairs, we were out of money. I needed more paint and wanted to buy new linoleum to replace the torn, ragged kitchen floor. All the fixing had cost my grandparents plenty more than they had planned to spend. My picky demands had already overburdened them and depleted their funds for renovation and repairs. And while Grandmother sympathized, she said she simply did not have the money to buy a new covering for the kitchen floor.

The kitchen linoleum was on my mind when Aunt Mary came over that day to help us clean. She was scraping dirt and debris from underneath the hot water heater in the kitchen.

"John, I want you to get on your hand and knees with this scraper and clean all that dirt from underneath that water heater," Aunt Mary said.

"Okay," I replied, taking the tool.

I began scraping with the metal spatula. But because no one could ever do housework to Aunt Mary's satisfaction, she was soon ordering me to put more elbow grease into it. Soon I was dislodging and flicking dirt from underneath the heater even more diligently, when the scraper seemed to get stuck on something. I pulled harder, harder . . .

Suddenly, out popped something that was the size of a playing card. But I could not immediately make it out. I looked closer, and closer still. Then I scooped it up.

"Oh my God," I said. "It's a wad of money."

I leafed through the stack of ten- and twenty-dollar bills, then began leaping weightlessly toward the ceiling—leaping and yelling.

"Thank you, Jesus! Thank you, Jesus! Thank you, God!"

Grandmother came running.

"What's the matter? What's the matter?" she asked, astonished.

"I was cleaning underneath the hot water heater and this wad of money popped out," I said, trying to catch my breath.

Grandmother's face lit up.

"How much is it?" Aunt Mary asked excitedly.

Grandmother and Aunt Mary stood there in the kitchen, watching as I counted the cash.

"It's $280," I said. "Two hundred eighty dollars! I can buy linoleum. I can buy my linoleum," I exclaimed.

I started doing a holy dance right on the spot. Grandmother's face broke into a wide grin, her arms started swinging the way they always did at True Vine on Sunday mornings whenever she was bubbling over with the spirit.

"Thank ya' Lord," she yelled. "Woo-oo-oo, my God, my God. I declare God loves you, John Foun-tainnn."

When Grandmother and I stopped dancing and praising the Lord, I grabbed the scraper once again upon Aunt Mary's suggestion and began flicking it around again underneath the water heater in search of more buried treasure. After my search turned up empty, Grandmother drove me to a home furnishings store down on Cermak Road, where I picked out a beautiful, glossy peach linoleum with floral designs to match our newly painted kitchen. The linoleum and a few more cans of paint took just about every penny I had. But to me that was only confirmation that God had given me the money exactly for that purpose.

"Oh well, I'm not worried. I'm sure there's more where that came from," I remarked to Grandmother after paying for everything, although I was then as broke as I had been an hour or two earlier.

About an hour later, after lugging the linoleum upstairs, I finally returned to my cleaning. I picked up my scraper and began finishing the task of removing the dirt and debris from underneath the water heater. Grandmother and Aunt Mary were in another room doing something else. I was still reeling from the experience of having money pop out of the floor, scraping nonchalantly when suddenly out popped a second wad. It was a wad of tens and twenties just like before. But this time it was $160. The ceremonials from earlier in the day took place again.

Sometime later that afternoon Aunt Mary asked for her cut, saying that I would not have found the money had she not suggested that I clean underneath the water heater. My response was that if the money had been meant for her, then she would have found it instead of me. I later offered her $40 from my new find.

"Nah, that's okay," she said, sounding somewhat ashamed. "God intended for you to have it."

I shoved the money back into my pocket, knowing that my family could well use it.

After Aunt Mary and Grandmother left the apartment that day, I cried. But unlike my usual tears, these were tears of joy. Maybe things were going to work out on Komensky after all, I thought to myself.

As for the money, I figured that the previous occupants likely had stashed their cash underneath the water heater and forgotten about it. It still didn't lessen the blessing as far as I was concerned. That they had forgotten about the money and I had found it in my hour of need after they were long gone was something that I took as more than coincidence.

Days later, my stepfather helped me lay the linoleum, and I added the finishing touches to the apartment, tightly bolting the security bars at the back window and back door.

In August 1981, we moved in. The apartment was nice. Everyone, especially Robin, was impressed with the job I had done. As Grandmother had promised, she stayed with me, right up until the last wall was painted and the linoleum was laid. The sunlight that spilled in from the kitchen windows seemed to wrap its arms around us. Everything was sparkling clean and fresh. Gone was the stench that had filled the apartment. There were no signs of roaches or mice or any such thing. The scent of pine cleaner, of fresh paint and new vinyl hung in the air.

But inasmuch as the apartment had undergone a transformation, in a sense, so had I. I felt a sense of empowerment in seeing the work of my own hands that had turned something so ugly into something so beautiful. I also felt a sense of self-sufficiency. Never again would I rely on others more than I would rely on myself, though it would still be a while before I learned to apply this lesson to other aspects of my life.

Even with our sparkling new place, life on Komensky did not start off perfectly. For a time, we did not have a refrigerator in the apartment. We had applied for a voucher with Public Aid, which furnished refrigerators to the poor. In the meantime, we kept our boys' milk cold in a Styrofoam cooler and I found it necessary to extend my beautification efforts to outside the building. One day I went next door to Mr. Newell's and borrowed the old man's garden tools. I dug up the front and back yards, flung grass seed, and watered the soil.

In time, we got a refrigerator and the grass began to sprout from the cracked dry ground where I thought grass might never grow again. Mr. Newell later admitted he was just as surprised to see grass growing next door again. Even a bed of flowers in front of our apartment building sprang up. Miss Hattie, who had lived on the first floor with her two children when we first moved in, had planted them.

It was eerie seeing those beautiful flowers, seeing that by the time they rose up from the ground, Miss Hattie was already dead and buried. She was found one morning raped and murdered a few blocks away. In the months before her murder, she showed evidence of mental illness and had taken to displaying obscene behavior in the middle of the street and talking to herself. In the spectrum of local happenings, her murder raised only a few eyebrows.

As night fell that first evening at our new apartment, I felt strangely at home and as if my young life had already come full circle. In being back on the block, I also wondered if I would ever leave again. This much I did know: I was a million miles away from my dreams and back where I had started.

That night, after the boys were settled in bed and my wife lay sleeping, I sauntered through the apartment in my bare feet, twisting the doorknobs and locks, making sure that my family was safe.

ID card text:

WRIGHT COLLEGE
CHICAGO, ILLINOIS 60634
"WRIGHT ANGLE STAFF"
FEATURE EDITOR
FOUNTAIN, John W.
1654 S. Komensky
Chgo, IL (23)

STUDENT'S SIGNATURE

SIGNATURE OF CAMPUS HEAD

THIS I.D. CARD IS FOR YOUR USE ONLY.
REPORT ITS LOSS TO THE COUNSELING
OFFICE. IF YOU WITHDRAW FROM THE
COLLEGE THIS I.D. CARD MUST BE RE-
TURNED TO THE COUNSELING OFFICE.

JAN. 1984
DATE ISSUED   SOCIAL SECURITY NO.

VALID THRU MAY 1984
(Validate Extensions on Reverse Side)

PART 3

Exodus

*And the Lord said, I have surely seen the affliction of my people
which are in Egypt, and have heard their cry by reason of their
taskmasters; for I know their sorrows; and I am come down to
deliver them . . .*

Exodus 3:7–8

CHAPTER 23

AID DAY

GHETTO LIFE was hard life. It wasn't just the poverty that weighed you down each day, but all the trimmings: the drugs, the gangs, the broken glass and gunshots that rang out in the middle of the night, the daily grinding of hope into yet another cup of despair that tasted bitter, like bad black coffee. It all seemed so inescapable. Even when an air of quietness hung over the neighborhood, you came to recognize it as the calm before the storm, an impasse in the usual chorus of chaos. I always felt on edge. And I was always looking over my shoulder and always worried that something was going to happen.

Late at night, I walked the floors of our apartment to make sure all inside our house were well. Like clockwork, around 3 A.M., I awoke. After making sure that everyone was safe and secure, I sometimes knelt besides my sons' beds, laid my hand on their heads and prayed over them, then went back to my room and climbed back into bed.

Patrolling the floors like a night watchman was something I had often done as a child, especially when my parents had gone out for the evening, as well as on those nights when there was no man in the house. Now I had no choice. I was the man, the watchman, the protector.

I have long understood that poverty summoned either the worst in people or the best and that any hope of surviving it lay in one's ability to get through the hell of one day without being consumed by the thought of facing another. *"One day at a time, sweet Jesus,"* was how the old saints faced life. At least, it was what they sang to keep on moving. I was still learning to cope. And there was nothing like having life as a teacher. But I still felt that there was something for me beyond life on the island of Komensky. I knew that I needed to find a life raft or build one for my family's escape, if we ever were to escape someday. What I did not understand then was how much whether we escaped would depend on the maturing of my own faith and the ability to believe for myself while depending less and less on the vicarious faith of those around me. The saints called it stretching out on faith. And I have learned that this is something that all people must do themselves.

If there was a bright side to being back in K-Town, it was that I knew a lot of the Negroes who lived there, including many of the gang-bangers and troublemakers, the dope dealers and the drugheads, the stick-up men and the general fare of do-nothings and thugs. After all, I had gone to school with many of them. Or else I had heard about certain individuals' reputations for committing crimes. That kind of information gets around a neighborhood. As a teenager, I had learned to avoid trouble whenever possible and how to spot predators even if I was seeing them for the first time. There was always something in their eyes, something about the way they stared at you as if trying to see straight through to your heart, size you up.

My position as guardian angel of my family was an unenviable one. I knew of guns being whipped out on fathers to keep them at bay, of mothers beaten down while trying to protect their children. I had witnessed the outbreak of mayhem and Negroes running from every direction to beat someone up for having whipped one of their relatives in an earlier fight. You had to protect your own. This was not a job for the police, who most often showed up after the smoke had cleared.

Once, my stepfather loaded his shotgun and sat on the porch as a sign to a group of thugs who lived at a house across the street that he was ready and willing to unleash one or both barrels on their butts. A few days earlier, this rowdy bunch had chased one of my cousins, who was visiting us. They even had the audacity to run into our building, all the way up the stairs, and pound on the front door, spitting obscenities and threats. Lucky for them, Daddy was not home at the time or there would have been a killing.

For weeks after that incident, my stepfather carried his shotgun openly to his car each morning and placed it in his trunk as he drove off to work. Then each evening, he climbed slowly out of his car, walked straight to his trunk, and pulled out his shotgun just as brazenly as he had carried it out into broad daylight hours earlier. Then, as everybody on the block looked on, he filled it with shells. Everybody on the block soon began saying, "That Eddie is crazy." That was exactly the image he wanted to project.

My stepfather might have handled the situation differently. Maybe he should have called the cops. But we all reasoned that the cops probably would not have done anything anyway. And everyone on the block would have thought us to be chicken, which would have made us fair game long after the cops left. Sometimes you just had to stand your ground, even if it came down to your having to take somebody out. The only thing that a truly bad Negro respected was fear. And the only thing that any really bad Negro feared was another bad Negro whom they perceived to be crazy enough to put a bullet in their head first.

Watching life unfold in the 'hood was sometimes like watching *Wild Kingdom* on television and seeing the lions pouncing on deer and antelope. To show any sign of weakness was to be eaten alive. By the time I moved back to K-Town, the atmosphere was pervasive.

A lot of brothers didn't respect the fact that some sisters were married. They might flirt with a man's wife while he walked with her, undress her with their eyes, and make no secret of their desires as they licked their chops when she passed by, sucking up the sweet smell of her perfume. They did not respect that maybe someone had a right to have a lawn and that they should not be trampling all over it or smoking reefers on someone else's porch, or blasting their music to kingdom come, or selling drugs out of their house, which drew more undesirable elements to the block. They did not respect that your children had a right to play outside without fear of being shot. That you shouldn't have to bar up the windows and doors of your house to keep them out, or that someone's wife, mother, or grandmother had a right to walk to the store without the fear of being raped or robbed.

The criminally minded in the neighborhood have always been in the minority, although they were responsible for wreaking most of the havoc against the law-abiding folks. Their terror, coupled with hardship and poverty and the siphoning of hope, worked against any kind of social stability that might otherwise have existed. We faced terrorists long before the term became popular. Except the terrorists we knew looked like us and talked like us, even though they seemed to hold so much hatred and disrespect for black folks that they might as well have been honorary members of the Ku Klux Klan.

I have long believed that it is impossible to love others if people do not first love themselves. And I was certain that many folks in K-Town did not love themselves. As a young man, I sometimes thought love to be the least abundant commodity in our neighborhood. At best, that meant there would be no great expression of love or respect for me and mine upon my return to K-Town.

Both Robin and I knew we had to survive it. So we made a pact to keep mostly to ourselves, to our church, and to the safety and refuge of our tidy apartment. We intended to do so for as long as was necessary. And from the looks of things, it would be necessary for a long time.

Morning arrived with a feeling of relief. I climbed out of bed, feeling more perky than usual. I got dressed and headed out of the door, bound for the currency exchange on Sixteenth Street and Pulaski Road. Today was "aid day" as everybody in the neighborhood called it. Aid day was the day when everyone who was on welfare in one form or another got his or her Public Aid check. It was always at the first of the month. After having plumb borrowed out, it felt good to get our monthly replenishment from the government. That translated into $400 a month, plus about $250 in food stamps. After paying rent, lights, gas, the telephone bill, and buying toiletries, which you could not buy with food stamps, after the currency exchange's tax for cashing my check, and after paying back the money we had borrowed from family members to make it to check day, there wasn't much left. I also faithfully set aside $50, which I gave to the church each month as my sacrifice to the Lord. I believed in the biblical principle of tithing, which said that believers should give 10 percent of all of their income to the church. My only income was Public Aid, so that was what I based my tithe on. Although we certainly could have used that $50 every month, it was my investment in the faith bank, and I believed that God would someday bless me for my faithfulness and sacrifice. I did not understand this fully until years later, but this act of faithful giving taught me to trust not so much in what I could see as in a power that I believed superseded even my sufferings and daily circumstance.

Grandpa always arrived early on aid day in the church van to take us grocery shopping. Net and her husband went shopping with us as well. Net was married to a no-good Negro whom everybody in the neighborhood had nicknamed the "Moocher" for his tendency to bum cigarettes, money, and just about anything he could from anyone who was so inclined to let him have it. The Moocher was the father of Net's child, and Mama hated him. She thought the Moocher to be a good-for-nothing bum with no job and no aspirations or home training. And that is putting it mildly. It had not helped matters any that Net had made elaborate plans to marry this dude without Mama's knowledge. It seems everybody knew they were getting married except Mama, although I was unaware that Mama knew nothing of the planned wedding until that Saturday of Net's big day when I called Mama to ask for a ride to the church.

"For what?" Mama asked.

"For Net's wedding," I replied matter-of-factly.

"Her what!" Mama screamed.

"Her, uh, her wedding. Ma, you didn't know?"

"No! I gotta go!" she said, hanging up the telephone.

The stuff hit the fan that day. But the wedding that had been secretly planned by Net with the help of Grandmother and some of Mama's sisters took place after all. They would all later explain that Net was intent on marrying "that boy" anyway and that Mama, even though Net was living in her home at the time, was being unreasonable in her insistence that Net not marry a man whom Mama rightly reasoned wasn't worth two dead flies. Actually, I had calculated his worth to not exceed one dead fly.

Mama vowed that she would never forgive her sisters and her mother for what they did, although her heart would soften over the years. On Net's big day, I had never seen Mama more distraught. She survived the ceremony with bloodshot eyes, tears, and intermittent sobs. Mama had to be carried out of the church, her body limp, her heart broken, and her daughter married to a bum.

Net and her husband lived upstairs on the third floor above our apartment at 1654, and we all went shopping on aid day in the church van. Since neither of us had our own car, Grandpa decided that he would take us shopping every month, no strings attached, though we sometimes rewarded him with a lean beef brisket. Grandpa knew we had to get our groceries somehow and that most of the ratty neighborhood grocery stores were rip-off joints. Even if we had taken the bus shopping, there would have been the extra expense and hassle of paying a gypsy cab to get our groceries home. I always thought Grandpa's volunteering to take us shopping such a kind and considerate act, so much so that years later I am still moved to tears that he thought enough to be there when I needed him for what in some people's eyes would be considered such a minuscule thing.

When Grandpa arrived, he honked his horn. We walked downstairs and piled into the van with our kids and all headed down on Randolph Street east of Ogden Avenue to the meat market, then eventually to Aldi's for canned goods and finally to Jewel Food Store for fresh produce and the last remaining items on our shopping list. It always bothered me the way a lot of people, blacks and whites alike, whispered and shot us ugly looks when they saw our shopping cart filled to the rim and us whipping out food stamps to pay for our groceries. I heard the nasty comments many times and could read the silent words spoken by that detestable look in their eyes:

"How come they got all that meat and steak and stuff when I can barely afford to feed my family? Shucks, I work every day and I can't afford steak," is what their eyes said. *"Them niggers getting over on the system. Look at that! Greedy bums—"*

I have always suspected that even if we had only beans and rice in our basket, some people still would have considered even that too much for good-for-nothing, welfare-loving Negroes like us. It's funny how people always made assumptions about folks on welfare. They figured that we all liked being on welfare and sucking up their tax dollars. I hated it. I despised going down to the welfare office every other month or brandishing my green Medicaid card at the hospital whenever our boys got sick. I abhorred being lumped into the same pitiful lot as the folks who lived for welfare and saw it as their due for generations to come. I hated being looked at like scum just because I was paying for groceries with food stamps. Although we sometimes had steak in our shopping cart, I would gladly have traded places with the folks spending cash. As I handed my food stamps to the cashier, I always fought hard to keep my head up. I also imagined that someday I would hand over a fistful of hard-earned cash for groceries rather than a book of food stamps and that I would never look down on someone for having to use food stamps. Nor would I ever allow anyone in my presence to put down someone who was spending food stamps. I vowed never to forget that feeling.

Shopping was a learning experience. We had to make our food last the entire month, which wasn't easy. That meant we had to plan our meals precisely, down to what vegetables we would place on the supper table. Once we got home, Robin and I washed and seasoned the meat, then divided it according to how much we ate and placed it in freezer bags. We always bought at least two gallons of milk and froze one. We also froze bread.

In buying groceries, we had to get lunch for the kids as well as snacks, although snacks were secondary. Besides, I had learned to make caramel corn from scratch, which was a relatively inexpensive treat. I had also learned to make cookies from scratch, both butter cookies and sugar cookies, as well as cornbread. Popcorn sprinkled with salt and covered with a little melted margarine or butter was a tasty standby whenever we wanted to treat our children. We always bought a couple of large bags of uncooked popcorn that we popped ourselves in vegetable oil in a big pot over a hot stove, which still tastes and smells better than any microwave popcorn. The popcorn lasted the entire month. And it made all the difference sometimes when our funds had been exhausted and aid day was still a week or more away. We always put away some food stamps for those inevitable times when things ran short or when the boys needed milk. But we always ended up borrowing.

We borrowed so much that I was ashamed—so ashamed that sometimes we were desperadoes by the time I got around to asking for help. I was proud like Mama, which was perhaps a little ironic since I was on the government dole, unemployed, and barely able to meet ends. For a long time, I did not want to accept anyone's help.

"I don't want nobody feeling sorry for me," I reasoned inside my head, occasionally allowing the words to spill out. "I don't want nothing from nobody! I don't want nobody thinking I'm poor."

By all indications I was poor. But as long as I had my sense of pride, no matter how false, I felt I could at least hold my head up, feel like a man. In time, my sons outgrew their shoes and their bunched toes puckered through the leather. They even developed corns. I could not afford to buy new shoes. We could barely afford a roof over our heads. My own shoes were ragged, so much so that the leather was peeling like flaky, dry skin. And I essentially had only one set of church clothes, a suit in which the lining on the inside of the jacket had worn out. I had one or two white shirts that I bleached, starched, and ironed stiff before church, which I sometimes attended several times a week. Grandmother told me many times that I was too proud and that everybody needed help sometimes.

"That's all right," Grandmother would say. "The Lord knows how to humble you."

In time, I learned to set my pride aside, especially since my pride was hurting my children and it hurt me more to see their toes bunched and corned. In time, Aunt Mary bought my sons shoes. Grandpa, who received an allowance for new work shoes each year from his job as a postal letter carrier at the Post Office, started taking me down to Chernin's Shoes on West Roosevelt Road, where he used his allotment on a new pair of expensive dress shoes for me. Sometimes after service or sometimes during service at True Vine, one of the old saints would walk up to me and shake my hand, quietly passing on ten- and twenty-dollar bills, which always seemed to happen at the most destitute of times. My resistance to receiving help slowly dissipated. And slowly my shame dissolved into gratefulness.

During the winter when the icy wind whipped through our storm windows and bit through the mortar and brick, we had to burn heat almost nonstop just to feel toasty. Even with plastic carefully tacked or taped around the window frames for insulation, our heating bill was astronomical and was easily $200 during a particularly cold month. The one or two times our gas was disconnected, Grandpa paid the bill for us. We always managed with the lights, in part because I learned how to reconnect them after the electricity man had shut off the power, a craft I had learned from my stepfather. It wasn't like stealing electricity, more like borrowing until we could pay, since the electricity still flowed through the meter, which monitored how much of it we used. Eventually, we managed to catch up on our bills.

We weren't the only ones on the block to fall victim to the disconnection man. Somebody was always getting his or her lights or gas turned off. The lucky folks were those whose electrical meters were on the inside and not the outside of their homes, which usually meant that someone had to let the dudes from Commonwealth Edison in to disconnect the power. But sometimes, in the most egregious of cases when someone in an apartment building had not paid the electric bill in a long time, the utility men climbed the electric poles and cut off the power to the entire property. The disconnection men from People's Gas sometimes showed up with a truck and digging crew that parked in front of someone's house or apartment building, then scanned the yard with a Geiger counter until they struck gold. Then they dug up some grass and soil until they found the natural gas shutoff switch for the property. Your business was definitely out in the street when the outside disconnection crews showed up.

It was better to let them in to shut your utilities off because then at least you had a chance of being able to turn them back on.

After learning that some people weren't above sawing off the locks that were put on gas meters during disconnection, the gas men sometimes carted away the entire meter and capped the pipes inside your house or apartment. But I knew of some folks who simply spent a few bucks on a flexible pipe and reconnected the gas line, despite the potential of blowing themselves to smithereens. Given the prospect of freezing, many chose to take the risk. Fortunately, the city eventually began preventing utility companies from disconnecting folks for nonpayment during the coldest winter months. The state also offered utility subsidies for the poor during the winter, apparently realizing that without it many of us simply weren't going to make it.

By the spring of 1981, I was spending a lot of my time at True Vine, cleaning, praying, going to Bible class, attending revivals and worship services. Although I started out at True Vine as a deacon, by then I had become a minister, a bona fide preacher of the Gospel, which I felt was my calling. This calling came to me in a less dramatic fashion than Grandpa's late-night visit from the Lord that led to the founding of True Vine. My gravitation toward the ministry as a preacher was a more gradual and subtle evolution from my growth as a Christian, my involvement in teaching Bible class, and the fire I felt in my belly whenever I stood before people to speak God's word. My calling, as church folks call it, manifested itself as a still, small voice and a kind of internal nudging to preach the Gospel. And I ultimately became as certain that God had called me to be a preacher of the Gospel as I was that I was born a man.

Some days passed quickly. Others crept by, particularly when money was short to nonexistent and we had received final notices from the gas or light companies. When I wasn't at True Vine, I was occupied doing odd jobs, cleaning our apartment, helping to cook, dressing or bathing our sons, studying my Sunday School lesson in preparation to teach my class, headed to or preparing to go to one church service or another. I was busy doing the things that stay-at-home moms fill their days with, only to have their husbands drill them about what they have been doing all day when they arrive home after a hard day's work, surmising that their wives have been doing nothing except watching soap operas. Sometimes I passed a few hours playing basketball, although this seemed more like therapy and the basketball court a respite from my worries.

I had all but given up on looking for a job, with the exception of the occasional lead from a friend or family member, which always turned out to be fruitless. I still did odd jobs for Uncle Gene at his building, which occasionally provided me with a few extra dollars. I probably could have gotten a job at some Burger King or McDonald's with relative ease. But without health benefits and with working at minimum wage, my family was better off being on welfare. If the welfare system could be seen as a disincentive to work, I also saw clearly how it could be perceived as being antifamily. Every penny I would have earned in a minimum-wage job would have been deducted against our check so that it would have been difficult, particularly with taxes being deducted from my wages and the added cost of work expenses, to maintain even our current living standard.

Truth was, it would have been better for Robin and the boys financially, if, given my economic status, they had been on aid by themselves. She would have received a fat welfare check without me. I knew folks for whom this was the case, women who understood that it was not economically advantageous for them to wed their live-in boyfriends and who managed just fine with a few extra, unreported, untraceable dollars that their boyfriends or their babies' daddies kicked in every month. So what did a sister like that need a husband for? That was how a lot of sisters figured it. Fortunately, Robin never thought that way. Either way, I would never have thought of abandoning ship, no matter how bad our finances were. I also figured that eventually something had to give.

CHAPTER 24

YOUTH NEWS

ROBIN AND I strolled down Pulaski Road, past Miller's greasy spoon and the Tasty Freeze, toward the El down on Twenty-first Street, in the morning sun. We were on our way to our summer jobs. It felt good to be going to work again, to stand on the elevated train platform with the few men in their suits and ties, and the crowd, mostly black women wearing nine-to-five faces, on their way to an assortment of jobs across the city. I was only twenty-one. But I felt older, much older. In fact, I felt old. Mostly, this was due to being married with children and being entangled in the web of adult responsibility to which only a handful of my old high school friends could relate. I had more in common with their parents. But by the city's standards, I was still young enough to qualify for its summer youth work program. It was Mama who initially brought this to my attention. I hadn't thought about working a city summer job, but according to the rules then in force, members of a family on welfare could work in the city's summer jobs program without their earnings being counted against their welfare grant. Robin and I both qualified for the summer youth jobs, which meant that we would be able to catch up on the gas bill before winter struck again and have a few extra dollars, which we could always use. Net agreed to baby-sit the boys while we worked.

In assigning youth employees, the administrators of the summer program had attempted to place us all in jobs that coincided with the interests we had listed on our applications. Robin, who had been interested in nursing, worked as a clerk at a West Side clinic. I had expressed an interest in writing. But even after finding myself assigned to Truman College on the city's North Side, where my job for the summer was to write articles and help produce a newspaper, I found it hard to believe that someone was actually going to pay me to do such a thing.

By this time, the summer of 1982, life was calmer. Perhaps we had begun to adjust to being married, to life on Komensky, and to being young parents with two children now, except by then Robin was pregnant again. In fact, she was five months' pregnant with our third child when we started our jobs that June. I don't know how it happened. Well, I do know in the sense of the biology and the mechanics of it all. What was unclear was how Robin had gotten pregnant once again while being on the pill. I routinely saw the pink pill pack on the dresser and had on occasion even seen her pop one of the tiny birth control pills into her mouth, usually before she went to bed at night. I was stunned at the news of her being pregnant again because I thought we had protection and that we both knew the last thing we needed was another child. Years later, I wondered whether Robin had not gotten pregnant on purpose. But once it was done, there was no use in crying about it. I didn't believe in abortions. Neither did Robin. I also believed the Bible, which says that children are a blessing. But the news of a third bun warming inside the Fountain oven troubled Mama. Like most other folks, she figured that with one child, I still had a chance of making it, that with two, it would be harder though not entirely impossible, but with three, the party was over.

The ride on the El each morning transported me past the gloomy ghetto landscape through the rhythmic streets of a vibrant metropolis filled with skyscrapers, rushing taxicabs, and the crush of bodies moving in every direction, all of them with purpose and a sense of urgency. I was glad to be in that number. And I felt energized by the mere fact that each morning I got to travel beyond the invisible walls of K-Town and to reacquaint myself with a world I had previously known, but in a sense had forgotten existed. The rickety squeal of the train over the steel tracks, the

jostling of commuters as the train rumbled and knocked along, the ruffl-
ing of a newspaper being folded by a businessman, and the shout of the
conductor announcing the next stop as the doors flung open each morning made me feel alive.

At Truman College, I encountered probably more than a hundred
youths from across the city with various assignments in the summer work
program at the Truman site. Only about a dozen or so workers were
assigned to the newspaper, *Youth News*. Most of my coworkers were
younger by at least a year or two. The group was about half male and half
female. A couple of the young women were mothers. But no one was
married with children, except for the instructor, Barbara McNairy, a kind
soft-spoken elementary school teacher. I reluctantly told the group that I
was married. For starters, it was none of their business. Also, I was so
young that people often looked at me with mouth agape and in amazement whenever I told them that I was married and already the father of
two. Heaven forbid they should find out that I had a third child on the
way. Some of the fellas on Komensky and even a few relatives had made
snide remarks about my status as a young husband and father. They even
joked that Robin and I were a "baby-making factory." That hurt. It also
made me begin to feel in a sense ashamed that I was married with children. What's weird about that is that so many so-called, cool
dudes—"playboys," as they called themselves—had sired babies from the
South Side to the West Side but took no responsibility for either their children or their babies' mamas. Yet no one ever dogged them out for their
unwillingness to assume even the slightest responsibility. But with me,
there always seemed to be some snide remark or other. Even at church
one Sunday morning during worship service, some people in the congregation snickered while others almost fell out of the pews laughing when
Grandpa remarked publicly from the pulpit, just before dismissal:

"Minister Fountain, you and Sister Robin don't need to have no more
children. Three is enough."

I wanted to shout back, "Even with our three, we're still three shy of
the six you had!"

Instead I sat silently embarrassed and angry, internalizing the laughter.

I saw nothing funny about our situation. At least we were married, which was a lot more than anyone could say about some of the single women in the church who either had babies or had aborted them or the sorry brothers who had left their children fatherless.

Nobody at Truman made a big deal about me being married. For some reason, a couple of the sisters sometimes called me Juicy John, which I didn't quite understand, although they usually said this with a twinkle in their eye. It felt good being out in the world again, being around people besides my wife and children and the folks at church. It also felt good to be earning my own money.

Among the *Youth News* staff was a guy named Ronnie Coleman. Like me, Ron was a preacher, although he was not married and was a member of a different denomination than I was. Ron was Apostolic, which was referred to as the Jesus-only church. I was COGIC. The difference between the two denominations boiled down to Ron's group believing that to be born again, people had to be water baptized "in Jesus' name," while we in the Church of God in Christ believed that baptizing "in the name of the Father, the Son, and the Holy Ghost" was enough to satisfy the Good Lord. In reality, there was really no difference between our faiths. I have long believed that denominations, which ascribed a certain set of doctrinal beliefs to groups of Christians, did more to separate Christendom than to unite it. Ron and I became good friends. And we both adored Mrs. McNairy, who happened to be Baptist. In fact, everyone liked Mrs. McNairy. She was one of those warm sincere people who could see some good in just about anybody, and who, if she had nothing good to say about someone, would choose to say nothing at all.

Working on the newspaper, my coworkers and I spent the first week or two coming up with story ideas and learning about writing. Mrs. McNairy basically rehashed a few rules of English, the kind of stuff that everybody should have learned in elementary school, such as the definition of subject, noun, and verb, and writing in complete sentences. Eventually, we went door-to-door to neighborhood businesses, selling ads. Mostly, Ron and I were the ones who sold the ads.

Once the ads were sold, we began reporting, writing, and editing our stories. I had not done any writing since my freshman year in college three years earlier, except for some church plays that I produced at True Vine. But my writing for *Youth News* seemed crisp and vivid, much more than the writings of my coworkers. Everyone, including Mrs. McNairy, was soon singing my praises. I was quickly pegged as the best writer in the group and voted in as editor in chief. As top dog, I helped edit and write the other students' stories, which boosted my sense of purpose as well as my self-esteem. It had been a long time since I had felt any self-worth outside the context of church or as a family man—so long since I had been able to concentrate on me.

In fact, the process of writing helped me to reconnect with a kind of creativity and empowerment that I had not realized had even been lost. It wasn't until then that I realized I had forgotten how much I loved writing. Whether this had transpired consciously or whether it occurred naturally as time and thought became consumed by the cares of life, I did not know. I only knew that the poetry and tapestry of creative thought and writing had stopped breathing. And now it was alive again.

The only blemish on the summer was a run-in with a woman named R. Dianne Wallace. A pretty woman, light-skinned with flowing hair and long legs, she was the director of the summer youth programs and the object of drool among all the fellas. Ms. Wallace seemed a little stuck-up to me, one of those sisters who thought they were God's gift to mankind. A lot of the young ladies "couldn't stand her," as they put it. I had limited dealings with her but did not like the way she seemed to talk down to the workers in the program or treat us as if we were all welfare recipients. Once that summer, Ms. Wallace came to the classroom where our newspaper group met daily to scold us for something or other. I said something, which I cannot recall exactly. Whatever it was, it rubbed her the wrong way.

"I'll have you know, young man, I have a degree from Southern Illinois University," she said in a smug bourgeois tone. "And youuu?"

On the defense, and somewhat wounded, I fired back.

"Well, I have a year at the University of Illinois in Champaign, which is probably worth about four years at Southern, the party school," I said. Pow!

Everybody laughed. Ms. Wallace huffed and puffed, and looked as if she might start crying right there in front of the class. That was that. End of war. Or so I thought.

By summer's end, I had written several articles, and like everyone else, I was eagerly awaiting the arrival of the newspaper hot off the presses. One of my articles was a somewhat flattering profile I had written earlier in the summer on Ms. Wallace. I had interviewed her in her office and wrote a piece about her role as director of the summer youth program and as an elementary school teacher during the academic year. About five of my articles were being published in the newspaper, the most of any on the *Youth News* staff. I could hardly wait to see my name in print on something other than an overdue bill or a welfare check.

Finally, the day came. It was the last day of work, a sunny August Friday when the newspapers showed up. I sat proudly and somewhat anxiously next to Ron as Mrs. McNairy handed out copies, waiting, like everyone else, to behold the beauty of all our hard work. It had been so much fun putting the newspaper together and writing stories that I was starting to envision writing as something I might enjoy doing someday for a living. Finally, a copy of *Youth News* made its way to my desk and into my hands, the smell of inked newsprint and paper rising to my nostrils. I hurriedly scanned page one for one of my stories, but found none. I flipped open the newspaper and scanned page two, then three, four, five.... But I could not find my name or any of the stories I had written. Meanwhile, there was the ring of excitement as other staffers located their stories. I sat stunned. Finally, I turned to Ron.

"Man, I don't see anything that I wrote in here," I said, puzzled.

"You're kidding, man," Ron said. "You wrote more than anybody here."

Ron began scouring the newspaper for my name.

"Hey, Mrs. McNairy, what happened to all John's stories?" he asked.

Mrs. McNairy stood at the front of the classroom speechless. Then suddenly somebody's eyes landed on my name.

"John, here's one of your stories on the front page," yelled a young woman.

I flipped to page one. There it was: a story above the fold. "How had I missed it?" I thought to myself. It was the profile on Ms. Wallace all right. But that still didn't explain what had happened to the rest of my work. I began reading the piece and quickly discovered that though it carried my byline, it was not the story I had written. "These are not my words," I said to myself. I sat stunned again for a moment, my mind racing, trying to make sense of it all. Finally, I turned to Mrs. McNairy.

"Mrs. McNairy, what's going on?" I asked. "I didn't write this. Someone changed this story. This isn't the story I wrote. What happened to all of my stories?"

"Ms. Wallace changed everything," Mrs. McNairy answered, sounding apologetic. "John, I begged her not to."

Everybody shook their head. I sank in my chair, trying to hold back the tears that surfaced instantly.

"Why would she do that?" Ron asked.

"I don't know," Mrs. McNairy answered. "Ms. Wallace wrote that story on page one and put your name on it," Mrs. McNairy explained to me. "I'm so sorry. I feel so bad, John. I'm so sorry."

There were no words to comfort me. Not only did I feel sad, but I was embarrassed that my stories had been obliterated and that the one that bore my name was a story I had not written. If Ms. Wallace's point was to prove that she was top dog, she had made her point well. If it was to hurt me, she had accomplished that, too. It wasn't just the absence of my work in this stupid, little jive-time giveaway newspaper that hurt so much. It was just that after finally finding something to feel good and proud about, there was somebody there to punch me in the gut and kick me in the shins. The newspaper was to be my trophy, a symbol of success to take back to the ghetto as evidence, if only proof to myself, that I had done something of note outside the walls of my own miserable world.

After everyone except Ron and I had filtered out of the classroom at Truman that last day of the summer program, Mrs. McNairy apologized once again, this time with tears streaming down her face. She walked us out into the hallway as we departed. She went on to say that Ms. Wallace did not like me for some reason and that she reckoned she had done all of this out of spite. I found all of this hard to digest, especially since Ms. Wallace hardly knew me and we had had such few dealings.

I wiped away my tears. Mrs. McNairy was still crying as we hugged good-bye.

"Don't worry, John," she said tearfully. "Don't worry about this little newspaper. I look to see your name in lights one day."

If that ever did happen, I wanted Ms. Wallace to see it, too.

After speaking with Mrs. McNairy in the hall, I walked away from Truman for the last time, feeling hollow and numb. I caught the train back to K-Town, feeling like a second-class citizen with a one-way ticket to nowhere, staring out the window, wiping away the tears, unsure of the future but knowing that in two months I would have yet another mouth to feed.

The saints had long urged me to be encouraged, saying that the darkest hour was always just before sunrise. Sooner or later, the sun had to shine again. It just had to.

CHAPTER 25

SHOTS FIRED

I WAS SITTING in the pulpit with the other preachers at True Vine that weeknight service when the telephone in the pastor's office could be heard ringing in the sanctuary. One of the sisters or deacons, I cannot remember who, hurried to answer the telephone so that it did not totally distract us from the purpose of our gathering. A few moments later, whoever had answered the telephone stood at the back of the church, motioning for Grandpa to come. People were always calling the church for one thing or another, money, a handout, prayer. Whatever the reason Grandpa was now being summoned, it seemed to have a different sense of urgency. I knew immediately that whatever the news on the telephone, it must have been serious to have caused a beckoning to the pastor to leave the pulpit during the middle of service. Grandpa climbed out of his chair, walked down the pulpit stairs, down the aisle of the sanctuary and disappeared into his office. My attention turned back to worship service.

I was spending a lot of time in church. There was Tuesday evening Bible study and Friday night worship service, choir rehearsal, or always during Christmas and Easter, play rehearsal. There was watch night service on New Year's Eve, sunrise service on Easter, the choir's third Saturday night musicals every month, always one service or another. We churched all day on Sunday, the mornings beginning with 9:30 Sunday School, then morning worship at noon, which lasted until 2:30 or 3:00 P.M. On those Sundays when a special afternoon service was planned—either one of the countless anniversaries called Women's Day, Men's Day, or choir and church anniversaries—we had just enough time to grab something to eat before it was time again to start prayer for the beginning of another service. Then for good measure, so as not to give place to the Devil, Grandpa most often insisted that we have our usual Sunday night service preceded by another Bible study class, which I headed. Called YPWW, it stood for Young People's Willing Worker, and Grandpa had appointed me president. It was always difficult to get people to come back to church or to stay for the 6:30 P.M. Bible study. I learned that nothing worked in luring the saints back to church like promising treats and playing Bible games. All of this worked to create a sense of excitement and anticipation.

Robin and I still didn't have a car. The church van rolled on Sunday mornings, but not Sunday evenings, which meant that Robin and the kids and I often had to walk back to True Vine. So we did, even on those days when it turned out that no one showed up except us and Grandpa and Grandmother. In those times, we talked a while, prayed, and went home comforted by Grandpa's assurances that God was going to bless us someday for our faithfulness. I also became a sponge for every ounce of positive encouragement that came my way, whether it was from other preacher's sermons—like the time Bishop Ford preached that sometimes we must "stoop to conquer." Or whether it was from simple words said in passing with a pat on the back, often without those people knowing how much their encouragement helped me. Like that time during one of our third Saturday night musicals when Guitar Jones Jr. remarked that he had heard a young man speaking on the radio who reminded him of me. He went on to say that I really had a gift in speaking and emceeing the way I did at church functions and that I had a real professional sense about myself. I stored his words like treasure in my heart. Meanwhile, I kept on keeping on, as the old saints would say.

My churching, as we called it, was nonstop. Sometimes True Vine visited other churches on Sunday or during the week when they were having their anniversaries, revivals, or district or state meetings, which sometimes lasted until 2 A.M. That did not include the fish and chicken fries on Saturdays, or any evangelism we did, or the monthlong nightly revivals we had every January where we sweated on the altar, clapping our hands and singing "Jesus-Jesus-Jesus" over and over again into the night until the Lord's spirit fell on us, causing some saints to roll on the floor and speak in tongues. Church life was all-consuming, but it kept me busy and on fire for the Lord.

Preparation for Sundays began on Monday when I started studying the next week's Sunday School lesson as well as the youth Bible study lesson, since Grandpa had also appointed me as a teacher in Sunday School. Most of the time, by Saturday I had read all the commentary and studied the Scriptures on my lessons and was busy making posters or creating some sort of visual aids for my classes. Then on Saturday afternoon, I went door-to-door on Komensky, asking parents if I could pick up their children in the morning for Sunday School. But by then, I had already cut my sons' hair and practiced playing my guitar, which I plucked during service.

As youth department president, I was responsible for fund-raising as well and for planning outreach and youth activities for the local church and also the district, which comprised several other churches in our jurisdiction. In the summer, I coordinated an outdoor carnival and festival, which I called "Summer Fun in the Son" and which everyone loved, the kids and adults alike. When I wasn't writing some new play for the young people to perform at church or studying my lessons and memorizing God's word, I sometimes cleaned the church. I had a key and would let myself in, sometimes carting a bottle of pine cleaner, bleach, and Ajax that I had purchased with my last few dollars, knowing that God's house needed cleaning, too, and believing that he would honor me someday if I honored him by giving my all. Sometimes Robin and the kids went with me. I always prayed before I scrubbed the toilets, mopped the bathroom and sanctuary's floors, dusted, and vacuumed: "Lord, let everything I do be done in your will and to your Glory." When I was done, I turned off the lights, locked up, and walked home. I still wonder sometimes whether the saints at True Vine ever knew that I was the mystery cleaner. I never told them, not wanting to make a big deal about it and feeling certain that the one who mattered most was sitting high and taking notes.

While the church activity occupied my time, prayer occupied my mind. Often, I prayed in my bathroom at home, kneeling over the tub, often for an hour at a time. Sometimes it was longer, depending on how the spirit moved me or how troubled I was. I prayed for a job, for strength, for blessings, for peace, for a closer walk with the Lord. Sometimes I prayed just to get through the moment. Although I was not fully aware of its significance at the time, I also created what was essentially my own faith network. That network included Christian radio and television programs as well as a repertoire of Scriptures, prayer with the church mothers on Tuesday and Friday mornings, and a twenty-four-hour hot line to my very own prayer partner. Whether it was 10 A.M. or 3 A.M., Grandmother always answered her telephone armed for battle.

"All right, baby darling, let's go to the Lord," she would say, starting to pray over the telephone within seconds of my call. "Father, you see this man, we speak peace right now, in the name of Jesus. Jeee-sus, we call on your name . . ."

Sometimes it was enough to hear the soothing sounds of WMBI-FM—the Moody Bible Institute radio station—to calm my nerves when the tempest was raging and the sense of hopelessness amid our constant state of financial strain was most overwhelming. The radio was a constant in our apartment. I knew every radio station, secular or Christian, that played Gospel music and what time it aired so that I could always tune in at any time, should I need inspiration and something to help soothe my mind and soul. There was WYCA with host Taft Harris every weeknight at 7 P.M. There was Reverend Maceo Woods at midnight, whose show always began with the deep, soulful, sung words, "The Lord will provide. I know the Lor-or-or-or-ord wi-i-i-il provi-i-i-i-ide." Reverend Milton Brunson was on from noon to 5 P.M. on Saturdays, followed by a few more hours of music hosted by Father Hayes and finally a review of the Sunday School lesson by Elder Willie James Campbell.

I also watched the *700 Club*. Back then, Pat Robertson and his cohost, Ben Kinchlow, talked a lot about reciprocity and the principle of giving, about God's faithfulness and his ability to bless and heal, both physically and fiscally. Sometimes they even gave a word of healing after they had prayed, describing on air as the Holy Spirit led them, the people and situations that God showed them that he was healing at that very moment. Many days I waited for them to describe me or my situation, to say that the Lord had showed them a young man on the West Side of Chicago who was on welfare and whom God was blessing and healing at that very moment. I imagined many times that I would have leaped from the sofa, shouting and praising God, if ever that happened. It never did. The word of healing never came, at least not in any instantaneous or miraculous moment, which was the way I later understood that many Christians expected faith to work—as if heaven was some cosmic candy machine and God was its operator. In time, I would understand that faith is 99-percent work and that just as Moses had to apply some elbow grease to lead his people out of Egypt, I was eventually going to have to get up off of my knees and do the same.

After being summoned to his office at church that night, Grandpa was not gone for long, but when he reemerged, the serious look in his eyes and the taut lines in his forehead and jaws said that something was wrong. He stood in the foyer just outside his office, staring toward the pulpit. He beckoned with his hand. I looked around, wondering whom he was calling until he pointed directly at me.

"Me?" I asked, touching a finger to my chest, my lips moving but making no sound.

Grandpa nodded.

"What for?" I wondered. "Was something wrong at home?"

The boys had come to church with me that night. But Robin, still pregnant and nearly due, wasn't feeling well and had stayed home. I sprang from my chair and hurried from the pulpit through the sanctuary.

"Something wrong?" I asked Grandpa.

"Nothing much. Come on, John, I just want you to take a ride with me," he answered.

We headed through the church's swinging wood doors and climbed into Grandpa's Cadillac. The air was dead silent. Warily, I asked again what was going on, where we were going.

"You've got an emergency at home," Grandpa answered.

"What?"

He offered no further detail.

Of course, there was the possibility that Robin was in labor. But I didn't get the sense that this was a baby call. I could not imagine what else might be wrong. I sensed from Grandpa's silence and the speed with which the car moved that whatever it was, it was very serious.

Weeks earlier, my family and I were sitting in the living room watching television one night when we heard the pop-pop-pop of a dozen or so firecrackers outside. It was well after the Fourth of July, so the popping sound startled us. But we didn't think much about it until we heard sirens wailing in the distance a short while later, which grew closer and closer until it was clear that the lights and sirens were all coming to Komensky. I ran to the window. In a few moments, squad cars were coming from everywhere. And I knew then that the popping sound must not have been firecrackers but gunshots.

I flicked off the lights inside our apartment. At least a half-dozen cops, most of them white, jumped out of their cars and ran up a dark gangway across the street. A paddy wagon arrived, its blue lights flashing. It pulled up and parked right across from the gangway. The cops' voices filtered in through the window with the breeze, though I could not make out anything they were saying. By then, other residents were watching as well from their porches, from windows, trying to find out what had happened. It was pretty clear that someone had been shot and was probably dead from the way the cops shuffled about without any sense of urgency.

After a while, two cops emerged from the darkness of the gangway into the glow of streetlights, moving in a hurry but with heavy, laborious steps, dragging a man by a fistful of his jacket gripped at the shoulders. I could not make out the details of the face of the man being dragged, but I could tell he was black. I could also tell he was dead by the way his head slumped, the way it just hung limp from his chest toward the earth, and the way the cops struggled under the strain of his weight, dead weight. The two cops finally made it to the back of the paddy wagon, where they hurled the body into the back like a slab of meat. It hit with a thud. They slammed the door shut. Bam! Just like that. Thud, bam, the disposal of trash.

I stood in the window, thinking that the cops had shot this brother to death and that nobody, at least no one on the block, had any idea what had happened. But judging from the beet-red faces of two harried white cops, it seemed clear that they had done the shooting. Even if the cops were right and he was wrong, the story of what happened would not amount to more than the words of some white cops against one dead nigger.

I did not even know the dead man's name. To this day, I still don't. But standing in the window, I could not shake the image of the white cops tossing this lifeless black body into the back of that paddy wagon as if it were road kill. As the cops scanned the ground with their flashlights apparently searching for something, I was so filled with anger that I suddenly yelled out of the window before I could catch myself, "Killers!"

A couple of the cops looked right up at my open window and shined their flashlights up at me without saying a word. Then they returned to scanning the ground a while longer before climbing into their cars finally and driving away. I watched as the last car rolled down the block, into the night, feeling a sense of powerlessness, if not altogether hopeless impotence.

I was feeling much the same way when Grandpa and I rounded the corner at Eighteenth Street and Komensky Avenue and saw the fleet of blue-and-white police cars parked outside my apartment building.

"Oh my God!" I gasped. "What happened? What's going on?"

Grandpa pulled to the curb and I jumped out of the car before it was even parked. I ran into the building and dashed up the stairs as fast as I could. My apartment door was open. I ran in, my heart and mind racing.

"What ... where's ... where's my wife? Where's my wife?" I said rushing toward the living room, where a swarm of police officers stood. I quickly scanned the room and saw Robin sitting on the couch. She looked shaken. I rushed over to her.

"She's all right," a police officer said.

"What happened?" I asked, shaken and angry.

Robin seemed too shaken to speak.

"Sir, someone shot through your window," a police officer said. "The bullet crashed through the glass and lodged in the floor there," he said, pointing.

"A bullet ... What? Awww man, you got to be kidding me," I said, trying to compose myself. "Where did it come from?"

The cops showed me the hole in the living room window. It was a hole about the size of a baseball. Then they showed me the round that had torn through it, a .22 caliber bullet they retrieved from the hardwood floor.

"It could have been fired from several blocks away," one cop explained. "You know how people shoot up in the air? Well, the bullet has to come down somewhere ..."

My eyes fell on the spot where the bullet had landed. And I was even more shaken. It was in front of the television, the same spot where our boys normally sprawled out on their bellies in the evening before bedtime each night to watch TV. I shook my head in disbelief. Robin had been lying on the couch watching television when she said she heard glass breaking, and then something hit the floor.

It turned out that the window through which the bullet entered our apartment was the same window from which I had yelled at the cops weeks earlier. I knew that we would never find out where the shot came from. But that didn't matter. What really mattered was that one of us could easily have been killed but that we had all been spared. No matter how troubling, I could not allow myself to dwell on it, if I was to maintain some degree of sanity. You could never afford to take it all in. You never fully ingested all the madness, at least not while you still lived in it, or it could incapacitate you. You saw it, but you didn't. You heard it, but you didn't. You convinced yourself that things were not so bad. That this was how life was. You counted your blessings. You moved on.

I hugged Robin. She said she was okay. The cops finished their report and left. Then Grandpa and I drove back to church. All the way back, I kept thinking that I had just one more thing to be thankful for—but I was convinced more than ever that I had to find a way to get my family away from here.

CHAPTER 26

THE VINE

THE AIR INSIDE our narrow storefront church felt like hot maple syrup. Grandmother's brown hands reached up toward the high white ceiling, the glowing globes, and the cobwebs, as if trying to pull down heaven and touch God.

"Praise yo' name Je-sus!" one church mother shouted.

"Hal-le-lu-jah," intoned another.

"Glo-raaaay!"

It was another Sunday service at True Vine, a weekly spit-spewing Pentecostal revival. After six days of enduring one thing or another among the travails of life in the ghetto, the saints usually sought rejuvenation through these teary testimonials and spirituals. Although I once had branded the whole business as snake oil, being of the mind that the spiritual powwows were no better than smoking weed or drinking cheap wine, I was of a different mind since life happened—marriage, two children, and another on the way by age twenty-one. It all led me to seek the intoxication of the spirit. Standing in front of the sanctuary, lifted up by the *uh-HUHs* and *Amens* of Grandmother and the little old ladies of the church, I testified:

"Giving honor to God, to the pastor and his wife, to all the elders, saints and friends..."

The congregation urged me on, the fingers of the organist fluttering over the keys.

"I-I-I don't know how I made it this week..."

Tears streamed down my face. Truth was, I couldn't see how I could make it through another. I can still hear Grandmother's soothing voice, "Ho-o-old on my darlin', hold on..."

Whenever I got so down that I found it hard to go on, when everything else in my faith network had failed to lift my spirits and I felt like dying more than I felt like living, the little fiery gray-haired ladies or the prayed-up young Christian sisters at church would tell me that God was going to bless me someday, if I could just hold out. They made these proclamations at the Tuesday and Friday morning prayer services. Ninety-nine percent of the time, I was the only man amid the "prayer warriors"—elderly women, including Grandmother, who basically rolled out of bed every morning and hit their knees calling on the name of the Lord.

Grandmother picked me up for prayer. And sometimes I rode on with her as she did her chores for the day. I actually liked hanging out with Grandmother, though often that meant running to keep up with her as she grabbed her purse and headed out the door to the rescue amid some new emergency, to True Vine or some church meeting or the countless trips to the sewing store down on Roosevelt Road for material for some new project: dresses for someone's wedding, quilts, scarves, suits. Grandmother was an intense worker, but she always carried a sweet disposition. She seldom raised her voice and always seemed willing to listen, although you could count on getting a good Scripture from her vast repertoire of Bible verses.

"They that wait upon the Lord shall renew their strength," Grandmother would say sometimes. "They shall mount up on wings as eagles."

"But when, Grandmother, is God going to help me?" I inquired many times, nearly in tears.

"Listen to what I tell you, John," she answered many times. "I ain't never known Him to fail. Grandmother wouldn't tell you nothin' wrong. Oh no, baby darling."

Then she would go back to stitching her quilt or pounding the dough for a peach cobbler, or working on one of the 10 million projects, usually for either the family or the church, that she was always involved in. I have never seen anybody more ready and willing to pray than Grandmother. She didn't mess around when it came to calling on Jesus. While spending the night at her house through the years, I had heard the telephone ring in the middle of the night, then Grandmother's raspy but soothing voice praying aloud, pleading for God to intervene in some situation for the caller on the other end. There was no preamble to prayer with Grandmother. It was like she had a hot line to heaven and that God was one of her bosom buddies. Sometimes we would be talking and she would share with me the things God had told her, about her children, about her grandchildren, the church, and other situations that she still believed God was going to work out in her favor. Sometimes she would say that God had said this or that. And I would wonder how come she got to hold such frequent discussions with the Lord when I had been calling on Him for years and had not heard so much as a whisper.

"Are you sure God talks?" I often wanted to know.

"He does," Grandmother would assure me. "He talks to me all the time."

"Why doesn't he talk to me?"

Grandmother would smile, sometimes without even looking up from her sewing, a silver thimble on her index finger, the needle in her hand, her hair sometimes still in rollers, still wearing a smock and house shoes.

"He does," she'd say. "Reach over and hand me that pair of scissors. You just have to learn to recognize his voice. Just keep on talking to Him, darlin'. Keep lovin' the Lawd."

Those words alone seemed to strike a fire in Grandmother.

"Thank ya!" she would exclaim. "He's a wonder-workin' savior. Sweet Je-sus!" Then she would sing a song, her voice filling the house, "Je-sus, You brought me all the way, and you carried my burdens every day . . ."

Within moments, Grandmother was as far removed from her house and her sewing and surroundings as the earth is from the heavens, at least in spirit. Her joy had an infectious presence on the mood at her house and upon everyone and everything around her.

If anybody was going to heaven, Grandmother was, and so was the band of little old ladies she mixed it up with in prayer. On Sunday, the church mothers wore beautiful, colorful hats and sat at the front of the sanctuary for all to see, looking like proud peacocks with their scarves draped across their knees, Bibles in hand, or their hands lifted toward heaven. They didn't take any mess, especially when it came to spiritual things. There was simply a clear dividing line between good and evil. And those who intended on walking with the Lord had better know it because they did not mind correcting them.

There was Mother Vaughn, Mother Chapman, Missionary Hawkins, Aunt Mary, Sister Crane, sometimes Aunt Scope and others. Few of the church mothers had an education beyond high school, most of the elder mothers having come up through the South at a time when hands were needed at home and in the field. But, man, they knew how to pray.

"Oh, Law-aw-awd. We praise yo' name. Ya' been maht-tee goo-ood... Ummmmm. Glo-raaay-to-yo'-name, Je-sus."

They didn't believe in women wearing pants, makeup, or showing any cleavage. They scolded some of the younger sisters for exposing knees and thighs and told them to drop their hems, take off their lipstick and colored fingernail polish. The brethren were not excluded from reproof, either. We could get a quick tongue-lashing for not helping our wives with the kids enough or for not bringing our families to Sunday School.

Their rebukes were given "in love," they assured us, although sometimes it sure didn't feel like it. But they would be the first to drop to their knees and go on a fast for you if you ever got into any serious trouble. I figured I needed them on my side, and they simply loved me to death for having the gumption to meet with them in prayer twice a week.

In addition to being a pastor's wife, Grandmother held the distinct honor of being district missionary, which meant she was in charge of a network of four or five churches. She and some of the other sisters decided to start the morning prayer so that God, in their words, would do something special for the district churches and their families. This was no women's social. It was business. And each morning that the women entered one of the churches in the district, they were stone-faced and purposed like they were going to go fifteen rounds with the Devil.

On those prayer mornings, usually inside one storefront sanctuary or another, we cried out to the Lord, eyes shut tight, as we laid our burdens at His feet. Afterward, we sang several of the many congregational songs, as we called them, that everybody knew by heart, like *"Jesus, you brought me all the way..."* Then without missing a beat, someone else would break out singing another song in soul-stirring a cappella: *"I love the Lord, I love the Lord, I love the Lord..."* Then we would segue into yet another, clapping and rejoicing. After the singing, we would hold a group testimonial session in which we each proclaimed what the Lord was doing in our lives. It was like a free therapy session.

On those mornings, as I washed my face and got dressed, I often wondered why I was seeking the counsel of a bunch of grannies or spending so much time on my knees when my situation seemed so desperate. It sometimes seemed so ineffectual to pour out my soul and never see any miracles or wonders, such as fire raining down from heaven or something more practical—like a job. There had been little miracles before, like the wads of tens and twenties that had popped from beneath the water heater while I was cleaning my apartment, like the times when a check arrived unexpectedly at Christmastime from the city's Neediest Children's Christmas Fund. The times when my chest was hurting and it felt as if my head would explode from all of my worrying until I found peace on my knees in prayer and the pain suddenly dissolved. Just making it month to month on our welfare check was in itself nothing short of miraculous. But I was still poor, still unable to take care of my family, still always needing something or someone to sustain me.

In exchange for my faithfulness to the church, the prayer warriors assured me that God would someday "pour you out a blessing you won't have room to receive."

"The greater the suffering, the bigger the blessing," Sister Crane, a short woman with the voice of an opera singer, used to say.

"God's gon' bless you mightily, Johnnn Foun-tain," Grandmother always assured me. "He's going to do something great in your life. I just hope I'm still around to see it."

Meanwhile, some of my friends thought I had turned religious fanatic. They laughed whenever they saw me on my way to church, either on Sunday mornings when we loaded into the church van, or on Sunday evenings when my family and I strolled back to church, or on the countless evenings that I emerged from my apartment building wearing a white shirt and tie and appearing bound again for church. Their chiding bothered me a lot. But given the pressure I was under, I needed something to cope. Given the alternatives of drinking, drugging, or womanizing, I figured I was better off wailing with the little old ladies.

I know now that many of my own initial misgivings about the prayer group really stemmed from manly young pride. Maybe what really irked me was that these women, in the twilight of life, had a strength and power that I greatly lacked. It was a power that still believed God looked out for the souls of wayward sons and daughters whose lives had ended up in shambles.

It would later be clear, at least in my own mind, that those morning storefront prayers taught me some things. Among them was that poverty is a matter of the spirit. I later realized that during most of my life, I wasn't poor—just broke. But for a long time, it was hard to see beyond the immediacy of my day-to-day needs.

"I don't know how I made it this week," I testified at True Vine one Sunday.

"I don't know how I'm going to make it . . ."

My knees felt weak, the world all around me becoming an agonizing blur.

"You can make it, brother!" a sister shouted.

"You can make it," intoned another. "Hold on to the Lord!"

The organ revved. The congregation clapped, raised their arms and voices in praise. And I began to feel the electricity.

"But I know God is going to make a way," I said, beginning to feel revived.

"His word said, Weeping may endure for a night, but joy comes in the morning!"

I began to leap and dance across the red carpet. Grandmother shouted, too.

It wasn't long before I finally began to realize that if joy and deliverance were to come on that proverbial morning, the night wasn't even close to being over. And that very thought was sometimes overwhelming.

With winter approaching, I was more depressed than I had ever been. I felt that sense of achy hollowness that accompanies the death of dreams, which happened all the time in the ghetto where valedictorians turned into crack addicts, church girls became prostitutes, and choirboys became pimps and pushers. There comes a point, perhaps it is a crossroads, at which you either move toward life or toward death. I was dying, despite all the prayer and churchgoing and faith talk. It all began to seem like a waste of time. And though I had managed to hold out until now, my faith was slipping.

Spending the summer working at Truman had only reconfirmed how far our island of Komensky really was from the rest of the world. And it left me feeling stranded, like Robinson Crusoe, only in the 'hood. The summer job had given me a glimpse of life and hope, but it was only temporary and my confinement to Komensky slapped me back to reality and a sense of futility. That was how I was feeling one morning after prayer that fall as Grandmother and I sat in her Cadillac outside my apartment building. I felt lost, as if I was never going to amount to anything and there was nothing Grandmother or her prayer warrior friends or Jesus or anyone else could do to alter my destiny, which more and more seemed like a life sentence to hard times in K-Town.

Grandmother and I had just come from prayer that morning, except I could not yet feel the medicinal effects. It was like that sometimes, especially on days when my troubles seemed particularly heavy, when the food had run out or the lights, telephone, or gas had been cut off.

I sat in the car with Grandmother, sullen and about ready to start sobbing.

"I'm tired, Grandmother," I said, my words slow and heavy. "I can't find a job, nothing. Man-n-n, even when people tell me somebody is hiring and I go there, they say they're not hiring. I ain't ever gonna find a job."

"Oh yes, you will, baby darlin'. You just keep on holding onto the Lord," Grandmother answered.

"I'm tired of holding onto the Lord, Grandmother. Why won't God bless me with a job now?" I asked. "I pay my tithes, I go to church, I live saved. Mannn! Other folks find jobs, they're blessed more than me, and they ain't even thinking about the Lord," I said bitterly.

Grandmother seemed unfazed by my tirade.

"The Bible says He rains on the just as well as the unjust," she answered, her voice steady but sympathetic.

"I can't even afford to buy my children shoes," I fired back. Tears welled up in my eyes. "If God loves me so much, why does He let me suffer so much?

She didn't answer. Maybe there was no answer.

"Grandmother, I just give up," I said tearfully. "I ain't even got no dreams no more. I give up, I just give up."

Grandmother looked at me, the car idling in the morning air. What happened next seemed less divine than earthly at the time, though I would later hearken back to it as the moment of my mortal resurrection. This time Grandmother did not offer to pray or break into a sanctified praise. She did not scold or even offer a dry shoulder. She did not speak in tongues or moan in the spirit. She spoke simple words that struck me in a way that few ever have.

"Wait a minute now, you can't stop dreaming or you start to die," she said, her words half sung. "Oh no, baby darlin'. You can't stop dreamin'."

Sitting there in that moment, I tried hard to recall my dreams, to remember what I had wanted to be before life happened. But I found no traces in my mind. The more I searched the corners of my mind, the more I encountered empty black spaces. And I was afraid, both startled and afraid, because I had not been so fully conscious of the extent to which my hope and dreams had dissipated until right then. Dead was the childhood dream of becoming a lawyer. So was the dream of someday buying my mother a home, of someday buying one for myself. It was as if life itself had been sucked out of me and, along with it, every dream I ever had. Maybe it should not have been a surprise. For without the antagonism of dreams, there was no nagging reminder of what I might have become, of how far off course my ship had drifted.

You can't stop dreaming or you start to die. Grandmother's words jarred me like smelling salts. *Or you start to die . . .*

In the hours and days that followed, Grandmother's words churned inside. And for the first time in a long time, I began to think seriously about what I might like to become someday, about the places I might like to go, about the kinds of possibilities that made me giddy just to think about. I gave myself permission to climb aboard the dream boat of my imagination, to take a temporary excursion from my island of constraint, poverty, and circumstance without feeling like I had to plot out the course or determine whether the journey was even feasible. It took some soul-searching. But eventually I found my dreams, lying like sunken treasure at the bottom of the sea of my subconscious, deep inside my heart.

I wasn't sure where those dreams would take me or how far. I still could not afford to buy shoes for my children, their toes bunched and half corned. My own shoes still had holes in the soles. My only suit was still so worn that the lining inside the jacket had withered. I still had no job and no prospects. We still had no car, no life insurance, no kitchen curtains, no checking account, and not even a single dime of savings.

But I had found hope. At least I had hope.

CHAPTER 27

AFTER BIRTH

WE WERE LYING in bed early that October morning when the pains came. But we were now old pros at this baby thing, this being the third time around. It clearly was time. I called my stepfather to borrow his car to take Robin to the hospital. Mama agreed to watch the boys. We got dressed, then grabbed Robin's bag for her stay in the hospital and walked downstairs, down the dark, quiet block to my parents' home. Soon Robin and I were headed off to the University of Illinois Hospital, one of the benefits of being on Public Aid and having a medical card. Her contractions weren't unbearable yet. But I could tell they were getting stronger from the way she grimaced and moaned.

We checked in at the hospital emergency room and were soon escorted to a room where Robin slipped into a hospital gown, one of those thin little back-out deals. The room was not big or fancy, just a boxy hospital room with four walls and two beds. Robin was in the bed closest to the door. The other bed was empty.

While Robin lay in bed, I slipped a gown over my clothes and put on a cap a nurse had handed me. For the first time, I was going to accompany Robin into the delivery room to witness the birth of our child. I had not watched our sons being born. In John-John's case, we weren't married yet. Being in the delivery room was something I figured was more for husbands than for boyfriends. I don't recall whether going into the delivery room had even been an option during Rashad's birth. Even if it had, I am not certain that the blood and guts and drama of birth were something I would have thought myself capable of handling at that time. But this time I was going all the way. I wanted to see this baby born and to be there by my wife's side rather than sit in some room, waiting for someone to wheel my baby out so that I could take a peek before he or she was whisked away to the nursery. Both Robin and I hoped for a girl this time around.

The doctor checked to see how much Robin had dilated. She still had a ways to go, he said. But Robin said she felt as if she could give birth at any second. Normally, I would have believed the doctor, except I figured that a woman working now on delivering her third child might well know her body better than any man, doctor or not.

Suddenly Robin screamed, "It's coming!"

The nurses rushed us to the delivery room, though once we got there the sense of urgency seemed to dissipate for a moment. The doctor had still not arrived. Within a few minutes, Robin yelled again, "It's coming!"

The baby wouldn't wait. Nurses were running. My eyes switched back and forth from them to Robin while holding her hand and hoping the doctor would burst through the door at any second. "Where is the doctor?" I wondered. "Where is the doggoned doctor?"

"He's not going to make it. Shoo-o-o-t!" yelled the nurse, standing at the foot of the bed. "I'm going to have to deliver this baby myself!" she said. "We can't wait . . . All right, hold on, I'm going to ask you to push in a minute."

With another contraction coming on, Robin suddenly grabbed me in a headlock.

"All right, push! Come on, push . . . That's it, keep pushing," the nurse said.

As Robin pushed, she squeezed my neck at the same time, choking the life out of me.

"Let her go so she can breathe!" another nurse yelled at me.

She had it all wrong. I was the one who needed air. Anyway I stood straight up, still holding onto Robin's hand, my head turning from her face—twisted and filled with pain—to her vagina, where soon I saw a little head covered with wet black hair suddenly emerging. Robin pushed, panted, strained, and squeezed my hand as if she were sinking into the sea with me as her life preserver. In those few minutes, it was as if Robin existed somewhere between life and death, as if she ceased to exist, at least not beyond any purpose other than that of bringing another life into this world. It was as if she were dying with each breath, holding onto nothing except my hand as I stroked her face, wiping away the sweat and tears. And it was there that I fell in love all over again, watching this woman give life to my child.

Finally, the baby's little wet head popped completely out. Robin caught her breath momentarily. Then it was time for one final push. The baby slid out into the nurse's latex hands. It was 6:45 A.M.

"It's a girl!" I said, watching in awe as the nurse held her wet little body securely. "It's a girl," I said over and over, the words resonating. "It's a girl..."

I stood there, crying like a big slob. Robin managed an exhausted smile, then whispered in my ear, "I love you."

"I love you, too."

An hour or so later, Robin rested quietly in her room. I needed to get home. It had been a long night and I was tired. I also needed to pick up the boys from Mama's. I kissed Robin good-bye and headed for the door. On my way out of the hospital, I stopped by the nursery. Our daughter lay sleeping in the transparent portable crib closest to the nursery window. On a little card taped to the front of the crib were her inked tiny footprints and the word, "Fountain."

I did not go into the nursery. I just stood there for a while alone in the hallway, lost in my thoughts and exhausted. The night had passed and a Sunday morning sun spilled into the hall. Music played softly over the hospital intercom, a song by Stevie Wonder, *Isn't she lovely?*

I started crying again, gazing at this new miracle, just a couple of hours old. Finally, I said good-bye to Rasheena Charee, then walked out into the morning sun, feeling that maybe I was not so poor after all, but also understanding perhaps more than ever that I needed to do something to give my children a brighter future.

Weeks later, when the last winds of fall had been swallowed by winter, I sat one afternoon in the powder-blue hallway of our apartment building on the stairs between the second and third floors. Net stood at the top of the wooden stairs. This had become our informal meeting place of sorts, a place where my sister and I solved the problems of the world and discussed our children or the difficulties of life. Net had given birth to her second child a week after Robin gave birth to our third. It was not long after my conversation with Grandmother, when she told me not to stop dreaming.

"Net, I've made a decision," I said.

"Oh yeah, what?"

"I've decided that I am going to go back to school."

"That's good," she replied, though sounding skeptical.

"I'm serious. I am going to go back to school," I said. "I'm going to be somebody." This was something I had not said in years, though I had often said this as a child to anyone who would listen and with enthusiasm and certainty.

"I'm going to be somebody, you'll see. You think I'm kidding?" I said, probably sounding as if I was trying to convince Net, although I was really speaking aloud more for my benefit than anyone else's.

"I believe you, for real," Net said, looking serious. "What are you going to study?"

"I'm not sure, maybe political science, maybe journalism. I really like writing. I don't know. Maybe I'll be on TV one day doing the news or something. We'll see."

"So when are you going to start?"

"In January. That's when the new semester starts. I already called up there. I've got to fill out my financial aid papers. But we're so poor that I know I'll qualify for every penny."

We both laughed.

"The only thing I'll have to worry about is buying my books the first semester 'cause my financial aid won't be approved by then," I said. "But I'll get it somehow. I ain't gonna worry about it."

As I had promised, one day that December, I caught the bus to Wilbur Wright College, where I had not been since dropping out of school three years earlier. The grades of "Incomplete" that I had received for not returning to take my finals that fall of 1979 had turned into F's. I looked at my transcript and wanted to cry, thinking about how badly I had screwed up my life.

I went ahead and registered that winter for a full load of classes for the spring semester to begin that January. And though the future still looked pretty bleak, I had already come through darker days.

CHAPTER 28

THE WRIGHT STUFF

THE HALLS OF Wilbur Wright College were clean and polished. They brimmed with students, black, white, and Hispanic. There was the sound of hurried feet and adult chatter. Students at Wright were generally a few years older than the batch of freshmen that typically landed on university campuses each year, though there were still quite a few eighteen- and nineteen-year-olds and evidence of the kind of youthful disinterest in academics that I had been guilty of myself as a freshman at Champaign. On the second floor near the gym stood the usual crowd of school loiterers. Most of them I figured to be jocks. And the slim attractive young women with the girlish smiles I figured to be their admirers.

Wright was located on the city's Northwest Side and had a reputation for being one of the best junior colleges in Chicago. It would have been easier for me to go to Malcolm X College, another junior college on the West Side, since it was a lot closer. But Wright was known as a better school. So I decided the hourlong ride on the bus each way was more worth my while, especially if someday I might want to transfer to a four-year college.

I enrolled that cold January of 1983 with a load of fifteen semester-hours. Robin's father gave me $150 to buy books, so at least I had one less thing to worry about.

I selected a variety of liberal arts courses at the suggestion of my college adviser. Initially, I worried that the several years' layoff from school had left my mind rusty. It turned out that the most difficult adjustment in returning to college was getting used to being out in the world again, being around people, sharing my thoughts in class, and pushing myself to study while balancing my other responsibilities amid my incessant worries. The first time I had enrolled in college, I was single. Now I was married with three children. And even though I was in school now, I still had the same stack of bills, the same fears about our safety and well-being, and the same worries over our lack of finances. In one sense, being back in school and having a family—with their future and stability potentially riding on every grade—sometimes felt overwhelming. But in another sense, it was motivational. I reasoned that I could not afford to fail. And I had at least one consolation: If I failed, how much worse off would we be?

Most difficult about school was that there was always studying to be done no matter how much I had completed. There was always some book to read, always research to do for some term paper or project, always the weight of studies on my shoulders and growing strife between Robin and me. Coupled with the responsibilities of fatherhood, it all felt overwhelming.

It was next to impossible to study during the day on Komensky, where car alarms blared, the bass of house and car stereos flooded the streets, and the yelling and screaming or other disruptive city sounds invaded our apartment. These sounds had always been there. But they seemed amplified now that I needed the peace and quiet requisite for study. Having two energetic sons and a new baby at home also did not make for the most conducive study environment. That Robin would not agree that the children needed to go to bed at a decent hour, say 8:30 P.M., also made studying at home next to impossible. I could have stayed at Wright after classes and studied, which I did sometimes. But if I studied at Wright or the public library, there was always the danger of coming home on the bus late at night and risking being accosted by the assortment of thugs, muggers, and gang-bangers who trolled the buses after dark for prey. So I chose to study at home, almost exclusively at night when the yelling or drunken chatter and all the tire screeching and the pulsating loud music and pounding bass that poured from passing cars finally melted into the silence of night. Sometimes I managed to nap for a couple hours before stumbling into the kitchen with my stack of books for my late-night study sessions.

At first I hated studying. It wasn't studying itself that I found most difficult—the act of cracking open a book, of reading, outlining, and taking notes. It was mastering the art of self-denial, of forcing myself to read when my body and mind wanted to sleep, of forbidding myself to turn on the television or climb back into bed. It was the task of dismissing the worries and all other thoughts from my mind so that I could concentrate on my studies. It was the difficulty of staying motivated when self-doubt crept in and the dim circumstances of my life seemed greater than the light of any dream.

Sometimes during the day when I heard the basketball pounding and some friend calling my name to go shoot hoops, it was hard to resist, though I did so, time and time again. It used to irk me the way my sister's husband walked around free as a bird, dribbling a basketball, chilling with the fellas on the porch on a spring or summer afternoon, seemingly without a care in the world. It bothered me that some of the guys on the block drove big expensive cars bought with money from the drugs they sold and that all the children and even some of the adults on Komensky gawked and oozed admiration when these drug dealers turned the corner and crept down the block in all of their hot-wax and shiny chrome glory.

It ate at me that while I went to school by day, studied all night, and walked with my wife and children back to church on Sunday evenings, many people looked upon me as an oddity worthy of ridicule and snickering, and at the same time they esteemed the drug dealer. I am not sure that this was done consciously but rather believe that it often stemmed from their obsession with material possessions and their belief that the tangible things in this life are more valuable than those things that are more invisible like faith, hope, and morality. In times when I felt most discouraged, I read the first chapter of Psalms, in the morning and late at night. I read it over and over again, so many times that I had committed the six verses of the chapter to memory:

"Blessed is the man . . ." I would recite. *"And he shall be like a tree planted by the rivers of water, that bringeth forth his fruit in his season; his leaf also shall not wither; and whatsoever he doeth shall prosper."*

The words resonated: *And whatsoever he doeth shall prosper. And whatsoever he doeth shall prosper.*

So I studied. As night gave way to dawn, as the sun's red morning light crept through the edges of the window shades and spilled into the kitchen, and as the birds began their daily song, I pored over my textbooks, believing that they would lead me to a brighter day.

Professor Berman was spouting eloquently as usual, pacing back and forth inside the second-floor classroom at Wright. Mr. Berman was a white-haired white man with a voice that rolled like thunder. He had an intimidating presence that said, "Pay attention in my class or else." Sometimes he seemed more like a drill sergeant than a social science professor, the way he exploded into his presentation of the lesson once the bell sounded. He also had a strong sense of sarcasm, which he used unsparingly in his ribbing of students when it was obvious to him that they had not done the assigned reading. If you did not want to be embarrassed in Professor Berman's class, then you read. Or else you simply did not come to class. I read, not because I did not want to be embarrassed but because I loved social science and particularly Professor Berman's passion for teaching, which made the statistics and anthropological theories come alive.

In fact, I was so hungry for education after my three-year hiatus that I sopped up every word. Social science and human ecology were my favorite subjects. That was probably because they were the two classes in which I found the most immediate relevance and application to my life. But I am just as sure that my grasp of the material and enthusiasm about going to class had something to do with the professors teaching both classes.

In human ecology, Professor Garrett was every bit as passionate as Professor Berman and intent on his students' learning the lessons of the classroom and applying them to our daily lives. A lanky man who wore glasses and often a white lab coat, which made him look like a mad scientist when he was ranting and all riled up, Professor Garrett was obsessed with healthy living and with trying to convert the nutritionally damned. He ribbed us for our poor eating habits, for our consumption of fast food, and even for drinking tap water, which he considered to be polluted. Mr. Garrett drank pure spring water, he assured us. Sometimes he held up a plastic container of water that looked so clear and pure that I could imagine it had been scooped from the rivers of God. Mr. Garrett had a way of making potato chips, fast food, and processed food sound disgusting and unfit for human consumption.

"Fat chips, that's what they are, fat chips . . . Dis-gust-ing! You're going to die eating this stuff . . . You're all going to die. I'm not kidding you, you're going to die," he would tell the class, launching into one of his tirades. "Read the labels, re-e-e-ad the labels, and find out what's in this stuff.

"Why do you use deodorant, do you know what's in that stuff? What do you notice about starving people in Third World countries, huh, what do you notice? I'll tell you what you notice: They all have bald heads and big bellies. What do you see all across America, huh, wha-da-ya see? I'll tell you what you see: bald heads and big bellies. And guess what? If bald heads and big bellies are a sign of poor nutrition in Third World countries, it says the same thing about America.

"You're all going to die, consuming all of these empty calories and this diseased food and water. You're going to die young, unless you stop, now!"

Professor Garrett went on and on and on. Sometimes students' eyes glazed over. Occasionally, some brave student fed up with his doomsday jawing would interrupt him, which was like dangling blood-dripping red meat in front of a hungry lion.

Professor Garrett's teachings had an effect on me. It made me take note of what I was eating and to begin to incorporate more fruits and vegetables into my diet, to stop eating fast food and to start taking a multivitamin and supplements. Ultimately, his teachings had the effect of helping me to see my neighborhood with regard to health and well-being in a new light. For the first time, I began to wonder why there were so many greasy spoons in K-Town instead of health food stores, decent restaurants where you might buy a greaseless deli sandwich, or corner cafés, like the juice and bagel joints in white neighborhoods. And why was there so much obesity in my community? Why were there no health clubs? Why did folks in my neighborhood generally not exercise? Why were black folks in such poor health? In my case, Professor Garrett's ranting and raving created a monster. At least I began to think more critically and to seek to better understand the world and my place in it.

Still, no single class provoked me more than social science. On those afternoons that I sat in Professor Berman's class, having done the assigned readings, I was eager for his sparring sessions to begin. The bell sounded and he began firing questions, slowly at first, then rapid-fire. When he spoke, it was as if a light kept popping on inside my head and as if he were looking through a microscope at the social intimacies of my world.

One afternoon while sitting in social science class during the fall of 1983, Mr. Berman said something that stunned me, although I later realized that it was a mere statement of fact. What he said was that given a certain set of determinants such as poverty, income, and education, social scientists could generally predict someone's life cycle and whether he or she would end up as a teen parent, a homicide statistic, a drug addict, or stuck in poverty for life. He said that he could predict with a relative degree of scientific certainty the likelihood of poor black teenagers getting pregnant with a second child within two years of having the first, their likelihood of falling into the welfare system, and the likelihood of the cycle of poverty being passed on from generation to generation.

For a moment, I felt naked sitting there in class, naked and ashamed. It was as if Professor Berman had been spying on my life. He seemed to be reciting for the entire class my life story and those of other people I knew through his social scientific crystal ball. Even as I sat there while Professor Berman rambled on, I began to feel sick inside, realizing in a way what I never had before—how deep a hole I was in, and that the odds were that I would never be able to climb out.

Whatever the odds, I decided to try to stay positive. That meant staying busy rather than giving in to self-doubts or dwelling on the many reasons I should not succeed. I began writing for the school newspaper, the *Wright Angle*. The summer at Truman had rekindled my passion for writing, which seemed to flow naturally from somewhere within and stirred my creative juices. I began writing news stories, then a profile or two. I eventually gravitated toward features. Writing features felt most natural, particularly because of the focus on detail and seemingly limitless boundaries in both subject and approach to writing. Eventually, I was named features editor and began spending more time at Wright editing stories, laying out the newspaper, assigning stories as well as writing my own. The school newspaper was a supplement to my journalism and writing classes at Wright. The more I wrote and discovered journalism, the more certain I was that I was moving in the direction that I thought I ought to be moving in, which was to become a journalist.

Initially, when I had told Mama about my desire to major in journalism, she suggested that I major in business or in something having to do with computers.

"Journalism seems tough," Mama said. "Why do you want to major in journalism? It's going to be hard to find a job in journalism. You're not going to make any money. Why don't you major in business?"

I know that Mama meant well, as did the folks at church. But while Mama supported my decision to go back to school, some folks in my family and at church thought I had just about lost my mind for deciding to go to school rather than hold out for a nine-to-five. In fact, they began whispering that with a family, I had no business being in school and that I probably had not been looking for a job as diligently as I had made it seem. Their whisperings hurt. But Robin at least knew the truth about how I had searched for a job and had shared in my tears and sorrow each time I returned home empty-handed. Her knowing the truth was all that mattered, anyway.

"Maybe college is what I am supposed to do," I reasoned within myself. "Maybe I can't find a job because I'm supposed to go back to school. Maybe that man at the bank, who had refused to give me the teller job years earlier, was onto something. Maybe my ending up back on Komensky was where I needed to be for a reason."

Since moving back, my neighbor Mr. Newell and I had become good friends, sitting sometimes on his porch, talking for hours into the evening as the sun was going down. We talked about his days in the South, about the white man, about the black man, about K-Town and how much it had changed, about how bad it had gotten. Mr. Newell was still kicking around his garden, though his steps were considerably slower and his lawn less green than I remembered and protected by a wire-and-pole fence to dissuade people from walking on it. I often borrowed Mr. Newell's garden tools, which he entrusted to no one else on the block. He was happy that I had planted grass next door. And he often told me how proud he was to see me taking care of the building where we lived and to see me taking care of my family and going to church. He was proud that I wasn't hanging out in the streets.

"Just keep on doing good, Johnny," Mr. Newell would say, puffing his pipe. "The Good Lord will take care of you. Just keep on doing good. You're all right, Johnny. You're all right."

There was a kind of strength that I took from Mr. Newell's admiration. It encouraged me in the same way that John-John's kindergarten teacher, Mrs. Thomas, had. Once, after we had come back from a field trip that I had chaperoned, she told me how she bragged on me to her Evanston friends when they were ranting on about how bad K-Town was, how there were only single women raising children and no decent men around, no hope. Mrs. Thomas said she told them about the father of one her students, a positive young brother who wasn't hooked on drugs, who loved God and was taking care of his family and was enrolled in school. Her words moved me to tears and made me want to run on.

What's funny is that once I had made up my mind to go back to school, to redeem the time, and when I finally began to feel a sense of purpose, it seemed that every other week, someone had some new interesting job prospect for me. I always felt obliged to apply for the job rather than face the possible implications of not applying and more whisperings. So I kept applying for jobs as they came up. But I also kept going to school and studying, convinced that education would prove to be the better way in the long run.

Still, I could not shake the feeling that I was more or less a failure. Deep inside, I still burned with shame and I reasoned that I was less of a man for not being able to provide for my family other than through welfare and odd jobs no matter how much Mama, Robin, and Grandmother said to the contrary.

"You're a good man, John Foun-tain, I deee-clare you are," Grandmother would say sometimes.

"If all your problems are money problems," Mama often said, "you don't have any problems because one day you'll have money. You'll see."

But my financial inability wore on my psyche. It gnawed at me and gave me migraines. And the shame I felt was always there when I woke up in the morning and when I went to bed at night. I felt it every time I looked into my children's eyes or cradled them in my arms and wanted to be able to give them more than just my love.

Going back to school did help ease my burden. Just enrolling gave me a renewed sense of empowerment. For somewhere between Robin and the kids and the endless disconnection notices, I had lost faith in myself. And now that I had found it again, it gave me life and sustenance, the strength to climb out of bed in the morning and to get through another day. But what I recognized even back then, even with my newfound strength, was that I was still holding on by a thread.

It was an average school morning. I climbed onto the bus on Pulaski Road. But as I walked past the rows, and the shadows occupying the seats, my mind somewhere between my worries and my studies, I was startled by a familiar voice.

"John!" the voice called.

"John!" the voice called again.

I looked toward where the voice had come from. Sitting in the back a few feet away from me was a friendly face, a familiar face. It was one of my high school classmates, Dorian.

"Dorian, what up, man?" I said excitedly. "What up, boy?"

Like me, Dorian had gone to St. Mel all four years. We had not seen each other since graduation day nearly five years earlier. We both broke into smiles. We slapped fives and fingered out a soul brother handshake, looking each other over.

In high school, Dorian was always a pressed young man, dark and handsome with clean white teeth. But he had always been a little on the corny side, not a jock, not a ladies' man, smart though not at the top of the class. He was a relatively quiet guy and laid back. But I always had the sense that even though he had been named "Best Dressed" in the senior yearbook and had a lot going for himself, he was envious of the guys who got better grades, played sports, and enjoyed more popularity with the ladies. Even though I got along with Dorian, I sensed that he was always in competition, that he was out to prove he was smarter or a better dresser—just plain better. Or I sensed at least that he was one of those people in life who were always waiting for you to fall so that they could laugh and make themselves feel better in the company of your misery.

"Dorian, what's been up, man?" I said that morning, genuine in my delight to see him.

"Nothing, man, I'm on my way to school," he answered. "What's happening, John, man, long time no see," Dorian said. "So what's been up with you, man? What you doing now? I heard you got married?"

It seemed like a million questions all at once. And suddenly, I felt a rush of embarrassment as I scanned Dorian's neatly pressed slacks and shirt, his tidy Afro and spit-shined shoes, in contrast to my worn slacks and shoes, my poor man's apparel. Dorian looked as *GQ* as ever. I felt like crawling underneath a seat as I sat there on the bus, squirming and not really wanting to answer Dorian's questions but knowing full well that he probably already knew most of the answers anyway and that he took pleasure in my pathetic poverty. I could see it in his eyes.

Some people in the 'hood were like that. It was as if they were always circling overhead like vultures, waiting for you to take that last breath and lie down and die so that they could tear the flesh from your carcass. On Komensky, a couple of guys I grew up with joked that the only things I did, now that I was married with a family, was play basketball and go to church. That wasn't entirely true. But it wasn't about truth. They meant it to sting. I sensed as much with Dorian.

I heard you got married. Dorian's words hung in the air.

"Yeah, man, I'm married," I answered finally, the shame pushing my head down and my pride nudging me to hold it up. "Yeah, me and Robin got married almost four years ago."

"How many kids y'all got?"

I hesitated. "Three," I answered.

Dorian snickered, his eyes lighting up with laughter. The peppering of questions continued, sapping me of dignity and pride and the ability to simply say to Dorian, "None of your stinking business."

"You working?" he asked.

Nope. The complete answer was, "No, we're on welfare." But I would never tell any of my friends that.

"Nah, man," I answered, "I'm in school."

Dorian looked ready at any moment to burst into laughter. I was on the verge of tears.

"Where you at?"

"Wright, uhhh, Wright Junior College," I answered.

At last, Dorian could not hold it any longer. He laughed out loud and laughed and laughed until finally he regained his composure just long enough to tell me that he was finishing up with a business or accounting degree or something at Loyola University downtown. Finally, the bus stopped at Lake Street and Pulaski, Dorian's stop for the train toward downtown and his four-year university. He rose to his feet, toting his satchel, smiling proudly and looking smug.

"All right, John, later, man."

"Later," I said.

Dorian got off and the bus slowly pulled away. I rode on to Wright, sitting on the back of the bus, wiping away the tears.

CHAPTER 29

CHAMPAIGN DREAMS

TIME PASSED more quickly than I might ever have imagined. After two semesters at Wright, I was looking at a third and at earning my associate's degree by the end of the spring, once I had transferred the hours I had earned during my freshman year at the University of Illinois. I had not yet made any plans beyond earning my two-year degree at Wright. In fact, that December I was still thinking that I might go out and look for a job. With an associate's degree in high school teaching, I thought that maybe I could get a job at a public school as a teacher's aide. Or perhaps I would apply for admission to one of several four-year colleges and universities in the city, such as Loyola or DePaul. I wasn't sure.

I had done well so far at Wright, earning no lower than a B in the more than thirty semester-hours I had taken. I had even earned an A in physical science and a B in physics, both classes that I had dreaded in high school. The same classes I had once found boring, I now found intriguing. As much as I thought that my freshman-year grades might hurt me in applying for admission to a four-year college, I reasoned that my success in college this time around would weigh more in my favor.

With two semesters complete, I felt that I was on a mission with no time to waste. I also had a greater appreciation for having been given a second chance. Once, I had sworn to Robin that if I ever got the opportunity to go back to school, I would make the most of it. I had. With graduation from Wright just months away, it was time to make more plans for the future. I wasn't sure which direction I needed to take, and I found few possibilities in my still limited scope.

But one day that winter, the telephone in our apartment rang. It was Mama.

Mama and I talked often, especially when she sensed that Robin and I were not getting along or that my money was short, which sometimes seemed like an everyday thing. Mama could always sense when I was particularly troubled. Whether it was the heaviness in my voice, or that tired short-circuited look in my eyes, or the way I sometimes withdrew from the world and sat quietly alone in my own thoughts in a room full of people, I do not know. Mama could always sense when things with me were not good.

For years, I was miserable in our marriage and haunted by Mama's warnings about Robin. I came to understand Mama's reservations perfectly well and was comforted only by the knowledge that I had not gone out looking for a wife at age nineteen, and that even if I had, I surely would not have known what to look for. I married my high school sweetheart, whom I happened to fall in love with and whom I happened to impregnate—twice. The winds of consequence and the currents of life carried us down that proverbial creek without a paddle.

I later came to believe that we often cannot help falling in love with someone and that sometimes we fall in love with the wrong people, meaning people who are all wrong for us. I further came to think that there exists on this earth someone for almost everyone, a soul mate, though whether you ever find each other is a different matter. Although I loved Robin deeply, and for many years could not imagine life without her, I increasingly came to see our marriage as my cross to bear. Often, I felt as if I were carrying dead weight up an icy mountain, understanding with each step I took that unless Robin ever decided to help me scale that mountain, there was only so far I would ever be able to climb.

It was a long time before I understood how much Robin resented me, although her venom was most likely aimed at what I represented in her eyes: a father more than a husband. In Robin's eyes, I was a control freak. In some ways I was. In a sense, I had to be. Given the state of our finances and the need to sustain our family, I took control of all of our financial affairs. I paid all the bills, worked out the budget, made the arrangements with bill collectors when there was not enough money to pay our bills. I insisted that we keep our house clean. I took Robin grocery shopping and tried to teach her all the things that Mama had taught me. How to buy in bulk, to compare unit prices, to stay away from cereals that offered no nutritional value, only sugar, to keep a running tally on how much you were spending so there would be no surprises once you got to the cashier. I bought clippers and insisted that I cut the boys hair myself to reduce our expenses rather than spend money on a barber. It was my suggestion that we should eat supper as a family at a certain time each evening. I insisted that the children be put to bed at a certain time each night and that we did not need to spend money on expensive brand-name apparel. That we should keep our apartment clean, should not let our children sleep over at other people's houses, and should go to church on Sundays and take our children to Sunday School. On most of these points and more, Robin resisted, though she had begun to do the laundry on her own, which consisted of having her mother pick her up and washing our clothes at her family's house.

There was not much that Robin did not fight me on, no matter how gingerly I made suggestions for our family and our affairs. Her resistance was sometimes passive, if not subversive. She simply would not cook until or unless she felt like it, or she would not clean, or she simply sat silently gazing at the television with a look that said, "I'm not going to do it and you can't make me." Sometimes she protested outright.

"Why do we have to eat at a certain time?" she'd say.

"We don't have to, Robin. I just think it's a good thing," I would answer. "It's good family time and as the kids get older, they'll be playing ball and involved in other things in school. Look Robin, if we do this now, we can establish a family time. And they'll know that this is the time that we all come together at home."

"That's so stupid. I don't agree. Uh-uh, I don't agree. Why we gotta eat dinner together? My family didn't eat dinner together..."

"And look at 'em!" I'd yell.

"Whaaat-ev-errr, John," Robin would fire back.

"Look, Robin, I'm just asking you to trust me on this. Why don't we try it?"

"No! I don't agree."

"What don't you agree with, huh? Please tell me what you don't agree with."

"We don't have to sit down at any certain time to eat dinner. Uh-uh. You just think you're always right."

"Robin, I'm not trying to be always right."

"Yes you are, John. You and your family always think y'all right."

Right or wrong, Robin and I seldom agreed, and the rift between us widened to battles over even the simplest of things.

When I told my sons that I wanted them to go to college when they grew up, in the next breath, Robin remarked, "Why they gotta be like you? Why they gotta go to college, just because you went to college?"

When I encouraged my sons to play basketball, she interjected, "Why they gotta play basketball just because you play basketball? Maybe they don't want to play basketball."

Robin always seemed to be in competition for our children's affections and more intent on being a friend than a parent. So in the children's eyes I became the strict parent, the enforcer, the brute. I did not understand the extent of the damage that was being done to my relationship with my children or the seeds of resentment and resistance she was planting. Nor did I understand how much my children had learned to respond and relate to me in the same ways their mother did.

In time I came to understand that for Robin, any attempt to establish order, a routine, or structure in our household was deemed an attempt to control her. And there was nothing I could say or do to help her see it any differently.

I thought about divorce many times. And each time, it was thoughts of my children that led me back to my good senses. I could not imagine my world without them, although increasingly I could imagine a world without their mother. And no matter how much I loved her, I felt that this might be necessary to save my own life.

I have never considered myself to be a Mama's boy. But often, when I seemed at the end of my rope, when life's pressures weighed heavily and Robin was threatening again to go back home to her father's, or when it seemed easier to simply just take a walk one day away from our apartment and my bills and all of my responsibilities and never come back, Mama never failed to encourage me. Even as I sat on the living room heater sometimes, unable to stop the flow of tears, I never had to worry about "acting like a man" or even hearing Mama say, "I told you so." She listened without judgment and without beating me up emotionally. She always told me in that reassuring voice that everything would be all right.

"Just get a good night's sleep, John, try not to worry, it'll work out. Things always look better in the morning, you'll see," Mama would say.

Sometimes they didn't. But just knowing that Mama was there when I needed to talk and that she was someone who would always love me whether I was a rich man, poor man, beggar man, or thief sometimes helped me get through the night.

"Hey, Ma," I answered the telephone that winter day.

"How's it going?"

"Okay," I said, feeling upbeat.

We were talking about my upcoming graduation and about my plans after finishing at Wright when Mama popped the question.

"John, I wanna ask you something."

"What?"

"Okay, uh, have you ever thought about going back to Champaign?" Mama asked, her voice filled with caution.

"To Champaign?" I asked. "For what?"

"To finish school," she said. "Have you ever thought about going back down to Champaign to finish school?"

"To Champaign, how, Ma?" I responded, truly unable to comprehend why on earth she would be talking to me about going back to Champaign.

"I just thought..."

Suddenly, I exploded.

"How can I go back to Champaign to school, Ma? I got a family. I couldn't make it there by myself, now I've got a wife and three kids on welfare. Nah, I ain't thought about going back to Champaign. How am I gonna even think about going back to Champaign, Ma?"

"I just thought that maybe you should think about it," Mama said. "I mean, you're finishing up at Wright. You might as well...I've heard of older married people going back to school. You can do it, John, I know you can."

"I can't, Ma, I can't. Ma, I gotta go."

"Okay, John. Bye."

I slammed the receiver down. Moments later, I was still seething. Then my anger melted into sorrow and my sorrow into tears. Truth was that somewhere deep inside, the dream of graduating from the University of Illinois in Champaign still lived. I had not thought about the possibility of returning to Champaign because it seemed to lie so clearly outside the realm of possibility. Except for the hope of seeing Jeff or my youngest sister, Meredith, or perhaps even my own children someday go to the University of Illinois, the Champaign dream was dead. I stood in the kitchen, feeling only pain and the warm salty tears that I seemed to have cried now for the millionth time.

In the weeks that followed, something strange happened. I began having a dream that seemed so real that it sometimes made me sit up in bed late at night, then shake my wife and tell her that I had had the dream once again. In the dream, I could see myself as well as my surroundings with great clarity. I was back in Champaign.

Soon I began to wonder whether God wasn't trying to tell me something. Finally, one afternoon, hours after having had the dream again, I picked up the telephone, figuring that it wouldn't hurt to call the University of Illinois to at least make an inquiry about going back to school. I was nervous as I punched the numbers from memory with my right index finger: 1-2-1-7-3-3-3 ...

"Office of Admissions," a lady's voice rang on the other end.

I explained that I was a former student who had dropped out years earlier and that I was now interested in returning to school. She asked me two questions: Had it been less than five years since I left? And had I left the university in good standing? The answer to both was yes.

"Then readmission is automatic," she said.

I hung up the telephone and started jumping up and down.

"Yes! Yes!"

Robin came running.

"What's wrong? What's wrong?"

I told Robin what the woman in the Office of Admissions had said and how I believed it to be a sign that God was opening the door for me to return to Champaign. I was laughing and crying and praising God. I felt more alive than I had in a long time. I also felt as if for the first time in a long time, I could scale any mountain. Maybe that new sense of power I felt—the faith that now filled me—had always been there somewhere inside and I had just had to find it. I don't know. But what I did know was that where I had once relied on the prayer warriors and the saints at True Vine to help me through my long days and nights, I was becoming less and less dependent on them and more reliant on hearing the Lord for myself.

In the days that followed my call to the Office of Admissions, I couldn't help but recall that final semester years earlier at the University of Illinois, when I was on academic probation, my father had been killed, and I wanted to quit school. I recalled that sense of compulsion, that almost supernatural urging that would not let me quit that semester. If I had given up back then, my readmission would not have been automatic and instead of my miracle, I might instead have had more misery. And I understood that I had made it through that semester by the grace of God.

What amazed me most was how that grace or favor—which always has kept me from being totally consumed by my own folly—always seemed to be there whenever I needed it most, despite my ignorance, shortcomings, or mistakes. It sometimes seemed as if someone was watching over me. There was, even before I recognized it as God, this unexplainable feeling of warmth that seemed to wrap its arms around me and fill me so completely in my most troubled times.

Sometime that winter, I began to believe that maybe I could make it back to the University of Illinois, though I knew that with a family, the road was going to be tough. There were the issues of still owing the university money, finding housing for my family, and how to manage the tuition and somehow buy an automobile, which we would need in order to get to the grocery store as well as to other places. In Champaign, we wouldn't be able to rely on Grandpa. When I told Grandpa one day while sitting on the passenger side of his car that I was going to go back to school in Champaign and take my family with me, he laughed.

"Oh yeah?" he replied, not meaning any harm and likely more stunned by my announcement than anything else.

His response hurt. But years later, I imagined I might have reacted the same way if a grandson in such a predicament as mine had said the same to me. When I told Grandmother of our plans, she wondered, as did many of the saints who didn't want to lose our presence in the church, why I could not attend one of the many fine academic institutions in Chicago.

By then, I was starting to realize that as much as the saints had been a blessing and my salvation, they had carried me as far as they could. And while I would always have their prayers and the uplifting experience of those Tuesday and Friday morning crying sessions with Grandmother and the prayer warriors, I had begun to understand that our destinies led to different paths. Their dreams were not my dreams, and my dreams were not theirs. And though we were in many ways one and they had nursed me to a state of viability and health, it was time for me to be in a sense born again, to sever the spiritual and social umbilical cord and to follow and fulfill my own calling.

"I'm going to talk to God about you leaving, see what the Lord has to say about that," Grandmother said one day. "You have to be careful moving a family like that. There aren't any schools here you could go to? We need y'all here at the church. We really need y'all. You're a big help to Grandpa."

"I could go to a school here, Grandmother," I answered. "But it has always been my dream to earn a degree from the University of Illinois. Plus, if I stay here, there are too many distractions."

"Oh yeah?"

"Yeah, Grandmother. I think I need to get away. It'll be good for the kids, for all of us. It'll be a totally different lifestyle living in a college town."

"It just don't seem to me that you really have to leave," Grandmother scolded. "I'm going to pray about it and see if God won't keep you here. We'll see what the Lord has to say about it. I'm gon' have a little talk with Jesus."

Something rose up inside me.

"Grandmother, the Bible said that God will give you the desires of your heart," I responded. "My desire is to go back to the University of Illinois. That's my desire. So you can pray, Grandmother, but I think God is going to answer my prayer."

"Okay," Grandmother said, laughing.

"Okay," I laughed.

I knew Grandmother meant no harm and only wished the best for me. She didn't want to have to say good-bye. Neither did I. But time and Champaign dreams seemed to be calling my name.

In subsequent weeks, something else strange happened. Those dreams that I had been having at night—the dreams about being on campus in Champaign that roused me from my sleep—they stopped. After I made the call to the Admissions Office that day, I never had another.

The car rumbled down University Avenue as Robin, her father, and I scouted out the land. It was our third trip to Champaign that spring in search of housing. We had a handful of listings and had exhausted all of our prospects with no good fortune. It had been the case that either the apartments we looked at were not up to par or the landlord was not interested in renting to a family. I had decided that this would be our last trip to Champaign. Either we found housing or I would abandon any dream of returning to school. It was getting pretty late for securing housing for the upcoming fall semester. And without anything that looked even remotely promising, hope was slipping fast.

I had already received my acceptance letter from the University of Illinois and was nearing the end of my final semester at Wright. I was graduating in a few weeks and had won an award from the Illinois Community College Journalism Association for an editorial I had published in the *Wright Angle*. I took special delight in the award, given that my colleagues had met and decided on which articles to submit for the annual contest without any consultation from me, even though I was features editor. They had submitted much of their own writing and only one piece that I had authored. But I was the only one who had won an award—touché.

The prospect of leaving Wright and the friends I made held some sadness for me. But the thought of earning my associate's degree and having done well in my classes made me feel good and proud. Most of my classmates were not planning to go on to four-year colleges, which I thought to be somewhat of a waste since many of them were far less encumbered than I. For me, there were four other souls to consider.

This trip to Champaign, like all the previous ones, seemed to be heading for failure, but then we remembered something that one of the prospective landlords had told us. He had mentioned something about the university having married-student housing and that he thought the name of the place was Orchard Downs. We decided to investigate. We stopped and asked students on the street about Orchard Downs; most said they had never heard of it. A few said they had but did not know where it was. Finally, we hit the jackpot. An older gentleman we stopped knew all about it.

"Go south on Lincoln until you get to Florida Avenue, and hang a left, and keep going, you'll run dead into it on your right," he said.

As we drove down Lincoln Avenue, I felt a rush of excitement that grew even more as we headed east on Florida, past the university president's mansion and finally to a sign that read, "Married Student Housing." I had a good feeling about this Orchard Downs place. But I was guarded as we made the right turn onto the grounds and headed for the housing office. Inside, I encountered an older white gentleman who turned out to be the housing manager. His name was Jack Smith. I explained that I was a returning student and that we were in search of housing for the fall. He asked us to follow him in his truck.

We trailed the white truck on a winding road past rows of short red-brick apartment buildings that looked like military housing. The units looked small and not very appealing. In fact, they reminded me of some of the projects in Chicago, except much cleaner and in much better shape. The good feeling that I had started to get when we first arrived at Orchard Downs was starting to fade. Then suddenly, at the end of a windy road, tall white-frame buildings emerged like castles surrounded by vast green fields.

"Oh my God, this is so nice," I exclaimed.

Robin's eyes lit up. We were both excited and could hardly contain ourselves as we climbed out of the car and followed Mr. Smith inside to one of the three-story apartment buildings that held twelve units each. The apartment itself was only two bedrooms but had a decent-sized living room, an eat-in kitchen, and a small terrace. It was a quaint little place that was not as spacious as our apartment on Komensky. But what it lacked in size, it more than made up for by its serene setting and the manicured fields of green, speckled with playground equipment that surrounded it. We could tell immediately that it was a different world from Komensky altogether by the way the children's bikes were strewn across the courtyard and how even the adult bikes were unchained. There were scents of spices, the likes of which I had never smelled before, coming from apartments. There were people of all nationalities going to and from buildings: Asian, white, and black. There was something about this place that gave me an immediate feeling of homeliness and peace and the sense that here was where my family and I belonged. We loved it.

"This is really nice. We really like it," I said to Mr. Smith. "So, uh, how do we get an apartment?"

"Well, unfortunately, I have to say that we have a waiting list that is one to two years long," he answered. "You're more than welcome to put in an application. But at this late date, I can't promise you anything."

"I wish I had known about family housing earlier," I said, unable to hide my disappointment.

"The university should have sent you something about it after you received your acceptance letter."

"Maybe they did," I said. "But I don't remember seeing it."

"Well, I'm really sorry," Mr. Smith said sincerely. "We have people who have been on the waiting list since last year. Again, you folks are welcome to put in an application. But, I have to be honest. It doesn't look real hopeful for this fall."

"Okay," I said. "Let's do that."

We drove back to the office and filled out an application. I thanked Mr. Smith for showing us the place and said good-bye. Robin and I climbed back into the car and headed home, feeling down but not entirely defeated.

"Don't worry," I said to Robin. "If God wants us to be here, He'll open up the door."

I prayed silently on the way home. In the days that followed, I prayed some more and also fretted some. I realized that Orchard Downs was our best hope, if not our only hope. My mind was laced with doubts. Had I been wrong about God opening the door for me to go back to Champaign? What would we do now? I had been afraid all along to get my hopes up too high, and now I stood to have them crushed. What was I thinking anyway, believing I could go back to Champaign?

"Lord, please hear my cry, oh God, I know that you are able to do all things," I prayed. "Please give us that apartment, oh God. Please open the door."

Finally, a few weeks after our trip to Champaign, the telephone rang one day.

"John Fountain?" asked the voice on the other end.

"Yes, this is he."

"This is Jack Smith from the Married Student Housing at the University of Illinois in Champaign..."

My heart pounded fast.

"Yes, Mr. Smith, how are you?"

"Fine, Mr. Fountain," he answered. "I have good news. We have an apartment for you."

"Excuse me, you, uh, you what?"

He laughed.

"You're in luck. We have an apartment for you," he said again. "Are you interested?"

"Yes! Yes!" I exclaimed.

"Well, it's that unit you wanted. If you'll go ahead and give a verbal commitment, I'll go ahead and mail you a housing contract."

"Yes, we'll take it."

"Okay, we'll get it in the mail today," Mr. Smith said. "Congratulations."

Tears welled up in my eyes.

"Thank you, sir," I said. "Thank you."

I hung up the telephone and shared the news with Robin. We both jumped up and down, laughing and crying and praising God. We called our parents and shared the news.

The road ahead still led to the Red Sea. But I could glimpse dry land on the other side and the miracle winds were starting to blow.

I climbed onto the southbound Pulaski Bus at Congress, headed home after a late night in the photo lab at Wright. The semester was just about over and graduation imminent. I had a satchel full of books and several folders full of black-and-white photographs and papers in another, the 35-millimeter camera I had rented from the school for a photojournalism class strung across my shoulder. I was tired. I sauntered to the back of the bus.

To my surprise, there was a young man whom I had grown up with in K-Town, sitting on the bench seat all the way at the rear of the bus with another young man whom I did not know. The young man I knew wore his hair in a Superfly do. Except his was a really bad conk, probably one of those do-it-yourself jobs that came in a box. Never mind that this was 1984, about a decade since the emergence of the Superfly-pimp-daddy look. His do was definitely outdated. But such was the look of a thug.

"What's up, man?" I said, nodding.

He spoke and nodded back. I sat nearby in one of the seats at the back of the bus that faced sideways rather than forward, giving me a view directly out of a side window instead of facing toward the front of the bus, the other passengers, and the driver. I was so tired that I quickly began dozing, which I rarely did, largely because that was not safe. But because I knew this guy on the bus, I felt a little more comfortable than usual. I dozed in and out for several blocks. At Arthington Street, a few blocks from where I had gotten on the bus, a few young men climbed aboard and strode to the back.

"Hey, what's up, man?" one of them said to the young man sitting next to the guy I knew.

"What's up?" the young man responded, as if he was seeing a long-lost friend.

The two men started laughing and talking loudly, but nothing out of the usual, as the bus rolled. Suddenly, with the bus nearly at Roosevelt, which is five blocks from where I would be getting off the bus and walking toward home, the young man I knew stood up and walked toward the back door, though he faced the back of the bus and seemed to be intentionally blocking the aisle. I quickly got the sense that something was wrong. I don't know how I knew. It was the same feeling that had come over me nearly every time when as a child I sensed I was about to be robbed by someone who had passed me on the street moments earlier and had spoken to me as they walked by. I just knew.

"Throw down, man," the dude with the bad conk yelled to the other young man he had been sitting next to at the back of the bus. "Throw down!"

The man sitting at the back of the bus looked at me. He looked dead into my eyes. I knew then exactly what was going on. It was a stickup. It didn't matter that it was on a public bus. This kind of thing happened all the time. Even if folks saw somebody getting mugged, they turned their heads rather than risking drawing attention to themselves or getting involved in someone else's fight.

"Throw down, man," the slick-headed dude I knew shouted again angrily.

"I can't, man," he finally answered, looking directly at me. "I can't."

"Man, I don't believe you. I give you my stuff and then you ain't gonna throw down."

"I can't," he repeated.

"Man, give me my stuff!"

His stuff, I knew, meant his gun. Just then he walked back toward his friend to retrieve his stuff. I knew I had to make a break. Nobody else on the bus, including the driver said a word or appeared to be coming to my aid. In fact, they stared straight ahead as if everything were normal. I reasoned that there was not much time and that this dude was likely to shoot me right then and there on the spot and take my rented camera and whatever few dollars I had in my pocket. For a moment, I was frozen in disbelief that someone I knew would try and stick me up. I knew this dude's brothers, sisters, and cousins, and even where his family lived. But Mama had always warned me that you had to be leery of the folks you knew. And I figured that because I knew my stickup man, there would be little recourse in a robbery other than to kill me. I didn't mind being robbed. I didn't want to be shot. I quickly snapped out of the fog and made my way to the bus's back door, not quite sure what to do but sure that I had to escape.

The bus driver pulled away from the stop at Fillmore Street headed toward Roosevelt Road. With the bus in motion, I pulled the emergency lever. The door flung open. I jumped off the bus into the draft and the night. My feet hit the ground, then my body and head. I have never known whether I lost consciousness that night. But I have always believed that I must have, since by the time I looked up from the middle of the street, I could see the red brake lights of the bus flash as it pulled into the stop at Roosevelt Road. My pictures and papers were sailing on the wind. My hands were scraped badly from my fall and my heart beat with the kind of excitement and fear that fills anyone who has narrowly escaped death. I collected what I could of my things, including my camera, which was dented, and which I would later learn was damaged beyond repair.

For a long time after the incident that night, I was sore physically. And for a long time, I was angry that this guy whom I knew and had played softball with as a child would have tried to rob me, angry that black folks preyed on one another, angry that even if I was trying to do something positive to help myself and my family, I reasoned that there was always going to be some fool trying to pull me down, giving me grief and misery, and seeing my criminal abstinence and my attempt to be a decent human being as signs of weakness. It made me mad that black folks were always talking about white folks trying to keep the brothers down. And yet every time I had been robbed, nearly every time I had had cause to fear loss of life and limb, and nearly every time I had stared into the eyes of the enemy, the enemy was someone who looked a lot like me.

Our terrorists were homegrown. They were the brothers. Not all the brothers, but far too many of us. It made me mad that we too often seemed to be our own worst enemy and that too often we were willing to excuse ourselves from accountability and responsibility as we laid the blame for our own shortcomings on slavery and racism. And though I knew the effects of both all too well and did believe that the "white man" was behind the guns and drugs that filled our neighborhood, I have also always understood that there was no poverty, no promise of filthy lucre, nor anyone or anything in this world that could make anyone sell drugs or stick a gun in someone's face and demand their wallet or purse.

A few days after the foiled robbery attempt, my would-be assailant had the nerve to show up on the block to visit his relatives. I reasoned that he was also there to show he was not afraid and to serve a silent warning not to call the cops. I never filed a police report, though this had less to do with fear of retaliation than it did with my sense that any criminal charges would not have amounted to much of anything. For a while, I had visions of simply quietly stalking this guy one night, of walking up to him and putting a gun to his dome and pulling the trigger. I imagined that his death would not have created much notice at all and that cops would likely not have investigated vigorously, surmising that he probably got what was coming to him. I have sometimes had difficulty imagining that I would ever have regretted it.

For a while I was angry with God. I couldn't help but wonder, if He loved me so much, why did He allow this to happen to me? Why now? My day of deliverance seemed so close, and yet I could only wonder whether I would live to see it. In my distress, I meditated on a Bible verse that had carried me through so many difficult times before, one that the saints had had inscribed on the red Bible they had given me as a gift one year:

> *Trust in the Lord with all thine heart and lean not to thine own*
> *understanding. In all thy ways acknowledge him and he shall*
> *direct thy paths.* (Proverbs 3:5–6)

I stood filled with joy and expectation to testify at True Vine one Sunday that spring. "Giving honor to God, to the pastor..." I testified. "I thank God for being here. I thank Him for opening the door for me to go back to school in Champaign...I thank God that He has allowed me to be accepted to school..."

"Amen!" the saints shouted.

"...Then we had applied for this apartment and the man told us that there was a two-year waiting list..."

"Uh-huh, testify," the saints urged.

"But I want you to know that he called us a few weeks later and said, 'I have an apartment for you.'"

"Hallelujah!" the saint's voices rang out. "Thank you, Jesus!"

I continued testifying.

"But there's one more thing I need God to do for me in order for us to move to Champaign. I need the Lord to bless me with a car," I exclaimed.

There were no hallelujahs or Amens this time, only nervous smiles and doubts glazing over their faces. But I was fired up now.

"I know God's going to bless me with a car! I don't know how He's going to do it. But I know he will!"

Grandmother leaped to her feet. She was smiling and radiating with joy, though years later she would admit to me that my declaration that God was going to bless me with a car had her a little worried, she said, because "I knew I didn't have no money to help you at the time."

"I said to myself, 'Help him, Lord,'" Grandmother recalled.

But whether anyone else believed at that point no longer mattered. What mattered was that I believed. After all of my tears and self-doubts, after all the morning prayers and revivals, after enduring the sometimes seemingly endless trials and hardship of life, after all the little miracles that had sustained me when I was at the end of my rope, I was now walking by my own faith. And God seemed closer and more real than ever before.

"I know He's going to bless me with a car!" I shouted.

Grandmother's arms began swinging, the way they always did when she was revving up to rejoice. I began leaping, praising God and dancing. Grandmother joined in. The organ piped. The saints clapped. And "I got a feeling," as the saints often sang on Sunday mornings, "that everything's gonna be all right."

CHAPTER 30

FAREWELL TO K-TOWN

MY CAP AND GOWN were black. I wore them proudly, standing before the crowd made up mostly of grinning mothers and fathers with cameras that clicked throughout the ceremony. Robin was there with our three kids. My baby, Rasheena, was already going on two. A pretty little girl with thick braids and a head full of barrettes, she sat on Robin's lap. Mama was there, as was my stepfather as well as Jeff, Net, Meredith, and Robin's mother. At twenty-three, I was finally graduating from college. Actually, I was receiving a Diploma in Arts in journalism that day and would be awarded my associate's degree once Wright had received a transcript of my freshman-year grades from the University of Illinois. That would happen as soon as I paid my long overdue bill at the University of Illinois that had accumulated penalties and interest.

My family all seemed very proud, but no one was prouder than I was on that spring day in 1984. After the ceremony, I introduced my family to a few of my classmates and professors, who said glowing things about me, including what a promising a future I had. I remember standing there, trying to process it all and wondering if they were just saying these things to be nice or if they actually meant them.

After the ceremony, Mama held a reception at her house. There was a great big spread of fried chicken, potato salad, cakes, and other soul foods. There weren't many people at Mama's. Not that the whole Hagler clan wasn't invited. They probably had some church function to attend. I cannot recall. But it seemed even then that the further I moved toward success and self-sufficiency and the more I embraced education and ventured into the wider world, the greater the gap between my extended family and me became, and the more it became clear that I would have to walk that road without them. They didn't understand this obsession of mine with education and my wanting to move all the way to Champaign, as if I was deserting them and maybe feeling they were no longer good enough for me, that I no longer needed them. Except that wasn't the case. I needed them, only in a different way. I wasn't leaving True Vine and Chicago out of spite but to try to better myself and to benefit my family. There was a part of me that hoped to return to True Vine someday and work in the ministry alongside the other Hagler men. But I came to understand that a lot of black folks, especially church folks, were narrow-minded when it came to education. They had a tendency to pooh-pooh the things of the world, and they failed to recognize the potential benefits to God's people and the furthering of the Gospel, which is every good Christian's aim. It was as if they believed that education, spirituality, and faith could not coexist. Maybe they were afraid that once someone ventured long enough and far enough away to see all that the world has to offer, they would become brainwashed by the Devil and would never want to come back. I wished the saints and some of my other family members who had prayed with me and helped me through all those difficult times had been there at the graduation or at Mama's place afterward to share my moment. But as we sat around, eating and celebrating my big day, I was more moved by the relatives who were in attendance than by those who were not.

My education was already paying off. I landed a summer job as a proofreader at Commerce Clearing House, or CCH, a publishing company on the city's far Northwest Side. The plan to move to Champaign was in full swing. But there was still much work to do, and we still needed to find a car. It was the last hurdle, the last miracle I needed to return to Champaign.

As I cut a slice of graduation cake, I dreamed of cutting another in a few years. Everybody clapped. I took a bite. It tasted so sweet.

Working the third shift as a proofreader was rough. The late-night ride to CCH on the Pulaski bus was the worst part. Every thug and stickup man, it seemed, trolled the buses late at night, looking for victims, or vicks, as we called them. As a teenager, I had ridden the bus without fear. I came home late many nights from Robin's house when we were dating and hadn't given even a second thought to being mugged or otherwise attacked. I don't know if this was because I was too young and naive to understand the dangers, or if now that I had a wife and children, I was aware that there was much more to lose. I was also still grappling with the near miss that night when I jumped off the moving bus to escape being mugged or worse. So I was probably more on edge than usual.

CCH was located on Pulaski Road at Peterson Avenue, which was as far north as the Pulaski bus traveled. That meant going from 1600 South to 6000 North—rolling through perilous West Side neighborhoods where you never knew who or what was going to get on the bus or whether some fracas was going to break out—through Hispanic and white neighborhoods where there were few passengers at night. The farther away from home the bus traveled in its nightly northward journey, the safer I felt. But only after the Pulaski bus crossed Chicago Avenue, two dozen city blocks from where my ride began, did I begin to sink into my seat next to my bag lunch with some degree of comfort for the remaining portion of my trip to work.

Work was from 11 P.M. to 7 A.M. I sat at my desk, usually paired up with one woman or another, galley proofs spread before us. Although there were other men who worked the graveyard shift, there was only one other man in my department. Most of the women were thirty to fifty years old. Some of them were single or divorced mothers, most of them white. The way it worked was that one of us read aloud while the other followed along silently, calling out anything that didn't jibe. The job was incredibly boring, especially come 5 A.M., having spent the entire night reading from a bunch of law books. Truth is, the job would have been boring even if we had been proofing mystery novels, because while you were proofing, there was no time for comprehension. It was like reading in another language, calling out all punctuation, capital letters, and paragraph breaks—everything.

We read all night long, with two coffee breaks and a half hour for lunch. I lived for the final coffee break, which carried me through the last few hours of reading. Sometimes I dozed, my speech slurring as the tiredness and boredom crept in and the natural rhythm of my biological clock yielded to the craving for rest. There sometimes was no remedy for the achy tiredness. I started drinking my coffee black, though I was not entirely sure it helped.

Although I was happy to have a job, I could not see working at CCH for any extended period of time. It seemed like a typical thankless low-level job where folks were always scrambling to get ahead. Except I had the sense that the folks in my department would never get very far, simply because of the nature of the job. They were proofreaders, not editors or lawyers. And many of them were unhappy, from what I could tell from the conversations I had with them. One woman, who sometimes gave me a ride part of the way home, explained that as far as she could tell, the body never adjusts to working the third shift, that human beings are simply on a natural time clock that dictates that one should be sleeping during night hours instead of working. She had been working the third shift for years and still her body was in withdrawal. She even had the ulcers to prove it. It was details like these that made me even more grateful to be headed to the University of Illinois. But there was still that business of buying a car. And the clock was ticking.

Early each morning as I rode the Pulaski bus home from work, I passed a used car and repair shop, called True Line, on the west side of Pulaski Road just south of Sixteenth Street. The shop had a car lot that was barely visible from the streets. Most of their crown jewels were parked curbside along Pulaski Road, earmarked by "For Sale" signs and the hot gloss that glistened in the summer sun.

At the beginning of summer, each morning I got off the bus at Eighteenth Street and walked back to the auto shop, surveying their collection of cars before trudging home to catch some shut-eye. Sometimes I talked to the owners, two white guys named Lenny and Larry. I inquired about a particular vehicle or asked when they were expecting to get a new fleet in. Lenny and Larry were brothers and essentially the last white guys standing in this part of K-Town. Long ago, their family had bought several buildings on Pulaski and opened the auto repair shop. The family had endured the turbulent 1960s and stayed even after the fires in 1968 had set the West Side ablaze. Lenny and Larry seemed like good guys, serious, decent kind of folks. They didn't say a whole lot but had developed a kind of street savvy that allowed them to do their business all these years and go home each night to their families. They seemed like the kind of guys you could trust, if ever you were going to buy a used car. But strangely, before now I had never noticed that the repair shop, also known as Ziebart, which had been there all those years around the corner from my house, also sold cars.

In the same way that I had felt compelled to call the University of Illinois Admissions Office, in the same way that I had felt we would get that apartment in Orchard Downs, I also had a feeling that I was destined to buy a car from the brothers at True Line. I said as much to Robin, going as far as saying that whenever I saw the car that was meant to be ours I would know it. Robin's faith was not as strong. I had begun collecting empty boxes from grocery stores in preparation for our move. The charge of doing much of the packing of clothes and small items was Robin's. But more than halfway through the summer and with little savings, still no prospects for a car, and no further word from the Lord, Robin stopped packing.

"Robin, go ahead and pack," I said. "Girl, we're leaving here."

"How?" she asked. "We still don't have a car."

"I don't know, Robin. But I'll tell you what, we're leaving here. You think God has allowed us to get this far just so we can be disappointed?"

"I don't know. I guess not," Robin said.

"Listen, God is going to bless us with a car. I don't know how. I don't know when. But I know He will," I said, trying to encourage Robin, who was also handling getting the kid's records for transfer to a new school.

As I spoke, I felt a sense of conviction, a spark in my spirit that seemed to energize my every word. I felt the way I did during the course of my preaching, when all the nervousness suddenly vanished and the words began to flow from my soul rather than from the script before me, and I seemed to transcend my own conscious knowledge and abilities and tap into something much greater.

"Keep packing," I said with fire and tears in my eyes. "We're moving. God's gonna bless us with a car even if we don't get it until the day before we leave."

That would be cutting it close. And it was actually my hope that our set of wheels would arrive sooner to stave off my own doubts.

Sometime in early August, one of the True Line brothers came over to me and said, "Man, you've been coming around here all summer, when are you going to buy a car?"

"Soon," I said, although I could not bring myself to tell him that I did not have any money. "Soon."

I was half asleep as the bus rolled down Pulaski Road one morning in August. New-student week and the date of our scheduled departure from K-Town was less than three weeks away and I still did not have a car. The boxes inside our apartment were stacked neatly in anticipation of our exodus. As the bus rolled past True Line, I caught a glimpse of a car that made me do a double take. It was a shiny rust-colored sedan.

"Oh God!" I said to myself almost immediately. "That's my car! That's it!"

Somehow I just knew. The bus couldn't stop fast enough. I climbed off at Eighteenth Street and ran back to True Line. I peeked inside through the car's window. It was a midsized car that looked brand new and big enough for my family. It was a 1979 Mercury Zephyr. It looked sweet with its polished chrome trim and metallic coat. It had not even a speck of rust. I ran inside excitedly and asked one of the brothers if I could see the car. He handed me the keys. I opened the door and voilà! The inside was a deep tan and leathery. It smelled like new. The odometer read less than

40,000 miles. I stuck the key into the ignition. It fired right up, and I took it for a spin around the block. The engine purred. It drove like brand new. I headed back to the shop, where Lenny poured on the sales pitch.

"So what kind of car did you say you're looking for?" Lenny asked.

"Oh, just something that will get me back and forth from Champaign to Chicago occasionally, something to get the groceries, you know, a decent car that's going to last me until I'm done with school."

"You're lookin' at it. I'm telling you, this car is in great condition, as you can see. It's clean, it's got low miles, it's in mint condition," he continued. "I'm telling you, listen to me, you buy this car, it will never quit, it's reliable. In fact, I promise you . . . where are you planning to go to school?" he asked.

"University of Illinois in Champaign."

"I promise you that when you graduate from the University of Illinois, it'll still be running and you can trade it in, or just keep it. This will be a great car for you," Lenny said, still trying to secure a sale.

I was sold from the moment I laid eyes on it.

"Now," I thought, "if I can just come up with several thousand dollars."

Lenny and Larry, like any good used car salesmen, assured me that financing was available. That was the good news. The bad news was that I was in a temporary job and still had little money for a down payment. I took an application with a promise to put down $1,500 as a down payment, $300 of which I could see and $1,200 of which I was going to have to depend on the Lord to provide. But the deal ultimately hinged on whether I could get financed for the bulk of the cost.

I went home and told Robin the news, then took her up to see the car. I also prayed for direction. I had my stepfather check out the car, and he agreed that it was in excellent condition. Then I called Uncle Gene and asked him for a favor, the kind that sons usually ask of fathers. I asked for a $1,200 loan so that I could buy a car. There was a moment of silence on the telephone. Then he asked me where I planned to buy the car, how much it cost, and whether I could get the financing. He said he would get back to me. In the meantime, I called Robin's father, Bob, to ask if he would cosign for me. I do not know why I did not ask Grandpa. But I do know that some people were automatically eliminated because I needed someone with good credit, particularly since I had no credit. I figured from everything I knew about Bob that his credit was in decent shape and that he might be inclined to help me, since he, and not anyone else, had given me $150 for books when I first went back to school. When I asked Bob about cosigning for the car, he did not hesitate in saying yes. A few days later, Uncle Gene called back with good news. He would lend me the money, which I promised to pay back in full around the first week in September. Now all I needed was for my financing to be approved. That is what it had come down to: a loan officer's decision on our exodus-mobile.

Faith had brought us this far, but I wasn't sure that it was strong enough to carry me through this time. Given my temporary employment status and lack of credit history, a denial was the only logical conclusion. I tried to reason that given every other obstacle that had been removed in my effort to return to school—gaining readmittance to the university, getting an apartment in Champaign and a job that summer, having done well at Wright—there was no cause to doubt that God could work one more miracle. I did not doubt that he could. The question in my mind was whether he would. How embarrassing it would be to go back to the saints and say that we hadn't gotten a car after all. What would my family say? What would Robin think? And what was I going to do, if I didn't go back to Champaign after all? I had put all my eggs in one basket, stretched out on faith, and believed God when no one else, not even my wife, believed. Where I once had spent hours on my knees at home and crying out to God with Grandmother and the prayer warriors, building my faith—planting seeds of faith—I had gotten up off my knees to take faith by the reins. I had gone back to Wright when it would have been easier to stay at home and sulk. I endured even in those times when I felt I could not go on, when money was low and our gas or electricity or telephone was disconnected yet again. I sacrificed, studied, and kept returning to class. I held onto God sometimes with tears in my eyes, sometimes with tears streaming down my face, but always with the belief that He was my only hope. Ultimately, I reasoned that there was nothing else to do now except leave it in God's hands. So I prayed and waited each day for word. With each day drawing closer to the date of our move, but still no word on our car, I prayed. I hoped and I prayed.

We were only days before our move when the telephone rang. I answered.

"Mr. Fountain?"

"Yes?"

"This is Lenny from True Line."

"How you doing?"

"Good," he answered.

My heart beat fast. I knew he had an answer on the loan. This was it. We were moving on, or not. There was no more use in praying. The deal was done.

As the voice on the other end started up again, I was almost too afraid to listen.

"So when do you want to come pick up your car?"

"I've been approved?" I asked.

"Yep, all we need is for you and your cosigner to come by and sign."

"Yes, yes!" I said excitedly.

"Congratulations," he said laughing. "Again, all we need is for you and your cosigner to come in and it's your car."

"I'll call him and see when is good and let you know as soon as possible."

"Sounds good. See you soon."

I hung up the phone.

"Thank you, Je-sus! Thank you, Jesus! Robinnn!" I screamed. "We've been approved. They said I can come and pick up the car!"

We rejoiced and cried. It felt surreal.

When I arrived to pick up the car that Saturday morning, it glistened even more brightly than it had on the day that I had first seen it. Robin's father and I signed, and I shook Lenny's hand, then climbed into our Mercury Zephyr. I drove south down to Eighteenth Street and made a right, rounding the corner and slowly driving the one block west to Komensky, where yellow sawhorses blocked off the street as they always did on the day of the annual Block Club party. I parked at the corner and climbed out as everyone stared in amazement. John, of all people, had a new car.

The block's celebration had already begun. So had the one for the Fountain family. Tomorrow we would be leaving. And just as I had said to Robin weeks earlier, though I hardly thought it to be prophetic at the time, the Lord had blessed us with our exodus-mobile on the day before we were to leave, once again in the nick of time.

Sunday morning arrived bright and early. Daddy and Jeff and Robin's brother, Lamont, and their father, Bob, as well as my cousin Michael showed up to help me load our furniture and other belongings onto the back of an open-cover truck driven by one of Robin's uncles.

I was a mix of emotions as I carried the boxes and furniture down the stairs to the truck that morning. Normally, I would have been preparing to go to Sunday School at True Vine. The Sunday before, Grandpa had called my family and me up front to the altar and laid hands on us while the saints all joined him in prayer. He prayed that God would keep and protect us as we began our new life in Champaign. Grandmother exhorted, "Get your learning, but don't lose your burning."

I had already said most of my good-byes. I said good-bye to Mr. Newell and to my Public Aid caseworker, whose eyes were filled with tears as she wished me the best, saying it was rare that she had seen a client do what I was doing in going back to school. I had said good-bye to my coworkers at CCH, who bid me Godspeed, and to John-John's kindergarten teacher, Mrs. Thomas, who cried and hugged me and wished us well. It was as if I was gaining release from a prison boot camp and everyone who had watched my transformation or rooted for me along the way felt a vested interest.

While preparing to move, I had not had much time to dwell on the idea of leaving K-Town and how I might feel should that day ever come. I had been too busy planning my escape to think about those whom I would miss and about the good times, the memories of playing softball on the vacant lot as a boy with Huckey, Mercury, and J-Rat and all the other fellas. I had not had time to reflect on the years of Block Club parties or the apple days in Mr. Newell's backyard, on life at the compound and the evenings of Home Run Inn pizza at Grandmother's house and traveling by caravan with the Hagler clan to Kankakee in the days when our family was close. I hadn't really had time to reflect on all the blood, sweat, and tears that went into fixing up the apartment on Komensky for my family, planting grass, and the joy of watching it grow. But as I carried our belongings that Sunday morning to the truck, I was filled with a mix of emotions, with the joy of moving on but also the pain of having to say good-bye. For I sensed that this time I was saying good-bye for good.

After everything was loaded onto the truck, Robin and I and the kids gathered near the front door of our apartment, near the bathroom where I had offered up so many prayers on so many sleepless nights, near the kitchen where I had studied often until dawn. We held hands and prayed.

"Lord, we thank you for this place, for all that you have done, for making a way out of no way, for being our provider," I prayed, as tears streamed down my face and the weight of the world seemed lifted off my shoulders. "Lord, I thank you for my wife and children. We thank you for leading me back to school, for blessing us with a car.

"Now, Lord, go with us to Champaign...Bless us and keep us... Amen."

I took one last look around the apartment, moving slowly from room to room, taking in deep breaths and quietly reflecting. Then we walked downstairs, climbed into our car, and drove about a hundred yards away to Mama's house. I needed to say good-bye to Mama alone.

"Y'all all packed up and ready to go?" Mama asked, greeting me at the door of her apartment.

"Yep, we're loaded," I said, smiling.

"John, I'm just so glad you are going back to school," Mama said, beaming and bubbling over. "I knew you could. I always knew you could. John, you can do anything you put your mind to. I'm just so happy for you."

"Thanks, Ma," I said, my words choked with emotion. There was something else I needed to tell her. My voice cracked. "Ma, uh, I, uh...I just want to thank you too, Ma, for, uh, for believing in me and for being there when I needed you. I know that when you first mentioned the idea of me going back to Champaign, I got so angry and said some things that I shouldn't have," I said, sitting in my usual crying spot on the living room heater.

"That's okay, John, I understand."

"Nah, Ma, I'm sorry. I just couldn't see it. I just couldn't see how I could go back."

"I know," she comforted me. "That's what mothers are for. I've always wanted what was best for you. I know that I may not have always done what was best, but it was the best I knew how to do. All any parent can ever do is their best."

"You done all right, Ma," I said.

Mama was fighting back tears.

Silence.

"Well, they're waiting for me downstairs, I better get going," I said finally.

Mama followed me out into the hall, where we hugged good-bye, a rush of sadness sweeping over me.

"Ma, I'm gonna make y'all proud," I said.

"John," Mama said, crying, "you already have. You already have."

I dried my eyes and then walked downstairs. Mama didn't follow. She walked back inside. I suspect that she watched from the window. I walked out into the morning light and climbed into my new car. Years later, Mama told me that she realized that day that I would probably never again live in Chicago. What I had not told Mama about that day was that somewhere in the back of my mind I also reckoned the same.

As we pulled away from the curb, the rickety truck loaded with our life's possessions, I felt like the Beverly Hillbillies. As we rounded the corner of Komensky Avenue and drove north on Pulaski Road, down to Roosevelt Road, past True Vine, bound for miles of highway, I had a feeling that the road, no matter how uncertain, led to a bright future and that the worst was behind us. But this one thing I was sure of: It was the Lord who had brought us out.

★

Late that evening, long after the truck had been unloaded and all of our helpers had gone back to Chicago, Robin and I and the kids were alone in our new apartment. I set up the beds so we would have someplace to sleep.

As night fell, there was only the sound of crickets, no sirens, and no gunshots, only darkness, the stars, and green meadows. I took in a deep breath and exhaled, the worries of a lifetime seeming to disappear into thin air. When I finally climbed into bed that night, I drifted quickly off to sleep. It was a deep restful sleep, uninterrupted by the midnight walking of the floors and the checking of locks on doors.

It was the best I had slept in years.

PART 4

REVELATION

I know thy works: behold, I have set before thee an open door,
and no man can shut it: for thou hast a little strength, and hast
kept my word, and hast not denied my name.

Revelation 3:8

CHAPTER 31

ANN ARBOR BLUES

November 1999

IT WAS COLD, so cold. The chill of a Chicago winter hung in the air outside like crisp snowflakes. The tour bus pulled off the Kennedy Expressway to avoid the snarling traffic on a frigid Friday afternoon. The bus, carrying about a dozen journalists in a fellowship program at the University of Michigan in Ann Arbor, was filled with chatter, though I sat mostly silent, staring out of the window, my heart racing and memories flashing across my mind like a strobe light. We had arrived a day earlier for a weekend tour of the Windy City with its towering skyscrapers, sparkling Magnificent Mile, and shimmering waters of Lake Michigan. I was one of the journalists, and this time, one of the tourists. After years of living away from Chicago, carried by my work as a journalist to many places and having seen many faces, I had come back home. At least I was headed in that direction. But it felt strange, so strange.

Earlier that day we had taken a tour of public housing projects, one of the planned stops on the fellowship's annual trip to Chicago. As we stared out of the bus window—first at the Robert Taylor Homes on the South Side and a short while later at Cabrini-Green—the projects seemed every bit as dilapidated and hopeless as I remembered. So much had happened to me and yet so little had changed.

Only four years earlier, on my thirty-fifth birthday, I stood in my dining room in Fairfax County, Virginia, surrounded by my new wife and new friends and the glow of thirty-five candles on my cake. I stood above the cake on the verge of tears, though not understanding what lay at the root of my sorrow. It took me nights to unearth the reason for my sadness, which was that the people gathered around my birthday cake had been strangers only a few years earlier and that by my thirty-fifth birthday, my childhood friends had already become ghosts. Some were dead or dying by other's hands or by their own, dwelling in a state of inebriation, crippled by drugs or alcohol, like a friend I had seen in passing on visits back home in recent years. So bad off was he, his skin jaundiced and putrid, that he walked with a cane. Once I saw him walking: The wind blew and he fell down. In turning thirty-five, I had become an elder. I was struck more and more by my own mortality. The years seemed to be slowly slipping away, and time seemed to be more of an enemy the older I got. But as I made my way down memory lane time and time again, I increasingly missed K-Town and the faces of the old neighborhood. The more I thought about home, the more I longed for it.

On many Sunday mornings while sitting in church in Virginia, I daydreamed of returning to Chicago to help Grandpa at True Vine. I also longed to spend time with Mama, with my brother and sisters, and with Grandmother, trading laughter and conversation more frequently with family and making more memories before it was too late. I was convinced that time was not on our side.

The more time I spent away from Chicago, the more I felt I needed to get back home. I do not know whether it was romanticizing the way I remembered life there or the sense that there was some lasting connection, some source of energy and strength or wholeness that I felt whenever I was back home that seemed to be driving me to return. I just wanted to go back home. Many nights I prayed toward that end, but there was no immediate answer.

In the spring of 1999, I applied for and received a Michigan Journalism

Fellowship, which boiled down to having a year off work with pay and full run of the university. For me, it was a needed break from the daily grind and the chance to exorcise the ghosts of my past or at least to find clarity about where I had been, where I had ended up, and perhaps most important, where I was going. Except it has been said that once you leave home, you can never go back. They say it is this way because home changes, and inevitably, so do we.

When I left Chicago for Champaign in 1984, Robin and I were still married. But our move to Champaign did little to cure our marital problems. I was never under the impression that it would, but I did think that moving to the more relaxed and stimulating atmosphere of a small college town would make life better for us all. I knew that it would also provide Robin with the opportunity to go to school as well, given the proximity of the local junior college and the general climate of academic pursuit in the atmosphere of life on campus. Mama had given us both a talking-to before we left Chicago that fall. She said that my being in school would cause me to grow in ways that I might not fully understand until many years later and that Robin and I needed to grow together. Mama said she knew of cases where certain spouses had gone back to school only to awaken one morning to find that they had outgrown their partner and their marriage was on the rocks.

"Make your wife a part of everything you do," Mama had said. "You need to encourage her to go back to school. She may not want to at first. But keep encouraging her, John."

Robin agreed finally to go back to school. Within a few months after we moved to Champaign, she earned her GED. Then she began taking classes at Parkland College, where Arty had gone years earlier. She took a few classes at first, then a full load. For a while, Robin seemed happier, though never fully at peace.

During the summers, I took my family with me on journalism internships, paid jobs as a reporter that I had learned about on the bulletin board in the basement of Gregory Hall, where the College of Communications is located. Early on, I had decided that I should apply for internships but mainly in Chicago, given that I had a family. It was hard to think of gallivanting off for an internship somewhere across the country and leaving my wife and children behind. I remember standing one day in the basement of Gregory Hall as I scanned the bulletin board and saying to myself that I could never take an internship at the *Washington Post* or the *New York Times* because both newspapers were in large cities, where I figured that the only places we could afford to live would likely be unsafe and unlivable. I remember feeling hurt as I accepted the notion that I might never know whether I was good enough to work at either newspaper, which nearly every student-journalist I knew saw as the pinnacle of American newspaper journalism. But I couldn't fathom the idea of spending summers away from my children as I chased my dreams.

So off we went. During the summer of '86 I worked at *Pioneer Press Newspapers* in Chicago, and we occupied the upstairs apartment in Robin's parents' house, where her grandfather had once lived. During the following summer when I worked at the *Chicago Sun-Times*, we lived with my parents. In 1988, we spread our wings, loading up our car and driving out to California, where I interned at the *Modesto Bee* and had secured in advance a nice two-bedroom apartment in a complex with an outdoor swimming pool and sauna. My editors at the *Bee* as well as the other two reporting interns were stunned to discover that I was married with three children and even more stunned to learn that they had come with me all the way out to California. I had learned early on not to offer information about my family situation, partly to avoid folks feeling sorry for me, and also the inevitable barrage of questions about how we were "making it." In my interviews the folks at the *Bee* had not asked about my family situation, and I had not volunteered information. I wanted to be judged on my performance and on my ability, not on anyone's perceptions. And I figured that I would likely not get that opportunity if it were known that I was "encumbered" by a wife and children, that I was not the usual young, happy-go-lucky intern. But in all of my internships, I never met any intern who worked harder or displayed more dedication than I did.

In the summer of '89, with one graduate degree in hand but still in graduate school studying political science at the University of Illinois, we were headed to Pittsburgh for an internship at the *Wall Street Journal's* bureau there. Robin had always looked forward to our summers with a sense of expectation and adventure, or so it had seemed to me. But on the day before we were to leave for Pittsburgh, it became clear that something was wrong. For starters, she had not packed any of the kids' clothes or hers. After I pressed her, she finally admitted that she did not want to go. I remember feeling stunned, mostly because she had not said a single word to me until that very moment. Now she said only that she preferred to stay in Champaign, or in Chicago with her parents, until I returned. There was no explanation, only passive resistance. In the end, Robin decided to go to Pittsburgh, though it soon became clear that it would have been better if she had stayed behind. The summer was filled with gripes and arguing and our general disdain for each other as well as the sense that our marriage had come to an impasse.

Early one cool evening in Pittsburgh that summer, I took the kids out for a stroll. As we walked near the basketball court in the complex where we lived, I asked them if they understood the meaning of "divorce." They did not. I explained as best as I could. "It's when mommies and daddies decide they can no longer live together," I began. There were no more questions. They cried. So did I. Then we strolled back to the apartment, the winds of change whispering on a summer night.

Looking back, with regard to my dreams, it was as if in some ways Robin had been a bystander. Although she never discouraged me, and most often supported my decisions at least by her words, I later realized that she never truly embraced my vision. Whether she did not have the faith to see what I could, or whether it was the difficulty of always having to delay gratification when it seemed that relatives and friends were living the high life—and quick to rub it in—or whether it was something else, I do not know. I later understood that sometimes there is a root of unhappiness buried deep inside some people that can breed a kind of general discontentment with life and that, like cancer, it will ultimately consume you if it is not cut out. And that such is a job for God, not man. As much as I wished to save our marriage, I began to believe that it was inevitably doomed, though maybe it was not Robin's fault or mine. Maybe it was the case that ultimately we grew apart. That was never part of my dream. In my dream, Robin and I would have had three more children and lived happily ever after. In reality, we split up in late 1989.

That fall I was hired as an intern at the *Chicago Tribune*, having held similar positions at the *Champaign News-Gazette, Pioneer Press Newspapers* in suburban Chicago, the *Chicago Sun-Times*, the *Modesto Bee*, and the *Wall Street Journal*, while earning my bachelor's and master's degrees from the University of Illinois. Unlike my previous internships, when we had all gone for the ride, this time I packed my bags, then kissed my children and our life as a family good-bye, though I never intended it to turn out that way. But even as I drove north to Chicago, promising to return to Champaign on weekends, I sensed a change in the wind, a cold inevitable death of a season and of love lost somewhere along the rugged road to the Promised Land. Robin and I would never live together as husband and wife again.

I had always looked at divorce shamefully, even though it was not uncommon in my own family. With the exception of Grandmother and Grandpa and Uncle Gene and Aunt Emma, everyone else in the immediate Hagler family had been divorced. That didn't ease my angst. Getting a divorce made me feel like a failure and as if everyone I knew at work or otherwise was pointing the finger and disparaging me for it. It didn't help that I soon acquired the label "playboy" for my frequent dating and being labeled a "dog"—as in a man who only uses women for sex, then dumps them once he is done, neither of which were entirely true. It was hard for me to reconcile the two John Fountains, the one who had been a family man and a faithful husband, and the other, whom most of my friends perceived as a "ladies' man," who sported a gold-hoop earring—a new ornament of my rebellion—and hung out at downtown dance clubs. I had undergone a metamorphosis. I thought that the earring would help me shed the physical appearance of looking like a preacher, though it never seemed to work. Even with complete strangers, something about me was a dead giveaway.

"Man, anybody ever told you that you look like a preacher?" some dude once remarked at the Baja Beach Club, ruining the rest of my night.

One of my colleagues at the *Tribune* once took a jab at me in a column about men who wore earrings, saying that he knew a "so-called" minister who wore an earring. I understood the dichotomy and how it must have seemed. The colleague, who was also a black man, had learned that I was supposed to be a minister in the church. Having made no grand public proclamation that my life and identity were in shambles, my lifestyle was called into question on public pages. He later apologized. But the hurt and embarrassment had already been inflicted.

The day our divorce was to be made final, Robin and I sat in a small office outside a judge's chambers inside the Richard J. Daley Center in the fall of 1991. Although we had talked from time to time about getting back together, it never happened. In fact, the last time I approached Robin about that possibility, she promptly declined. She had a new boyfriend by then and was no longer interested in me. She suggested instead that we continue to live separately and do our own thing.

"We don't have to get divorced," she said. "We should just stay married and live apart."

I knew where that could end up. Unwilling to linger in a state of limbo that I figured with Robin could last a lifetime, and wanting simply to get on with life, I told her that we were either going to be married, or not.

The divorce papers lay on a table before us that day. Neither of us said much of anything. I half hoped that Robin would say she didn't want to go through with the divorce, that we would walk out of the judge's office teary-eyed and hugging. But as I sat there looking at Robin, she seemed to have changed, to have become a different person in the time we had been apart. She dressed differently. More stylish, perhaps ghetto-fabulous is the more appropriate description. She talked more streetlike, her voice mixed with more twang and slang than I ever recalled.

Like Robin, I had also assembled my own collection of ghetto-fabulous threads. I seldom went to church anymore, partied at dance clubs, and started drinking with great regularity. Liquor and ladies worked like a strong sedative and had long since replaced prayer. I was disillusioned with the church and angry with God. I felt that in many ways God had somehow failed me and that for all the times I had prayed for him to fix my marriage, he never answered.

As much as marriage had not come with a how-to manual, neither had divorce. We muddled through it, although our muddling was often at the expense of our children. I got custody of the boys, who were then thirteen and eleven, and Robin got Rasheena, who was almost nine. I did not want it this way and would gladly have taken custody of our daughter, though Robin would never have agreed to this. I figured that in time, I would have all three of the children. I didn't take on custody so much because it was something that I wanted to do but because I thought it was necessary to save my children, particularly my sons, who were most at risk in a city where young black men were being devoured by the elements of urban life. I always knew that a divorce would be bad for them, though I never knew how bad. And though I do regret even the slightest pain that I ever caused my children during my breakup with their mother, I have never regretted the decision to file for divorce. Nothing solidified that feeling more than the words Robin spoke to me one day, years after our divorce.

"Nigger," she remarked, with more than a tinge of bitterness, "I knew you when you weren't nothing."

I replied without much hesitation: "You never knew me."

Although Robin's eyes were dry and clear that day we signed the divorce papers, I was crying. It felt as if someone I knew had died. At home that night, I drifted off to sleep, still feeling pain.

In the morning, when I awoke alone in my bed in my apartment in Oak Park, a suburb west of Chicago, where my boys and I were starting over, the sound of birds singing drifted in through an open window. I opened my eyes to the sunshine that beamed like a glistening diamond through my blinds, as the reality that my marriage to Robin was finally over settled in.

The sun had never shone so brightly.

By the spring of 1992, I was a full-fledged reporter for the *Chicago Tribune*, and I had been given the temporary assignment to cover one of the

Democratic presidential hopefuls, Bill Clinton, the governor of Arkansas. I could hardly believe I was covering the campaign. "I'm a long way from K-Town," I thought to myself sometimes while sitting on the plane with the reporters, all the Secret Service agents, and Mr. and Mrs. Clinton. I counted it a blessing to be there on the campaign and an answer to hard work and my prayers for opportunity. And I was beginning again to see God's hand in my life, though it was still far from being perfect. What surprised me most was that I could see how God had been there all along, in the times when I had been drunk and driving and somehow always managed to get home without killing myself or anyone else. I could see his hand of mercy in that I had not blown my brains out when, in those times during my divorce when the strain seemed too much to bear, I had replayed the scenario over and over again in my mind and contemplated suicide. I saw God's hand of protection in that I had not contracted HIV or some other disease. In fact, looking back, there had been many episodes in my life that made the hairs on my limbs stand at attention but that also led me to believe that someone must have been looking out for me; despite a life turned upside down, I still had my sanity. And it was clear in my mind that I owed that all to God. The idea that He could love me that much, even though I had walked away from Him and from the principles of righteous living, over time drew me back to God. His faithfulness to me in spite of myself was what I found most astounding.

As I climbed off the airplane at Midway Airport after a full day on the campaign trail with Governor Clinton, I was tired and thinking of taking a pass on the day's last scheduled campaign stop, at a South Side elementary school. For no reason in particular, I changed my mind at the last minute.

I was standing in a crowded room inside the school, waiting for Governor Clinton to enter, when I looked up from my reporter's pad and was stunned into near speechlessness. There, about fifteen feet away, stood a tall, slender woman with glasses whom I recognized clearly. But I could not believe my eyes. I had not seen her in ten years. And I was certainly no longer that young man on welfare, working for a summer newspaper called *Youth News*. It was R. Diane Wallace, standing just a few feet away.

"Thank you, God. Thank you, God," I said to myself, beaming and feeling instantly revived.

In my dreams, I had imagined for years that I would someday meet Ms. Wallace again. I even told friends and family about the woman at Truman College who had squashed my hopes like a bug during that summer I worked on the *Youth News* newspaper. It was never that I wanted to tell her off, but rather I hoped to come face-to-face with her in some glorious moment, to say that I had made it in spite of her. I had given up that hope over the years, but now, out of the blue, there she was in the flesh.

I was barely able to keep myself composed. But I decided that I would wait until after Governor Clinton's speech to approach Ms. Wallace. And when I did get the chance to speak with her, I figured that it would be more appropriate to pull her aside and say my piece rather than embarrassing her in front of anyone.

Soon after the speech, I looked up and she was gone. "Oh no," I thought. I rushed out of the room into a nearby hallway, afraid that I had missed the moment of reckoning. But no sooner had I entered the hallway than I spotted Ms. Wallace, standing a few feet away, smiling and chatting with an astute-looking, middle-aged black gentleman dressed in a suit. So much for the chance to speak with her alone. It was now or never. I walked up to them.

"Excuse me, uh, Ms. Wallace?" I asked.

"Yes," she said looking up.

"I am—"

She interrupted: "You're one of my former students," she mused, smiling widely.

"Nope. Uhhh, some years ago," I began explaining, "I was in a program at Truman—"

She interrupted again.

"I know who-o-o you ar-r-re," she said, her jaw dropping and her eyes widening. There was complete silence. She stood speechless.

"I'm John Fountain," I said, speaking calmly and plainly, every word carefully chosen. "A few years ago you did something that I thought was really cruel and that hurt me really deeply. But I want you to know that since then, I went back to school and earned my associate's, then I went back to the University of Illinois and I earned my bachelor's and master's." I continued for a few moments, reciting my résumé while she stood there appearing to be in a state of shock.

"And I just want you to know that every time I thought about giving up, I thought of you and I kept going."

"My brother, it sounds like you're still angry, like you still have some issues there," the man standing next to Ms. Wallace interrupted abruptly.

"Nah, man, I ain't mad. I just don't want her to do to some other young person what she did to me or to destroy someone else's life," I said. "I made it. They might not."

He smiled as if he were impressed, then handed me his business card. He turned out to be the superintendent of Ms. Wallace's school district. I smiled back and handed both of them one of my red, white, and blue *Tribune* business cards. I did so with the same pride with which I had given one to my old St. Mel classmate Dorian, who had snickered on the bus that morning years earlier about me being a student at Wright and presuming me to be out for the count. I had encountered Dorian one evening while picking up a pizza at Home Run Inn. I was sharp as a tack, educated and paid. We chatted briefly, and I told him what I had done since we had last seen each other that morning on the bus years earlier when I was on my way to Wright and he was headed to Loyola. Dorian was congratulatory. But he looked dumbfounded, as if maybe he was seeing a ghost. I handed him a business card, then I picked up my pizza, smiled, and walked away. Now, encountering Ms. Wallace, I felt like Michael Corleone at the end of *The Godfather*, settling all family business.

"Have a good day," I said to Ms. Wallace and her supervisor. Then I turned and walked away.

The next morning, I climbed aboard the press bus to the tune of Mike Frisby, the *Boston Globe* reporter, calling me teasingly.

"Hey, Front-Page Fountain!" Frisby yelled. "Front-Page Fountain!"

"What are you talking about, man?" I replied, knowing that I had filed notes on the previous day's campaigning, though unaware that any of my notes had been transformed into a story. "I don't have a story on the front page."

"Yes you do, man," he said holding up the *Tribune* with my name as clear as day on the story that ran on page one.

"I guess you're right, man," I said, taking my seat on the press bus. I smiled as I sat there, willing to bet that Ms. Wallace had also gotten the *Tribune* that morning and had seen the name John W. Fountain splashed on page one of a real newspaper.

Months later, on the sunny Saturday afternoon of August 29, 1992, I got married for the second time, to Monica Copeland, a colleague at the *Tribune* whom I had met two years earlier. Less than a month later we moved to England, where Monica had won a scholarship to study. We both took a leave of absence from the paper, and my sons soon joined us there in a little countryside town called Lewes. With my life settling down again, I still had many unresolved issues, demons that vexed me. In the meantime, I found life in Lewes—playing basketball and taking strolls on the downs—to be a soothing balm.

Although I returned to the *Tribune* the following year, the time had come to move on. In late 1994 came an offer to join the *Washington Post*, a newspaper I had never dared dream I might write for. I said yes, and we packed up and headed east, though it was without my eldest son, John, now sixteen years old, who begged me to allow him to live with his mother and sister. Tearfully, I relented.

Not long after moving to Virginia, I decided to call my father's mother, Autherine Jackson, in Evergreen, Alabama, and reintroduce myself. Actually, it was more like introducing myself for the first time. The only time that we had met previously was that brief encounter sixteen years earlier when I had gone to Evergreen for my father's funeral. I wanted to answer questions about my father and investigate his side of my family, which up until then was a complete unknown to me. I told Mrs. Jackson that I wanted to come to Evergreen again, and she seemed delighted at the thought of my visiting with the family. I also sensed her shock after all those years, to one day pick up the telephone and hear the voice on the other end introduce himself as John Fountain.

In July, Monica, Rashad, and I loaded up the car for the trip from Virginia to Alabama. Although I was on a search for answers, I was not sure that I knew all the questions. The closer we drew to Evergreen, the more I worried about whether my father's folks would consider me to be family or whether they would simply see me as some mixed-up young man struggling with childhood anxiety over his father's absence in his life. I also wondered whether I could handle being in Alabama, where I had not been since the funeral in 1979. The closer we got, the more the internal struggle boiled inside and the more old feelings, memories, and past hurts seemed to surface, as if my life were flashing before my eyes.

"Babe, I don't know if I can handle this," I said to Monica, who was then five months' pregnant.

"John, it'll be all right. Your father's mother seemed happy when you called, right?"

"Yeah."

"And when you told her that you wanted to come and visit, what did she say?"

I sighed. "I know, I know, I just don't understand why nobody down here ever called me or came to see me or anything. I mean it was almost like I didn't exist. I don't want them thinking that I want nothing from 'em," I said, my anger percolating, though mostly at the root of it was hurt. Hurt and pain.

"All I want is a picture of my dad, and to ask my grandmother some questions," I huffed.

"It'll be all right, John," Monica said, rubbing my hand. "It'll be all right."

Driving into Evergreen was like driving through a cloud of smoke into the past. The roads looked strangely familiar, as the events of 1979 seemed to come back to life. There was the police station uptown where Mama, my stepfather, Net, and I had gone to get a copy of the police report. Soon we rounded the corner on Highway 31 South, where my father had been shot like a missile through the windshield of his car when it was hit by the truck. We traveled north a piece until I spotted the narrow driveway where my father's car had rolled just a few feet onto the highway into harm's way before the awful wreck happened. Then we drove up the driveway toward the little redbrick, single-story house where my father had spent his last hours here on earth, stupefying his mind and soul, and where his mother, my grandmother, still lived. I knocked on the door and she emerged, a frail, thin woman with butterscotch skin and big glasses. I hugged her and we went inside and talked for a while.

Our conversation was filled with questions, which rolled slowly and painfully from my lips. Questions about who my father's father was, about why my father never came to see me, and about my father and family's medical history, which in time had become more important for my own longevity and the well-being of my children.

"I don't know why he didn't come and see you," Mrs. Jackson said, speaking plain and honest. "We all knew about you and your sister. But you know Gwen," she said, referring to my mother. "That girl could be so mean."

I sat there thinking that she had some nerve saying anything about my mama. But I allowed her to continue uninterrupted.

"I don't know," she continued. "You know, your daddy had a drinking problem. I just could never get him to leave that stuff alone. He was okay as long as he didn't drink. But when he drank..."

I listened to Mrs. Jackson talk for a little while about how my father was forced to live with her mother because his stepfather did not want him living there with his siblings and mother. She spoke of some of her other sons or relatives who had drinking problems, about another relative who was killed in an automobile accident, about one whose legs, she said, were amputated because of drinking and diabetes, about one sad tragedy after another. The more she talked, the more the anger and pain of a lifetime seemed to fall off me like dead dry skin. And I began to wonder what might have happened to me if my troubled father, so vexed by all of his demons that tormented not only him but also possessed his family, had been in my life. I knew how my life without him had turned out. And though less than perfect, I was not an alcoholic. I had a steady and respectable job. I had managed to go back to college and earn my degrees despite my hardship. I believed in family and loved my children, who would never know the pain of not knowing their father's love or suffer the image of me to be reduced to a shadow in a foggy mirror.

All that time I had thought myself to be deprived by not having known my natural father. But sitting there in the living room, where his mother's only picture of him hung in an oval frame, for the first time in my life I understood that I was better for not having known him. I actually thanked God for my not having known the man and for having given me the good sense to latch onto the best that was in the men who were in my life.

I was the sum total of them all.

From my grandfather, I took his love for God and family and his stewardship. From Uncle Gene, I took his humor and oomph for masculinity and manhood. From my stepfather, I took his kindness toward children, his love of the blues, and his knack for do-it-yourself fix-up jobs. From Mr. Adams, I took his zest for education and the belief that it had the power to change my life, his perseverance and indomitable back-the-freak-up presence as a black male. From some men who crossed my path, I took the fire that for me symbolizes black manhood. And from others, the gentle hand, tenderheartedness, and righteousness that is our eternal flame. From my father, even in his absence, or perhaps because of it, what I took was the memory of a father walking hand in hand with a son, the smell of cinnamon gum, and a pact that I made with myself to be a better man than he was. As my anger seeped from my pores, from my heart and soul, I was also filled with sympathy and sorrow for my father, whom I was beginning to see as a troubled boy who grew up to be a troubled man whose troubles eventually swallowed him whole.

Before we left Evergreen that next morning, there was one last stop to make on my journey. I needed to go by Long Corner Cemetery to see where my father was buried. Mrs. Jackson said that one of her sons would need to take me by the cemetery to help me find the grave, which was not marked by a headstone. And so my father's younger brother, Billy, led me toward the grave site, and after a while, narrowed my father's resting place to one of several nameless white slates covered by weeds and grass.

"I think it's this one," he said, looking puzzled. "But I can't say for sure."

I stood above the grave, teary-eyed. Then I squatted. Billy and my wife and son walked away so that I could make my peace.

I had not been able to cry at my father's funeral. But sixteen years later, the tears began to pour. They flowed freely as I began to have that long-overdue conversation that I had always dreamed of having with my father. Much of what I said at the grave site that day remains a blur, though I do recall telling him who I was, telling him about the man I had become.

It was only those words that I found most liberating that I clearly remember saying. "I love you, Dad," I said, wiping away tears, "and I forgive you."

With that said, I climbed into my car and drove out of Long Corner Cemetery, away from Evergreen, away from death and back toward life.

With Chicago only a three-and-a-half hour drive west on Interstate 94 from Ann Arbor, Rasheena (who had moved to Virginia to live with us in late 1996); Monica; our three-year-old daughter, Imani; and I visited family and friends frequently. (Rashad, now nineteen, was working, and John, now twenty-one, was working and going to City College—both of them in Chicago.) The saints at True Vine were happy to see us back home, especially Grandmother, who was still healthy and spry but contemplating hip-replacement surgery. True Vine had long since moved from the storefront on Roosevelt Road. Back in 1988, the old True Vine caught fire and was badly damaged. I was in school in Champaign at the time. But everyone said Grandpa cried like a baby as he stood there that night, helplessly watching the flames. For a while, the fire left the saints at True Vine displaced, but the Lord works in mysterious ways. With the insurance money, along with the nest egg Grandpa had put aside and what seemed like a million chicken- and fish-dinner sales—in addition to the donations by True Vine's members—they bought a beautiful church in the western suburb of Bellwood.

The church was brown brick with a white steeple and a big bell that Uncle Gene sometimes rang on Sunday mornings at the start of Sunday

School. The church had a huge kitchen and dining room, classrooms, and a balcony with enough seating for more than 500 people. The sanctuary was adorned with stained glass windows, natural wood beams, and a high ceiling with white ceiling fans and no cobwebs. They even added air-conditioning.

Grandmother was largely responsible for getting the new church building. True Vine's members all made the necessary financial sacrifices, but it was Grandmother who provided the faith. One evening while sitting in their car outside a big fancy Lutheran church, Grandmother simply said with the surety with which she always spoke when the Lord had revealed something to her, "Honey, I think we can get it." That was all that Grandpa needed to hear.

Whenever we visited True Vine, Grandpa and Uncle Gene, who sat in the pulpit, were always the first to spot us entering the doors of the sanctuary. My eyes automatically drifted to the front of the church, across from where the church mothers sat to an orange cushiony chair near the pews where Grandmother always sat. When Grandmother spotted me, her face lit up. There was something instantly reaffirming about the smile and nod she gave me. It was like the feeling of security and peace all those times I spent the night at their house while growing up. Grandmother was always glad to see me. I was always glad to see her and grateful that the Good Lord had kept her around to see my success.

On my way to the pulpit to join the other ministers, I always paused momentarily to hug Grandmother and kiss her face. After church, I always shared with her the latest news of what was going on in my life. "That's nice," Grandmother would say, smiling proudly. Her main concern, though, was not my latest accomplishment but: "Do you still have your burning?"

"Keep on lovin' the Lord," she would say.

Most of my secular success was lost on my family. Their sometimes less-than-impressed responses used to bother me. But I later came to see the good in that. It had a sobering effect on me and helped me to keep my professional success in proper perspective, to never get so caught up in the rat race that I would forget the days of welfare, the mornings of prayer with Grandmother and the prayer warriors, and that long before I ever became a big-city journalist, the God who designed the universe cared enough to hear the cries of a ghetto boy. Grandmother and Grandpa were proud simply to know that I was living a decent, principled, and God-fearing life, even if I was far from perfect.

Ever since I moved away to go back to school in Champaign, Grandmother and I talked much less frequently than we used to in those times when she was fasting and sending up prayers for me in the middle of the night or carting me to prayer meeting on those Tuesday and Friday mornings. But our closeness never faded. And I always understood that one of her greatest wishes for me was that I return home someday and assume my rightful place at True Vine in the pulpit next to Grandpa, Uncle Gene, and the other preachers. I promised Grandmother that I would be back someday, even if I wasn't sure how or when. More than anyone, Grandmother looked forward to that day.

In addition to the opportunity to spend time at True Vine, being closer to Chicago also meant getting to see Mama. She still lived on Komensky, in the same redbrick building at 1634. The other building of the compound, where Robin and I had lived, was long gone, reduced to yet another vacant lot. It had burned down years earlier, set ablaze late one night by an arsonist whom the police never caught. Net and her children and the other folks who lived in the building at the time, including Aunt Clotee and her daughter Marcy, narrowly escaped with their lives as the building, doused with gasoline, popped and crackled into oblivion.

It was clear that the old neighborhood bore only a fraction of resemblance to its glory years, when lawns were lush and green and there was a sense of community even amid the poverty. Most of the families that lived on the block when Grandpa and Grandmother bought that first building more than fifty years earlier were long gone. Whatever fragile sense of peace there had been in K-Town, amid the violence and despair of the larger neighborhood, had clearly disintegrated. But I could not help but wonder if my having spent so much time away from K-Town did not also color the lens through which I now saw my old neighborhood. I'm sure it did.

Either way, what I saw during my visits back to K-Town was enough to make a grown man cry.

The little girls danced in the street, bumping, grinding, making love in the wind. The thumping sound of bass poured from powerful stereo speakers that someone had brought outside. The song was up-tempo, a repetitive mix of drums and bass known as house music. This particular song carried only one lyric, a single expletive repeated over and over. The music seemed almost spiritual. It ran up and down the 1600 block of South Komensky Avenue, like a summer breeze on that day of the annual Block Club party.

Mama stood in her yard, shaking her head. She talked in a hushed voice about what a shame it was for the girls to be dancing like that to that music while some of the girls' mamas and daddies stood there all the while laughing and urging them on the way that Mama and Clotee had done when I used to dance the Bird and the Funky Chicken. The new dances had different names and were filled with gyrations. The Tootsie Roll and Butterfly were among the latest. But none seemed more popular than the Booty Clap, a dance aptly described by its name, which leaves nothing to the imagination.

"Look at that. Can you believe they're just standing there letting their little girls shake their tails?" Mama said. She shook her head in disgust.

All you could do was to look, or not.

As I scanned the block, I recognized few of the faces. It was as if I was in a different place altogether than where I grew up. I barely knew anyone, which, it turned out, was not a new feeling for Mama and other longtime residents of the block who also wondered where all the new folks moving in were coming from. Most were young folks in their twenties, already saddled with more little crumb snatchers than you could count. And it had quickly become clear to Mama and everyone else that most of the newcomers didn't work regular jobs. You could tell this by the way that they spent their days strolling up and down the block. They brought other changes as well. Or it may have been that some changes on the block had attracted a new breed of residents while at the same time causing the old heads to flee and what remained of any moral fabric and fiber to seem to disappear.

Komensky felt dead. There seemed to be less a rhythm to life on the block than a pulsating, never-ending noise that emanated from its core like the music that poured from the speakers, enticing the little girls to dance.

My friend Robert was among the few who chose to stay on Komensky, where his mother and grandparents have lived for as long as I can remember. A studious-looking and soft-spoken young man who wears glasses, Rob is the same age as my brother, Jeff. But as we grew older, he and I became friends. Rob worked at a school as a custodian and is married with three children. And in my mind, he came to symbolize the best hope for communities like K-Town.

As I watched Rob standing over a grill that day of the Block Club party, smoke blowing, the children waiting anxiously for the hot dogs to brown, he reminded me of Old Man Newell, who had passed away years earlier.

"What up, Rob?" I said, strolling across the street and slapping hands, slipping into the vernacular as smoothly as my car shifts into drive.

"Ain't nothing going on, Fountain. What up with you, boy?" he answered.

"Nothin', Rob, man, just chillin'."

"Y'all back up this way now, Fountain, or you just visiting your mama?" he asked. "You still working for that newspaper in, uh-h-h, where is that?"

"Washington," I answered without much thought. Even my family had trouble keeping up with all of my moves.

"Yeah, that's right. You know I be forgetting stuff, man. I'm getting old, my mind ain't like it used to be," Rob said, exaggerating some. Rob laughed, poking his glasses back up snugly to his face.

I told him about the fellowship at Michigan. And we talked for a while about the whereabouts of old friends, about who was in jail and who wasn't, about how much things had changed.

"Everybody just want to do their own thing," Rob said, poking the hot dogs. "Man, Fountain, it's so bad now, I have to pay these doggoned kids to get them to help me clean up the vacant lots and pick the paper and stuff up off the street. You try to keep things as nice as you can. That's all you can do."

"Yeah, man, that's true," I said, the bass from the vulgar music still pounding.

"Fountain, you know I bought Old Man Newell's house?" Rob said.

I didn't know. "Yeah, man?" I responded.

"Yeah, Fountain, it needs a lot of work," he continued, "but I'm gon' fix it up for my family. I'm gon' take my time and make it real nice. I ain't in no hurry."

"That's cool man, congrats, congrats," I said looking up the street at the old house. "Hey man, what ever happened to Mr. Newell's old apple tree?"

"It's still back there," Robert answered to my surprise. "Wanna go see it?"

We were just about to head to Old Man Newell's place when two other childhood friends, Carl and Cookie, walked up. We exchanged "what ups" and handshakes, and then Rob and I told them where we were headed.

"Is that tree still back there after all these years?" Carl asked, his eyes lighting up.

Cookie and Carl said they wanted to go and see the tree, too. We reminisced along the way.

We entered the yard through the old silver gate and walked down the cracked concrete walkway to the backyard. And just as Rob had promised, there it was, the apple tree, or what was left of it. It seemed smaller than I had remembered, and barren. We stood there gazing, the four of us, speechless for a minute, then reminiscing aloud some more. Then suddenly Rob made his announcement.

"I'm going to chop it down," Rob said.

There was a flurry of protests.

"Chop it down?"

"For what?"

"Why, man?"

"Man, I don't want that mess in my yard," Rob answered without hesitation. "I'm gon' build me a garage."

"Man-n-n, do you know how long it will take for a tree like that to grow?" I asked.

Rob laughed. "Man, I'm gonna chop it down," he said again. He laughed some more.

Soon we were all laughing, laughing and still gazing up at the tree, except I wasn't laughing on the inside. I understood that there was more at risk than the life of Old Man Newell's tree, that in its very existence lay a symbol of life and hope for us all.

I decided not to push the issue at the moment for fear of sounding mushy in front of the fellas. I didn't want to seem all bent out of shape over some old tree. So I decided that I would call Rob later to explain.

In the meantime, the tree of life would be safe.

With each cycle of the bus's wheels, I grew more anxious, although there was something pleasant about passing familiar haunts, and riding down streets, past corners and places that I knew like the back of my hand. Actually seeing the projects again, and recalling memories of the way some poor people in the city had to live, was depressing. Being a tourist only made me feel worse. It was as if the journalism fellows and I were the safari enthusiasts, studying the natives from a safe distance. This was not how the tour was intended, for sure. But I could not imagine that the people who saw us studying them from the bus saw us any other way. We came for the ghetto tour, like the tourists who each summer in New York City buy the Harlem bus tour package, complete with a hand-clapping, foot-stomping, hallelujah service at a local black Pentecostal church on Sunday morning and afterward a soul-food dinner at Sylvia's on 125th Street. But at least they get off the bus.

I wanted to season the despair with hope. So I set up a tour of my alma mater, Providence-St. Mel, which survived the Chicago Catholic archdiocese's attempt to shut it down after my senior year twenty-one years earlier and eventually became an independent private school that still sends 100 percent of its graduates to college. After touring the projects, St. Mel was the next stop.

As we rolled down Madison Street, past the United Center where the Bulls and Blackhawks play, the landscape quickly changed to bald vacant lots and abandoned buildings standing like dusty fixtures in a ghost town that died many years ago. But there were miniature pockets of hope and renewal. A few old gray stone buildings, immaculately kept, shone like roses amid thorns. A cluster of new townhouses on Monroe Street stood proudly. Finally, we rounded the corner to St. Mel, the castlelike, beige brick building that towers above Garfield Park and is surrounded by emerald grass that I am still convinced grows greener than anywhere else on the West Side.

My journalist friends were impressed with Mr. Adams and St. Mel, as well as the student escorts who showed us around the school before we retired across the street to Mr. Adams's new house for a wine-and-cheese reception.

As we boarded the bus, my friends talked about the hope of a school like St. Mel and about the hopelessness of the housing projects we had seen earlier that day. They spoke in solemn tones about the visible devastation at the projects and across much of the place I once knew as home. It hurt. Not their words as much as the truth.

As the tour bus rolled away from the West Side, I settled into my seat and stared quietly out the window, looking back over the years. Ever since going off to Champaign, I had often found myself looking back and longing for home. And in my mind, "home" always meant Chicago, the West Side, Sixteenth and Komensky. Despite its hardship and challenges, I missed it. Even when working at the *Tribune* and living in Oak Park, I sometimes took late-night drives through K-Town, tears falling from my eyes while crawling down the street under the glare of the streetlights and the silent stillness of the night. And while driving sometimes, it was as if I could see the faces of my friends and hear their voices ringing over and over in my mind.

I missed the faces and the voices of friends and family, the summer nights of playing hide-and-seek under a florescent moon. I missed sitting on the porch with the fellas, talking trash and dreaming our big dreams until Mama's voice cracked the night: "Joh-ohnnn."

I missed catching apples when Arty and the other boys climbed up in Old Man Newell's tree and made it rain. For all that Komensky was not, it was where I remembered walking hand in hand with my dad. It was where the Hagler clan had made a home, where I had lived longer than anyplace else on this earth and had made many fond memories. It was home.

Maybe when I was struggling, I had been too caught up to appreciate it. When I was planning my escape, maybe I was too busy. When I was a child, maybe I was too young. And when it made a turn for the worse, maybe I had been too pessimistic to still see the hope.

Or maybe this yearning was born out of the rejection I often felt in white suburbia. Maybe it was the long stares in the grocery store lanes and checkout lines, the unfriendliness of my white neighbors, or my own submersion in a mostly white world where in order to survive, I often felt that I had to be less black. Maybe it was my weariness of mental boxing.

Or perhaps it was my desire to live where I wanted and where I simply felt most comfortable being black. Maybe it was my desire to be able to live where I grew up, to walk out of my home and see familiar faces, and to walk in familiar places.

Or maybe I just felt lost.

Finally, the tour bus reached downtown and the canyons of skyscrapers. I walked toward the exit, a million thoughts swirling inside my head, like the wind. I stumbled out into the cold.

Later that winter, I was sitting in class at the University of Michigan one night surrounded by students and a professor, James Chaffers, who sometimes wore a dashiki and played cerebral jazz compositions or African music on cassette during class. Professor Chaffers, an architect by training, taught a class entitled "Urban Redevelopment and Social Justice." It was one of several classes I had picked out. It sounded interesting and fit the subject of study I had carved out for myself for my fellowship year: "Inner-City Poverty and Race."

In Chaffers's class, we spent a lot of time defining concepts like "family," "justice," "love," "space," and "hope." We discussed ways of redesigning inner-city neighborhoods, which happened to be where many of the black kids in class were from. We also talked of rebuilding community, not buildings of brick and mortar, but habitats of faith and hope where people could feel and be whole. It soon became clear to me that as much as I was struggling with trying to find my way back home, so were many of the young people in my class. Sometimes they were moved to tears as they spoke of their desire to be able to live where they grew up, to meld their success and hopes with their past, and to make the world, or their corner of it, a better place.

While sitting in class one of those cold nights in Ann Arbor, the idea popped into my head to move back to Komensky, if only for a while, maybe to write about my life and where I had grown up.

"Wow!" I thought to myself, sitting in Chaffers's class, as I pondered the idea of moving back to K-Town for maybe a month, taking my computer with me and finding old friends to interview while also recording my observations of life on Komensky.

But in the back of my mind, I got to thinking, "Mannn, you must be crazy."

I was still wavering late that spring of 2000, when a friend suggested that between the end of the fellowship and returning to the daily grind of newspaper deadlines I make the journey back to my neighborhood, if only just for me.

"If you don't do it now, John," he said, "you never will."

One Sunday morning that May, I packed my bags and my computer and climbed into my car. I headed west toward home with a head filled with questions and a heart longing for answers.

CHAPTER 32

Sweet Home Chicago

It is cool outside. Cool and quiet, gray and rainy. A soft rain falls this morning outside this second-floor window at Mama's place, onto the green limbs of the big tree outside 1634 South Komensky Avenue. In front of that old tree, a house used to stand. That house next door was where Mr. Black and his family lived when I was a young child. The vacant lot that stands in its place is part of a wild field of vacant lots usually laden with rubbish and trash from trucks that occasionally dump there. Stray dogs turn over garbage cans and rummage through trash there, but mostly neighbors and passersby simply use it as their personal dumping ground. On rare occasions, usually after the lot is particularly strewn with litter or debris, Rob manages to scrounge up a few people to clean it. Most of the time, it grows wild with litter, glass, and untamed grass.

I have been up since 8:30. The children's voices rose to my bedroom window as they passed by the house on their way to school this morning, making laughter and indecipherable chatter. I remember the schoolchildren's symphony as being among the first sounds of life each morning on Komensky. I embraced them, as I lay half awake.

I did not sleep well last night, every few hours rising from my bed to peek through my bedroom curtain, across the vacant lot, to the curb where I had parked Aunt Brenda's white Pontiac Grand Am to make sure it was still there. Aunt Brenda was kind enough to let me borrow the car, and I don't want it to get stolen. The car doesn't have an alarm and I forgot to have Aunt Brenda show me how to use the Club, a device used to lock the steering wheel, making a car harder to steal. It lay on the driver's side floor. But the car made it through the night.

As I lay in bed this morning, I could not help but wonder if my anxiety about my aunt's car possibly being stolen was not a fear that comes from being away from home so long and maybe having bought into the stereotype about poor neighborhoods. Truth is, I never really remember anyone on the block's car getting stolen, though I surely know that everyone around here has a car alarm and that insurance companies jack up the rates for neighborhoods like this. Maybe my fear is justified.

I cannot keep from engaging in these mental gymnastics, trying to decipher what is the truth of life in the ghetto and what is myth perpetuated by the fears of those who have never lived here. It is as if I am in a tug-of-war with myself and against myself, with who I was and who I have become, with what home once was and what home has now become. Maybe it is also a war between what I have become and what home has become. Someday I'll figure it out. But right now, this morning, I just want breakfast.

My parents are already gone. The house is still. I wash my face in the bathroom. I must have washed here at least a thousand times, though not in the same sink. Years ago, when we were still teenagers, Net mistakenly laid a hot comb on the white porcelain sink, then shrieked for dear life when she saw the top of it crack up into pieces under the heat and assumed that Mama was going to kill her. Mama yelled and cursed some, but Net was spared. Anyway, the cracked white porcelain sink was eventually replaced with a beige one. Everything else in Mama's apartment feels and looks the same, except for newer furniture, more freshly painted walls, and new kitchen tile. This is home. But I still feel more like a visitor.

I have decided to drive to a restaurant for breakfast. Even for short distances, driving is safer. You can avoid the drug dealers this way, at least not have contact with them the way you would if you had to walk past them, through them.

Mama has never driven and catches the bus whenever my stepfather isn't chauffeuring her. Most days she's on the bus. So each afternoon, she climbs off the Pulaski Road bus into the mix, never quite knowing whether she will step into a shoot-out or a scuffle or the sales pitch of some young entrepreneur, "Rocks! Blows!"

Once, a couple of years ago, Mama was riding home on the Pulaski Road bus. Around Madison Street, about sixteen blocks north of home but still in the heart of the West Side, Mama and other passengers watched as several gun-wielding teens chased down another kid. They caught the boy in the middle of the street, in the middle of rush hour, in the middle of a bustling shopping district, in broad daylight and pumped him full of bullets. The bus rolled on.

Mama has seen her share of gun battles, her helping of death and drug deals, and she has been subjected to the terrorism of thugs while hoofing it on foot and on public transportation. It bothers me. No, it frightens me that she walks the two blocks home from the bus stop each day after work. She used to ride down to the Eighteenth Street bus stop to avoid the main drug thoroughfare at Sixteenth Street. But it no longer matters. On Eighteenth Street, the drug traffic is like the checkout line on Saturday morning. And avoiding becoming a victim of the drama, even as a passerby, is a roll of the dice.

Sometimes I have wondered how Mama does it. I have at times over the years suggested to her that she learn to drive, that she get herself a car. For that matter, why not pack up and move?

I have always suspected that she never saw how bad things were, which is something you can't afford to do if you are going to live there with some degree of sanity.

At a Block Club party years earlier, I had brought my sons by Mama's place and left them there to enjoy the festivities while I went to get a haircut. The party was jumping when I left. Adults were playing cards. Children raced and jumped rope in the street. When I returned about an hour later, an eerie quiet had enveloped the block and I could sense that something was wrong. But this was hard to tell from the calm look on people's faces. I was standing near the fence in the front yard outside Mama's house when suddenly I noticed some lights flashing and the police pawing over something in the alley, beyond the vacant lot.

"What's going on?" I asked.

"Oh somebody's dead back there," Mama said nonchalantly. "The drug boys had a shoot-out when you left."

Suddenly, a chorus of excited voices filled in the gaps, about how they were running and diving over each other to get out of the line of fire of the drug dealers, who dashed through the vacant lot with guns blazing in broad daylight on a block filled with children. The body in the alley had been a casualty, though nameless, faceless, and far enough removed from everyone's front doorstep so that Mama and her neighbors could still claim some degree of immunity and life could return to normal. A few minutes after they conveyed the story of the shooting, still only minutes after the gun battle had ended, someone unfolded a card table and Mama and several others resumed their game of bid whist in the open night air, even as police yards away were scooping up the remains of the dead man. Whenever I asked Mama why she had not moved away in all these years, she always shrugged, and replied, "It's home."

So Mama walks and rides the bus whenever Daddy or Jeff or I can't take her. Her steps have gotten more laborious over the years, as she has suffered several heart attacks and now has diabetes. Sometimes while visiting, I have watched Mama hobbling in her white Reeboks down the block toward home. It is not a full hobble, for you cannot afford to give hint of weakness in the wild. Hers is more of a sway, a swagger perhaps, with an aura of cockiness—or is it indifference?—or perhaps numbness to the dangers all around, like a gazelle walking past a pride of already feasting lions. Whatever that is, I used to have it. But I am not sure I do anymore. At least I have not needed to summon it for a while. If Mama is a gazelle, then I imagine that I am the occasional naturalist passing through, so obviously out of place as to never draw any more attention than an acknowledging glance from the inhabitants as long as I don't get too close and pose no threat.

In some ways, I no longer seem to fit. It was about seven years ago when I became painfully aware of my expired status. I was standing outside on Komensky, with some of the fellas, including Jeff, chugging beers and chilling one warm summer night when we'd run out of beer. It was my turn to buy, so I spoke right up. I offered to walk around the corner to the store to get another case of brews. Before I could get the words out of my mouth, Rob spoke up.

"Hey, man, we better go with you. 'Cause, man, you don't know some of these younguns around here."

"Yeah," Jeff laughed. "We'll go around there with you."

I was half embarrassed, thinking for a moment that they were taking me for a chump. What? They think I can't handle myself? That I'm going to get vicked, as in victimized, walking a block and a half from home, around the corner, to the same store, although now a liquor store, where Net and I bought candy and bubble gum as kids? They had to be kidding, right?

They weren't. And in the end, I decided not to protest. Instead I took the block-and-a-half drive to the store escorted by my bodyguards.

This morning I am driving.

I round the corner of Komensky at Sixteenth Street and head east one block toward Pulaski Road, the skyscrapers of downtown this morning hidden by gray clouds. Already, shop is open. The drug dealers stand on the corners, eyeing the traffic flow, pacing back and forth ready to dispense their CODs.

Then there are the women and men with wanting eyes, the crack heads, "hypes" or "rock stars," as addicts are called. The unhealthy dark skin, the aimless gait. They look like zombies and congregate just before sunrise like creatures in *Night of the Living Dead*.

It is eerie to see the dealers doing business so early in the morning. Drugs used to be sold secretly from apartments or houses, eventually detectable only because of the incessant and ultimately burgeoning traffic that spelled "drug house." Back then, dealers were never this brazen or bold.

Waiting for the light at the corner of Sixteenth and Pulaski, I look across Pulaski Road, where Pine Valley Restaurant has sat for as far back as I can remember. For a moment, I consider eating there. The drug dealers mill about. The light turns green. I turn right and head to McDonald's, sixteen blocks distant, away from K-Town, in the cold and rain.

Rashad came over this evening. He has been calling me a lot over the last few days. That same morning that I packed up and drove here to Chicago, his girlfriend gave birth to a baby girl. At nineteen, Rashad is a father now, making me a grandfather at thirty-nine. And I suspect that he is probably already beginning to feel the weight and responsibility of fatherhood, maybe even beginning to understand for the first time a bit of what it has meant for me to be a father to him. I could be wrong. I ask him what's on his mind.

"Nothing," he answers.

"Is everything okay?"

"Yep," he says, smiling.

We talk some, about nothing in particular. We exchange idle chitchat while leaning on the fading silver fence outside, where I had often stood with my arms spread wide as a child looking up at the night sky.

A few other neighbors sit outside this mild spring evening. Across the street, where Miss Hazel—who is Rob's mother—lives, the porch is full. Three little boys glide up and down the sidewalk on roller blades. Behind us, in the alley, a few kids shoot baskets on the last edges of daylight. It reminds me of the alley ball I played while growing up, although back then we could rarely afford a real basketball hoop. Instead we removed the spokes from a bicycle rim, nailed it to a telephone pole, and played until the sun had given way to the moon, to nightfall and the emergence of rats. Alley ball was rougher than regular basketball. It was elbow-flailing, trash-talking, scruffy, anything-goes-basketball in which we positioned the rim at a height that allowed for plenty of dunking for a five-foot-five moderate jumper like me.

This evening Komensky is relatively quiet, calm even. I tell my son that this is the way it used to be when I would sit out on the porch with my friends, Huckey and Recee, Michael and Ricky, and some of the two dozen or so boys who lived on the block. Back then, when gunshots suddenly rang out it was still something out of the ordinary.

There seems a constant edginess to life here now. From my vantage point, it is like watching tightrope walkers at a circus.

I worry about my sons. Both live in Chicago, on the West Side. I worry because I know they don't have to necessarily be involved in any illegal extracurricular activity to get caught up. A few years ago, I remember writing a story about a fifteen-year-old Chicago boy who was sitting on the steps of a church one Sunday with a friend a few blocks from home, eating fried chicken, when he was shot and killed by gang members because he looked like a member of a rival gang. I took John-John, who was being rebellious and disobedient at the time, to the boy's funeral, to try to strike the fear of God in him. So many funerals of black children have filled my career as a journalist. God forbid I should have to bury one of my own.

Rashad and I stand in the evening air, killing time. It is about 7:30 P.M., and quiet, still. Rashad and I talk and laugh. Then suddenly it happens.

Boom! Shhhhh!

The explosive sound comes from the south end of the block, where the drug boys hang around the corner on Pulaski Road. It sounds like a car crash. It is a fierce noise followed by an incredible gushing sound. Our heads immediately turn south toward Eighteenth Street. The folks on Miss Hazel's porch look up the street, too. As a child, I would have run to investigate the commotion. As a man, I know better.

"What was that?" I ask, startled.

"I don't know," Rashad answers, looking half scared, but managing a nervous laugh. "It sounded like maybe a car hit a fire hydrant."

Screams follow the explosion. Then suddenly, a man wearing a black shirt appears. He is running for his life, rounding the corner, and thank God, headed in the opposite direction from us. Another blur of a body isn't far off his heels. Then comes a trail of young men sprinting like the competitors in a 100-meter dash after Michael Johnson. Their faces are not visible. Just legs and torsos moving at lightning speed. They soon disappear about halfway down the block. A bunch of folks, mainly women and children, who had been enjoying the spring air, dart out after the crew, shouting excitedly in the same way we did as kids, when we flocked to the scene of an after-school fight.

"It's probably a hit-and-run," I speculate.

"Yeah," Rashad says.

Neither of us is convinced.

Minutes pass. But there are no sirens. Still, we don't venture down the street to investigate. We don't move an inch in that direction.

Finally, after maybe ten minutes have passed, sirens wail in the distance. They draw closer. We spot the flicker of red lights over on Pulaski Road. An ambulance appears at the end of the block and heads at a moderate pace south on Komensky Avenue, the wrong way on the one-way street, near where the runners had disappeared.

"Let's go check it out," I say, feeling only half adventurous.

Rashad does not answer. I motion as if I am headed down the block, then stop.

"I don't see no police down there. Man, forget that. I ain't getting in no mess."

Rashad laughs.

"Mannn, them Negroes crazy," I say. "Best to mind your own business."

After a while, the ambulance pulls away slowly. Then a police car emerges, crawling up Komensky north toward us from Nineteenth Street, with no lights flashing, no sense of urgency at all. The squad car makes a right at Eighteenth Street, the wrong way on a one-way street, toward the drug spot. It disappears. Slowly, people filter back onto their porches. Three little boys, about eight or nine years old, are headed our way.

"Hey, fellas," I say, "what happened down there?"

"Some guy ran into a tree," one brown-skinned youngster answers, his words rinsed with excitement. "They say, 'He dead.'"

"He dead," one of the other boys mutters with no detectable emotion.

"Thanks, fellas."

The boys walk away. I later hear a different story about a drug buy gone bad and the horrific details of a beating with a brick. With the excitement ended, things return to normal.

Upstairs, Meredith and Mama sit in the family room watching television. I give Mama a blow-by-blow of the events outside as her face contorts in varying degrees of horror, her body and hands jerking and shaking as if she were being shot repeatedly.

"We heard a crash a while ago," she says. "But when I looked out of the window and saw everybody just sitting still on Miss Hazel's porch, I figured nothing was going on."

Nothing was.

It's dark now. Rashad is about to head home. I hug my son good-bye and for the umpteenth time I say, "Be careful out here."

"I don't go nowhere but home and work," Rashad answers. "I don't be out in the streets."

He climbs into his car, headed away from K-Town.

From Mama's living room window and from walking around the neighborhood, I see the shells of people passing in the day and night, stumbling in a recognizable stupor up and down Komensky, Sixteenth Street, and Pulaski Road or idling on a corner. Some are familiar faces. I find myself studying the faces, looking deep into their eyes, trying to get beneath the thousand scars of their hard-knock-life masks in search of some semblance of someone I once knew.

I find amazing the grip that drugs have on people here. It is not that everyone is hooked. But those who are, as well as the drug dealers, make the streets unsafe for everyone else. Most good folks are prisoners in their own homes and seldom stray from the straight line from home to their cars, or from home to the bus or the El train and back again to their homes, which are fortified with dead-bolt locks and iron bars.

Nowadays, Mama keeps the outside door downstairs locked. When I was a boy, we seldom ever locked that door unless we were playing hide-and-seek and my cousins and I were hiding in the hallway. But Mama worries that some crackhead may lay wait in the hall to rob her, or maybe that the drug boys will use the hall to hide their stash.

I keep wondering what happened to Komensky. What happened that destroyed this community? What happened that made it so ripe for the drug dealer and so familiar with the Grim Reaper? I can't help but wonder whether the place I knew isn't gone forever and whether the lack of out-side intervention by city or federal officials or anyone with power enough to save this community isn't part of some grand conspiracy to let the neighborhood and everyone in it self-destruct and hemorrhage the way Native Americans did before the white man moved in to take their land.

There is so much disorder. Kids stand on the corner selling crack. Mamas and grandmas stroll through the streets, reeling from its effects. Artery-clogging greasy spoon joints fill the neighborhood, as do rotten-smelling neighborhood grocery stores. There is the absence of the ameni-ties that exist in abundance in functional neighborhoods. There is no coffee shop. No major supermarket. No drive-up bank teller. No outdoor café. One dine-in restaurant, if you dare. No Starbucks. No Kinko's. And, I'm starting to feel, no hope.

After a week here, I feel exhausted. It is as if I have been in a war zone. I am planning to drive home to Ann Arbor tonight. After a week I need a break, time to settle my mind.

Sunday is Mother's Day. I figure on buying Mama some flowers. In all my years, I have never known a flower shop to exist around here. But I know a great little spot on the North Side, not far from downtown.

Mama is still not home from work when I arrive back at her place with the flowers. I leave a vase filled with three dozen long-stem red roses on my desk next to my computer screen in the living room with a Mother's Day note. Then I climb into my car and head back to the interstate toward home for a little R&R.

The workout is cool, the conversation better. I pump iron at a home gym just a few blocks from Komensky with Big Mike, Rob's oldest brother, and another dude we grew up with named Kent. Kent's folks moved away from K-Town years ago. Kent's older brother, Jerry, and I were good friends. Jerry went by the nickname J-Rat. Sometimes we called him Biggie Rat after the 1970s cartoon character. J-Rat was a short muscular dude who was soft-spoken and walked with a wide-legged swagger that said, "Punk, I will beat you down."

Challenging Rat was always a mistake. He was one of those brothers that loved to get his fight on. Some guys loved fighting but were no good at it. Rat was good at it. He took on all comers: big, tall, short, small, old, young. And he had a small posse that he could call upon, including an older brother, Eddie B, who walked even cooler than Rat and seemed to like fighting just as much. Once, I was on my way to the store up on Eighteenth Street when I stumbled upon Rat fighting a big muscular dude in the middle of Pulaski Road. I ran back to Rat's house for reinforcements. Eddie B tore out of the house. But there was no need. Rat was handling his business quite well when we returned.

I have not seen Rat in years. Like many brothers I know from K-Town, Rat did prison time, for something or another. I never search for the complete details, mostly preferring to remember my friends the way they were, though I seldom see them anymore. Or is it possible that I no longer recognize some of them?

A few years ago, I was driving west on Sixteenth Street when I saw Rat, standing with some friends. I stopped the car in the middle of the street and called out his name. He came running. We exchanged handshakes and hugs. I have not seen him since. But tonight I do not want to trouble Kent with questions of his whereabouts, knowing that often family members do not want to rekindle the shame or the pain of a brother, cousin, or uncle gone astray.

Kent and Big Mike are a few years younger than I am. They were more Jeff's crew growing up. But manhood and survival has brought together those of us who are like-minded in the pursuit of life, liberty, and happiness.

It is already after 9 P.M. when we start pumping iron in a back room of the huge apartment that Kent and Mike, both on the mend from divorce, share. The apartment is on Douglas Boulevard, about ten blocks from

Komensky. Mike, a stout caramel-complexioned man with his hair pulled back in a ponytail and wearing small black-frame glasses, curls forty-pound dumbbells alternately in each hand. Kent and I swap places on the bench press, climbing our way to 275 pounds. Veterans of divorce, we reflect on the horrors of fatherhood made nearly unbearable by our babies' mamas' desire to control and wreck our lives, even at the expense of the children.

"Man-n-n, John, I was just talking about you the other day," Big Mike huffs in between sets. "I'm glad every time you come around, 'cause man, you always inspire me. It's good to know somebody who made it out and has done all right for their self."

I feel humbled. I don't know what to say.

"Mann, I just praise God. I'm glad that my kids by my ex is grown," I laugh. "Robin's kids. That's what I call them. Mannn, that woman put me through hell. My sons are twenty-one and nineteen. And my daughter will be eighteen in October. But she's a senior in high school and headed to college. Woo-o-o, mannn, it's almost over!"

"Mannn, I know you're glad," Big Mike says.

"For re-e-eal!" Kent snaps.

I continue. "Yeah, mannn, my daughter asked me the other day if I was gon' throw her a graduation party. I said nah, but I'm gon' throw me one."

We all laugh.

"Man, these women out here is a trip," Big Mike complains. "You try to be a good father and all they give you is hell."

"Man, what-choo talkin' bout? I feel you, man, I feel you," I say with the same fervor that I declare Amens in church on Sunday mornings.

Michael has two sets of twins, by two different women, six children in all. He was young sowing oats, he admits. He made some mistakes. Not the children. The women. The unprotected sex. But he has always loved his children, he says. He snatched up his twin sons when his ex left them on his mother's porch and cried when after he had cared for them for several months, she showed up again and they went back to live with their mother.

Kent was once happily married. The pictures of two beautiful daughters and a son, who is his spitting image, grace the top of his giant television. The marriage soured. They divorced.

All he and Mike want to do now is to fulfill the responsibility of taking care of their children. Not out of legal compulsion, but because of what a father feels in his gut when he first lays eyes on his baby. It isn't easy, we all agree, making confessions about how it tears at your heart that you can't be there to protect your children in the middle of the night. I talk about the times that I cried when I picked up my children for the weekend and they were unkempt and uncombed, and the stench of unwashed children filled my car. I've heard other men complain that there are times when their kids are cloaked with only a thin jacket in the dead of winter, even though they are faithful on the child support and the mama's hair is always fried, dyed, and laid to the side.

We trade war stories. About mamas using their children as pawns and threatening to send the children to live with their daddies as punishment, not to mention the fear of getting into a serious relationship with another woman after having suffered third-degree burns at the hands of the first one. Could it be we have children by the same women? It is amazing how much our stories jibe. Or sadly, not so amazing.

Kent chimes in.

"Man, you used to could depend on mama," he says. "Daddy would go out and do his dirt and mama would hold the house together until daddy came around."

"Uh-huh," Big Mike says, nodding and looking disgusted.

"Yeah, man, mama would get in there and make some potato patties," I add.

"Now, mama is the one who's scandalous, doing the stuff men used to do," Kent says.

"Man, we gotta form a club," Kent laughs.

"Shhh, man, I ought to write a screenplay, like that movie that the sisters all loved," I say. "You know the movie..."

"Yeah," Big Mike says. "I saw it the other night. What was the name of it?"

"*Waiting to Exhale!*" I shout.

"Yeah, man, that's it!" they both say almost simultaneously.

"Yeah, man, I'm gonna write a screenplay that all us brothers with children and crazy babies' mamas can relate to," I say.

"You can call it *Waiting to Explode!*" Kent announces.

The room thunders with laughter and the slapping of fives.

We lift and talk until almost midnight. We make several futile attempts to make our way toward the front door, but we keep talking, need to keep talking.

Finally, it is time. I head toward the stairs. Big Mike and Kent have to go to work in the morning. A few hours and a thousand complaints later, we all feel relieved. And they seem to take great comfort in the idea that at least one of us is about to end his bout with babies' mama drama. They say as much.

Mike walks me downstairs to my car to show me how to properly put on the Club before I head back to K-Town.

I can't get over the overwhelming sadness I feel in being back on Komensky, back in K-Town. There seems to be a hint of death wherever I go: on Sixteenth Street and Pulaski Road, altogether missing or wilting buildings; the young women, or at least shells of them in their high heels and miniskirts, with their beckoning eyes and slow, directionless steps.

I talked with Rob today about wanting to return, about wanting to write about home and wanting to "make a difference," and he seemed excited about the possibility of my coming home. He said he was sure that there would be people who would see me as some bourgeois, do-gooder Negro and would resent me. But Komensky was my block, he said, and I shouldn't worry about what folks might say.

I don't doubt that Rob, who has had squabbles with the local drug dealers hiding their stash beneath his hedges, has some self-interest in seeing a homeboy with a similar vision for a community that is whole, moving back to stake a claim. Still, I worry that no matter how much I might try, I stick out like a black man in white suburbia. That perhaps the only place that I cannot live as a black man in America, besides the enclaves of American society that remain exclusively white, is home. And I can't help but wonder if perhaps there may be only one thing left for me to do in K-Town. That is, to say one last good-bye.

For the first time in my life, Mama talked today of doing the same. She didn't say much, only that she was sick and tired of living on the edge, of hearing the gunshots and wondering how close to her doorstep the next body would drop. While Mama spoke, there was fear in her eyes—fear and weariness.

Spring is almost over now, summer nibbling on its final days. Miss Cartwright, my second-grade teacher at Mason Elementary School, sits across from me in a classroom at the school. A dark-skinned woman with an Afro and a warm smile, she doesn't look to have aged at all since that day when she threatened to call Mama because I was disturbing the other kids after having finished my class work early. That was thirty-two years ago. The only difference is that I now tower over Miss Cartwright, who used to seem a lot bigger. And the fear that I once held for this teacher, whom I always thought to be quick to beat down a smart-mouthed kid, has turned into respect.

Miss Cartwright is now known as Mrs. Ballard, her married name. For the last fifteen years, she has worn many hats, including that of assistant principal. She is still a straight shooter. She speaks with the plain, cold matter-of-factness of a homicide detective and the boldness of a preacher. Moments into our conversation, it is clear that she still has her fire, though she says that after forty years in Chicago public schools she is retiring at the end of the school year.

"I'm tired," she says.

She talks of the third grader who brought cocaine to school one day, of the gunfights in the neighborhood, of the former students gunned down over drugs, of the rise of tensions, anger, and hopelessness that smolder like a rumbling volcano.

"When I leave here every day, I see my children out here selling drugs to white men and white women in cars," she says. "These kids are angry. They're mad with the world when they get here."

I have stopped in to see Miss Cartwright periodically over the years. And she has always embraced me with a hug and the love and admonition that a mother gives to a son. I have come today seeking counsel, an answer to a single question: Can I come home again?

"When you say 'home,' are you talking about right where you were raised up?"

I nod.

"When you say 'home,' I thought you were talking about coming back to Chicago and getting involved. Now, I could see that. But I wouldn't live over here," she says, adding that a fellow teacher had asked her once to consider moving from the South Side neighborhood where she lives to K-Town, where she works.

"I said, 'You can't pay me to live over here,'" Miss Cartwright recalls. "I'll be honest. I said, 'I can't not sleep at night for people shooting all night long.' That doesn't make any sense.

"When you said 'coming home,' I was thinking you were talking about coming back to Chicago. Now if you went to an area where nobody knew you and you came back and helped in school and things, I don't see nothing wrong with that. But moving over here? Uh-uh.

"Number one, you wouldn't be happy over here. And I say, 'Self-preservation is the most important thing for anybody.' You have to be happy in order to help somebody else to be happy. You understand what I'm saying?"

I nod again.

"You couldn't be happy over here. 'Cause you know what life's about," she continues. "Now, if you had never been out of here, then you could just stay here. But all the places you've been and things you've done, how can you be happy here, in this area? You couldn't. Do you think you could?

"There's nobody over here that you really know and those that's over here, they don't even know who they are. They're so doped up and messed up. Most of the kids that have done well, they don't live over here, they're gone.

"I'm from Tennessee. There's nothing for me at home in Tennessee. I go there to visit. I always go see some of my relatives, some of my friends who live there. But I would never go back there to live."

I interject.

"You move beyond home, you take home with you," I say, still sounding as if I am trying to convince myself. "You make a new home."

We laugh and talk a while longer. We hug good-bye.

Although I planned to stay on Komensky for a month, after two weeks I know that it is time to go home, though I no longer know for certain where that is.

I stand on June 5 at Mason Elementary School in the same auditorium where I had once played my acoustic guitar as a child during a talent show. I have been invited back to give the commencement address to the eighth-grade graduating class of 2000—me, the kid who could not afford a 5-cent cookie to go with my free lunch, now a man and a successful writer. It seems surreal. The class's commencement theme—"My Endless Possibilities"—is something to which my own testimony speaks.

"Students, getting an eighth-grade diploma is not enough," I say during the speech in the packed auditorium. "You must finish high school, you've got to finish high school, you don't have an option." Applause.

"And after that, you've got to finish college. You must finish college."

More applause.

"But most of all, you must dream. For it is the seed of faith. If you don't dream, you die.

"You must plan. For planning is the fruit of faith. If you don't plan, you won't fully conceive your dreams.

"You must work. For work is the fuel of faith. If you don't work, you won't achieve your dreams.

"And you must endure, or last. For it is the fertilizer of faith.

"I want you to know that I haven't always been a reporter at the *Washington Post*."

Applause.

"But I want you to know that I've not always done that. I've been a janitor, I've been a security guard, I've been a dishwasher in a hospital, I've been a sandwich maker at Burger King.

"When I sometimes tell people when I go away that I could have been a gang member, that I could have been a drug dealer, and they say, 'No, John, not you. You couldn't have done that.' Yes I could have. All I had to do was make different decisions.

"So I say, 'Congratulations to you and Godspeed.'"

After the ceremony, and many handshakes, Monica, Imani, and I walk through the school's hall, bound for the cafeteria to ice my triumphant return to Mason with a stack of those fat, 5-cent butter cookies that I once could not afford. I suspect that the price has gone up some by now. With a pocketful of cash, it doesn't matter. And I can't wait to sink my teeth into about a dozen of 'em.

When we arrive at the lunchroom, I do not see or smell any sign of the cookies. When I inquire, a cafeteria worker informs me that the school system no longer provides butter, that it's too expensive. So without butter, they can no longer make the cookies, she kindly explains. Her words are numbing, in a sense.

I stroll out of the school into the sunshine and the middle of K-Town, laughing to myself, shaking my head, and thinking, "Man, how things have changed."

Grandmother hasn't been doing so well lately. Ever since the hip replacement surgery last October, she has been ill. She suffered several strokes that have stolen some of her memory and left her mostly in a state of unconsciousness. I have been waiting for Grandmother to get well enough, or to be awake enough, so that I might tell her about my returning to Chicago in a way that I could never have imagined: as a national correspondent for the *New York Times,* an offer that had come unsolicited at the end of my fellowship.

On the day I was in New York interviewing for a job at the *Times,* some of the editors and reporters I met in passing spoke glowingly about my grandmother, having read an autobiographical piece that I had written for the *Washington Post* a few years earlier. When I returned to my hotel room that evening, I had a message from home that Grandmother had suffered yet another stroke. A few days later, I was offered the job. And though I would have to spend the summer in New York, I was finally coming home. I couldn't wait to share the news with Grandmother.

A few weeks later, I visited Grandmother in the hospital on a day when she was conscious, though unable to speak because of the breathing tube. The monitors clicked and blinked. Grandmother's gray hair was pulled back, and she looked to be in some discomfort.

"Honey, look who's here. It's John," said Grandpa, who was spending every waking and sleeping moment by his wife's side at the hospital. "Open your eyes, honey. It's John."

Grandmother opened her eyes as Monica and I stood over her hospital bed. Her weary eyes widened with delight.

"Hey, Grandmother," I said, stroking her arm. "I've got some good news. I've been offered a job by the *New York Times* to be a national correspondent. Guess where?" Her eyes widened more. "Chicago," I said. "I'm coming home."

Grandmother's face lit up. She tried to talk.

"Don't try to talk, Grandmother," I said, stroking her arm and choking back tears. "I just want you to know that I am this only because of who you are. I thank you for your prayers, for believing in me when I couldn't believe in myself. I love you, Grandmother."

She tried to talk again, her lips moving, the tube in her throat strangling her words.

"It's all right Grandmother, I know. I know you love me, too."

I left the hospital that day, crying, and with my folks still praying to God for one more miracle.

CHAPTER 33

ONE LAST DANCE

THE SUMMER AIR was gentle, the breath of fall just beginning to blow. Monica and I strolled down the avenue on my way from Net's house to Mama's new house in the west suburb of Bellwood. We had come to Chicago on a house-hunting trip, though we were still not sure where in the area we would settle.

I was eager to see Mama's new house. It had been just four months since that evening in May when Mama first talked about moving away from K-Town. During the summer, she and my stepfather decided to look for a house, a little place in a quiet neighborhood in the suburbs. They both agreed that life on Komensky—the cycle of chaos and death—had gotten to be too much even for two war-hardened but battle-wearied veterans like themselves.

I always dreamed of being there on the day my folks left K-Town, when the last of the original settlers climbed onto their covered wagon and rode off into the sunset bound for a new Promised Land. I imagined that we would all shed tears and hug that day, wave good-bye to those friends we were leaving behind.

But I happened to be at a convention in Phoenix when that day arrived, and Mama could not stand to wait. A few days after their financing was approved, she nearly worked herself to death packing up their belongings so they could make their exodus as quickly as possible. My brother and sisters told me that the actual move happened really fast. Jeff and Daddy and some of his brothers ushered everything to a rented truck, and Mama drove away from K-Town, forty-four years after she had first arrived, the last of her sisters to buy her own house, worn, weary, and narrowly escaping, but still saddened to have to say good-bye.

I had heard much about Mama's new house, in which she had unpacked everything in about a week's time with little to no help, hung pictures on walls and started an eclectic collection of lemon everything, from ceramic lemons to lemon candles and towels to a lemon clock, all of which she set in place around her kitchen. I had heard about the huge basement that ran the length of the house and that got Mama all excited just thinking about the bid whist card parties she could hold there as well as our annual family Christmas Eve gathering, where all of her children and grandchildren opened gifts after dinner while she watched as if there was no greater joy. Their new house even had a garage and a lush lawn. And Mama marveled about how quiet the neighborhood was.

"John, it's so quiet," she told me over the telephone, her voice filled with girlish excitement. "It's just so quiet."

The town of Bellwood, some ten miles west of K-Town, is not just the new home of True Vine but also where most members of the Hagler clan have found their way over the last fifteen years. Everyone except Aunt Mary, who still lives on the West Side, made the westward migration, even Net, who lives just three blocks from Mama's new house. Uncle Gene lives in a neighboring suburb, five minutes away, as does Aunt Scope. Grandpa and Grandmother bought a house just spitting distance from the church soon after they bought the new church building. They sold their old house on Van Buren Avenue, where they lived for much of my life, and where I witnessed Grandmother quilting many days while moaning in the spirit, "Jeee-sus," and singing some old church song.

When we arrived on our house-hunting trip that September, Grandmother was still in the hospital. Mama had not yet gotten to show Grandmother the new spread. Grandmother's sickness and her brushes with death took a toll on everyone, but perhaps on no one more than Grandpa, who could not be pried from her side. Much of Grandpa's time was spent in tears, holding his wife's hand and wishing, praying, that she would get well.

After all that Grandmother's body had been through, after all the prayers and the laying on of hands, I was sure in my heart that she was not going to get better. And that was okay, because I believed she was going to a better place. It may be easier for a grandson to let go than for a husband, especially after more than sixty years of marriage. But there comes a season.

As I walked up to Mama's house, it felt strange to be visiting Mama at home someplace other than Komensky. Mama's house was every bit as nice as everyone had said. She took us on the grand tour and talked some about how good it felt to be finally away from K-Town.

"John, there just ain't no shooting, no car alarms going off all night," Mama gushed. "I just love it."

In the little time that she had been away, Mama had gone back only to get her hair done at a beauty shop on Sixteenth and Pulaski. It frightened her to walk past the drug boys and gang-bangers on the street to the point that she was considering finding a new beautician, in a safe neighborhood.

"Was it always that bad?" she asked.

"Uh, yeah, Ma," I answered.

"Why couldn't I see it?"

We both knew the answer.

Finally, it was time to leave. I told Mama for the umpteenth time how beautiful her house was and how happy I was for them, then I said good-bye.

As I walked that breezy summer night the three blocks to Net's house, the sky clear and twinkling with stars, I was struck by how much Bell-wood reminded me of a place that I once knew before drugs and gangs and the poison of hopelessness seeped in. In Mama's new neighborhood, the lawns were full and emerald, the houses, proud and brick. There were no sounds of gunshots. No sirens or bottles breaking. No drug dealers standing on corners. No yells of "Rocks! Blows! Ho's!" Only quiet and peace. A dog's barking echoed in the night as I walked toward my sister's house.

Then suddenly, I was startled by the sound of a bike approaching from behind in the dark. For a moment, old fears and my old sense of guardedness kicked in. Then I paused in my tracks and turned to see what or who was coming. It turned out to be nothing to be worried about, just two young boys, riding their bikes on a starlit night. I stepped aside as they pedaled by.

I took in a deep breath and stared up at the purple sky, moved to tears that Mama had found her perfect home, even if I was still searching.

Months later, I stood in the vacant apartment at 1634 South Komensky Avenue that was being gutted for renovation. It was no longer in the family. Soon after Mama moved away, Grandpa sold the building to Rob's brother David. David was kind enough one afternoon to let me walk around the place some. He told me of his plans, how he intended to lay new drywall, put in a new heating system, add air-conditioning, the whole nine. Then he disappeared, leaving me alone in the apartment as if he knew that I needed time by myself there. I stood in the living room, looking around at the walls, overcome by memories. It was as if I were saying good-bye to a longtime friend. It struck me that the apartment looked much smaller than I had always thought it to be, so much darker, dead even, like much of Komensky.

On one matter I never got back to Rob, as I had intended. And so, one day he took an ax to Old Man Newell's tree and chopped it down. Rob probably would have done this regardless of what I said anyway. In fact, he not only chopped down the tree but also butchered his hedges and offered to do the same for anyone else on the block free of charge. Puzzled, I asked him why. Rob's answer was simple: Trees and bushes make for good hideouts for drug stashes and stickup men.

Better a dead tree than a dead man.

★

The organ revved at True Vine. The church was packed. Nearly everyone was there, something that I could not remember since those days when the entire Hagler clan would climb into cars and race down to Kankakee to the smorgasbord. There was Aunt Mary, Aunt Scope, Uncle Gene and Mama, Aunt Clotee and Aunt Brenda, all the grandchildren with the exception of one, the great-grandchildren, all of our spouses, and the saints from far and near. Grandpa sat in the front row, near the rose-colored coffin, where Grandmother lay in an ivory-white habit that she had worn on special church occasions. Grandmother looked at peace in her white crown, under the soft glow of white lights.

After nearly two years in a state of unconsciousness, her body weary but not her soul, Grandmother closed her eyes early Sunday morning, January 6, 2002, hours after her eightieth birthday, after having spent all of sixty-five Christmases with her husband, and a lifetime of caring and praying for her family. Grandpa was there to the end, sitting endless days and nights, clinging to God's hand and his wife's until God's will was finally made clear.

A week after Grandmother died, the grandsons and great-grandsons carried her into True Vine from a white hearse. Grandpa wanted it that way. Grandmother would have wanted it that way. There were two services that Sunday, one for the local church and the other for the state—the jurisdictional network of churches—and all the saints with whom Grandmother had prayed, and cried, or worshiped and worked in the Church of God in Christ for most of her life.

They came all day long so that there was not room even in the basement, where closed-circuit televisions airing the services had been set up. I sat in True Vine's sanctuary next to Monica, unable to hold back the tears. The feeling of loss and sadness filled my chest. Although I had not expected Grandmother to recover, and had already said my good-bye, I had not expected the finality of her life to hit so hard.

As I stood in the pulpit to read a poem I had written in tribute to Grandmother, I asked all of my cousins to stand:

"Arty, Cheryl, Doris, Michael..."

They stood one by one, all of us grayer, balder, or rounder than we once were—the lines of age and life showing more on some of us than on others. After everyone stood, many of them with tears in their eyes, I read:

> The smell of peach cobbler
> Mixed with sugar, cinnamon and spice
> Our voices:
> "Grandmother, can we go outside?"
> A can of ice-cold Pepsi in Grandmother's warm hands
> On a hot summer's day
> Home Run Inn Pizza at Grandmother's place.
> The sewing machine, pounding, tapping soon after sunrise
> The light of God's love in Grandmother's eyes.
> Making mischief in Sunday School, testing the rules.
> Grandmother silently praying, maintaining her cool.
> Her purse at her side, rushing out the door.
> The worn out carpet on the passenger's side floor
> "Georrrge! Look out!"
> But seldom does she shout.
> She sings:
> "If you live right heaven belongs to you."
> She prays:
> "Trust in the Lord and He will see you through."
> The smell of Grandmother's dressing
> Of cornbread and sage,
> Her smiling face, loving grace
> Our many suits and dresses she made.
> The smell of Grandmother's peach cobbler
> Good right to the core.
> The comfort of her love and faith
> Of memories forevermore.
> We miss you
> Your grandchildren.

Although the funeral program read "Celebrating the Life of Mother Florence Geneva Hagler" and good Pentecostals are known for festive home-goings, complete with singing, hand-clapping, and dancing in the spirit, it seemed that nothing much could stop my tears. Just when I thought they had stopped, they would start flowing again.

As I sat there, recalling memories of Grandmother, of the many nights she prayed with me on the telephone when hope seemed lost, of that one morning after prayer while sitting in her car outside my apartment on Komensky when she told me to never stop dreaming, of how by example she led me gently to Jesus Christ, I also remembered how joyously she praised God, how she lived what she preached, how much she loved her family, and how much she loved me. As the organ revved, Guitar Jones twanged, and the drums beat, it was as if I could see Grandmother in my mind, dressed all up in her Sunday best, her hair flowing, and smiling in that joyous way she did whenever she felt God's spirit moving. And Grandmother was saying, "Don't y'all cry for me, I'm gone to be with Jesus!"

I closed my teary eyes. And I could see Grandmother even more clearly. I could see her feet getting loose and her arms flailing, her body twisting, the way she did whenever she danced on Sunday mornings in the spirit, when she danced with me in those times when all I was holding onto was faith and hope. With tears streaming down my face, I stood to my feet, lifted in the spirit. With tears in my eyes and joy in my broken heart, I danced. I shouted, "Hallelujah!" I praised God for Grandmother, for the memories of her that I will carry for as long as I live, for the grace He had shown the Hagler family along our journey, and for his son, Jesus Christ, the True Vine, in whom lies the promise that someday I will see Grandmother again. I cried.

Yes, I cried. And I danced.

EPILOGUE

ON BITTERSWEET DAYS, when I flip through my Rolodex at work, I find a few names of childhood friends. I search elsewhere for the lost souls. I tap out the letters of their names on the keys of my computer and hit return to scan the Illinois Department of Corrections prisoner search program on the Internet. Within a few seconds, their faces—scarred and hardened by time and by life—materialize on my screen along with their identification number, rap sheet, and next parole date. Not all of my friends can be found there. Some of us made it out—up—from K-Town. Most didn't. Many that I cannot find at the prison web site are dead—casualties of bad living, drugs, alcohol, gangs, the neighborhood's consumption. I made it out, though not without scars and only by faith.

Like every man, I needed to make my own journey away from home and ultimately back home again to see more clearly, to find clarity.

What I discovered along the way was faith. Real faith. A living faith more than an institutional faith, not dependent on church affiliation, religiosity, or church attendance, or even on Grandmother or Grandpa or anyone else, but ultimately on my own personal relationship with God. It is a faith found from within and to be celebrated among a body of believers whose ultimate hope lies not in what we can see but in the substance of things hoped for.

I also discovered that no matter how poor, no matter how dire life's circumstances, there is always hope, for as long as there is breath and faith. I learned that real faith is found not in the tangible, but in the ability to see beyond circumstances, no matter how bleak, and to observe oneself through the prism of possibility; that faith begins with the smallest seed of hope planted in a fertile heart; that it is faith and hope that is so severely lacking in poor communities. It became clear that poverty is a matter of the spirit and that its cure lies not in taking people out of the ghetto but in taking the ghetto out of people; that we as a people may rove from Promised Land to Promised Land until we have discovered that the Promised Land lies within us and ultimately in our willingness to stake a claim and to nurture, cultivate, and possess the land.

At the end of my first beginning, I was twenty-two, a college dropout, married with three children and living on welfare. My hope and my dreams were all but dead. Some wrote me off, counted me out. Now, years later, I am college educated, a successful journalist, married with children, a Pentecostal minister, sane, content, whole. It sometimes seems as if the two men are separate lives. But we are one and the same, and the melding of the two is reflective of what measure of miracles we all may bring to ourselves by faith. I believe in Jesus, the True Vine, who says in St. John 15:5: "I am the vine, ye are the branches: He that abideth in me, and I in him, the same bringeth forth much fruit: for without me ye can do nothing."

A vine must be rooted in soil, nursed by rain and sun. It must have somewhere to grow, support, and structure. Then its branches will spread freely over walls, rippling across thresholds, bearing fruit, growing beyond containment, boundaries, and imagination. Apart from the vine, a branch withers and dies. Without faith, such would have been my epitaph. I later realized that during most of my life I wasn't poor—just broke. I also realized that the biggest change I could ever make was changing me and that my greatest lack was never from within but from without.

Mine has been an unbelievable journey, one laden with potholes and pitfalls, with my own mistakes, miscues, and imperfections and peppered with my share of doubt, heartache, and disappointment. But God is sovereign, righteous, faithful, and He has become my best friend. And over the years I have discovered, just as Grandmother once promised, that God really does talk and that if I sit still, listen, and wait, I can hear Him. But when I have heard God speak, it has been in less than thunderous tones. Mostly, He speaks in a still small voice ringing from somewhere deep inside my soul. It has led me, reassured me, loved me, lifted me up, and given me strength to go on in those times when taking even one more step seemed impossible. And of all the things in life I have learned I can afford to live without, His love is the one thing that I cannot.

He has preserved me in spite of myself. And through it all, He has blessed and preserved my family. John-John and Rasheena are juniors at my alma mater, the University of Illinois at Champaign, both of them budding young writers. Rashad lives in Chicago and remains at the heart of my hopes and prayers for my children.

Not long ago, I stopped by Komensky. I still go by every now and then. It is a place with which I suspect I will always feel some connection. In my dreams, I hope to be able to live there again someday, but I am not sure that day will ever come. Although few of those I once knew remain, if I close my eyes, I can still see their faces, hear the voices of summer, still feel and smell the coming autumn on a breeze blowing through the branches of Mr. Newell's old apple tree. I can still see Mr. Newell, standing there proudly and smiling as we grab up his apples, still see Arty way up there in the tree, his wide bucktoothed smile.

Old Man Newell's place is looking good these days. Rob has fixed it up nicely, erected a tall wrought-iron fence, and built that garage he had been talking about, planted new grass, and made everything look like new.

Standing one afternoon in front of his house, Rob looked proud and contented, surveying the work of his hands. He bragged about how many tomatoes his garden had produced.

"That was some good soil Old Man Newell had," Rob said, laughing. "Fountain, you should have seen how many tomatoes came up. We had tomatoes for days. I gave them to everybody."

Then Rob pointed to a barren bunch of stubs in the front yard. It was a rose bush that Mr. Newell had planted many years ago. It had been spared. And it still bloomed each year, still emerged from the ground each summer into a velvet spray.

"Man, them roses keep coming back," Rob said. "Every year, they keep coming back."

As I stood there next to Rob, next to his bed of dormant roses, I understood that there is still hope in a place called K-Town, for a block called Komensky and for those who remain, that there is always hope.

There will always be hope.

ACKNOWLEDGMENTS

Although this book materialized over the last two years, it was written in various essays and unpublished ramblings over the last ten years, but not without the support and encouragement of some very special people:

I am grateful for Grandmother and Grandpa, whose prayers never ceased and whose hearts wished only good; for Mama, who gave me life and who believed in me before anyone else and through whose sacrifices I gained the tools to dream; for my three oldest children, John-John, Rashad, and Rasheena, whom I love dearly; for my sisters, Net and Meredith, my brother, Jeff, and Dad for their love and support; for the entire Hagler family—especially Aunt Clotee—whose blood and love for God runs in my veins; for the True Vine family and the prayer warriors and the testimonies of the saints; and for the people of Komensky—for the memories of gentler times.

I am especially grateful to Peter Osnos, whose faith in this project helped bring it to fruition. To Paul Golob, whose patience, prodding, editing, and encouragement coached me through the process of writing my first book. To David Patterson and the entire PublicAffairs staff for helping *True Vine* to materialize.

I am grateful to Paul J. Adams and Providence-St. Mel High School, where I learned to dream. I am grateful to Charles Eisendrath, who reminded me to dream again. To Professor James Chaffers, who helped me find my way home. Thanks to Jennifer Preston, whose words moved me in the direction of fulfilling this dream and was first to suggest that my memoir be called *True Vine*.

Thanks to Nichole Christian, Patrice Gaines, Tamara Jones, Deborah Heard, my dear friend Jane Ungari, Butch Staten, and Cousin Marcy, who read various and sundry versions of *True Vine*. Thanks to my crew at the Matteson, Illinois, Starbucks, especially Terri, Karen, Adu, Arthur, and Andrew, and every *barista* who passed through on my journey. A special thanks to Stephanie Gadlin and NOMMO of Chicago, a black writer's collective, who graciously listened to my drafts. Thanks to Professor Bob Reid at the University of Illinois, whose passion for journalism helped kindle my own flame.

Thank you, Robin, for the good times.

Last, but not least, I am grateful for three very special people without whom I would never have been able to complete this endeavor. For my youngest daughter, Imani, whose existence inspires me. For my youngest son, Malik, who is my earthly joy. And I am most grateful for my wife, Monica, who brought me life after death, and who patiently endured my early mornings, late nights, and weekends spent writing in between my travels on my day job. Thank you for your encouragement when completing this book seemed the impossible dream. Thank you for your tireless reading and editing over the last two years. We did it! I love you.

My praise and thanks to God are without saying. For without Him, I can do nothing.